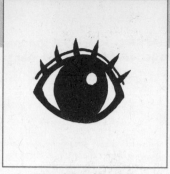

冨樫義博

Eye.

Yoshihiro Togashi

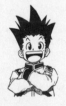

Yoshihiro Togashi's manga career began in 1986 at the age of 20, when he won the coveted Osamu Tezuka Award for new manga artists. He debuted in the Japanese **Weekly Shonen Jump** magazine in 1989 with the romantic comedy **Tende Shôwaru Cupid**. From 1990 to 1994 he wrote and drew the hit manga **YuYu Hakusho**, which was followed by the dark comedy science-fiction series **Level E**, and finally this adventure series, **Hunter x Hunter**, available from VIZ Media's SHONEN JUMP Advanced imprint. In 1999 he married the manga artist Naoko Takeuchi.

HUNTER X HUNTER Volume 35
SHONEN JUMP ADVANCED Manga Edition

STORY AND ART BY
YOSHIHIRO TOGASHI

English Adaptation & Translation/Lillian Olsen
Touch-up Art & Lettering/Mark McMurray
Design/Matt Hinrichs
Shonen Jump Series Editor/Urian Brown
Graphic Novel Editor/Shaenon K. Garrity

Printed in the U.S.A.

Published by VIZ Media, LLC
P.O. Box 77010
San Francisco, CA 94107

10 9 8 7 6 5 4 3 2 1
First printing, March 2019

VIZ MEDIA
viz.com

PARENTAL ADVISORY
HUNTER X HUNTER is rated T+ for Older Teen and is recommended for ages 16 and up. It contains realistic violence and mature language.

ratings.viz.com RATED T+ OLDER TEEN

SHONEN JUMP ADVANCED
shonenjump.com

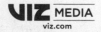

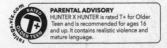

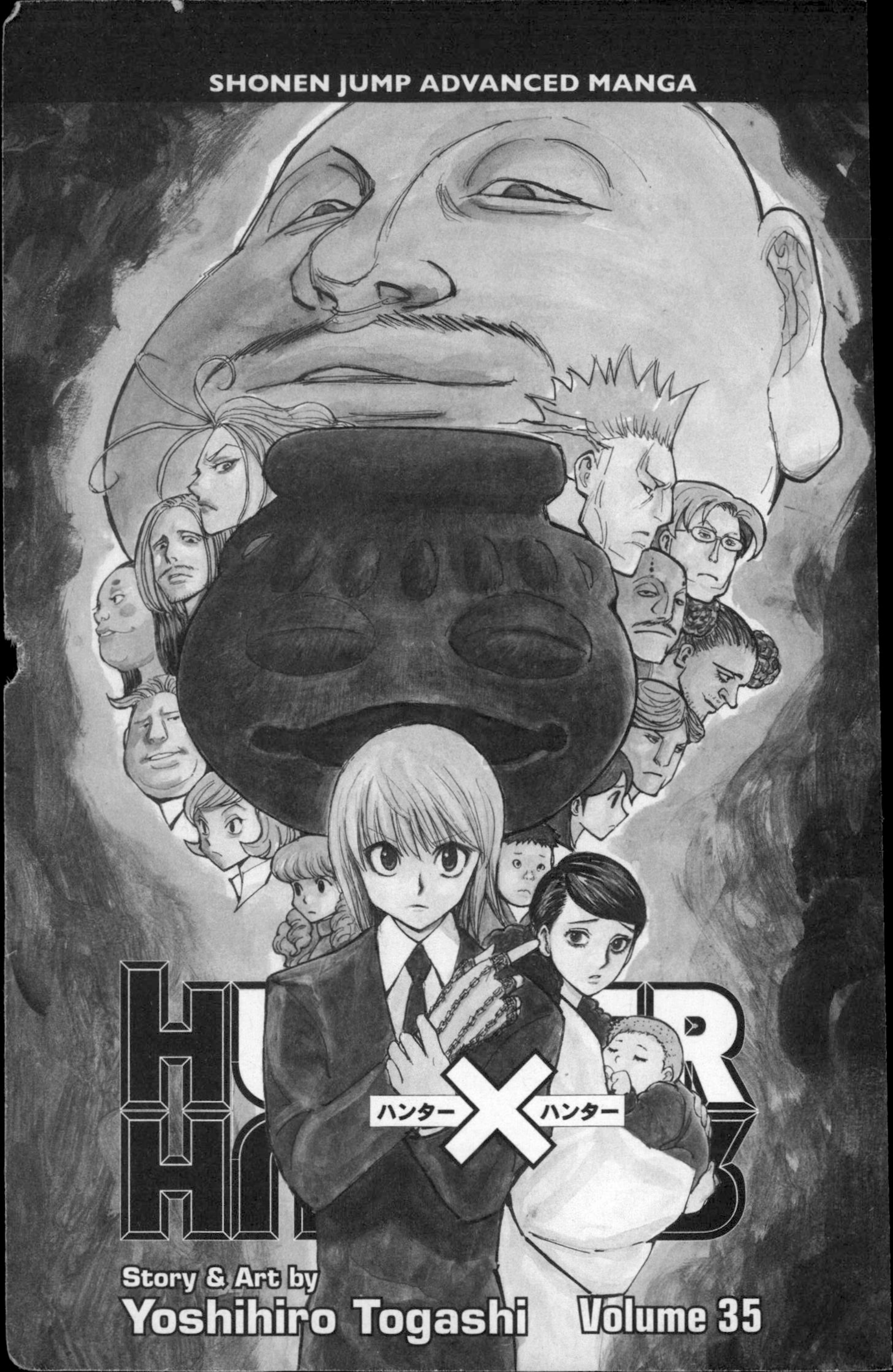
SHONEN JUMP ADVANCED MANGA
ハンター × ハンター
Story & Art by
Yoshihiro Togashi
Volume 35

CHARACTERS

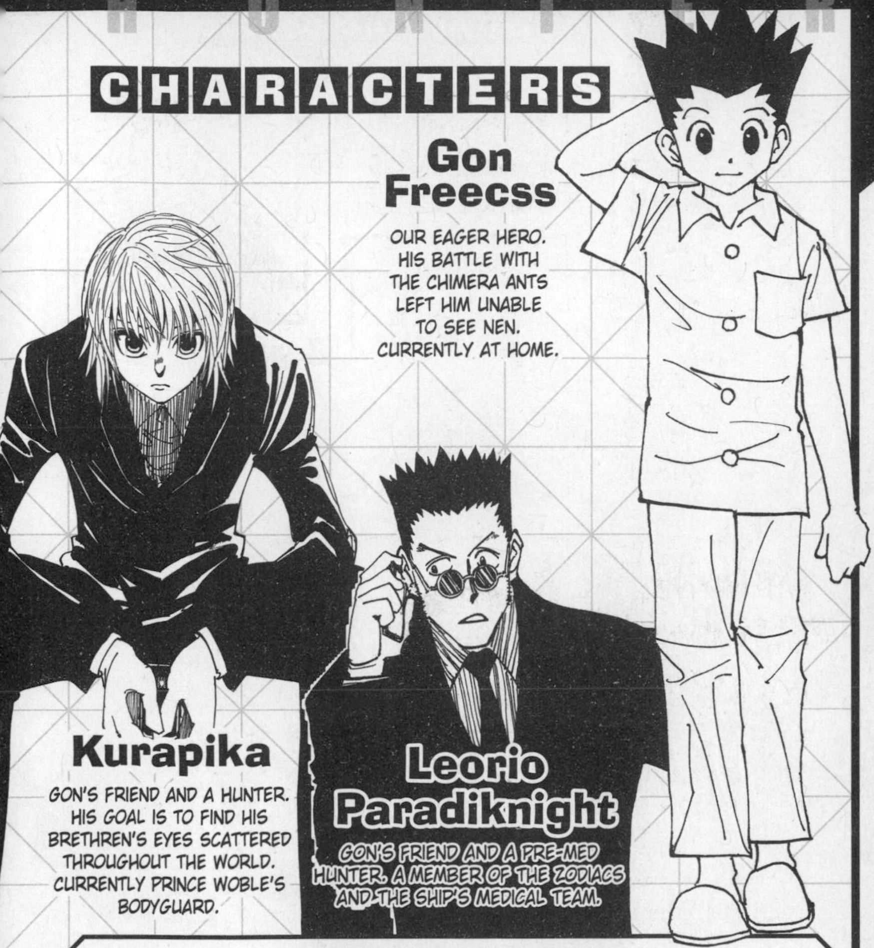

Gon Freecss

OUR EAGER HERO. HIS BATTLE WITH THE CHIMERA ANTS LEFT HIM UNABLE TO SEE NEN. CURRENTLY AT HOME.

Kurapika

GON'S FRIEND AND A HUNTER. HIS GOAL IS TO FIND HIS BRETHREN'S EYES SCATTERED THROUGHOUT THE WORLD. CURRENTLY PRINCE WOBLE'S BODYGUARD.

Leorio Paradiknight

GON'S FRIEND AND A PRE-MED HUNTER. A MEMBER OF THE ZODIACS AND THE SHIP'S MEDICAL TEAM.

The Story Thus Far

GON DREAMS OF BEING A HUNTER LIKE THE FATHER HE HARDLY REMEMBERS, THE GREAT GING FREECSS. HE PASSES THE HIGHLY SELECTIVE LICENSING EXAM AND JOINS THE RANKS OF THE HUNTERS.

THE HUNTERS ARE VICTORIOUS IN A DEVASTATING BATTLE AGAINST THE CHIMERA ANTS, BUT AT THE COST OF HUNTER ASSOCIATION CHAIRMAN NETERO'S LIFE. CHEADLE, A MEMBER OF AN ELITE HUNTER GROUP KNOWN AS THE ZODIACS, IS ELECTED CHAIRMAN IN HIS PLACE. THOUGH GON IS CRITICALLY WOUNDED, HE RECOVERS AND IS FINALLY REUNITED WITH HIS FATHER.

MEANWHILE, NETERO'S SON BEYOND ANNOUNCES A VOYAGE TO THE UNEXPLORED DARK CONTINENT. SEVERAL HUNTERS BOARD A SHIP TO THE DARK CONTINENT, ONLY TO FIND THEMSELVES IN THE MIDST OF A BATTLE FOR THE THRONE OF THE KAKIN KINGDOM. KURAPIKA IS HIRED AS A BODYGUARD TO THE YOUNGEST KAKIN PRINCE AND IS IMMEDIATELY SURROUNDED BY ASSASSINATIONS AND ESPIONAGE...

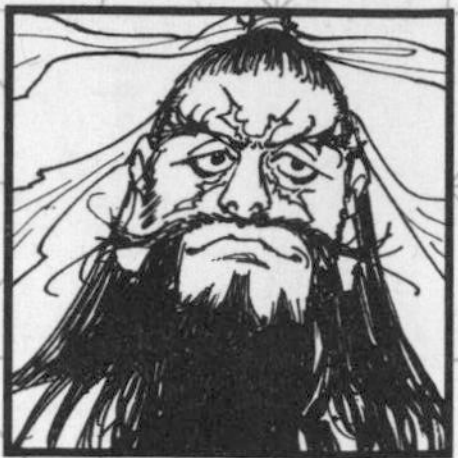

Beyond Netero

NETERO'S SON AND LEADER OF THE EXPEDITION TO THE DARK CONTINENT.

Pariston Hill

FORMER MEMBER OF THE HUNTER ASSOCIATION AND THE ZODIACS, NOW INTIMATELY INVOLVED IN BEYOND'S PLANS.

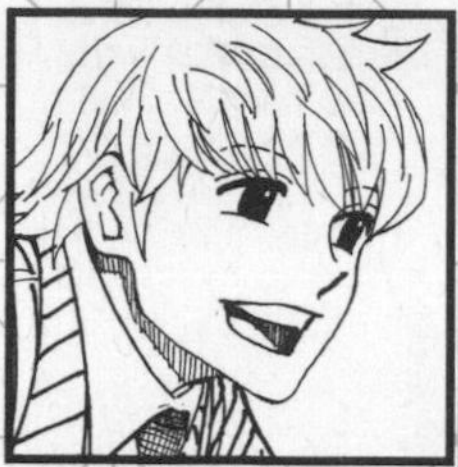

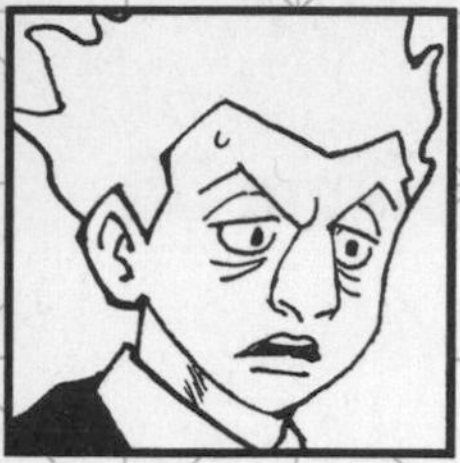

Bill

ONE OF THE PRINCE'S BODYGUARDS, HIRED THROUGH PARISTON. HE WAS NOT TOLD OF THE BATTLE FOR SUCCESSION.

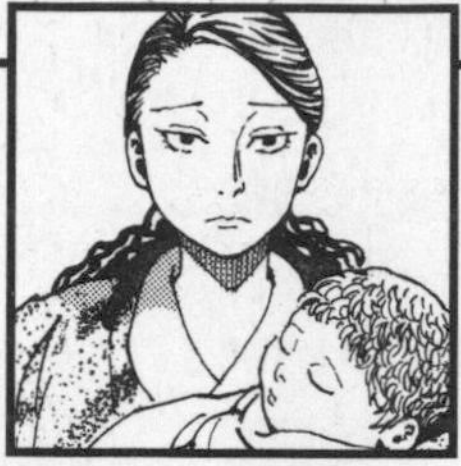

Prince Woble and Oito

THE 14TH PRINCE OF KAKIN AND HER MOTHER. KURAPIKA HAS BEEN HIRED TO PROTECT THEM.

Kakin Princes

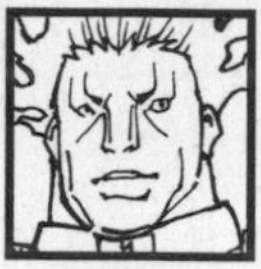

FIRST PRINCE BENJAMIN

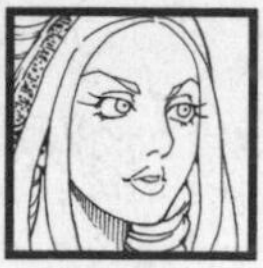

SECOND PRINCE CAMILLA

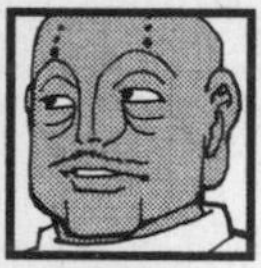

THIRD PRINCE ZHANGLEI

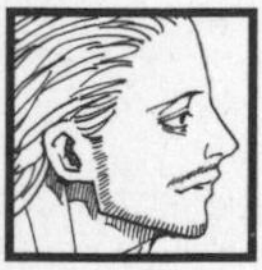

FOURTH PRINCE TSERRIEDNICH

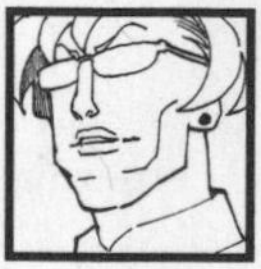

FIFTH PRINCE TUBEPPA

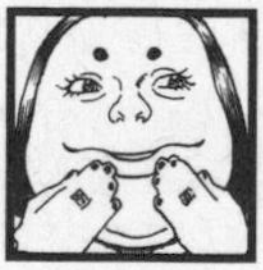

SIXTH PRINCE TYSON

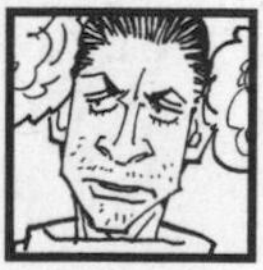

SEVENTH PRINCE LUZURUS

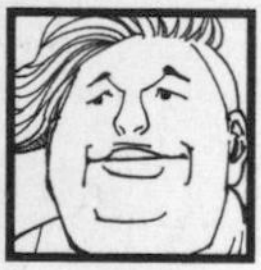

EIGHTH PRINCE SALÉ-SALÉ

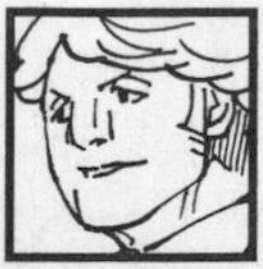

NINTH PRINCE HALKENBURG

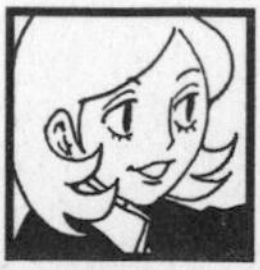

TENTH PRINCE KACHO

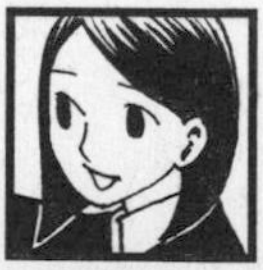

11TH PRINCE FUGETSU

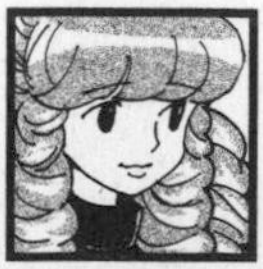

12TH PRINCE MOMOZE

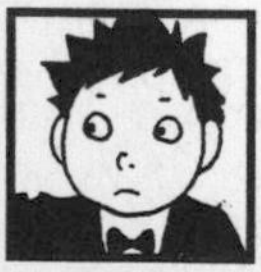

13TH PRINCE MARAYAM

HUNTER×HUNTER

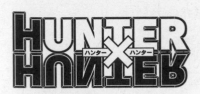

Volume 35

CONTENTS

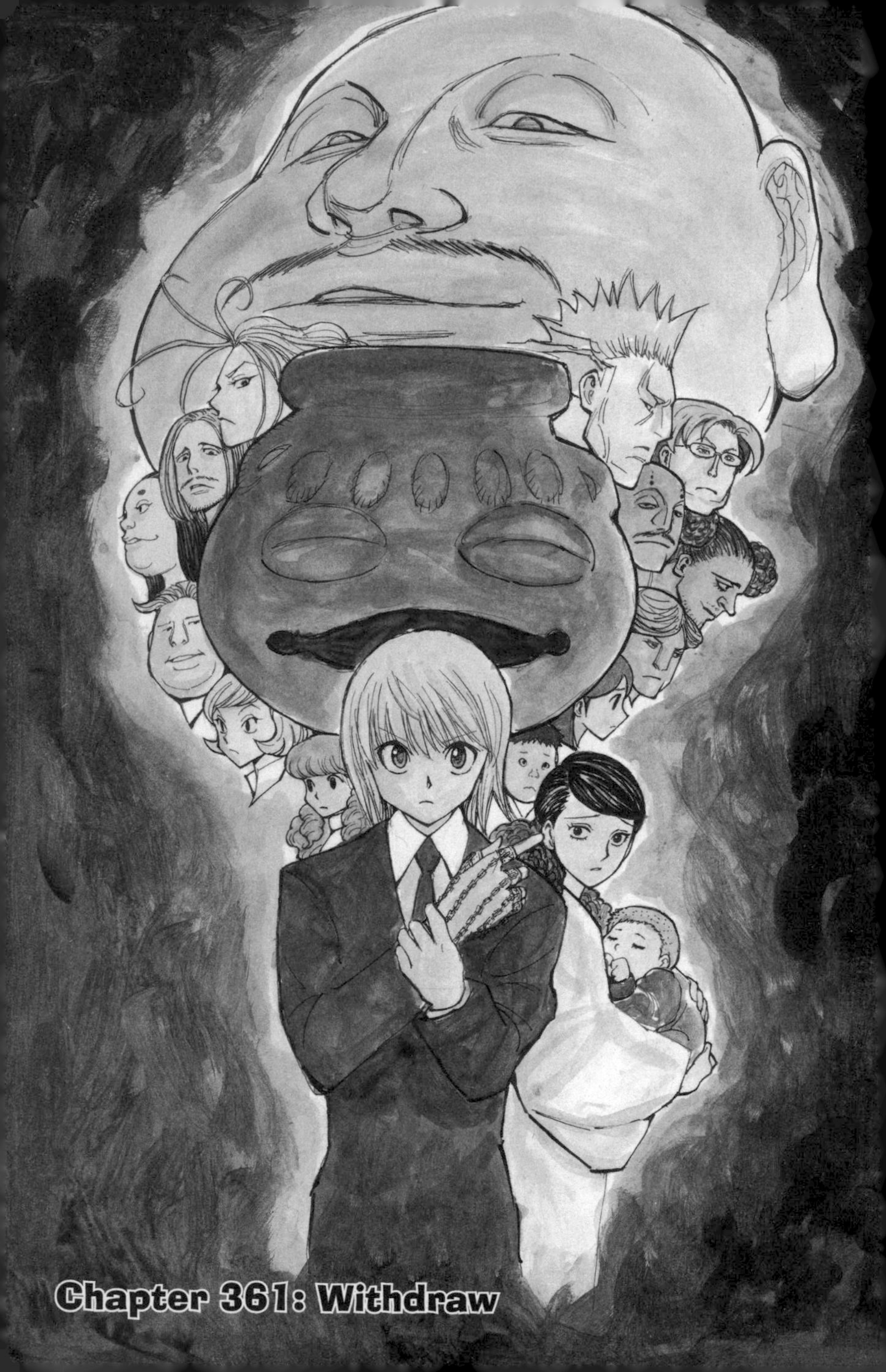
Chapter 361: Withdraw

Chapter 364 originally ran in a special issue of *Shonen Jump* magazine where all the artists hid a straw hat somewhere in their manga. I went overboard and hid a total of 14 items from different series. For those who are interested, I'm including the answers in bonus pages here. I also wrote new dialogue for the panels with word balloons.
Yoshihiro Togashi

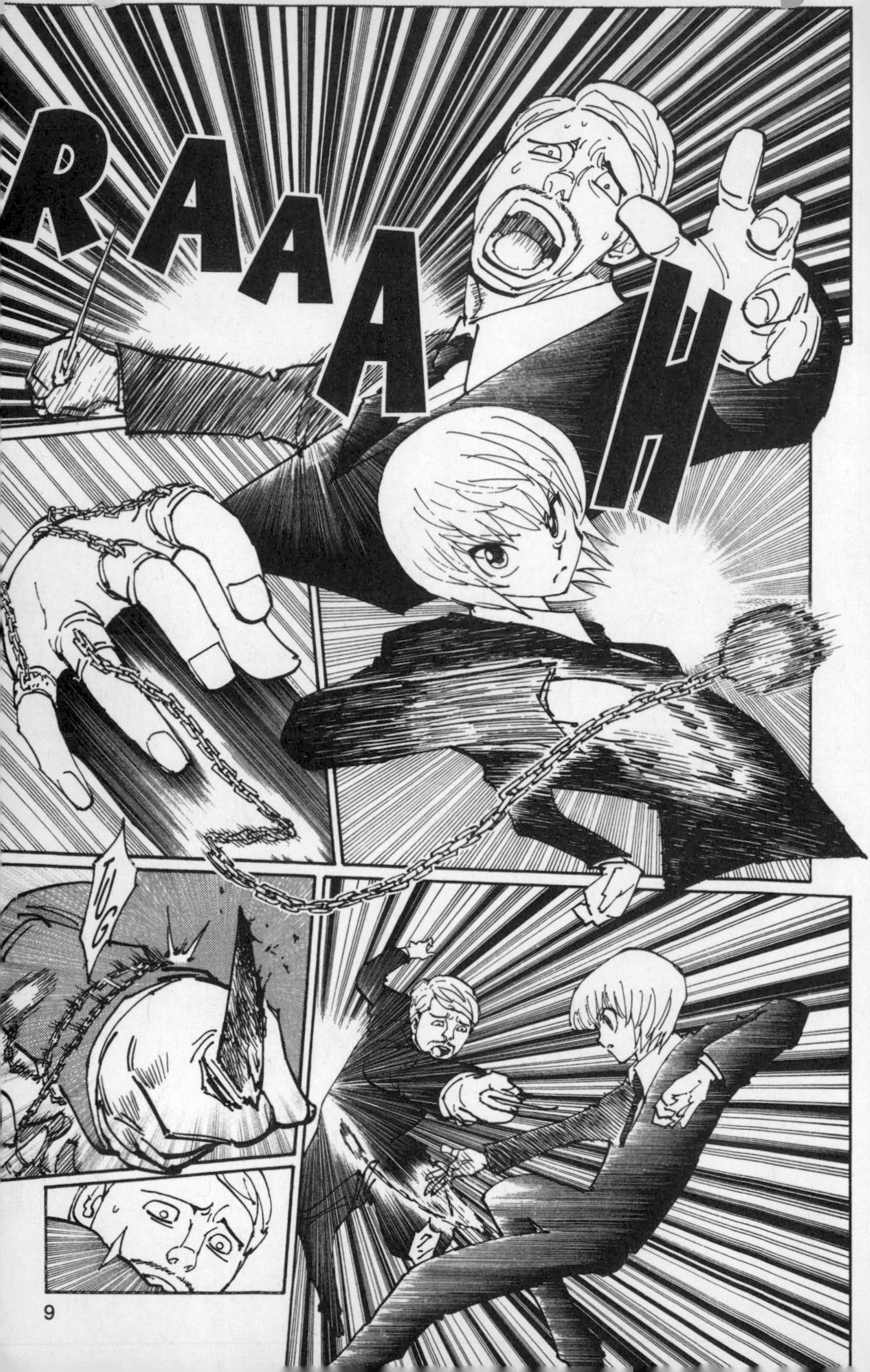
RAAAAH
TUG

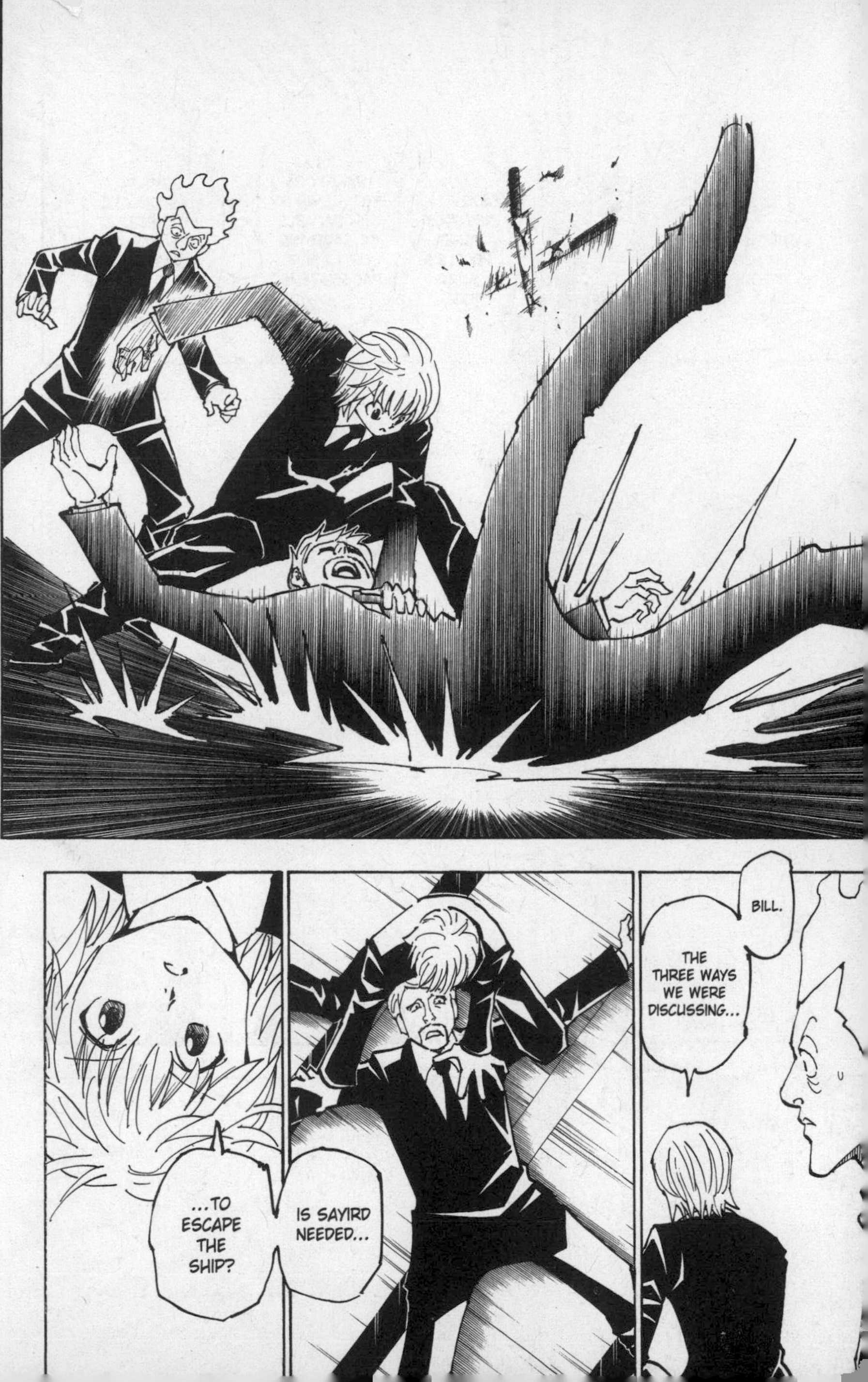
BILL.
THE THREE WAYS WE WERE DISCUSSING...
IS SAYIRD NEEDED...
...TO ESCAPE THE SHIP?

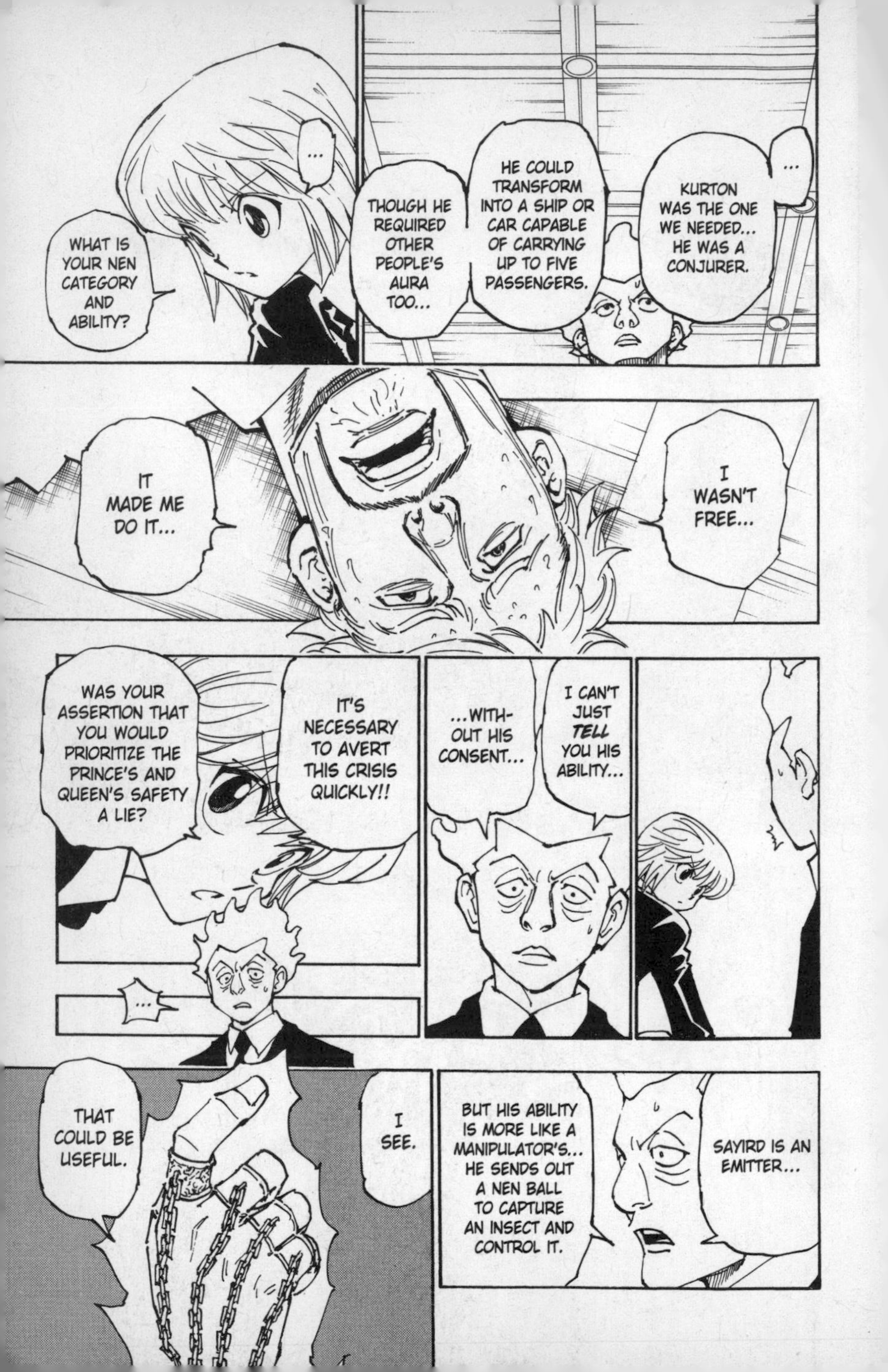
...
KURTON WAS THE ONE WE NEEDED... HE WAS A CONJURER.
HE COULD TRANSFORM INTO A SHIP OR CAR CAPABLE OF CARRYING UP TO FIVE PASSENGERS.
THOUGH HE REQUIRED OTHER PEOPLE'S AURA TOO...
...
WHAT IS YOUR NEN CATEGORY AND ABILITY?
I WASN'T FREE...
IT MADE ME DO IT...
I CAN'T JUST *TELL* YOU HIS ABILITY...
...WITH-OUT HIS CONSENT...
IT'S NECESSARY TO AVERT THIS CRISIS QUICKLY!!
WAS YOUR ASSERTION THAT YOU WOULD PRIORITIZE THE PRINCE'S AND QUEEN'S SAFETY A LIE?
...
SAYIRD IS AN EMITTER...
BUT HIS ABILITY IS MORE LIKE A MANIPULATOR'S... HE SENDS OUT A NEN BALL TO CAPTURE AN INSECT AND CONTROL IT.
I SEE.
THAT COULD BE USEFUL.

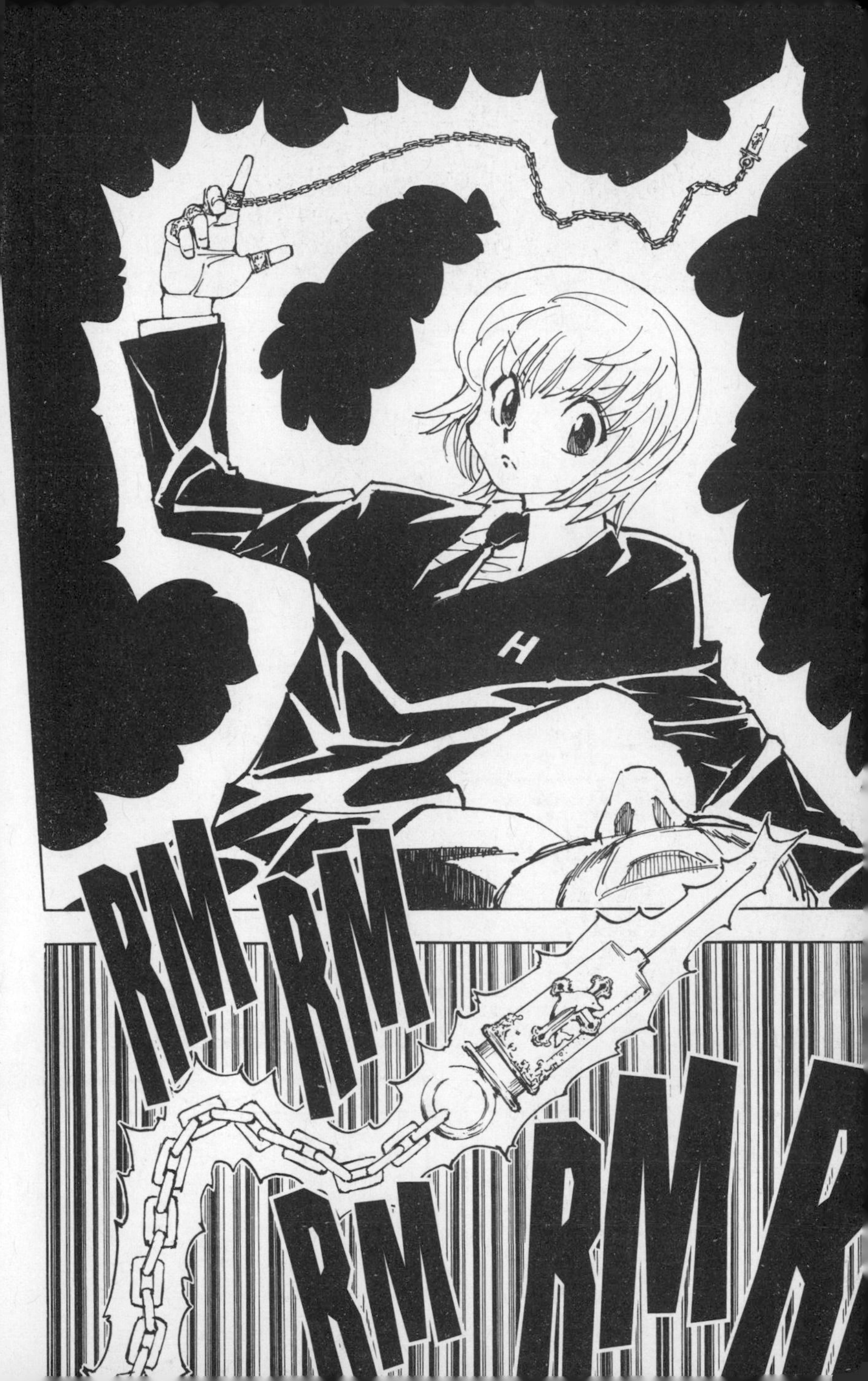
RM RM
RM RM R

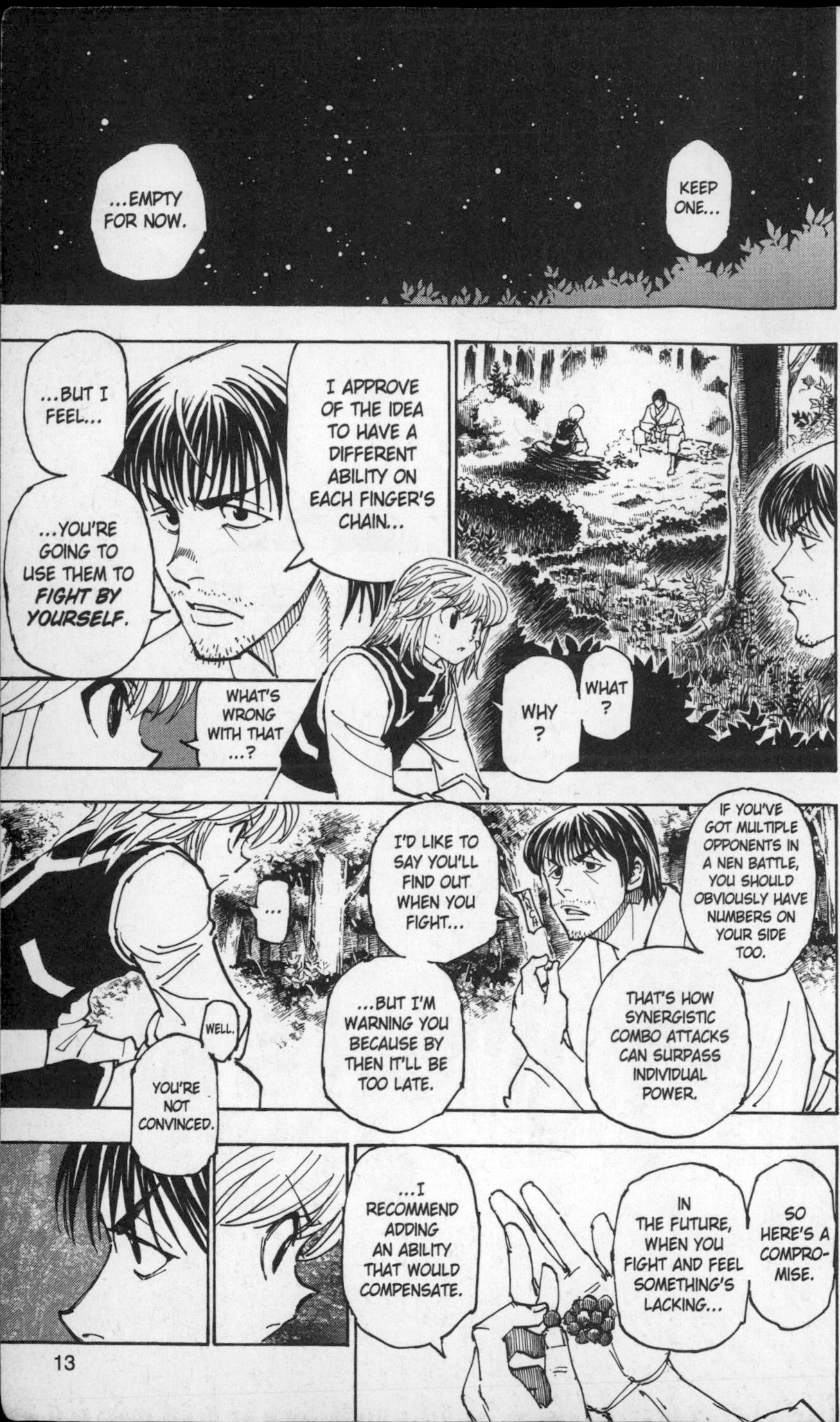
KEEP ONE...
...EMPTY FOR NOW.
WHAT?
WHY?
I APPROVE OF THE IDEA TO HAVE A DIFFERENT ABILITY ON EACH FINGER'S CHAIN...
...BUT I FEEL...
...YOU'RE GOING TO USE THEM TO *FIGHT BY YOURSELF*.
WHAT'S WRONG WITH THAT...?
IF YOU'VE GOT MULTIPLE OPPONENTS IN A NEN BATTLE, YOU SHOULD OBVIOUSLY HAVE NUMBERS ON YOUR SIDE TOO.
THAT'S HOW SYNERGISTIC COMBO ATTACKS CAN SURPASS INDIVIDUAL POWER.
I'D LIKE TO SAY YOU'LL FIND OUT WHEN YOU FIGHT...
...BUT I'M WARNING YOU BECAUSE BY THEN IT'LL BE TOO LATE.
...
WELL.
YOU'RE NOT CONVINCED.
SO HERE'S A COMPROMISE.
IN THE FUTURE, WHEN YOU FIGHT AND FEEL SOMETHING'S LACKING...
...I RECOMMEND ADDING AN ABILITY THAT WOULD COMPENSATE.

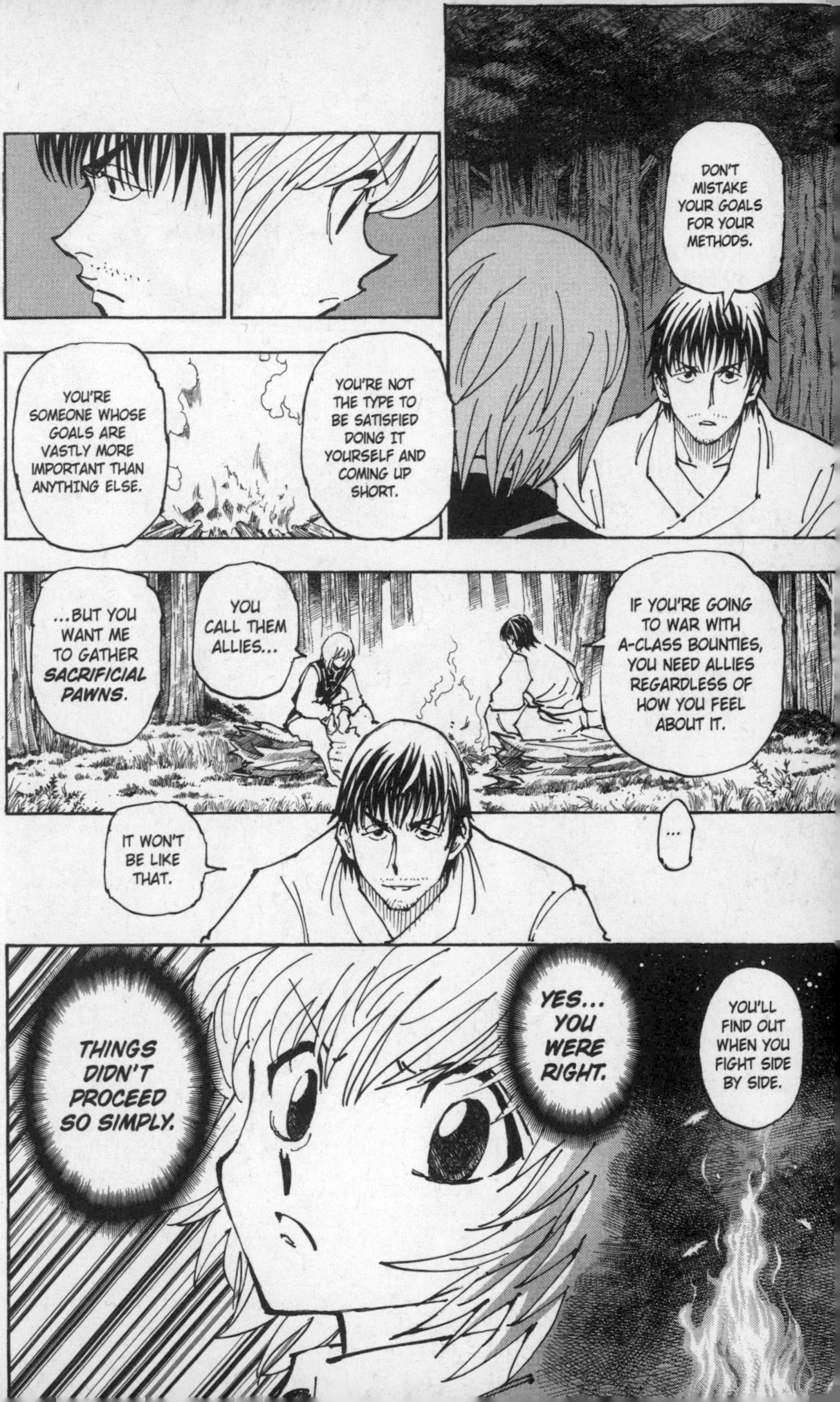
DON'T MISTAKE YOUR GOALS FOR YOUR METHODS.
YOU'RE NOT THE TYPE TO BE SATISFIED DOING IT YOURSELF AND COMING UP SHORT.
YOU'RE SOMEONE WHOSE GOALS ARE VASTLY MORE IMPORTANT THAN ANYTHING ELSE.
IF YOU'RE GOING TO WAR WITH A-CLASS BOUNTIES, YOU NEED ALLIES REGARDLESS OF HOW YOU FEEL ABOUT IT.
YOU CALL THEM ALLIES...
...BUT YOU WANT ME TO GATHER *SACRIFICIAL PAWNS.*
...
IT WON'T BE LIKE THAT.
YOU'LL FIND OUT WHEN YOU FIGHT SIDE BY SIDE.
YES... YOU WERE RIGHT.
THINGS DIDN'T PROCEED SO SIMPLY.

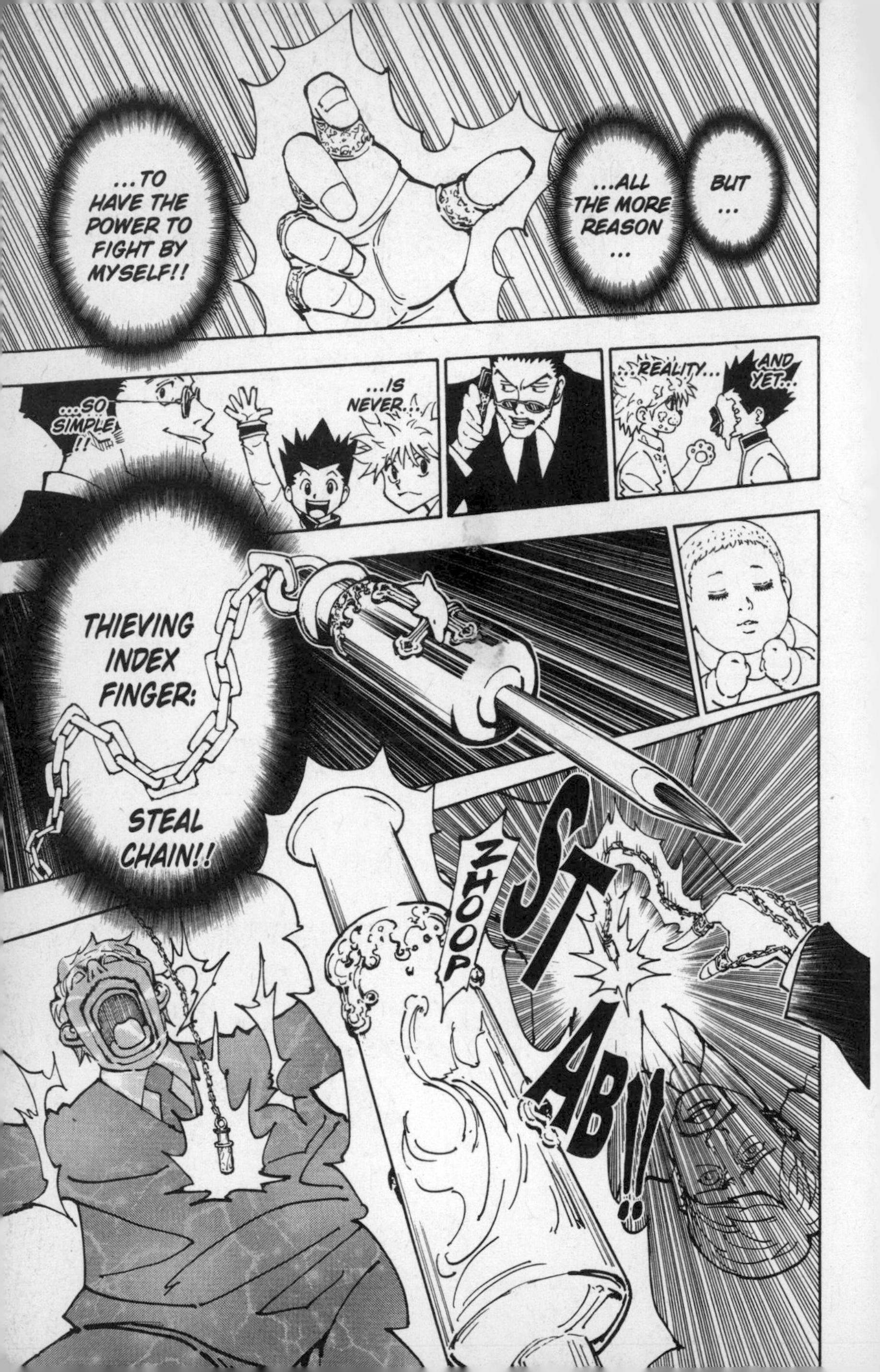
BUT ...
...ALL THE MORE REASON ...
...TO HAVE THE POWER TO FIGHT BY MYSELF!!
AND YET...
...REALITY...
...IS NEVER...
...SO SIMPLE!!
THIEVING INDEX FINGER:
STEAL CHAIN!!
STAB!!
ZHOOOP

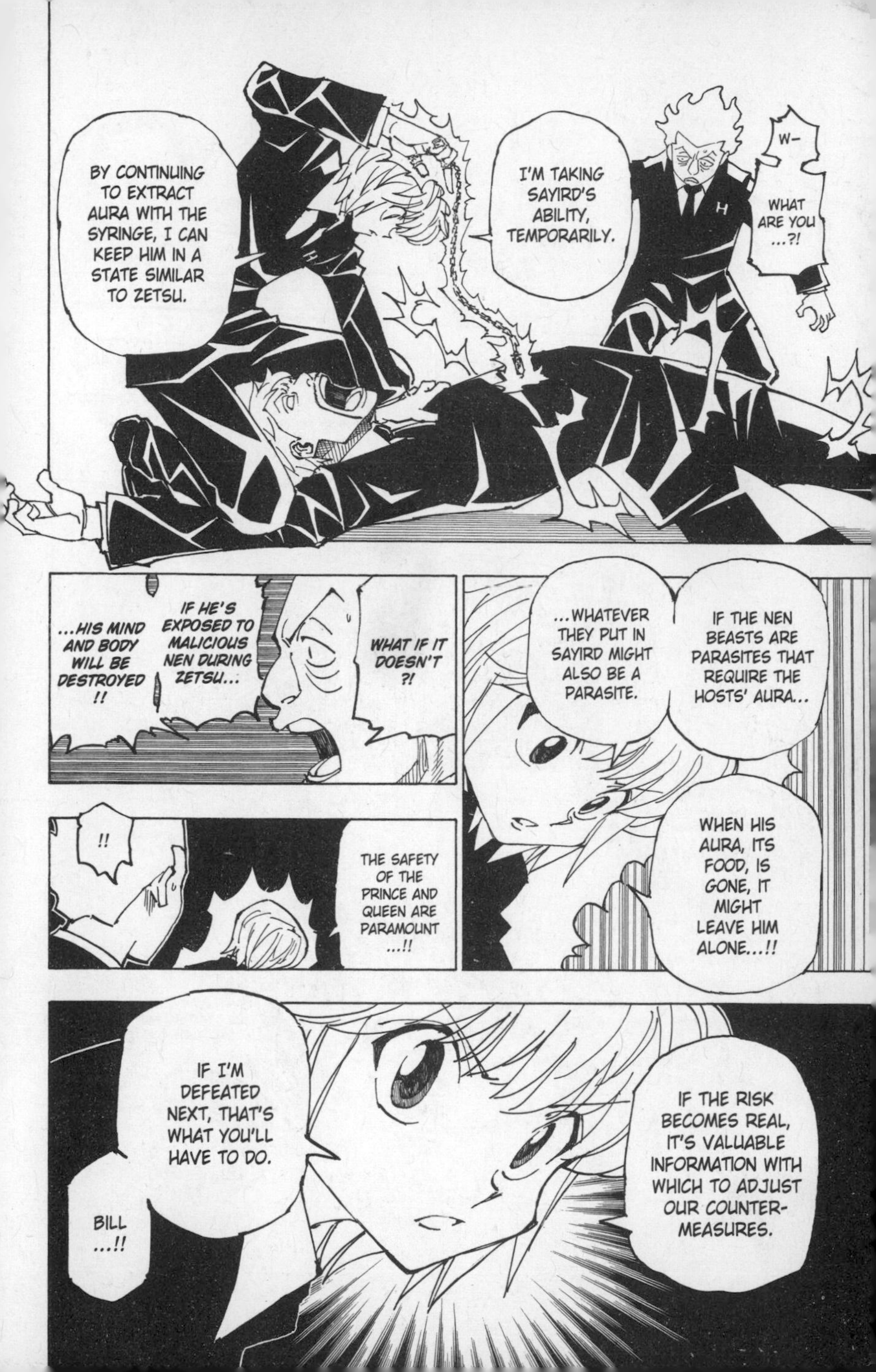
W—
WHAT ARE YOU ...?!
I'M TAKING SAYIRD'S ABILITY, TEMPORARILY.
BY CONTINUING TO EXTRACT AURA WITH THE SYRINGE, I CAN KEEP HIM IN A STATE SIMILAR TO ZETSU.
IF THE NEN BEASTS ARE PARASITES THAT REQUIRE THE HOSTS' AURA...
...WHATEVER THEY PUT IN SAYIRD MIGHT ALSO BE A PARASITE.
WHEN HIS AURA, ITS FOOD, IS GONE, IT MIGHT LEAVE HIM ALONE...!!
WHAT IF IT DOESN'T ?!
IF HE'S EXPOSED TO MALICIOUS NEN DURING ZETSU...
...HIS MIND AND BODY WILL BE DESTROYED !!
THE SAFETY OF THE PRINCE AND QUEEN ARE PARAMOUNT ...!!
!!
IF THE RISK BECOMES REAL, IT'S VALUABLE INFORMATION WITH WHICH TO ADJUST OUR COUNTER-MEASURES.
IF I'M DEFEATED NEXT, THAT'S WHAT YOU'LL HAVE TO DO.
BILL ...!!

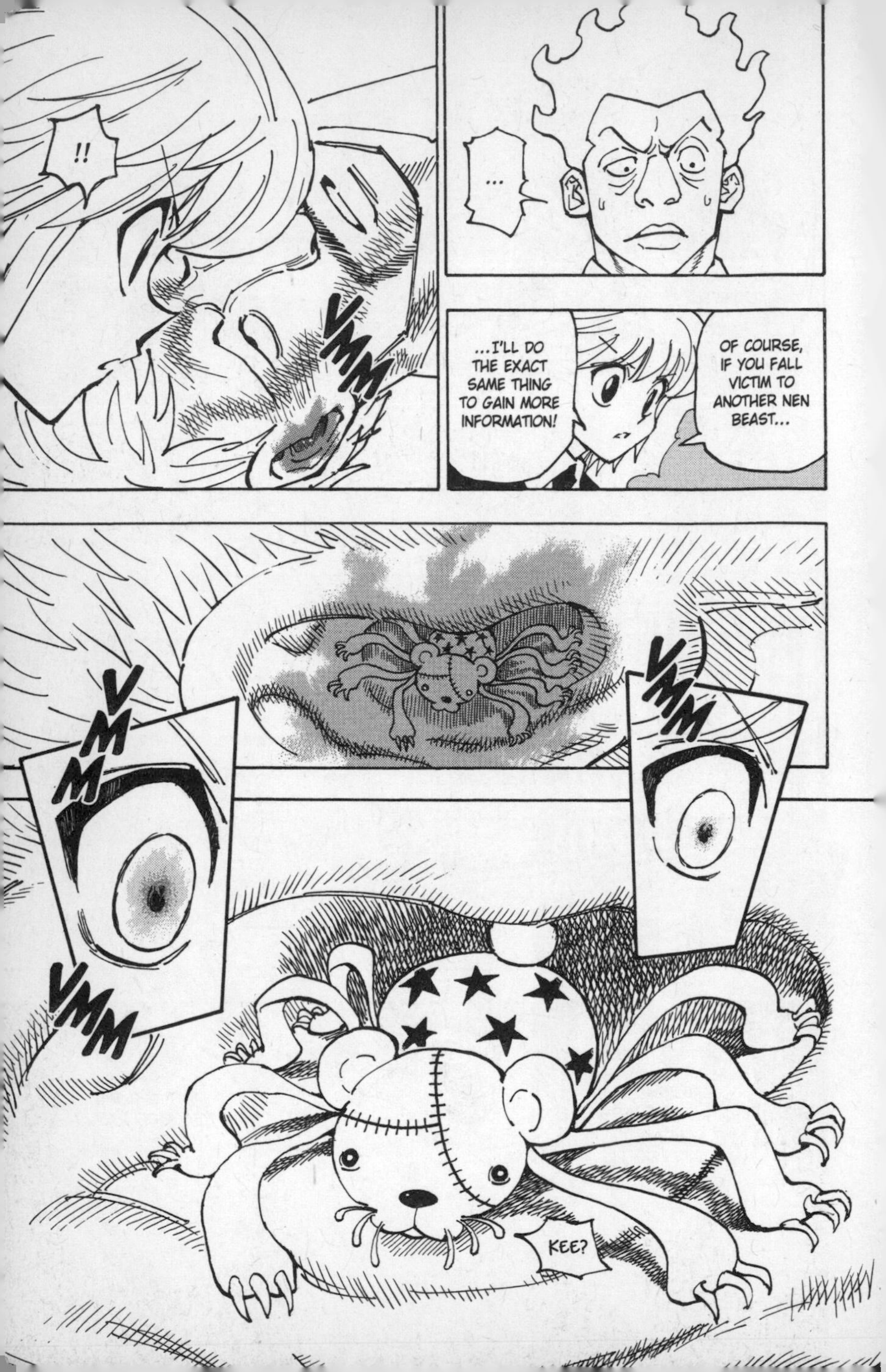
...
OF COURSE, IF YOU FALL VICTIM TO ANOTHER NEN BEAST...
...I'LL DO THE EXACT SAME THING TO GAIN MORE INFORMATION!
!!
VMM
VMM
VMMM
VMM
KEE?

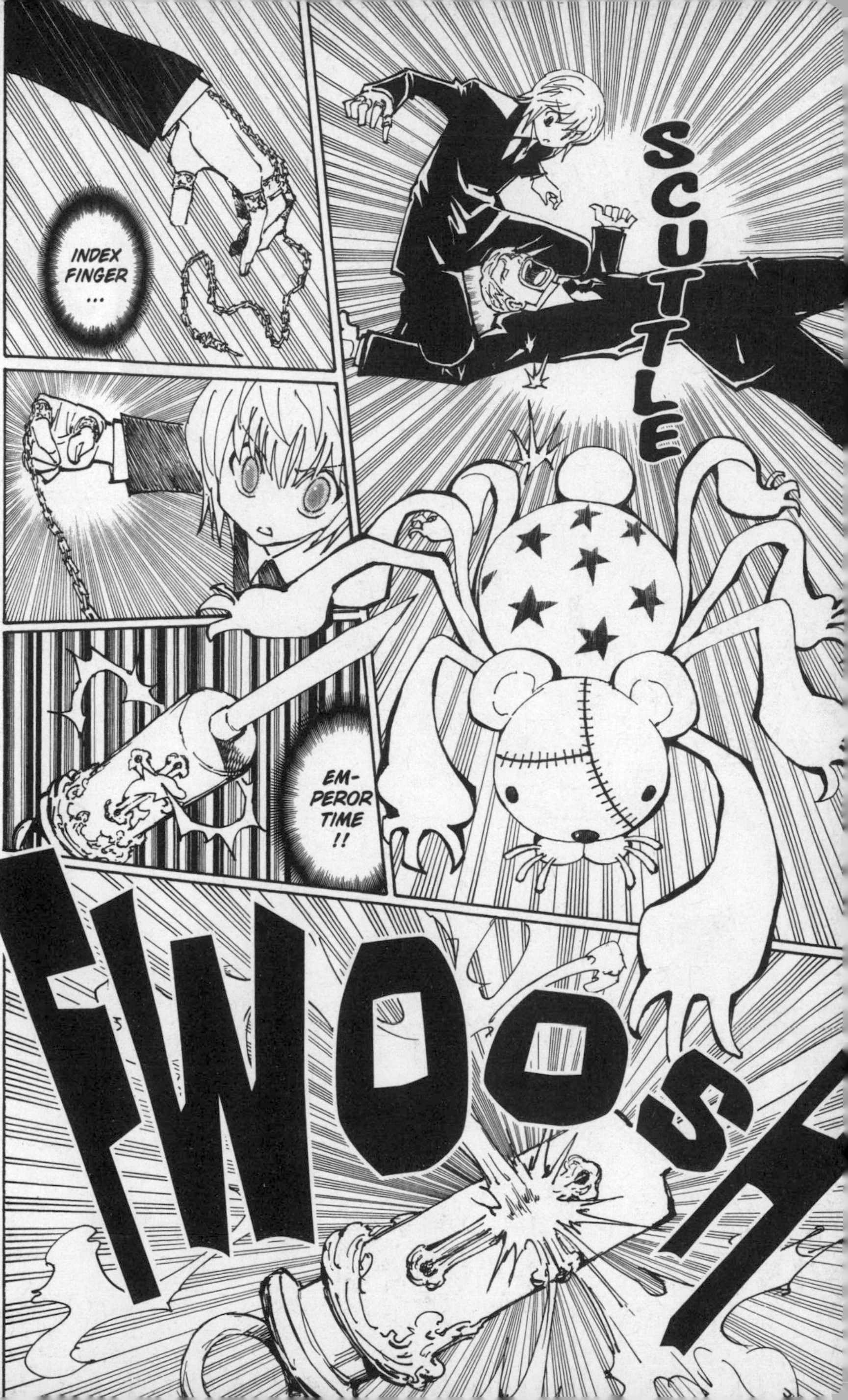
SCUTTLE
INDEX FINGER ...
EM-PEROR TIME !!
FWOOSH

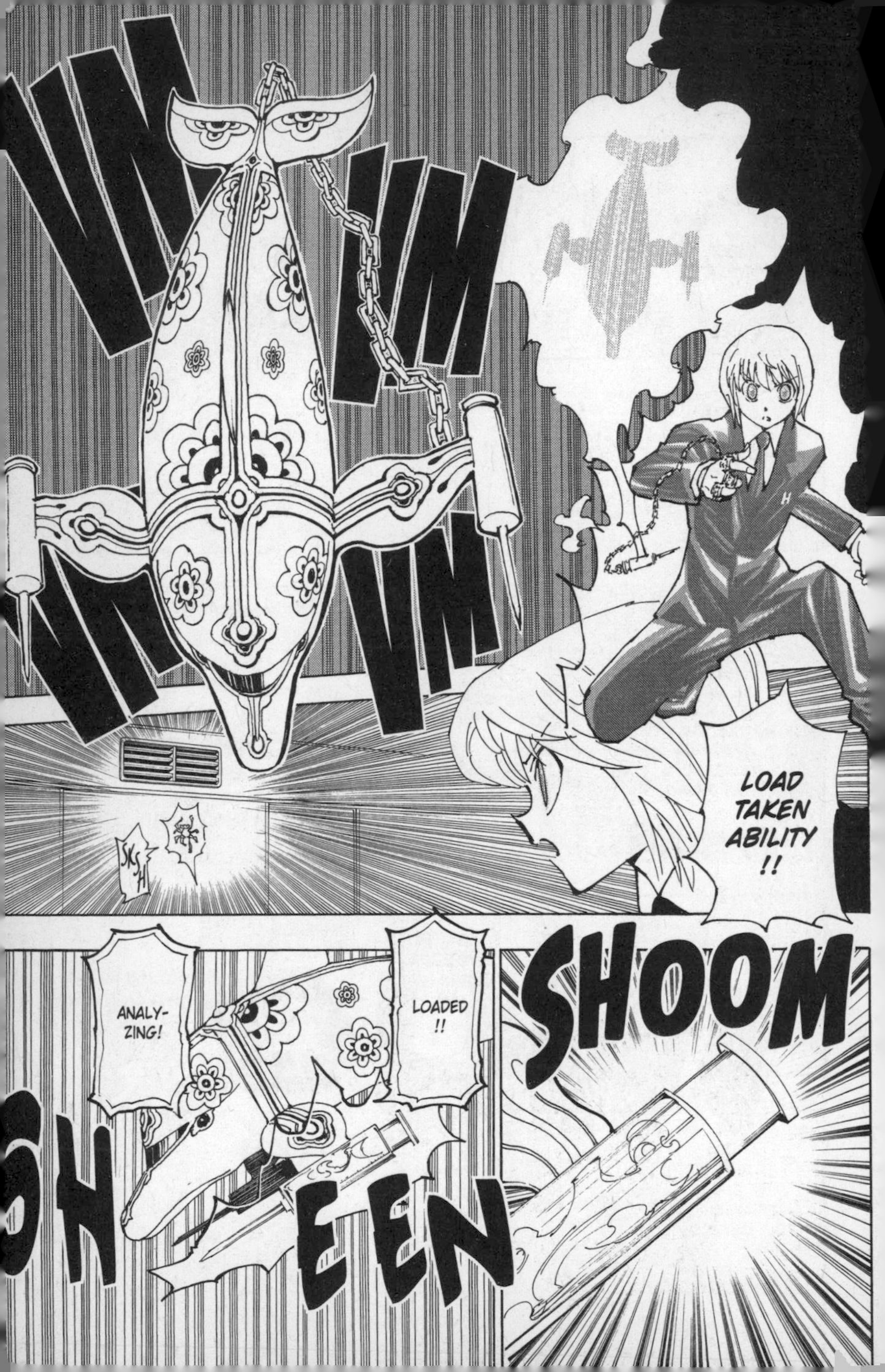

LOAD TAKEN ABILITY !!
VM
VM
SHOOM
LOADED !!
ANALY-ZING!
SH EEN

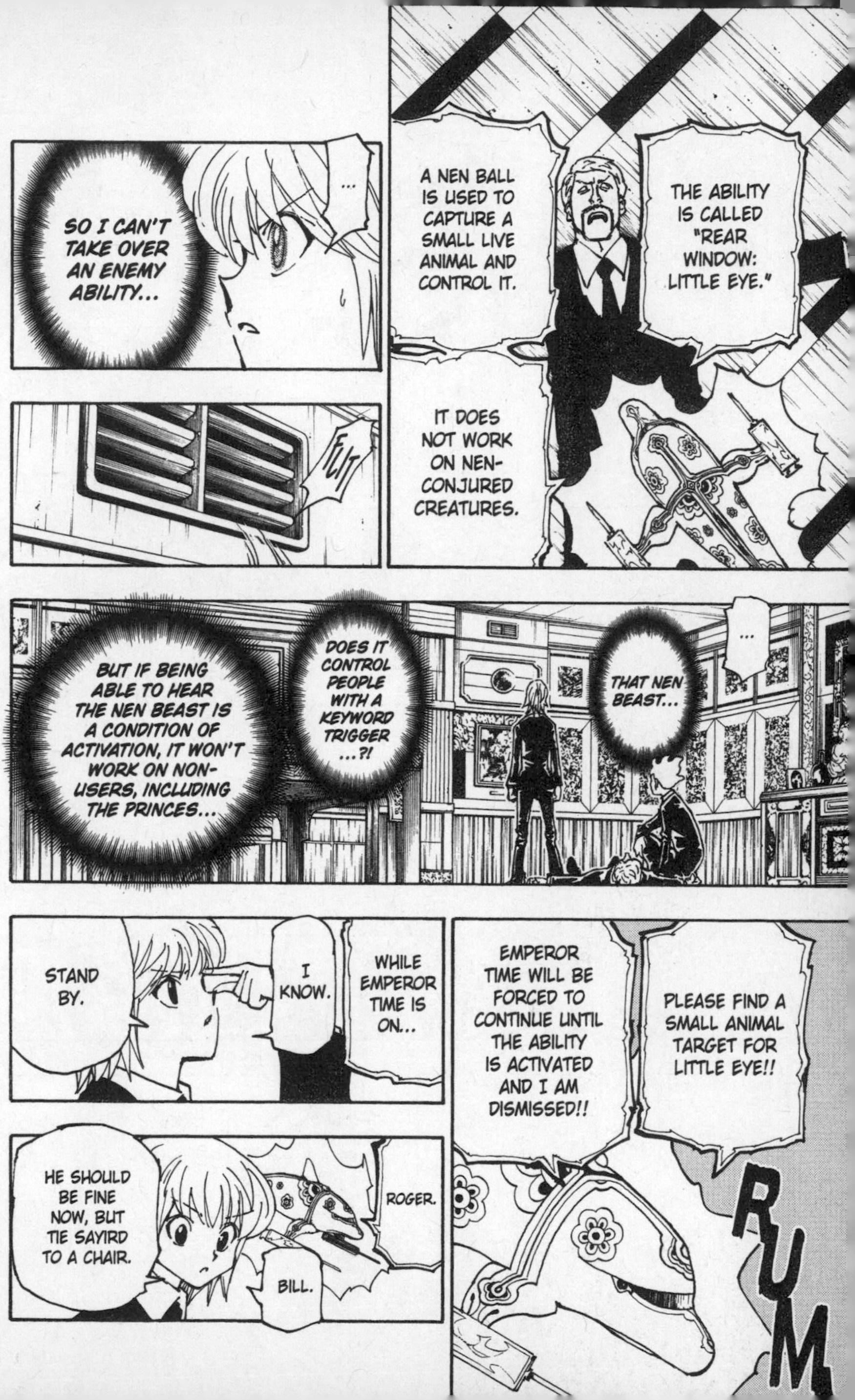
THE ABILITY IS CALLED "REAR WINDOW: LITTLE EYE."
A NEN BALL IS USED TO CAPTURE A SMALL LIVE ANIMAL AND CONTROL IT.
IT DOES NOT WORK ON NEN-CONJURED CREATURES.
...
SO I CAN'T TAKE OVER AN ENEMY ABILITY...
FLIT
...
THAT NEN BEAST...
DOES IT CONTROL PEOPLE WITH A KEYWORD TRIGGER ...?!
BUT IF BEING ABLE TO HEAR THE NEN BEAST IS A CONDITION OF ACTIVATION, IT WON'T WORK ON NON-USERS, INCLUDING THE PRINCES...
PLEASE FIND A SMALL ANIMAL TARGET FOR LITTLE EYE!!
EMPEROR TIME WILL BE FORCED TO CONTINUE UNTIL THE ABILITY IS ACTIVATED AND I AM DISMISSED!!
RUM
WHILE EMPEROR TIME IS ON...
I KNOW.
STAND BY.
ROGER.
HE SHOULD BE FINE NOW, BUT TIE SAYIRD TO A CHAIR.
BILL.

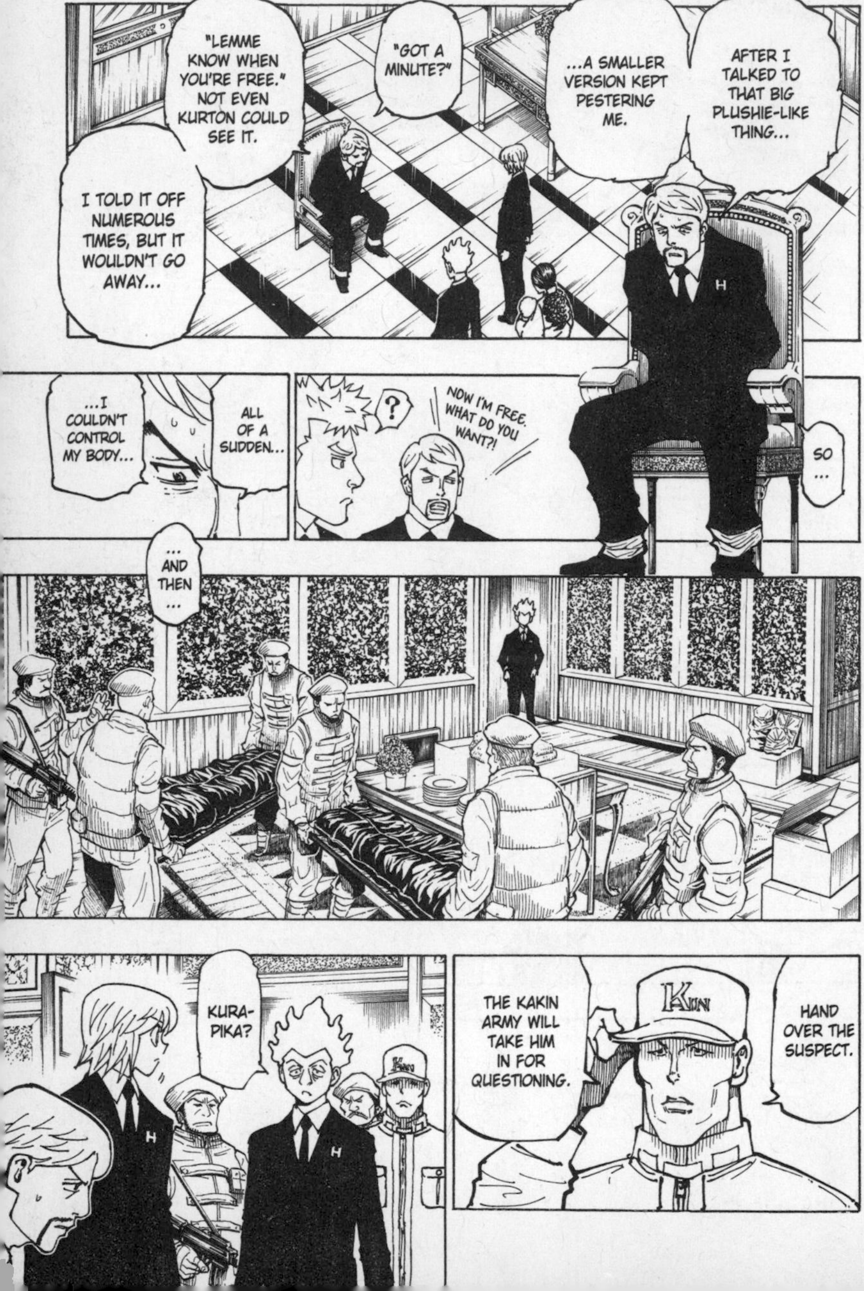
AFTER I TALKED TO THAT BIG PLUSHIE-LIKE THING...
...A SMALLER VERSION KEPT PESTERING ME.
"GOT A MINUTE?"
"LEMME KNOW WHEN YOU'RE FREE." NOT EVEN KURTON COULD SEE IT.
I TOLD IT OFF NUMEROUS TIMES, BUT IT WOULDN'T GO AWAY...
SO ...
NOW I'M FREE. WHAT DO YOU WANT?!
?
ALL OF A SUDDEN...
...I COULDN'T CONTROL MY BODY...
...AND THEN ...
HAND OVER THE SUSPECT.
THE KAKIN ARMY WILL TAKE HIM IN FOR QUESTIONING.
KURA-PIKA?

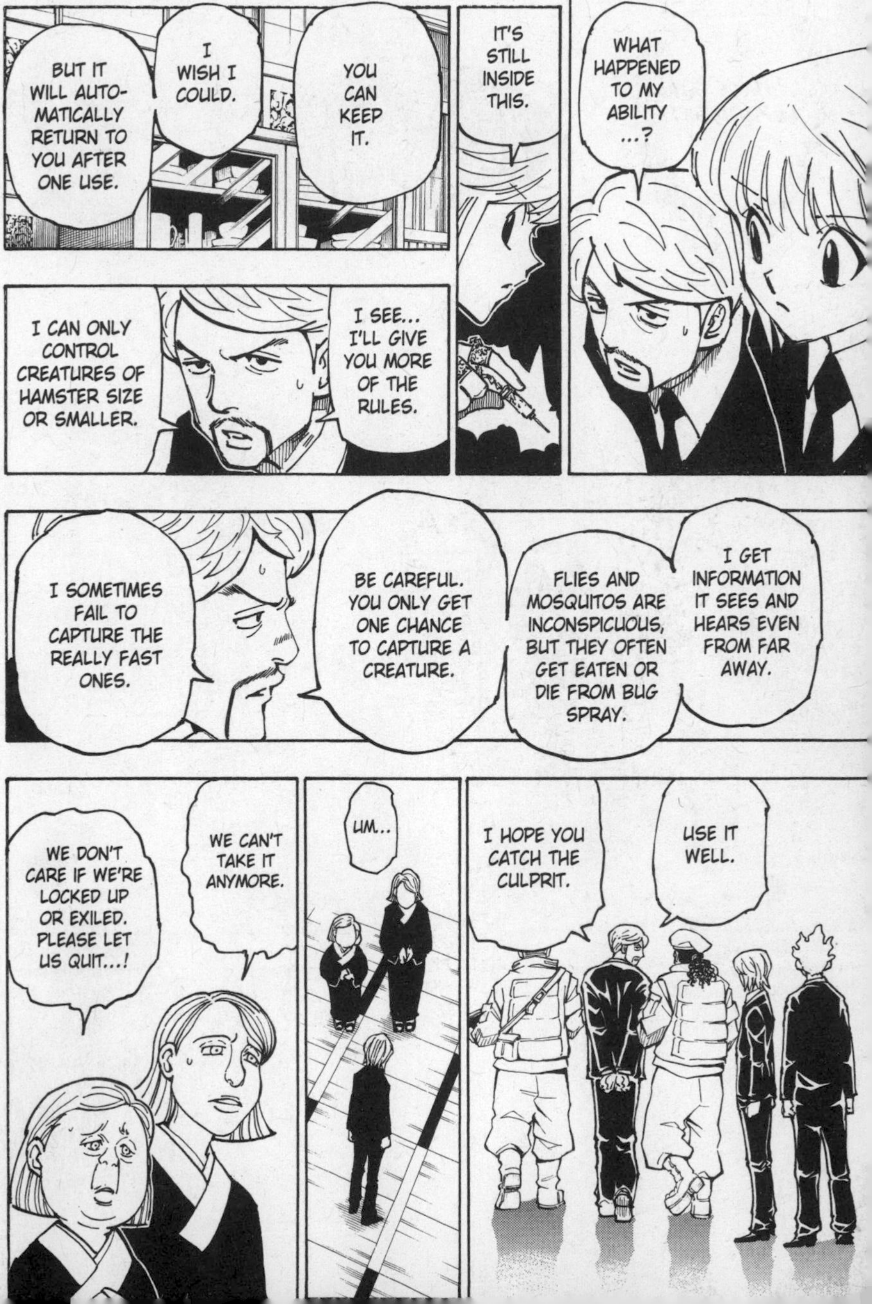
WHAT HAPPENED TO MY ABILITY ...?
IT'S STILL INSIDE THIS.
YOU CAN KEEP IT.
I WISH I COULD.
BUT IT WILL AUTO-MATICALLY RETURN TO YOU AFTER ONE USE.
I SEE... I'LL GIVE YOU MORE OF THE RULES.
I CAN ONLY CONTROL CREATURES OF HAMSTER SIZE OR SMALLER.
I GET INFORMATION IT SEES AND HEARS EVEN FROM FAR AWAY.
FLIES AND MOSQUITOS ARE INCONSPICUOUS, BUT THEY OFTEN GET EATEN OR DIE FROM BUG SPRAY.
BE CAREFUL. YOU ONLY GET ONE CHANCE TO CAPTURE A CREATURE.
I SOMETIMES FAIL TO CAPTURE THE REALLY FAST ONES.
USE IT WELL.
I HOPE YOU CATCH THE CULPRIT.
UM...
WE CAN'T TAKE IT ANYMORE.
WE DON'T CARE IF WE'RE LOCKED UP OR EXILED. PLEASE LET US QUIT...!

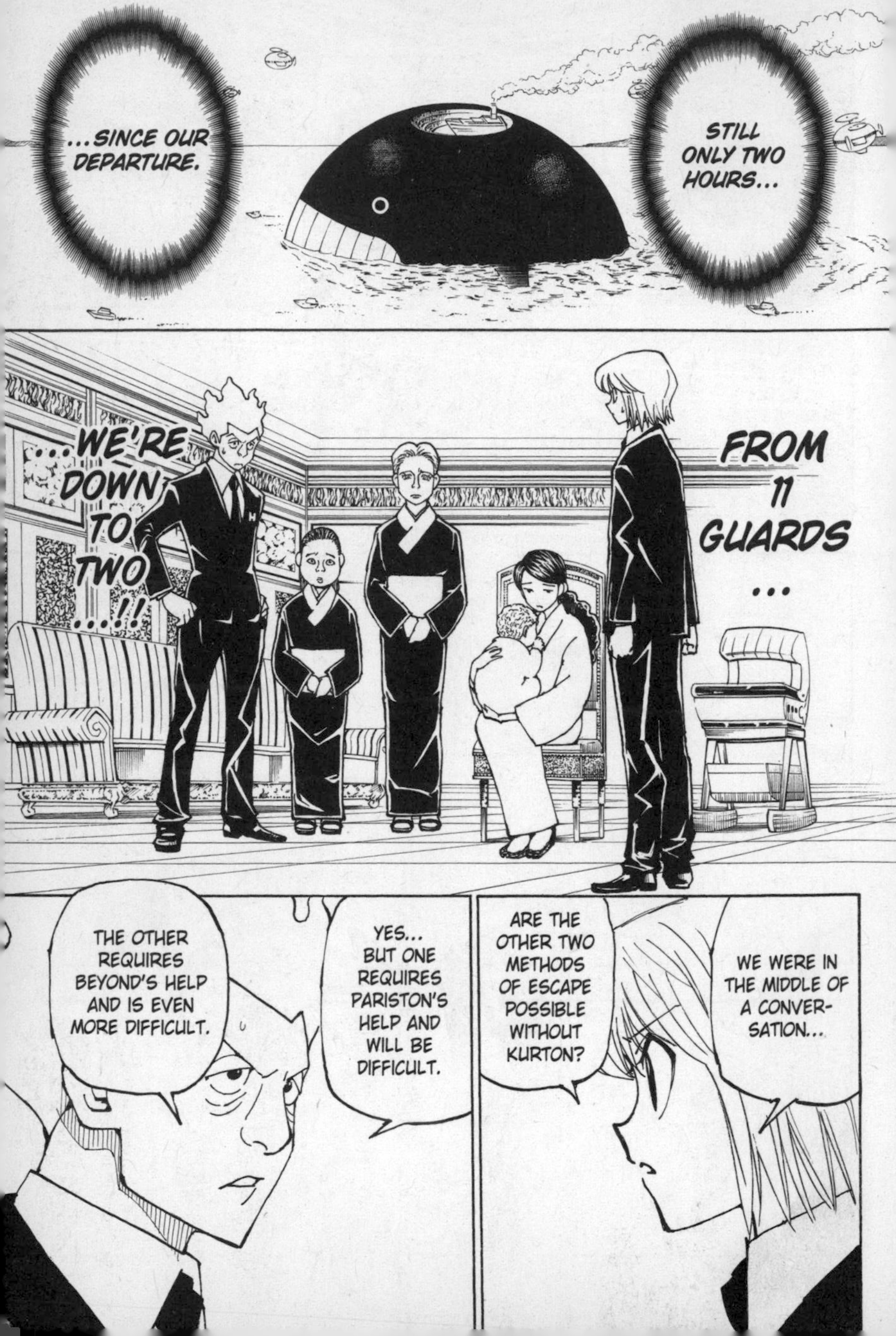
STILL ONLY TWO HOURS...
...SINCE OUR DEPARTURE.
FROM 11 GUARDS ...
...WE'RE DOWN TO TWO...!!
WE WERE IN THE MIDDLE OF A CONVERSATION...
ARE THE OTHER TWO METHODS OF ESCAPE POSSIBLE WITHOUT KURTON?
YES... BUT ONE REQUIRES PARISTON'S HELP AND WILL BE DIFFICULT.
THE OTHER REQUIRES BEYOND'S HELP AND IS EVEN MORE DIFFICULT.

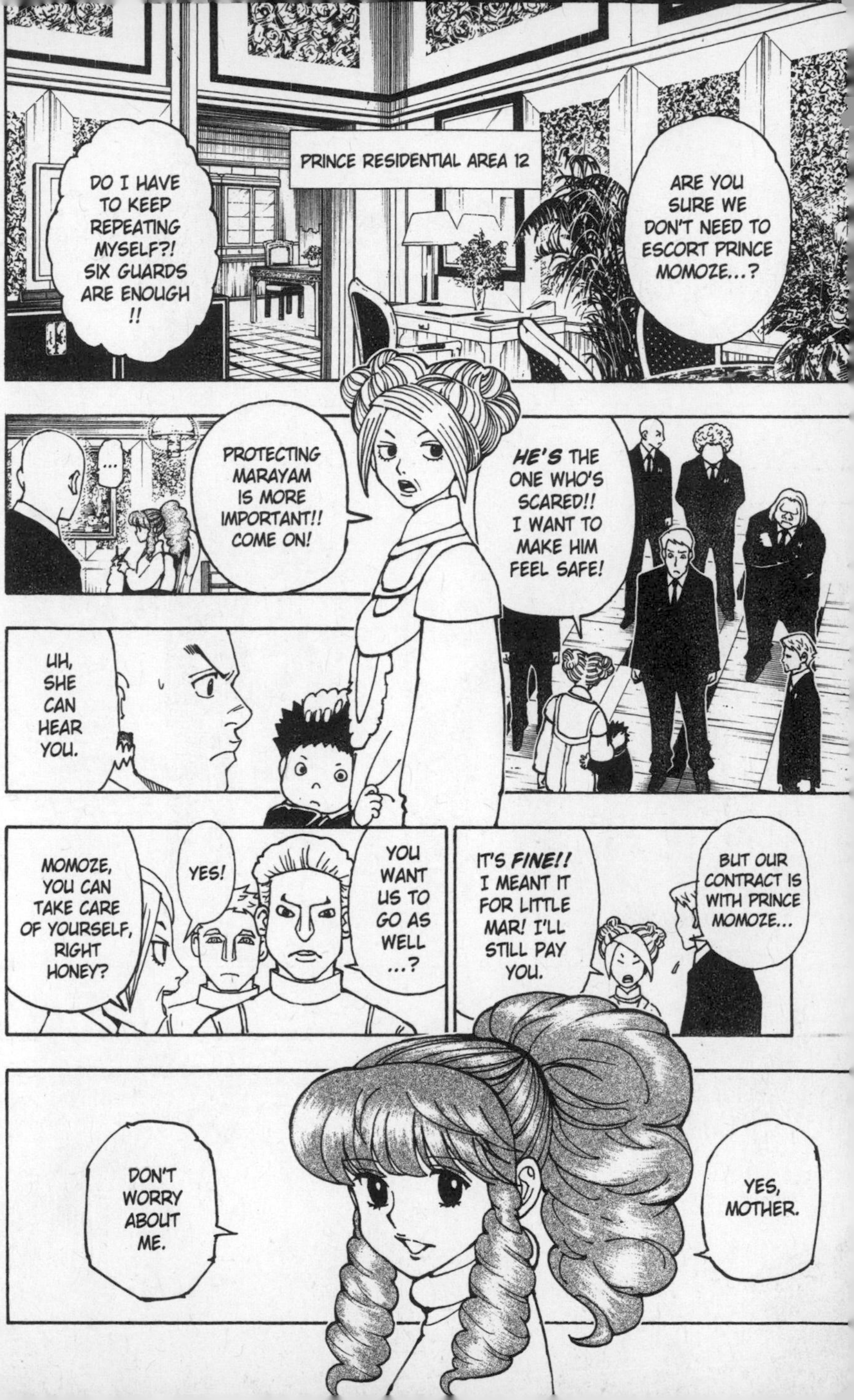
PRINCE RESIDENTIAL AREA 12
ARE YOU SURE WE DON'T NEED TO ESCORT PRINCE MOMOZE...?
DO I HAVE TO KEEP REPEATING MYSELF?! SIX GUARDS ARE ENOUGH!!
HE'S THE ONE WHO'S SCARED!! I WANT TO MAKE HIM FEEL SAFE!
PROTECTING MARAYAM IS MORE IMPORTANT!! COME ON!
...
UH, SHE CAN HEAR YOU.
BUT OUR CONTRACT IS WITH PRINCE MOMOZE...
IT'S FINE!! I MEANT IT FOR LITTLE MAR! I'LL STILL PAY YOU.
YOU WANT US TO GO AS WELL...?
YES!
MOMOZE, YOU CAN TAKE CARE OF YOURSELF, RIGHT HONEY?
YES, MOTHER.
DON'T WORRY ABOUT ME.

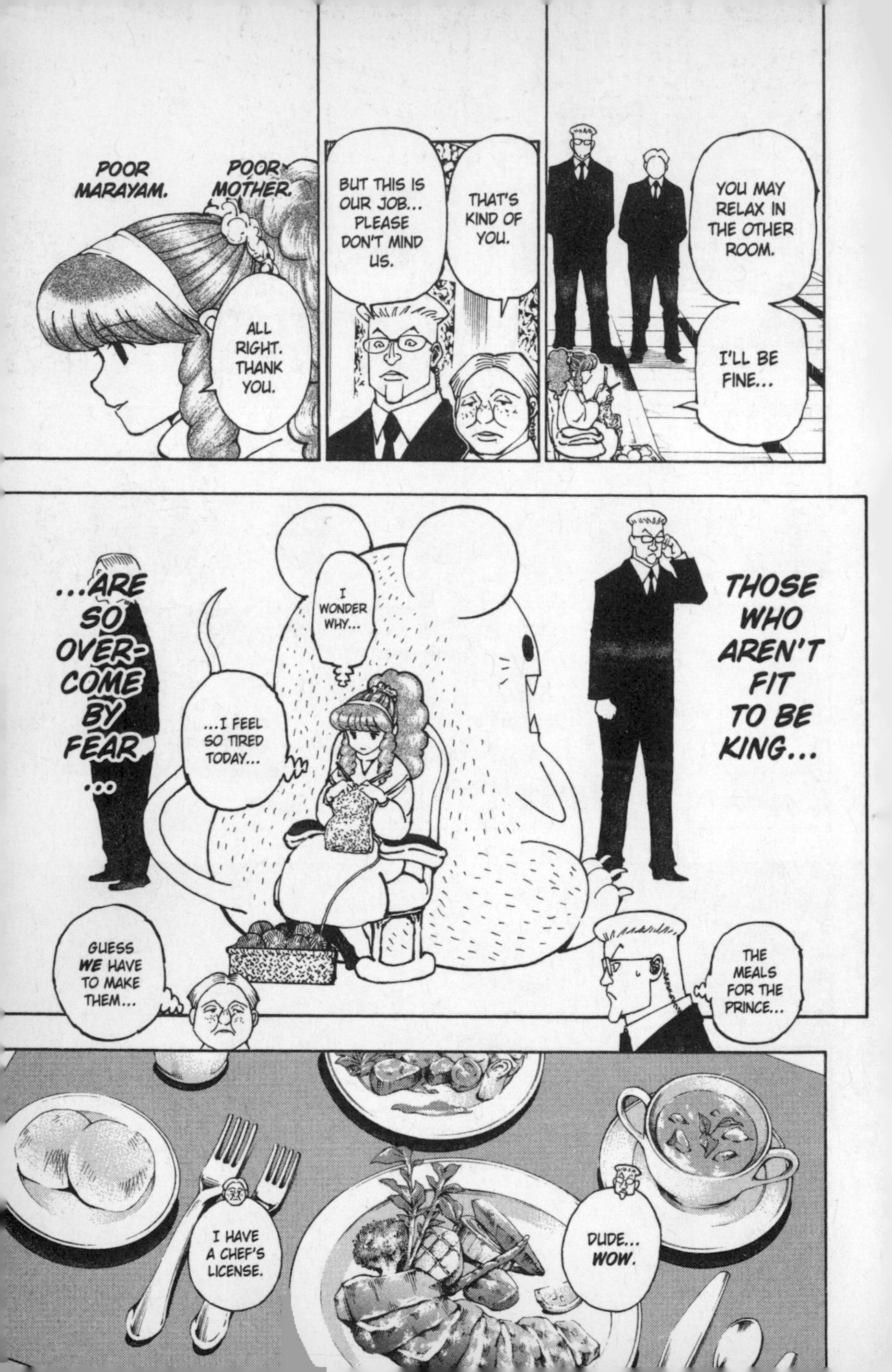
YOU MAY RELAX IN THE OTHER ROOM.
I'LL BE FINE...
THAT'S KIND OF YOU.
BUT THIS IS OUR JOB... PLEASE DON'T MIND US.
POOR MOTHER.
POOR MARAYAM.
ALL RIGHT. THANK YOU.
THOSE WHO AREN'T FIT TO BE KING...
I WONDER WHY...
...I FEEL SO TIRED TODAY...
...ARE SO OVER-COME BY FEAR...
THE MEALS FOR THE PRINCE...
GUESS WE HAVE TO MAKE THEM...
DUDE... WOW.
I HAVE A CHEF'S LICENSE.

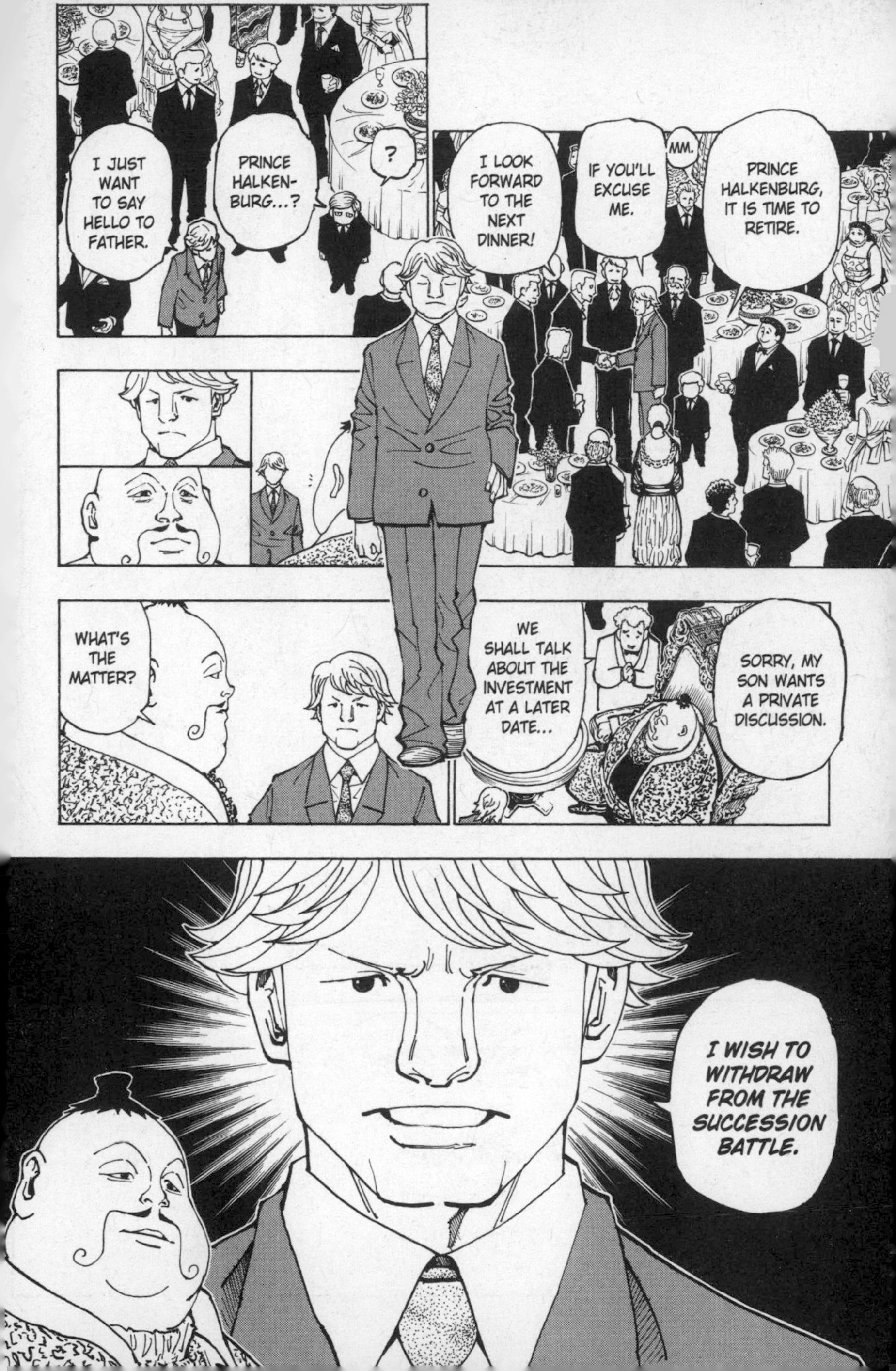
PRINCE HALKENBURG, IT IS TIME TO RETIRE.
MM.
IF YOU'LL EXCUSE ME.
I LOOK FORWARD TO THE NEXT DINNER!
?
PRINCE HALKEN-BURG...?
I JUST WANT TO SAY HELLO TO FATHER.
SORRY, MY SON WANTS A PRIVATE DISCUSSION.
WE SHALL TALK ABOUT THE INVESTMENT AT A LATER DATE...
WHAT'S THE MATTER?
I WISH TO WITHDRAW FROM THE SUCCESSION BATTLE.

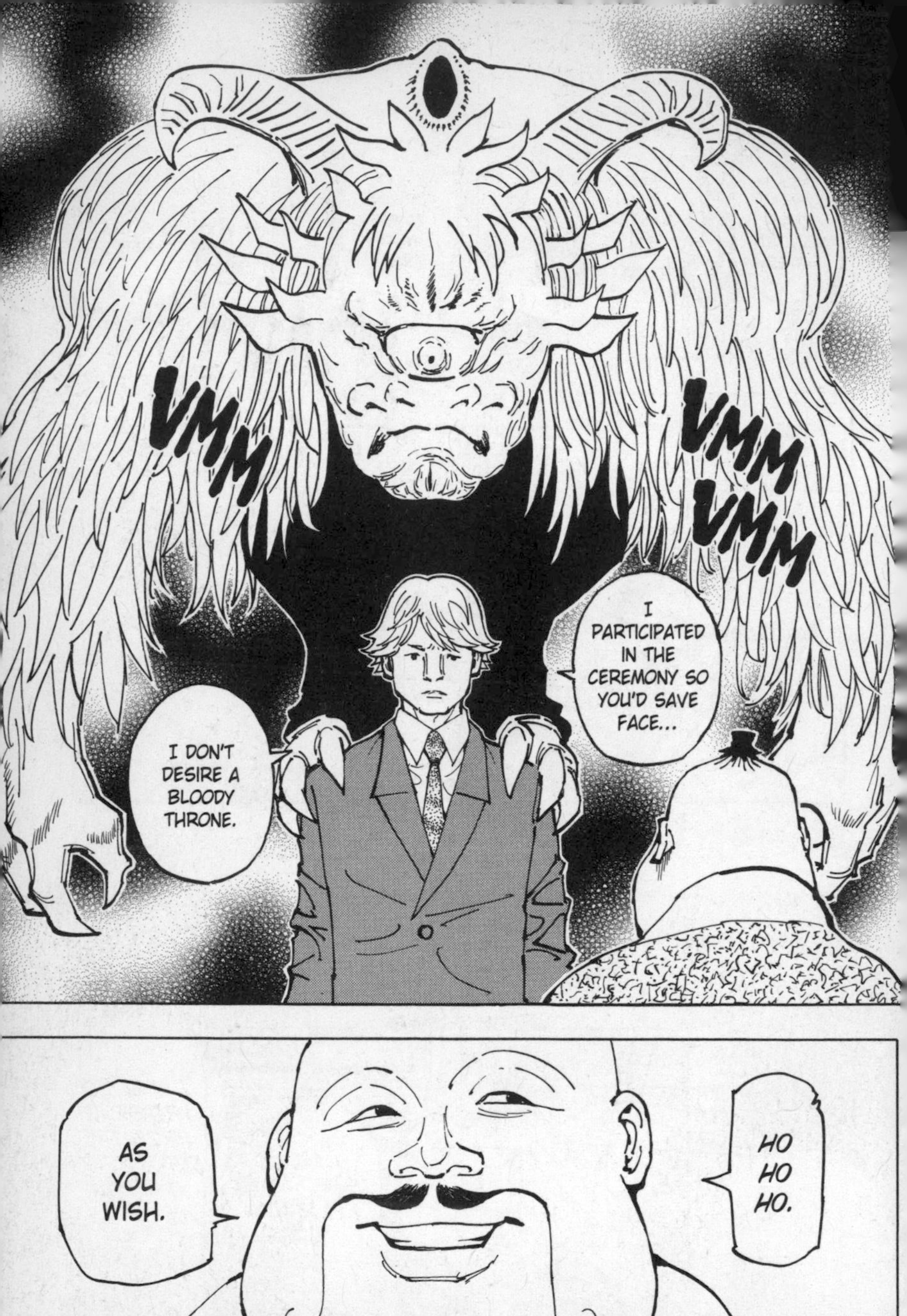
VMM VMM
VMM
I PARTICIPATED IN THE CEREMONY SO YOU'D SAVE FACE...
VMM
I DON'T DESIRE A BLOODY THRONE.
HO HO HO.
AS YOU WISH.

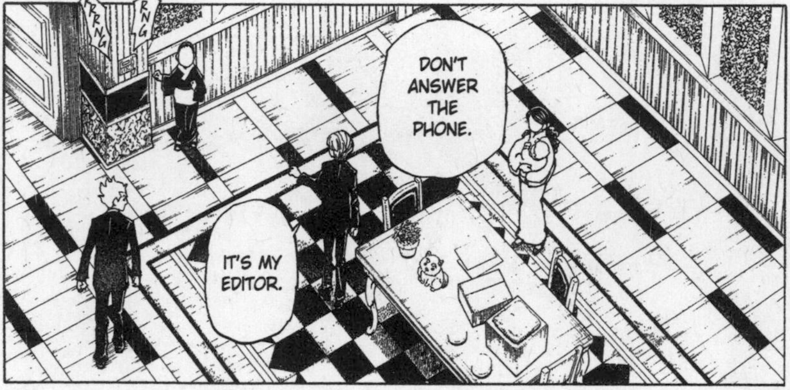
DON'T ANSWER THE PHONE.
RNG
RRRNG
IT'S MY EDITOR.

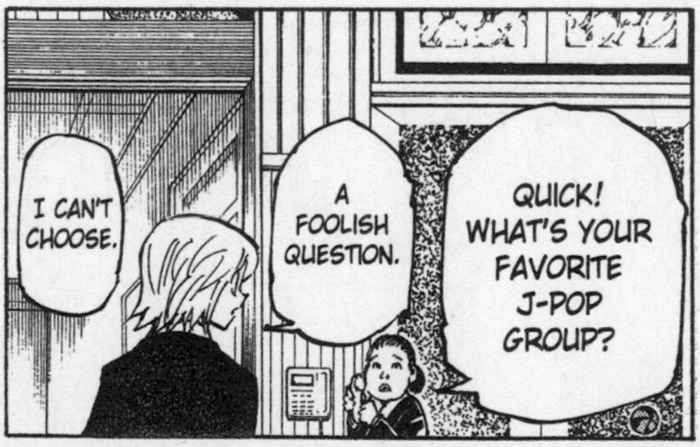
QUICK! WHAT'S YOUR FAVORITE J-POP GROUP?
A FOOLISH QUESTION.
I CAN'T CHOOSE.

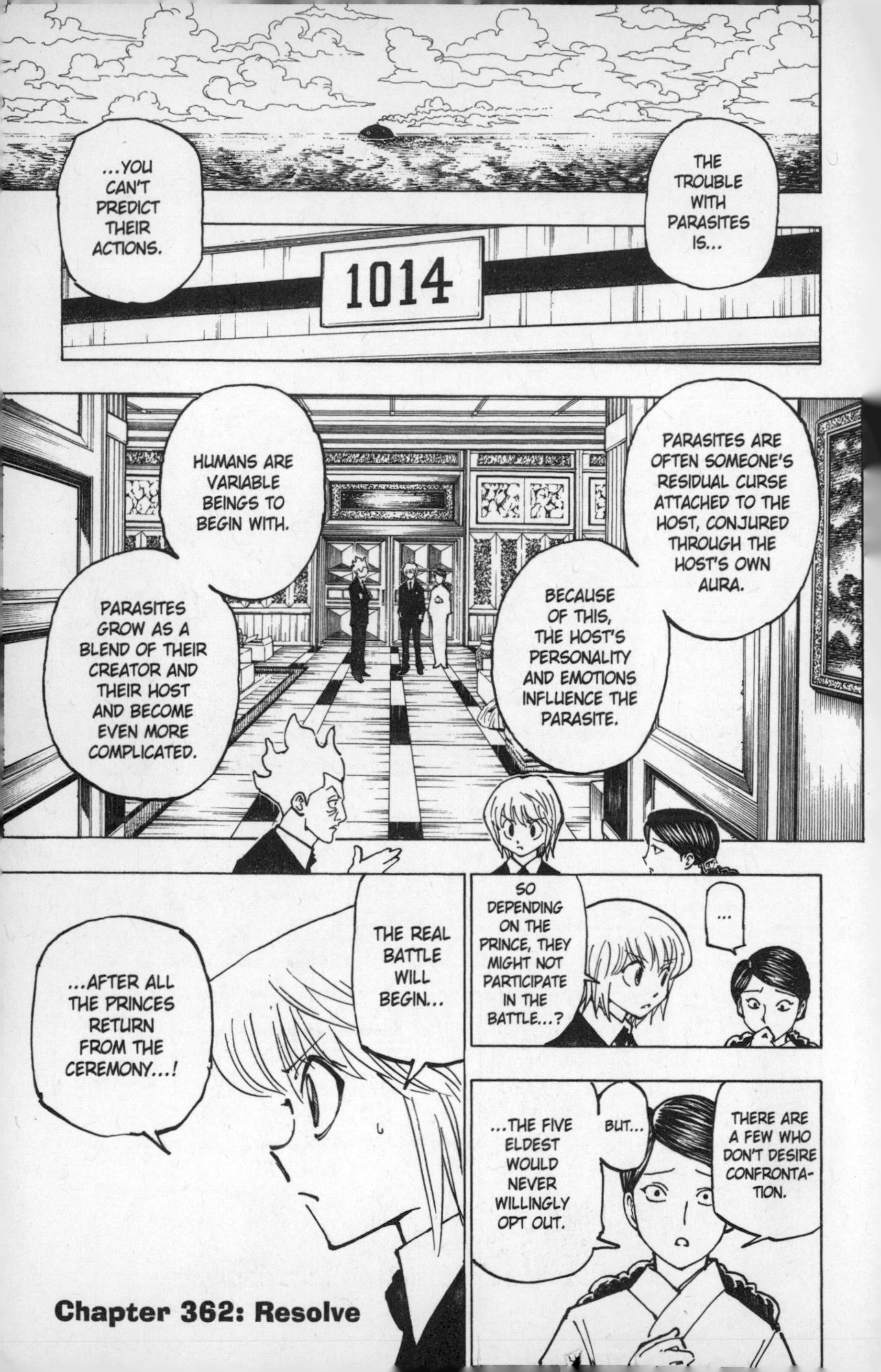
THE TROUBLE WITH PARASITES IS...
1014
...YOU CAN'T PREDICT THEIR ACTIONS.
PARASITES ARE OFTEN SOMEONE'S RESIDUAL CURSE ATTACHED TO THE HOST, CONJURED THROUGH THE HOST'S OWN AURA.
BECAUSE OF THIS, THE HOST'S PERSONALITY AND EMOTIONS INFLUENCE THE PARASITE.
HUMANS ARE VARIABLE BEINGS TO BEGIN WITH.
PARASITES GROW AS A BLEND OF THEIR CREATOR AND THEIR HOST AND BECOME EVEN MORE COMPLICATED.
...
SO DEPENDING ON THE PRINCE, THEY MIGHT NOT PARTICIPATE IN THE BATTLE...?
THERE ARE A FEW WHO DON'T DESIRE CONFRONTA-TION.
BUT...
...THE FIVE ELDEST WOULD NEVER WILLINGLY OPT OUT.
THE REAL BATTLE WILL BEGIN...
...AFTER ALL THE PRINCES RETURN FROM THE CEREMONY...!
Chapter 362: Resolve

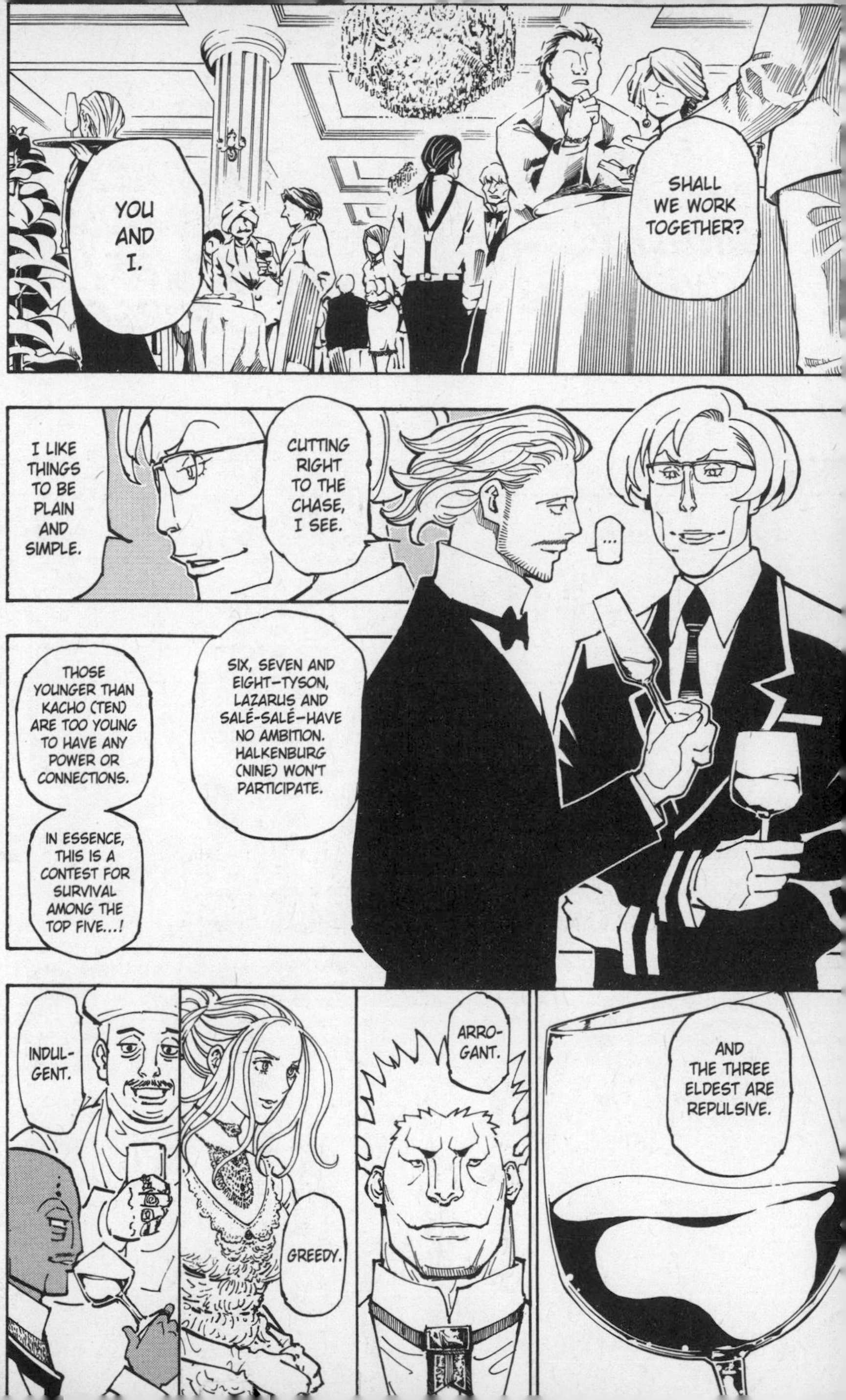
SHALL WE WORK TOGETHER?
YOU AND I.
...
CUTTING RIGHT TO THE CHASE, I SEE.
I LIKE THINGS TO BE PLAIN AND SIMPLE.
SIX, SEVEN AND EIGHT—TYSON, LAZARUS AND SALÉ-SALÉ—HAVE NO AMBITION. HALKENBURG (NINE) WON'T PARTICIPATE.
THOSE YOUNGER THAN KACHO (TEN) ARE TOO YOUNG TO HAVE ANY POWER OR CONNECTIONS.
IN ESSENCE, THIS IS A CONTEST FOR SURVIVAL AMONG THE TOP FIVE...!
AND THE THREE ELDEST ARE REPULSIVE.
ARRO-GANT.
GREEDY.
INDUL-GENT.

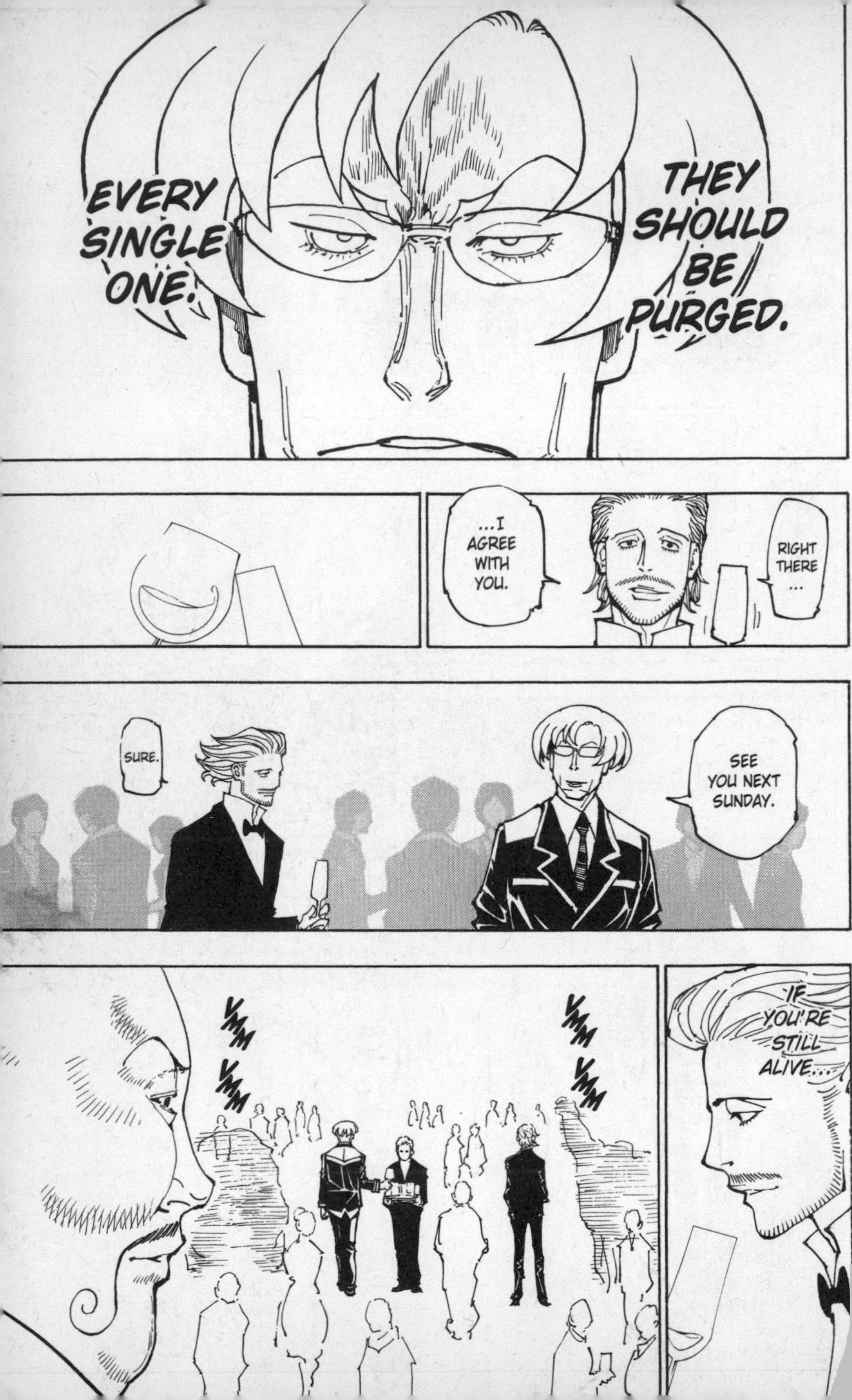
THEY SHOULD BE PURGED.
EVERY SINGLE ONE.
RIGHT THERE ...
...I AGREE WITH YOU.
SEE YOU NEXT SUNDAY.
SURE.
IF YOU'RE STILL ALIVE....
VMM VMM
VMM VMM

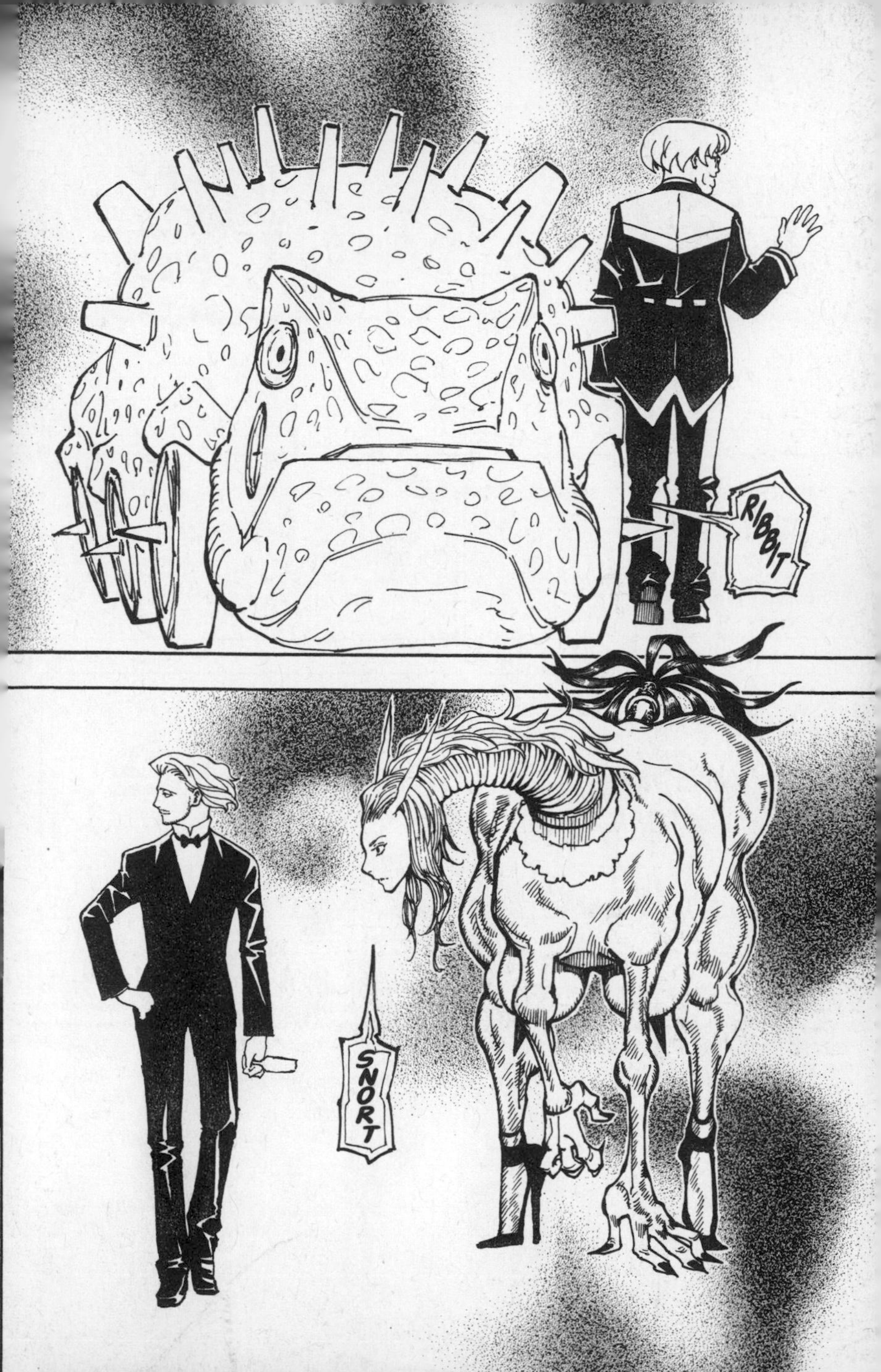
RIBBIT
SNORT

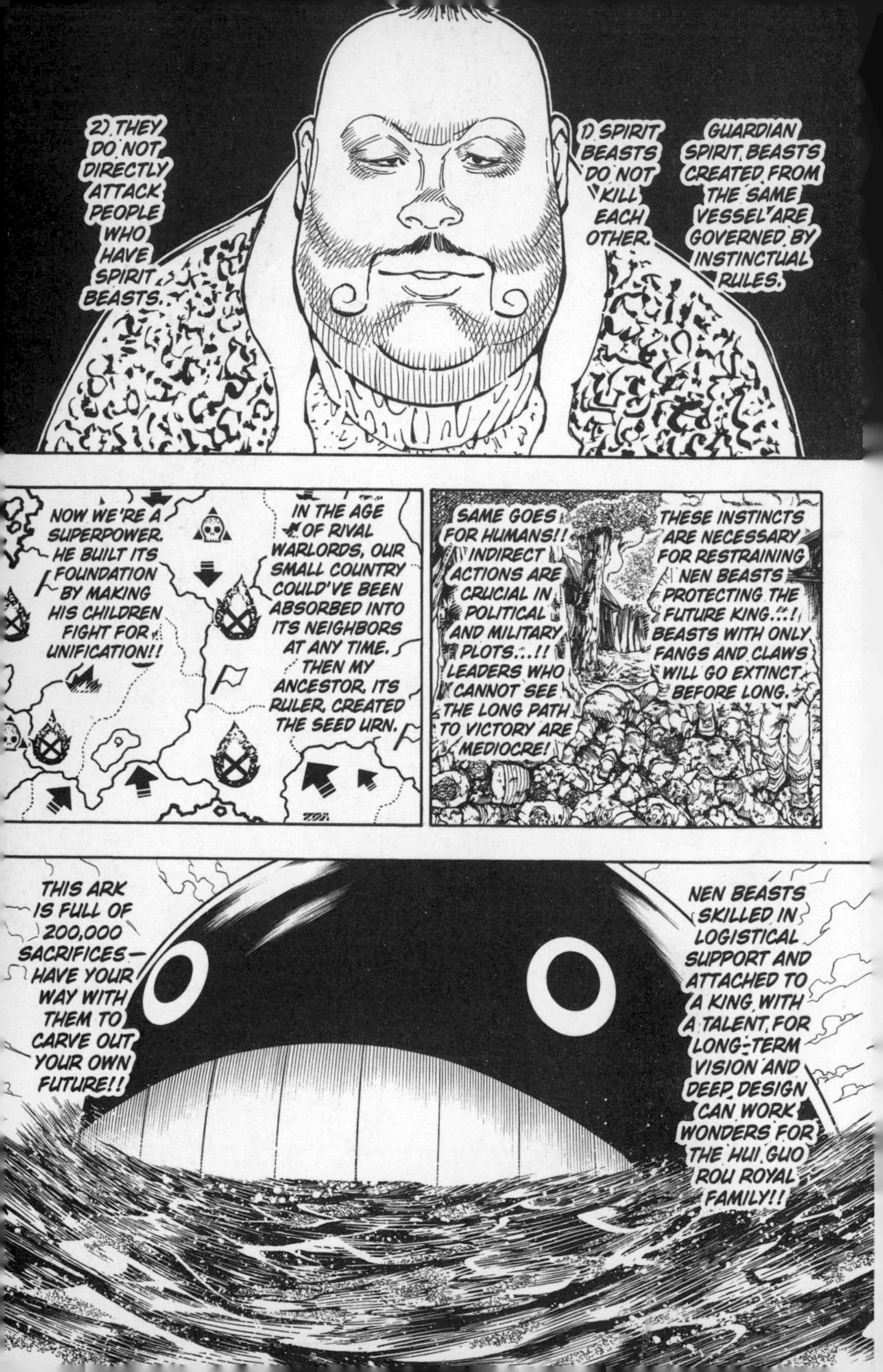
GUARDIAN SPIRIT BEASTS CREATED FROM THE SAME VESSEL ARE GOVERNED BY INSTINCTUAL RULES.
1) SPIRIT BEASTS DO NOT KILL EACH OTHER.
2) THEY DO NOT DIRECTLY ATTACK PEOPLE WHO HAVE SPIRIT BEASTS.
THESE INSTINCTS ARE NECESSARY FOR RESTRAINING NEN BEASTS PROTECTING THE FUTURE KING...! BEASTS WITH ONLY FANGS AND CLAWS WILL GO EXTINCT BEFORE LONG.
SAME GOES FOR HUMANS!! INDIRECT ACTIONS ARE CRUCIAL IN POLITICAL AND MILITARY PLOTS...!! LEADERS WHO CANNOT SEE THE LONG PATH TO VICTORY ARE MEDIOCRE!
IN THE AGE OF RIVAL WARLORDS, OUR SMALL COUNTRY COULD'VE BEEN ABSORBED INTO ITS NEIGHBORS AT ANY TIME. THEN MY ANCESTOR, ITS RULER, CREATED THE SEED URN.
NOW WE'RE A SUPERPOWER. HE BUILT ITS FOUNDATION BY MAKING HIS CHILDREN FIGHT FOR UNIFICATION!!
NEN BEASTS SKILLED IN LOGISTICAL SUPPORT AND ATTACHED TO A KING WITH A TALENT FOR LONG-TERM VISION AND DEEP DESIGN CAN WORK WONDERS FOR THE HUI GUO ROU ROYAL FAMILY!!
THIS ARK IS FULL OF 200,000 SACRIFICES— HAVE YOUR WAY WITH THEM TO CARVE OUT YOUR OWN FUTURE!!

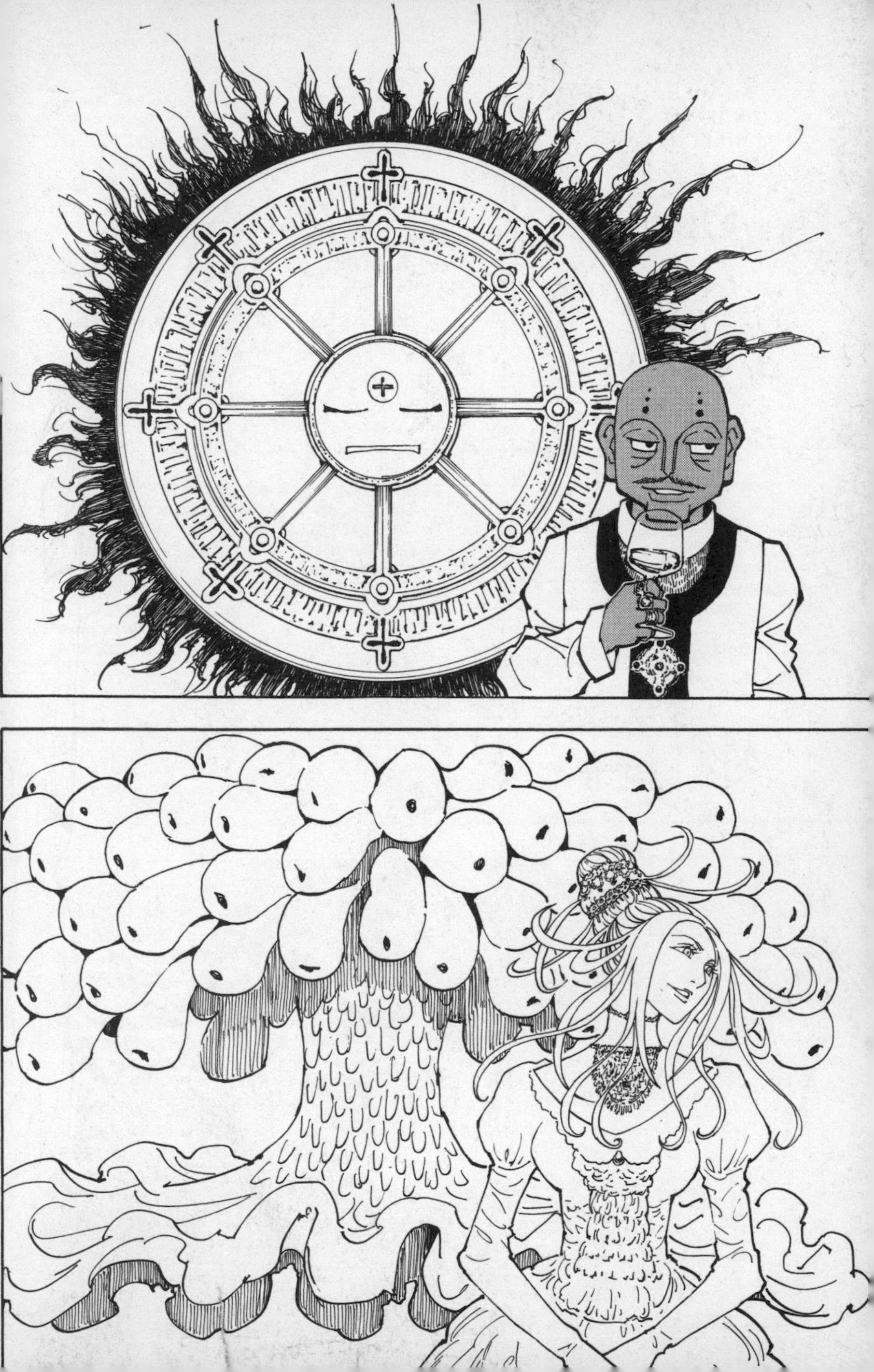

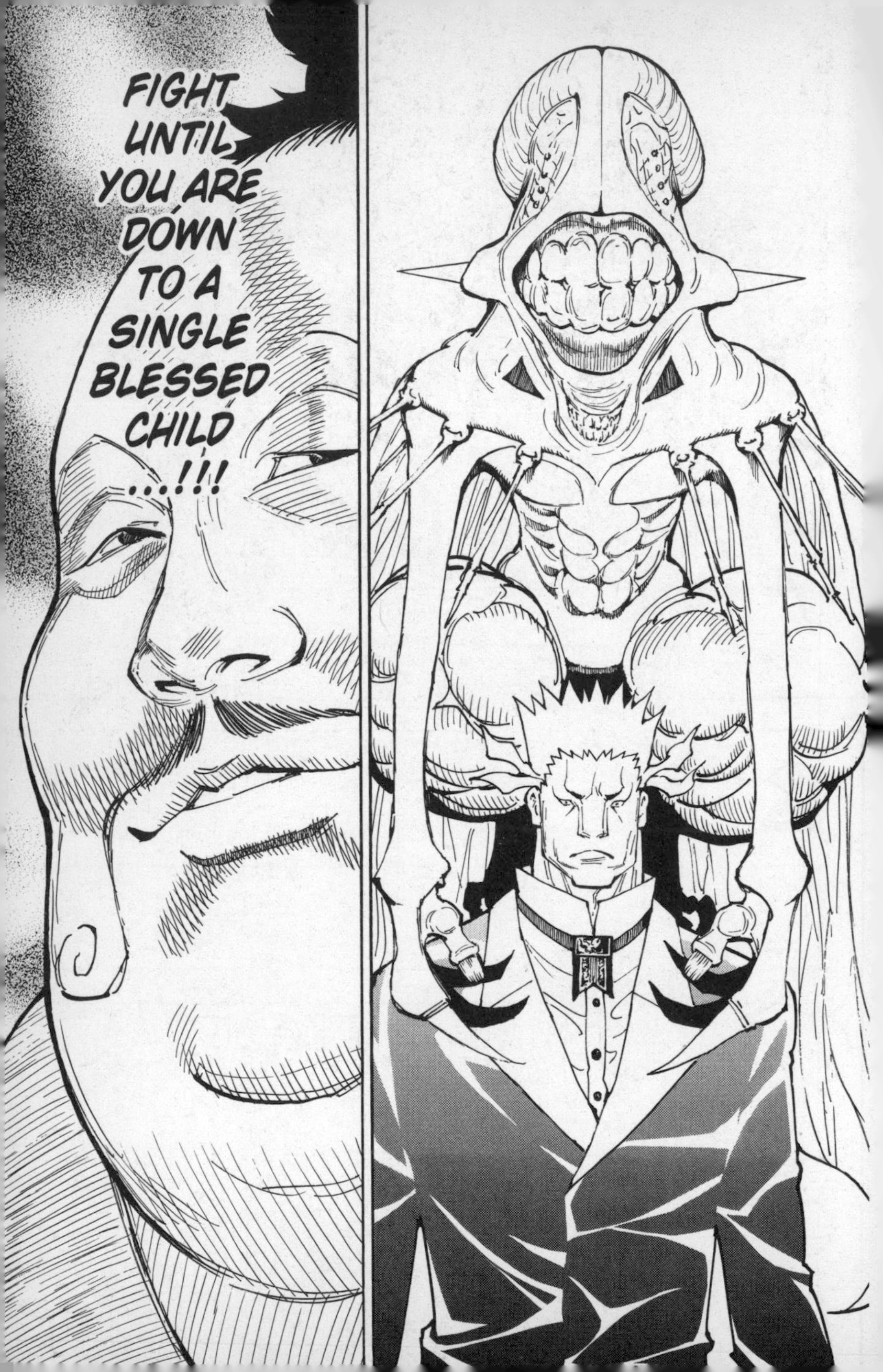
FIGHT UNTIL YOU ARE DOWN TO A SINGLE BLESSED CHILD ...!!!

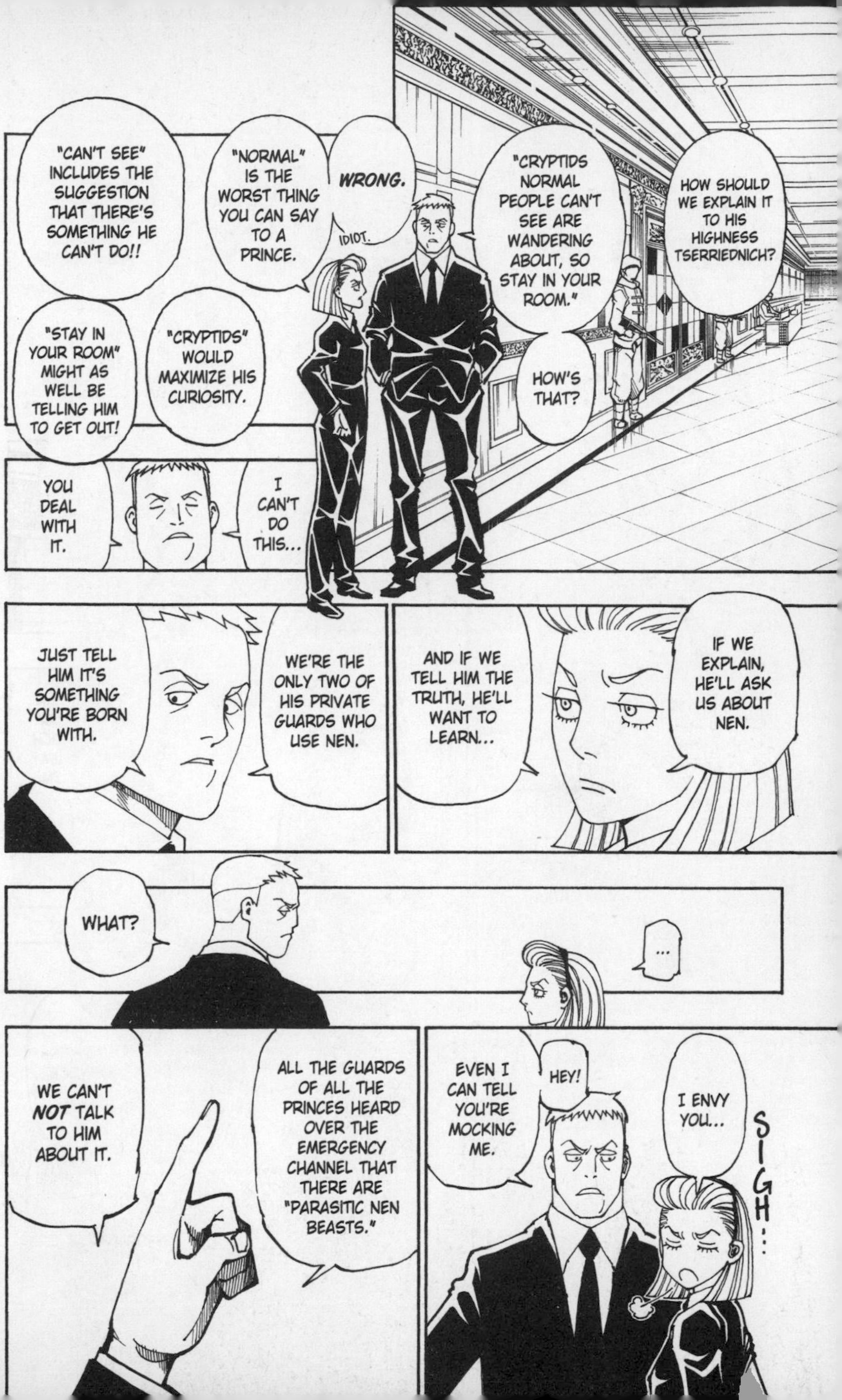
HOW SHOULD WE EXPLAIN IT TO HIS HIGHNESS TSERRIEDNICH?
"CRYPTIDS NORMAL PEOPLE CAN'T SEE ARE WANDERING ABOUT, SO STAY IN YOUR ROOM."
HOW'S THAT?
WRONG.
IDIOT.
"NORMAL" IS THE WORST THING YOU CAN SAY TO A PRINCE.
"CAN'T SEE" INCLUDES THE SUGGESTION THAT THERE'S SOMETHING HE CAN'T DO!!
"CRYPTIDS" WOULD MAXIMIZE HIS CURIOSITY.
"STAY IN YOUR ROOM" MIGHT AS WELL BE TELLING HIM TO GET OUT!
I CAN'T DO THIS...
YOU DEAL WITH IT.
IF WE EXPLAIN, HE'LL ASK US ABOUT NEN.
AND IF WE TELL HIM THE TRUTH, HE'LL WANT TO LEARN...
WE'RE THE ONLY TWO OF HIS PRIVATE GUARDS WHO USE NEN.
JUST TELL HIM IT'S SOMETHING YOU'RE BORN WITH.
...
WHAT?
I ENVY YOU...
SIGH..
HEY!
EVEN I CAN TELL YOU'RE MOCKING ME.
ALL THE GUARDS OF ALL THE PRINCES HEARD OVER THE EMERGENCY CHANNEL THAT THERE ARE "PARASITIC NEN BEASTS."
WE CAN'T *NOT* TALK TO HIM ABOUT IT.

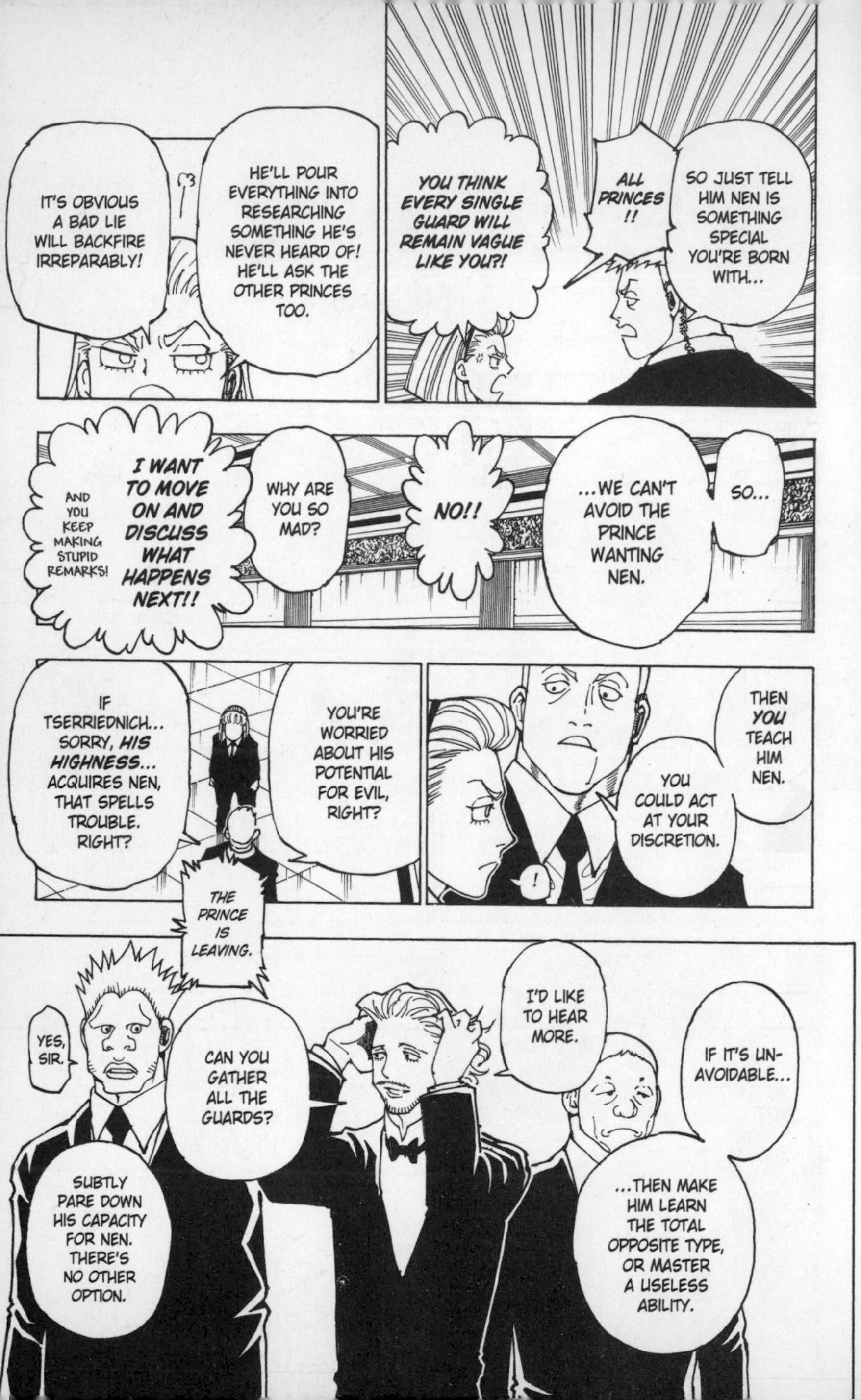
SO JUST TELL HIM NEN IS SOMETHING SPECIAL YOU'RE BORN WITH...
ALL PRINCES !!
YOU THINK EVERY SINGLE GUARD WILL REMAIN VAGUE LIKE YOU?!
HE'LL POUR EVERYTHING INTO RESEARCHING SOMETHING HE'S NEVER HEARD OF! HE'LL ASK THE OTHER PRINCES TOO.
IT'S OBVIOUS A BAD LIE WILL BACKFIRE IRREPARABLY!
SO...
...WE CAN'T AVOID THE PRINCE WANTING NEN.
NO!!
WHY ARE YOU SO MAD?
I WANT TO MOVE ON AND DISCUSS WHAT HAPPENS NEXT!!
AND YOU KEEP MAKING STUPID REMARKS!
THEN YOU TEACH HIM NEN.
YOU COULD ACT AT YOUR DISCRETION.
YOU'RE WORRIED ABOUT HIS POTENTIAL FOR EVIL, RIGHT?
IF TSERRIEDNICH... SORRY, HIS HIGHNESS... ACQUIRES NEN, THAT SPELLS TROUBLE. RIGHT?
THE PRINCE IS LEAVING.
IF IT'S UN-AVOIDABLE...
...THEN MAKE HIM LEARN THE TOTAL OPPOSITE TYPE, OR MASTER A USELESS ABILITY.
SUBTLY PARE DOWN HIS CAPACITY FOR NEN. THERE'S NO OTHER OPTION.
I'D LIKE TO HEAR MORE.
CAN YOU GATHER ALL THE GUARDS?
YES, SIR.

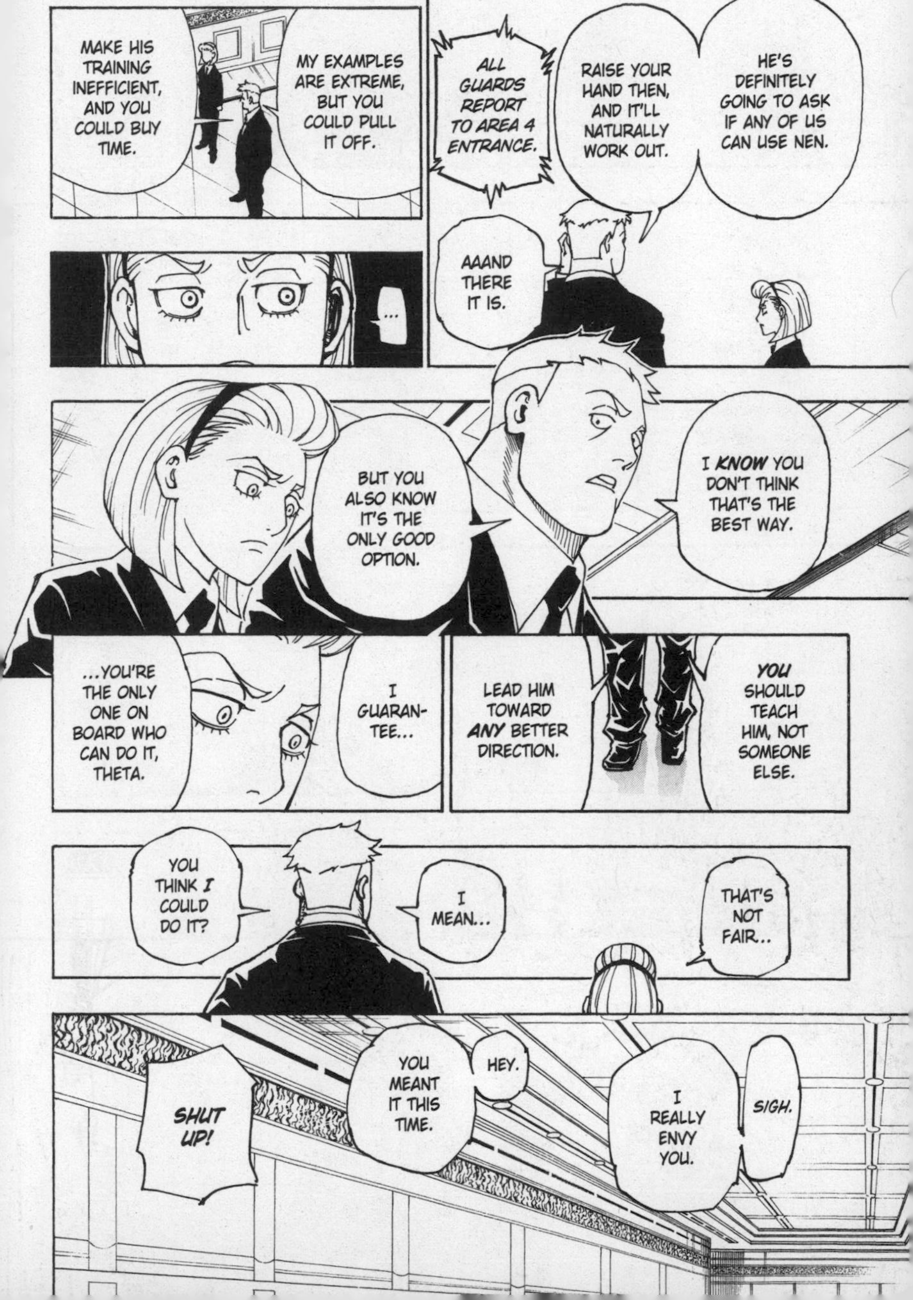
HE'S DEFINITELY GOING TO ASK IF ANY OF US CAN USE NEN.
RAISE YOUR HAND THEN, AND IT'LL NATURALLY WORK OUT.
ALL GUARDS REPORT TO AREA 4 ENTRANCE.
AAAND THERE IT IS.
MY EXAMPLES ARE EXTREME, BUT YOU COULD PULL IT OFF.
MAKE HIS TRAINING INEFFICIENT, AND YOU COULD BUY TIME.
...
I KNOW YOU DON'T THINK THAT'S THE BEST WAY.
BUT YOU ALSO KNOW IT'S THE ONLY GOOD OPTION.
YOU SHOULD TEACH HIM, NOT SOMEONE ELSE.
LEAD HIM TOWARD ANY BETTER DIRECTION.
I GUARAN-TEE...
...YOU'RE THE ONLY ONE ON BOARD WHO CAN DO IT, THETA.
THAT'S NOT FAIR...
I MEAN...
YOU THINK I COULD DO IT?
SIGH.
I REALLY ENVY YOU.
HEY.
YOU MEANT IT THIS TIME.
SHUT UP!

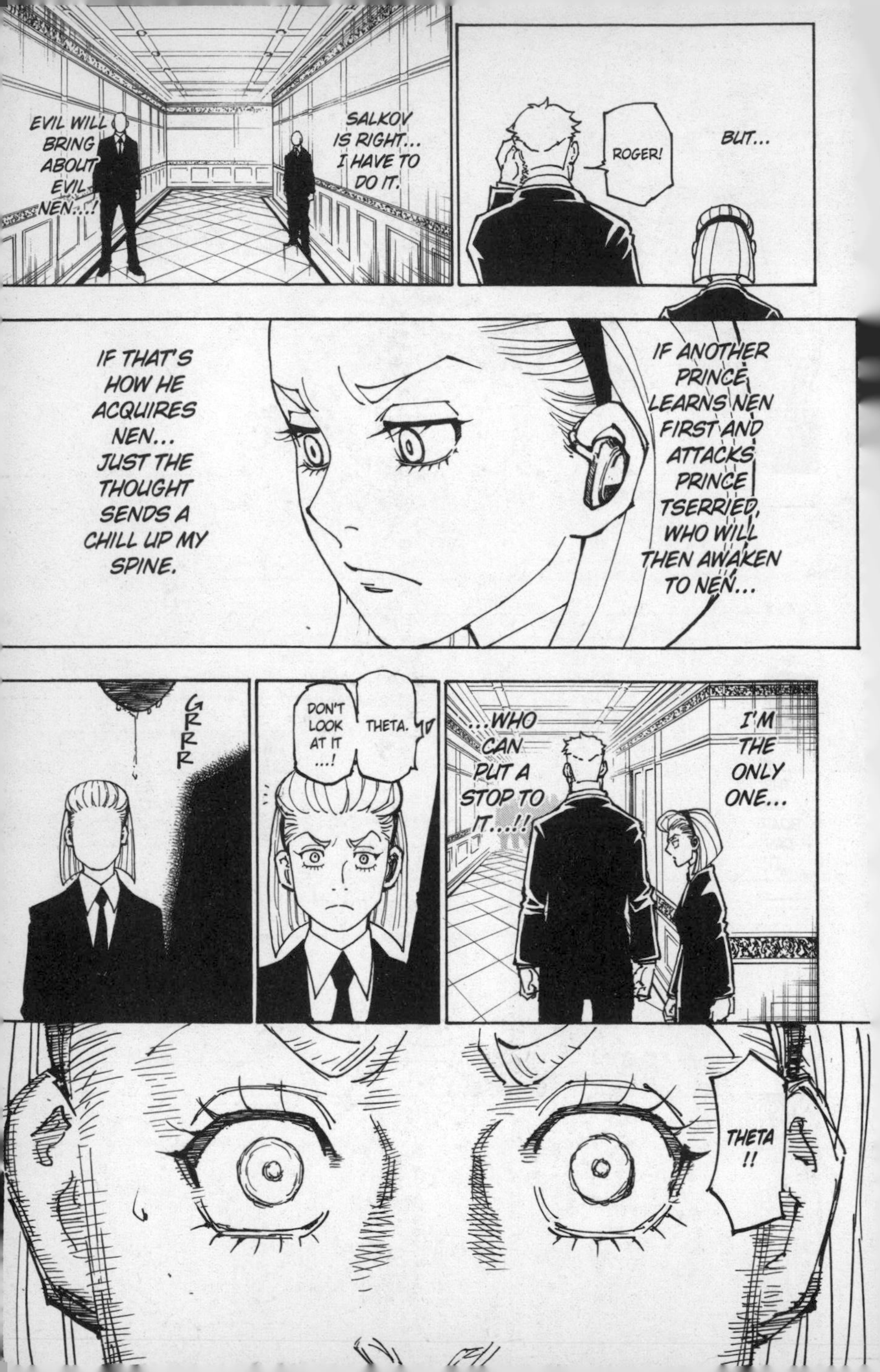
ROGER!
BUT...
SALKOV IS RIGHT... I HAVE TO DO IT.
EVIL WILL BRING ABOUT EVIL NEN...!
IF ANOTHER PRINCE LEARNS NEN FIRST AND ATTACKS PRINCE TSERRIED, WHO WILL THEN AWAKEN TO NEN...
IF THAT'S HOW HE ACQUIRES NEN... JUST THE THOUGHT SENDS A CHILL UP MY SPINE.
I'M THE ONLY ONE...
...WHO CAN PUT A STOP TO IT...!!
THETA.
DON'T LOOK AT IT...!
GRRR
THETA !!

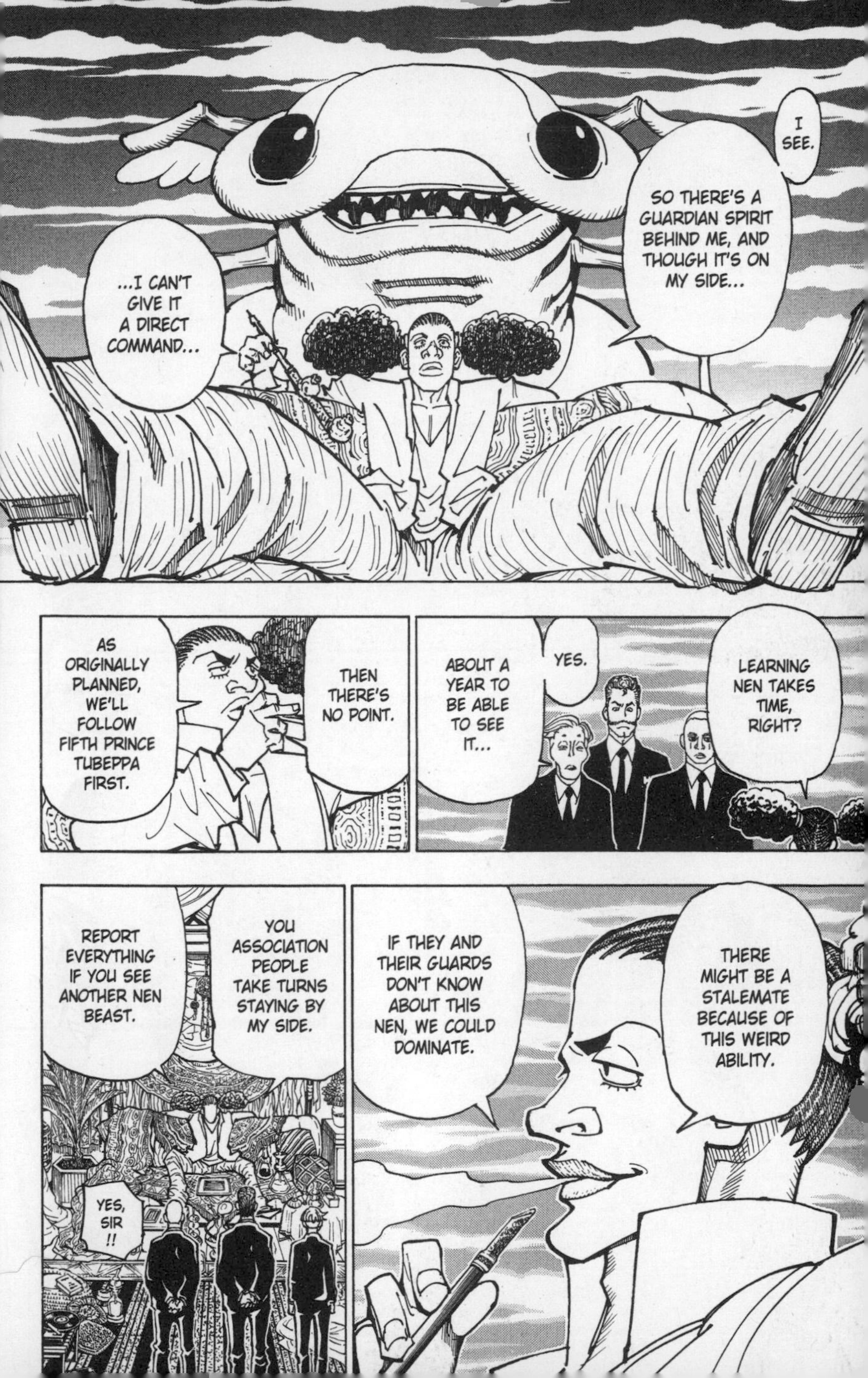
I SEE.
SO THERE'S A GUARDIAN SPIRIT BEHIND ME, AND THOUGH IT'S ON MY SIDE...
...I CAN'T GIVE IT A DIRECT COMMAND...
LEARNING NEN TAKES TIME, RIGHT?
YES.
ABOUT A YEAR TO BE ABLE TO SEE IT...
THEN THERE'S NO POINT.
AS ORIGINALLY PLANNED, WE'LL FOLLOW FIFTH PRINCE TUBEPPA FIRST.
THERE MIGHT BE A STALEMATE BECAUSE OF THIS WEIRD ABILITY.
IF THEY AND THEIR GUARDS DON'T KNOW ABOUT THIS NEN, WE COULD DOMINATE.
YOU ASSOCIATION PEOPLE TAKE TURNS STAYING BY MY SIDE.
REPORT EVERYTHING IF YOU SEE ANOTHER NEN BEAST.
YES, SIR!!

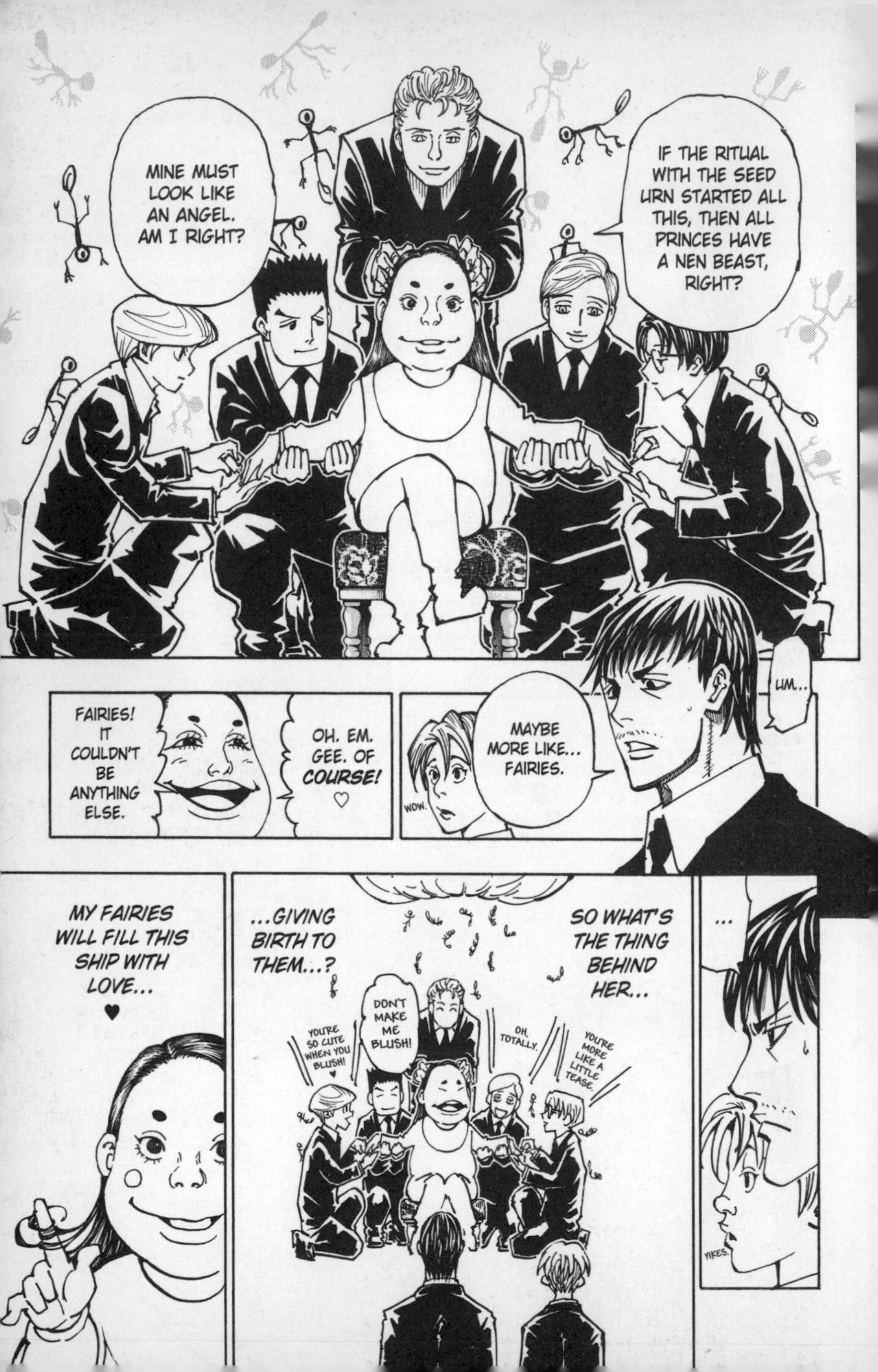
IF THE RITUAL WITH THE SEED URN STARTED ALL THIS, THEN ALL PRINCES HAVE A NEN BEAST, RIGHT?
MINE MUST LOOK LIKE AN ANGEL. AM I RIGHT?
UM...
MAYBE MORE LIKE... FAIRIES.
WOW.
OH. EM. GEE. OF COURSE! ♡
FAIRIES! IT COULDN'T BE ANYTHING ELSE.
...
YIKES.
SO WHAT'S THE THING BEHIND HER...
...GIVING BIRTH TO THEM...?
YOU'RE MORE LIKE A LITTLE TEASE.
OH, TOTALLY.
DON'T MAKE ME BLUSH!
YOU'RE SO CUTE WHEN YOU BLUSH! ♥
MY FAIRIES WILL FILL THIS SHIP WITH LOVE... ♥

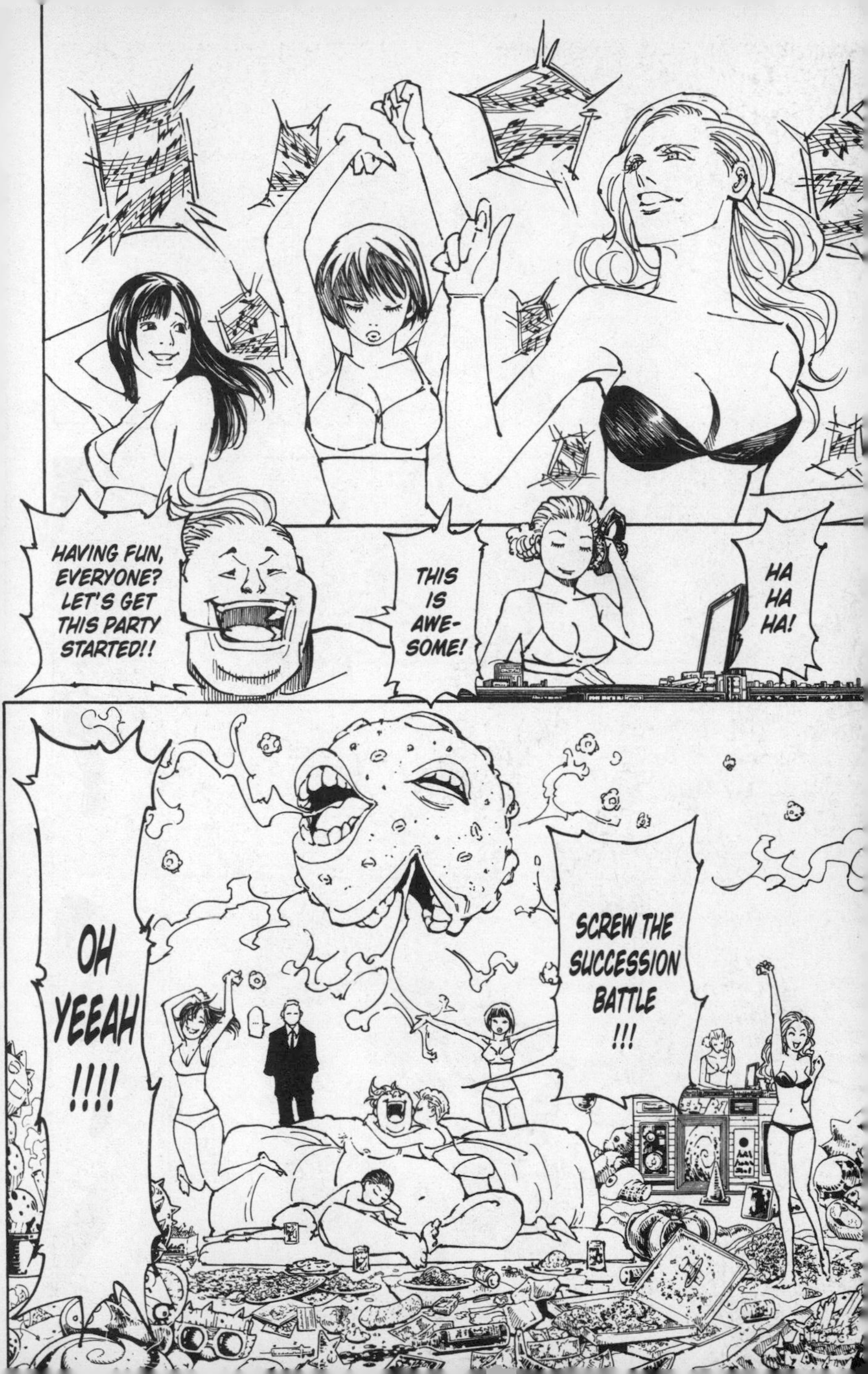
HA HA HA!
THIS IS AWESOME!
HAVING FUN, EVERYONE? LET'S GET THIS PARTY STARTED!!
SCREW THE SUCCESSION BATTLE!!!
...
OH YEEAH!!!!

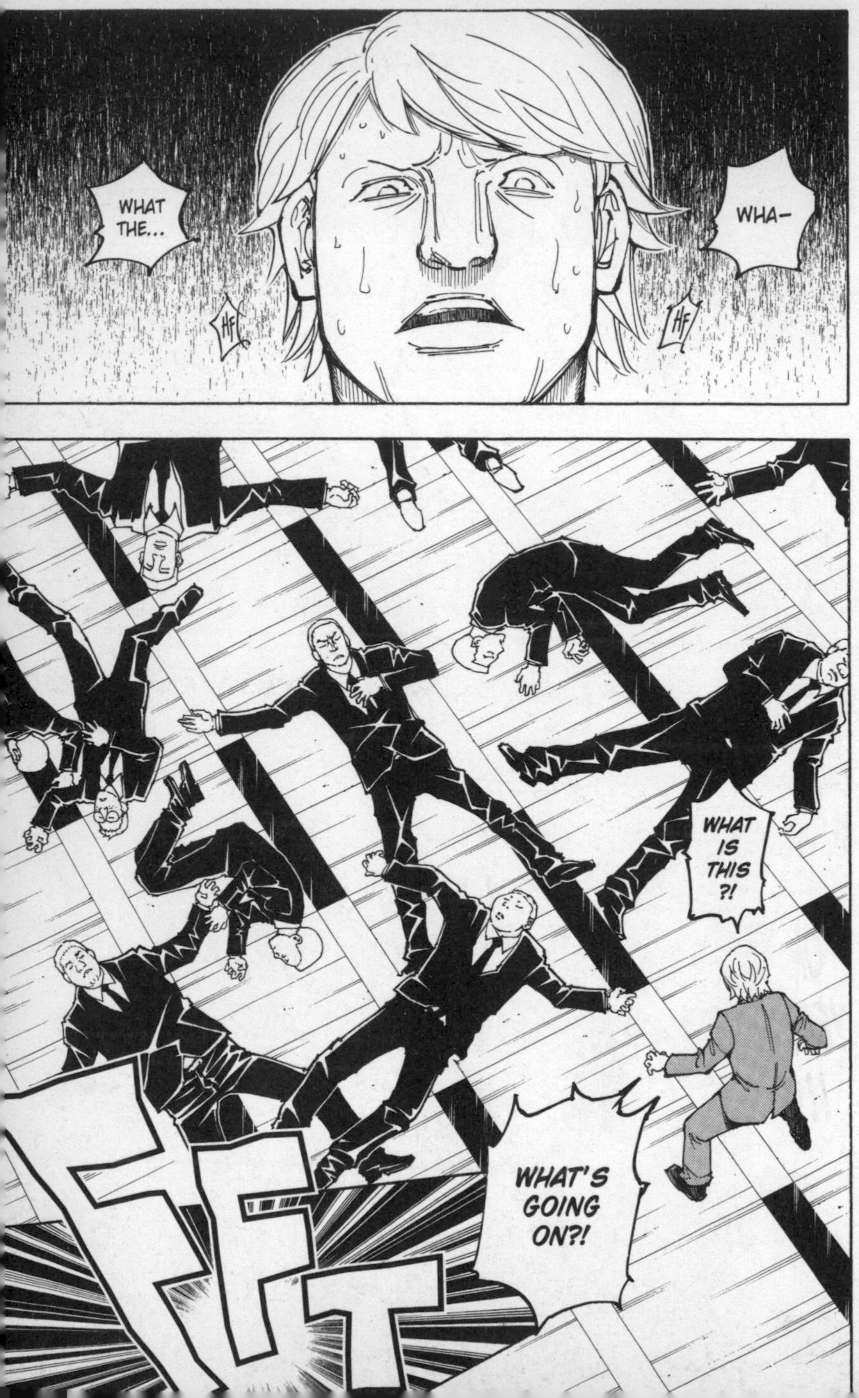
WHA-
HF
WHAT THE...
HF
WHAT IS THIS?!
WHAT'S GOING ON?!

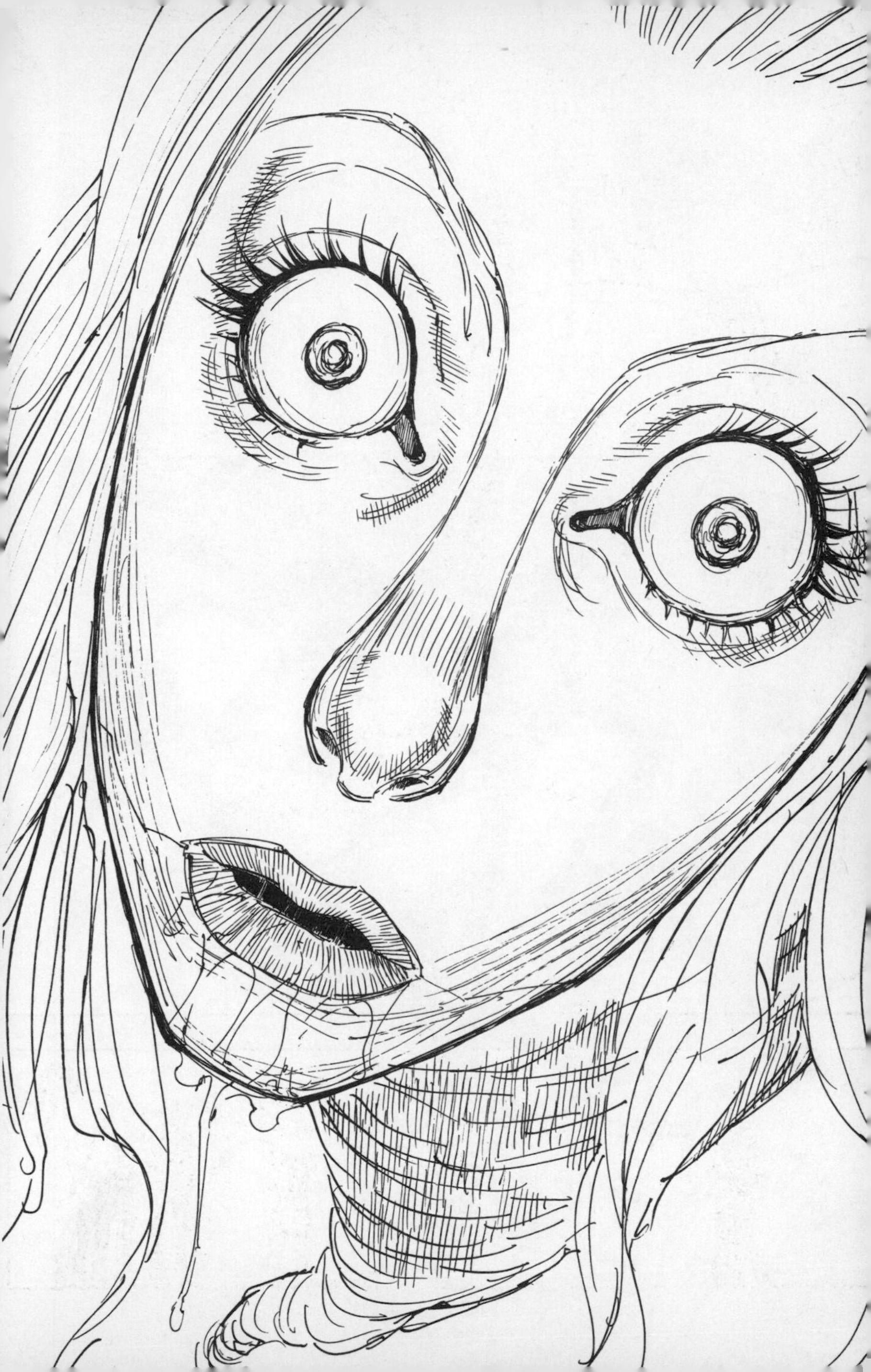

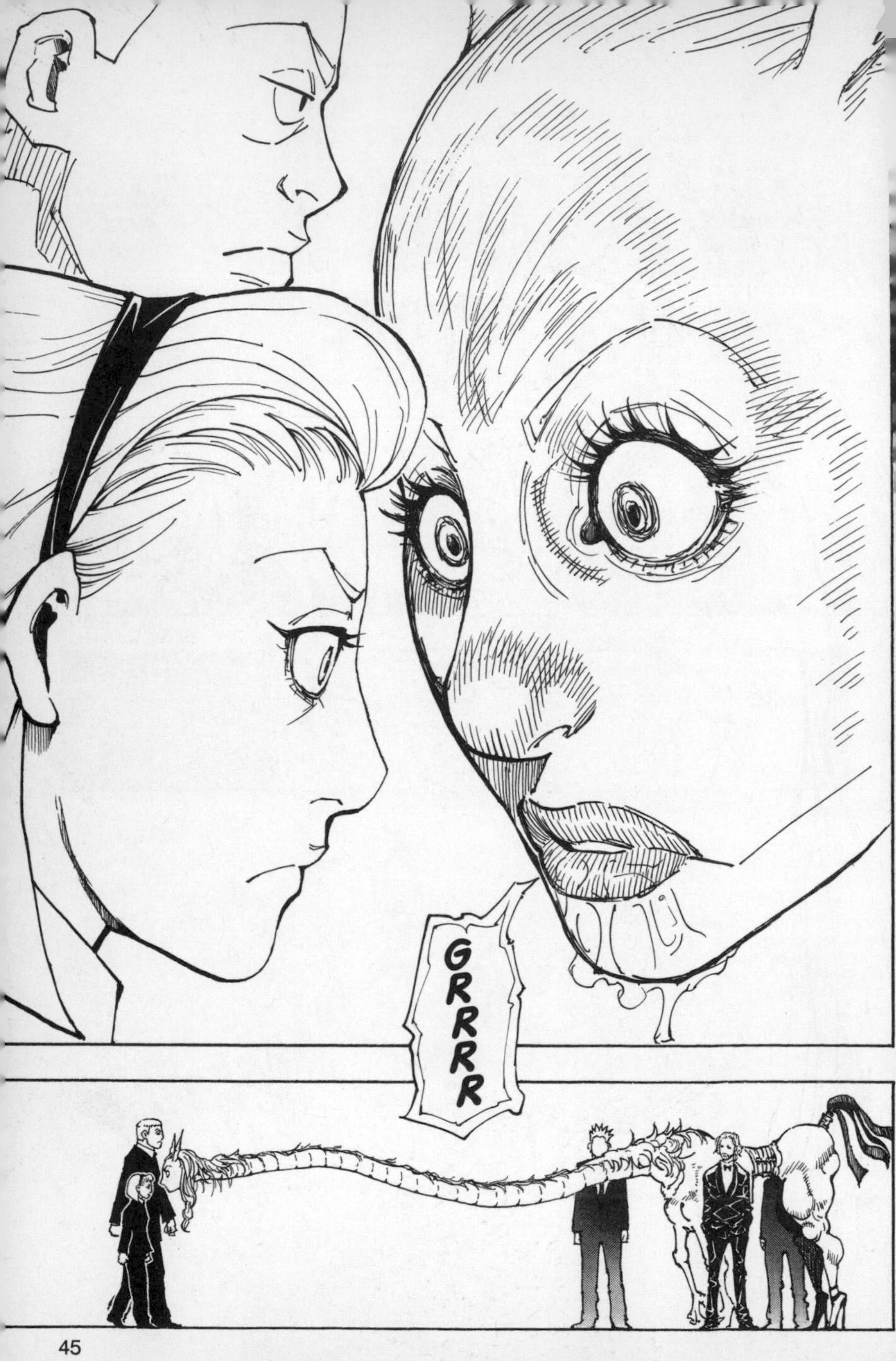
GRRRR

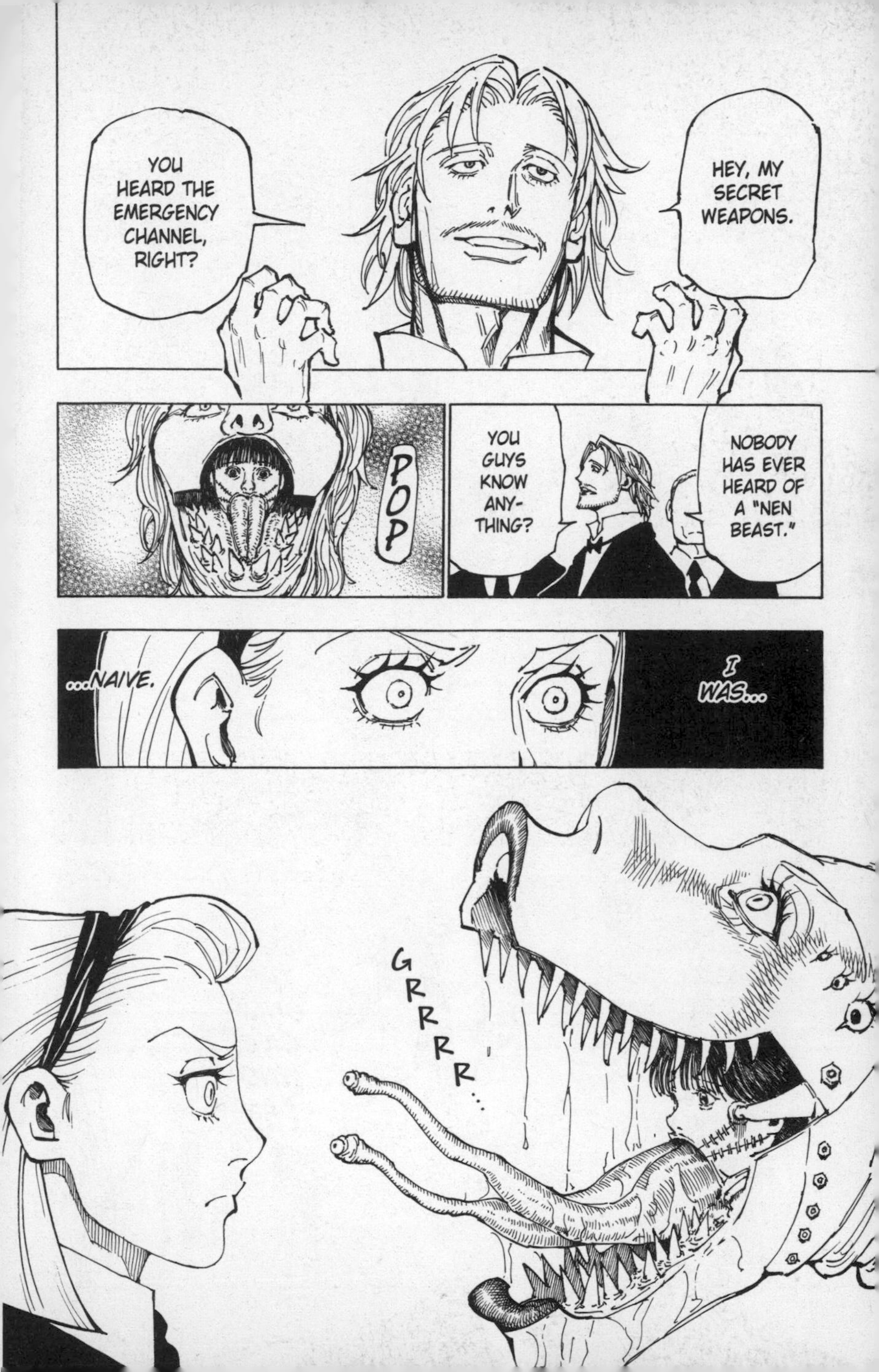
HEY, MY SECRET WEAPONS.
YOU HEARD THE EMERGENCY CHANNEL, RIGHT?
NOBODY HAS EVER HEARD OF A "NEN BEAST."
YOU GUYS KNOW ANY-THING?
POP
I WAS...
...NAIVE.
GRRRRR...

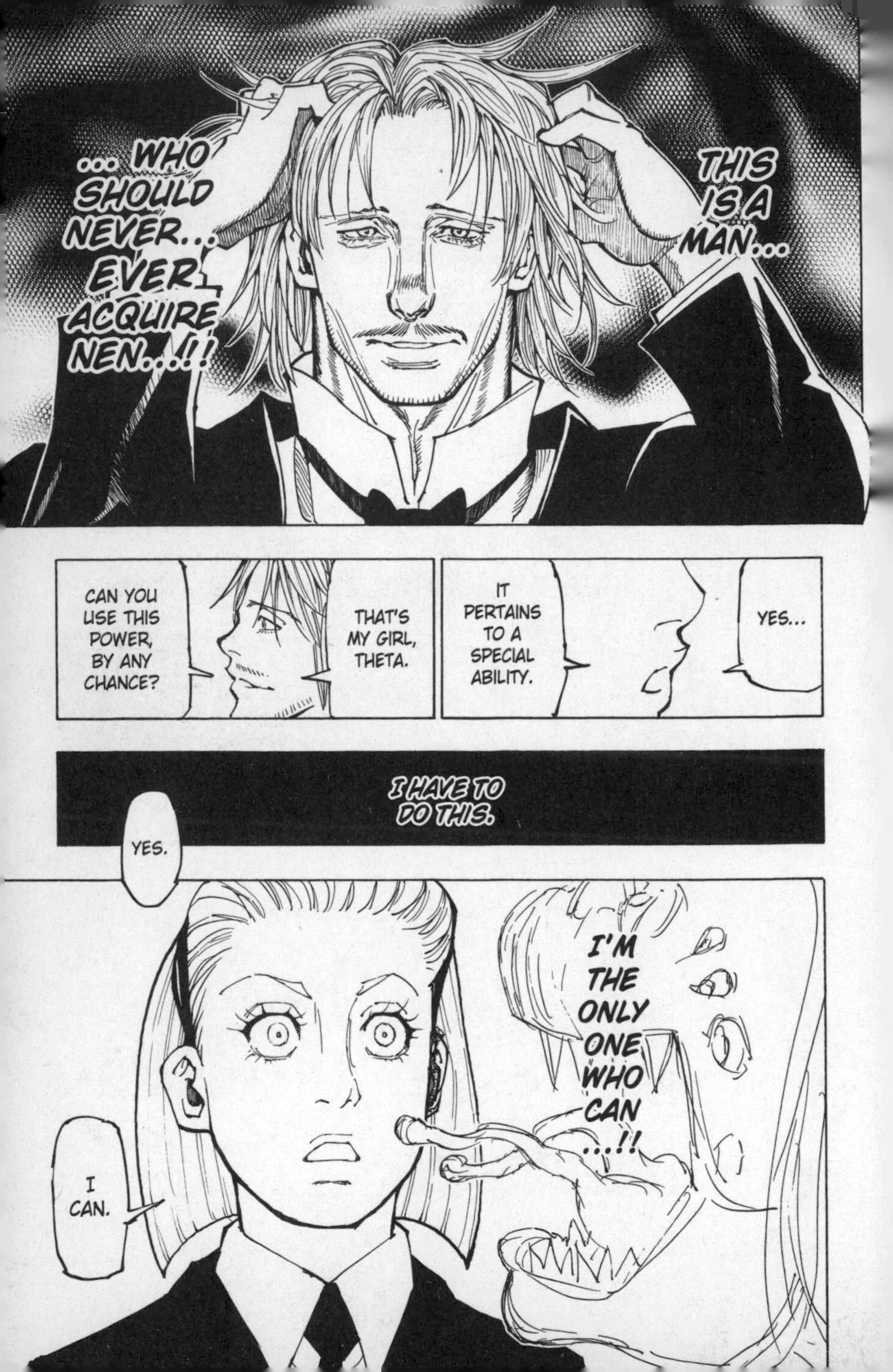
THIS IS A MAN...
... WHO SHOULD NEVER... EVER ACQUIRE NEN...!!
YES...
IT PERTAINS TO A SPECIAL ABILITY.
THAT'S MY GIRL, THETA.
CAN YOU USE THIS POWER, BY ANY CHANCE?
I HAVE TO DO THIS.
YES.
I'M THE ONLY ONE WHO CAN ...!!
I CAN.

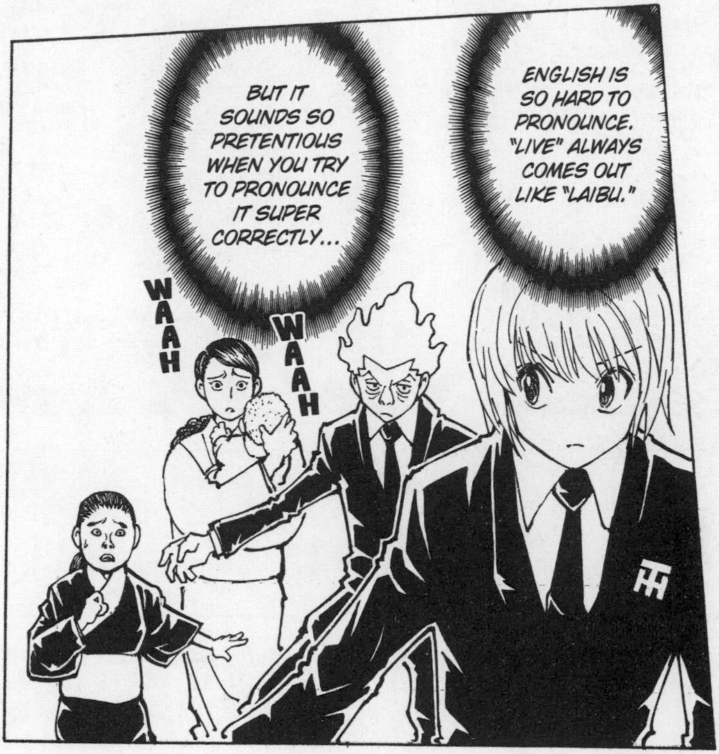
ENGLISH IS SO HARD TO PRONOUNCE. "LIVE" ALWAYS COMES OUT LIKE "LAIBU."
BUT IT SOUNDS SO PRETENTIOUS WHEN YOU TRY TO PRONOUNCE IT SUPER CORRECTLY...
WAAH
WAAH

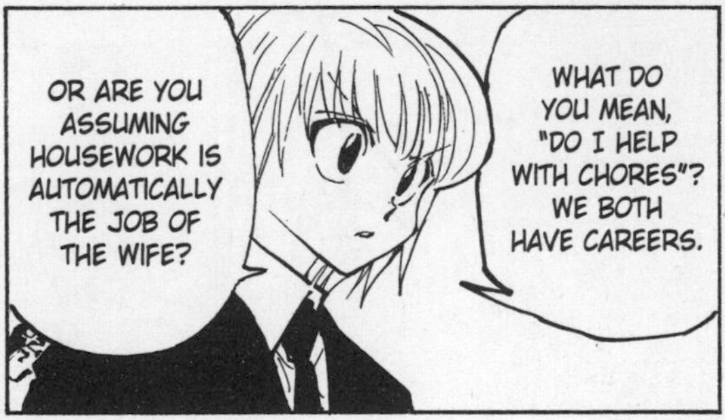
WHAT DO YOU MEAN, "DO I HELP WITH CHORES"? WE BOTH HAVE CAREERS.
OR ARE YOU ASSUMING HOUSEWORK IS AUTOMATICALLY THE JOB OF THE WIFE?

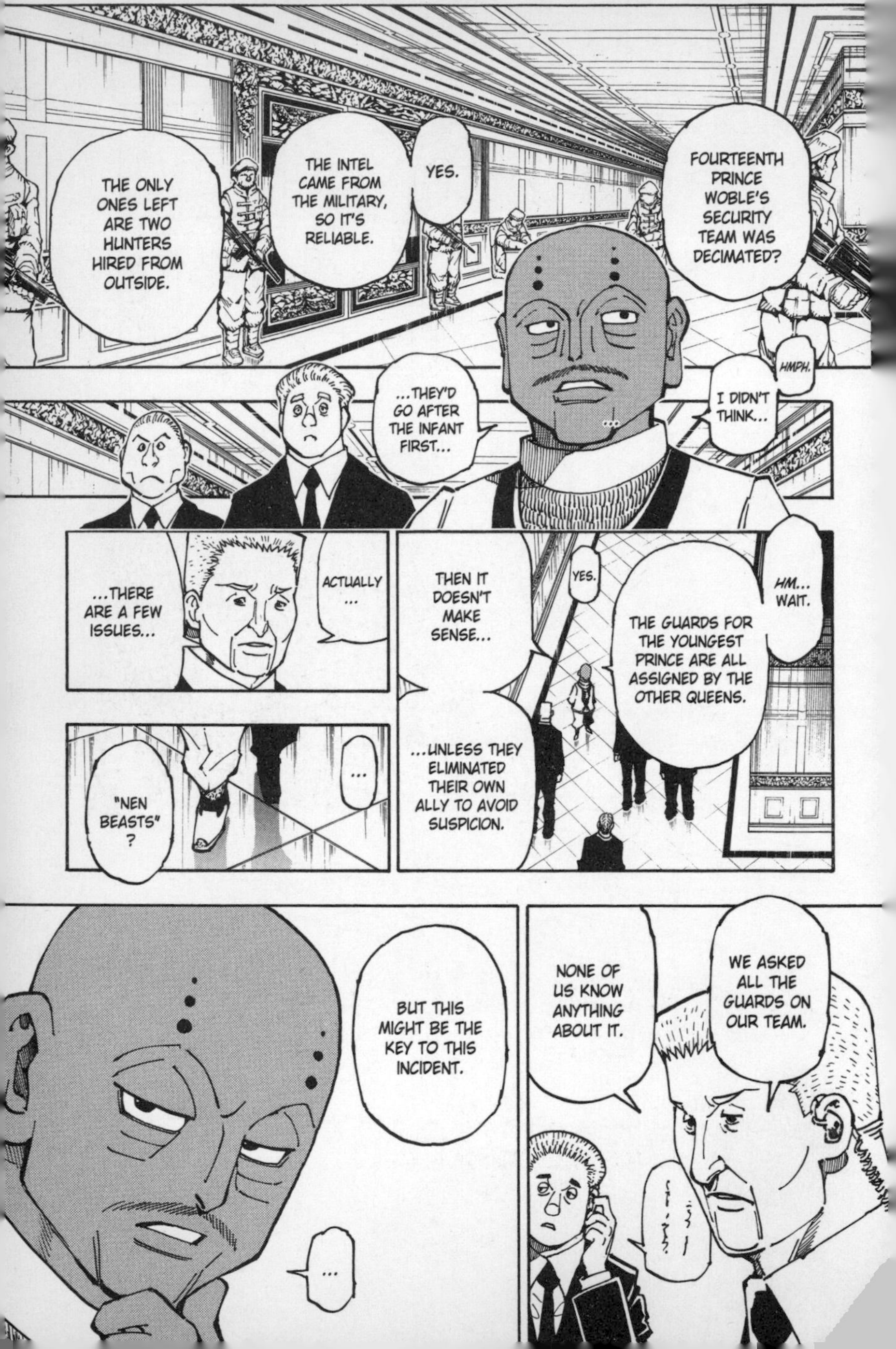
FOURTEENTH PRINCE WOBLE'S SECURITY TEAM WAS DECIMATED?
YES.
THE INTEL CAME FROM THE MILITARY, SO IT'S RELIABLE.
THE ONLY ONES LEFT ARE TWO HUNTERS HIRED FROM OUTSIDE.
HMPH.
I DIDN'T THINK...
...THEY'D GO AFTER THE INFANT FIRST...
HM... WAIT.
THE GUARDS FOR THE YOUNGEST PRINCE ARE ALL ASSIGNED BY THE OTHER QUEENS.
YES.
THEN IT DOESN'T MAKE SENSE...
...UNLESS THEY ELIMINATED THEIR OWN ALLY TO AVOID SUSPICION.
ACTUALLY ...
...THERE ARE A FEW ISSUES...
...
"NEN BEASTS" ?
WE ASKED ALL THE GUARDS ON OUR TEAM.
NONE OF US KNOW ANYTHING ABOUT IT.
BUT THIS MIGHT BE THE KEY TO THIS INCIDENT.
...

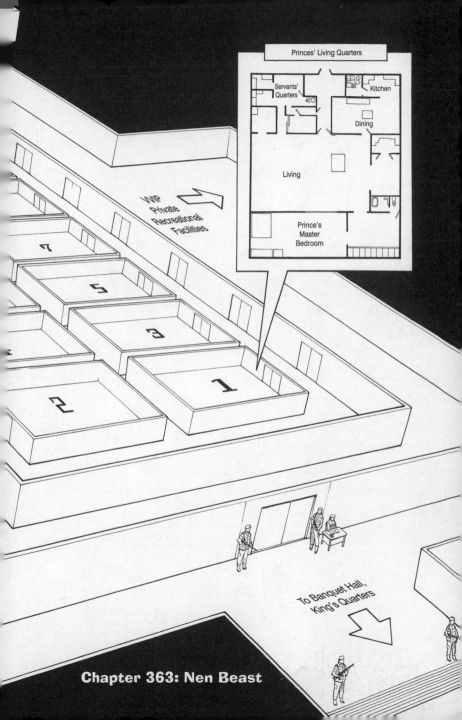

Princes' Living Quarters

Servants' Quarters

Kitchen

Dining

Living

Prince's Master Bedroom

VIP Private Recreational Facilities

7

5

3

1

2

To Banquet Hall, King's Quarters

Chapter 363: Nen Beast

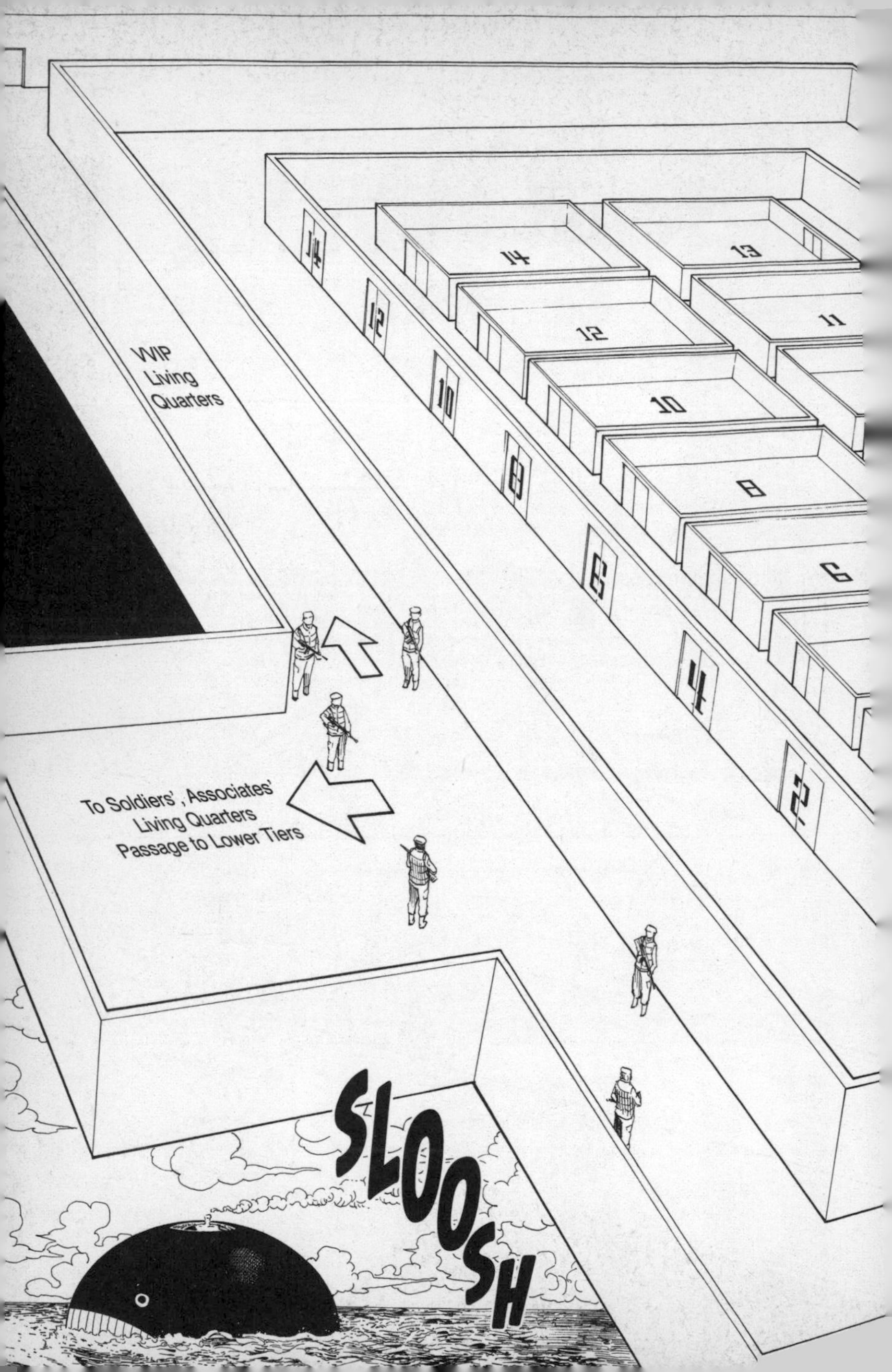
VVIP
Living
Quarters
To Soldiers', Associates'
Living Quarters
Passage to Lower Tiers
SLOOSH

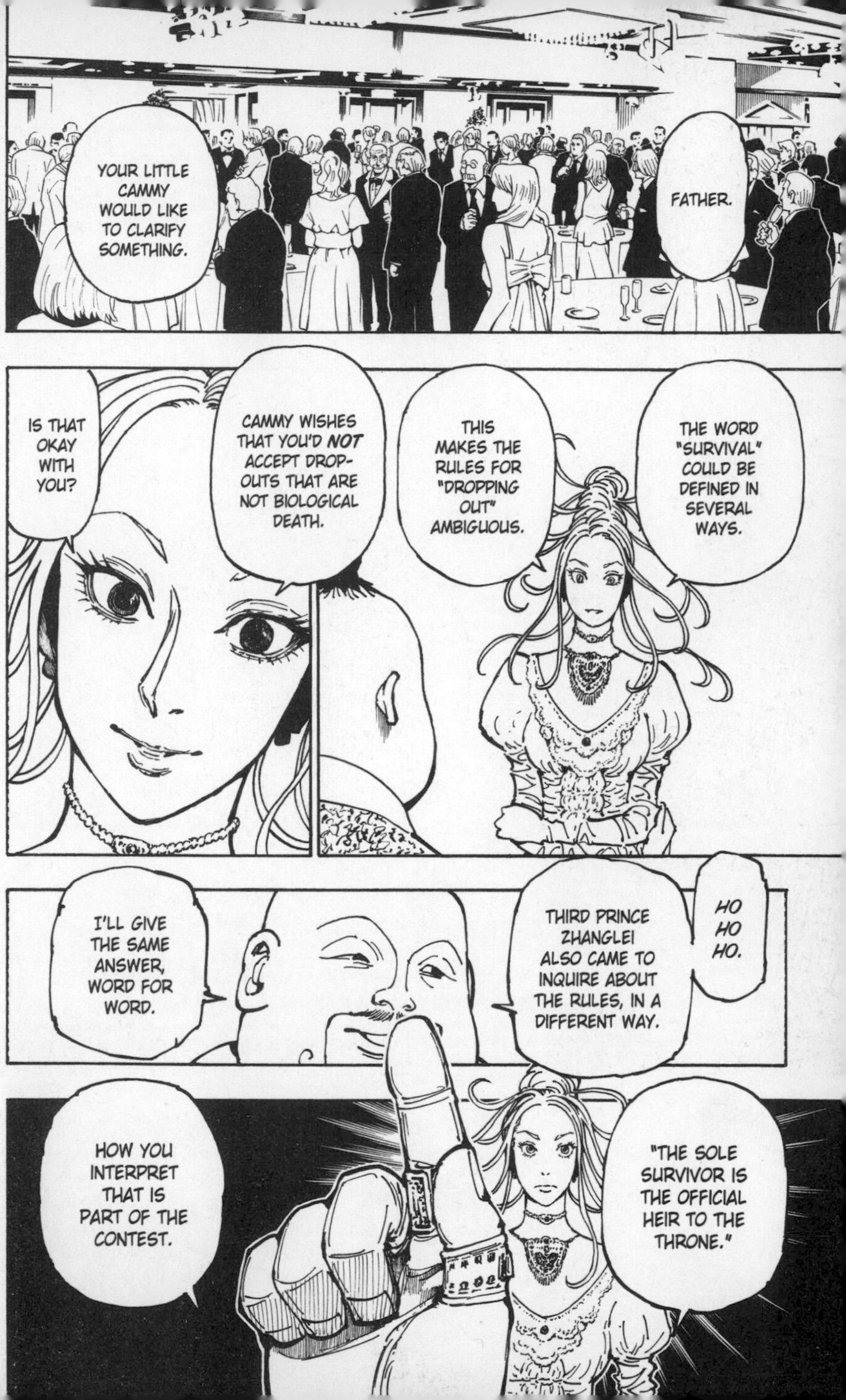
FATHER.
YOUR LITTLE CAMMY WOULD LIKE TO CLARIFY SOMETHING.
THE WORD "SURVIVAL" COULD BE DEFINED IN SEVERAL WAYS.
THIS MAKES THE RULES FOR "DROPPING OUT" AMBIGUOUS.
CAMMY WISHES THAT YOU'D ***NOT*** ACCEPT DROP-OUTS THAT ARE NOT BIOLOGICAL DEATH.
IS THAT OKAY WITH YOU?
HO HO HO.
THIRD PRINCE ZHANGLEI ALSO CAME TO INQUIRE ABOUT THE RULES, IN A DIFFERENT WAY.
I'LL GIVE THE SAME ANSWER, WORD FOR WORD.
"THE SOLE SURVIVOR IS THE OFFICIAL HEIR TO THE THRONE."
HOW YOU INTERPRET THAT IS PART OF THE CONTEST.

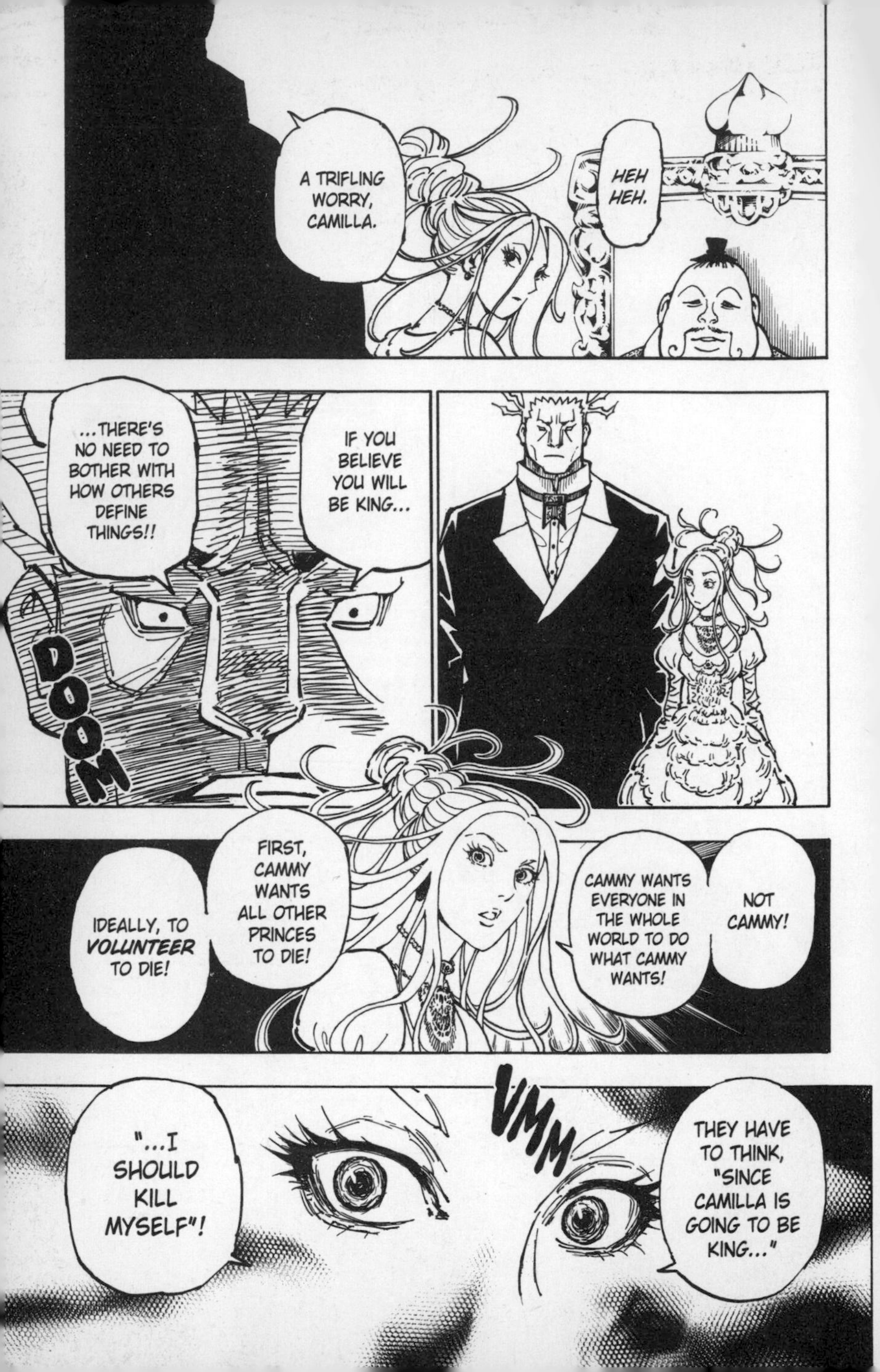
HEH HEH.
A TRIFLING WORRY, CAMILLA.
IF YOU BELIEVE YOU WILL BE KING...
...THERE'S NO NEED TO BOTHER WITH HOW OTHERS DEFINE THINGS!!
DOOM
NOT CAMMY!
CAMMY WANTS EVERYONE IN THE WHOLE WORLD TO DO WHAT CAMMY WANTS!
FIRST, CAMMY WANTS ALL OTHER PRINCES TO DIE!
IDEALLY, TO **VOLUNTEER** TO DIE!
UMM
THEY HAVE TO THINK, "SINCE CAMILLA IS GOING TO BE KING..."
"...I SHOULD KILL MYSELF"!

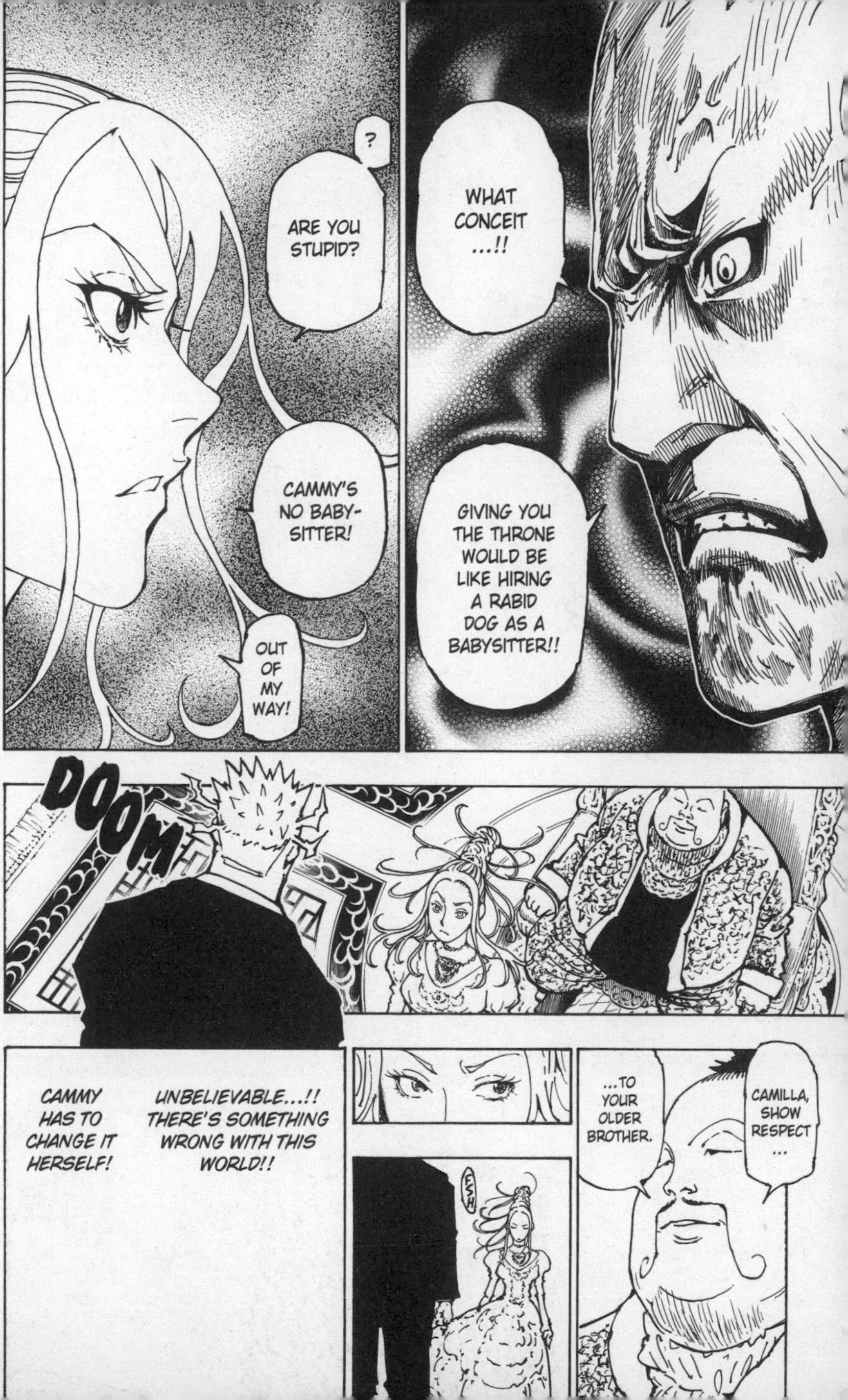
WHAT CONCEIT ...!!
GIVING YOU THE THRONE WOULD BE LIKE HIRING A RABID DOG AS A BABYSITTER!!
?
ARE YOU STUPID?
CAMMY'S NO BABY-SITTER!
OUT OF MY WAY!
DOOM
CAMILLA, SHOW RESPECT ...
...TO YOUR OLDER BROTHER.
FSH
UNBELIEVABLE...!! THERE'S SOMETHING WRONG WITH THIS WORLD!!
CAMMY HAS TO CHANGE IT HERSELF!

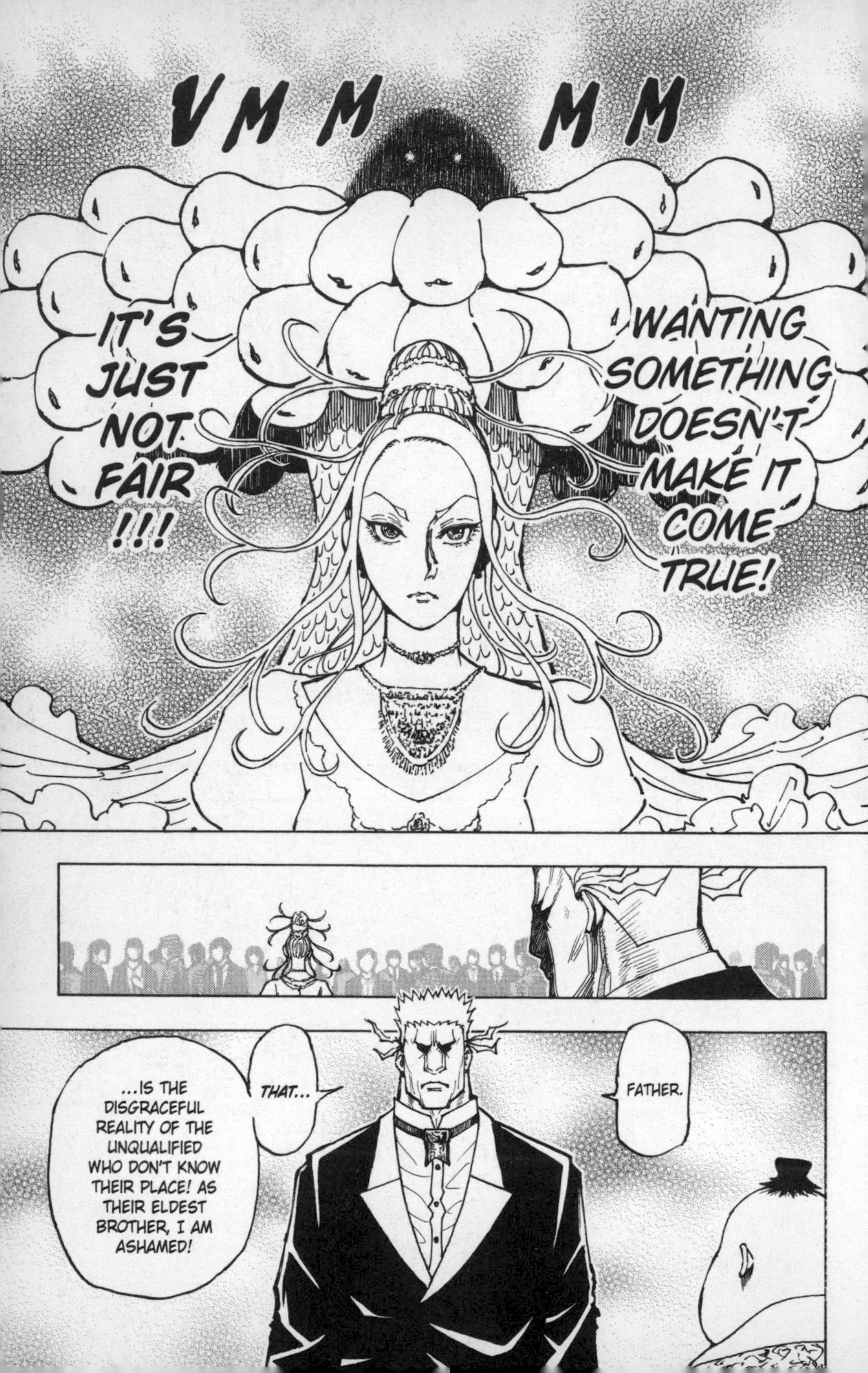
VMM MM
WANTING SOMETHING DOESN'T MAKE IT COME TRUE!
IT'S JUST NOT FAIR!!!
FATHER.
THAT...
...IS THE DISGRACEFUL REALITY OF THE UNQUALIFIED WHO DON'T KNOW THEIR PLACE! AS THEIR ELDEST BROTHER, I AM ASHAMED!

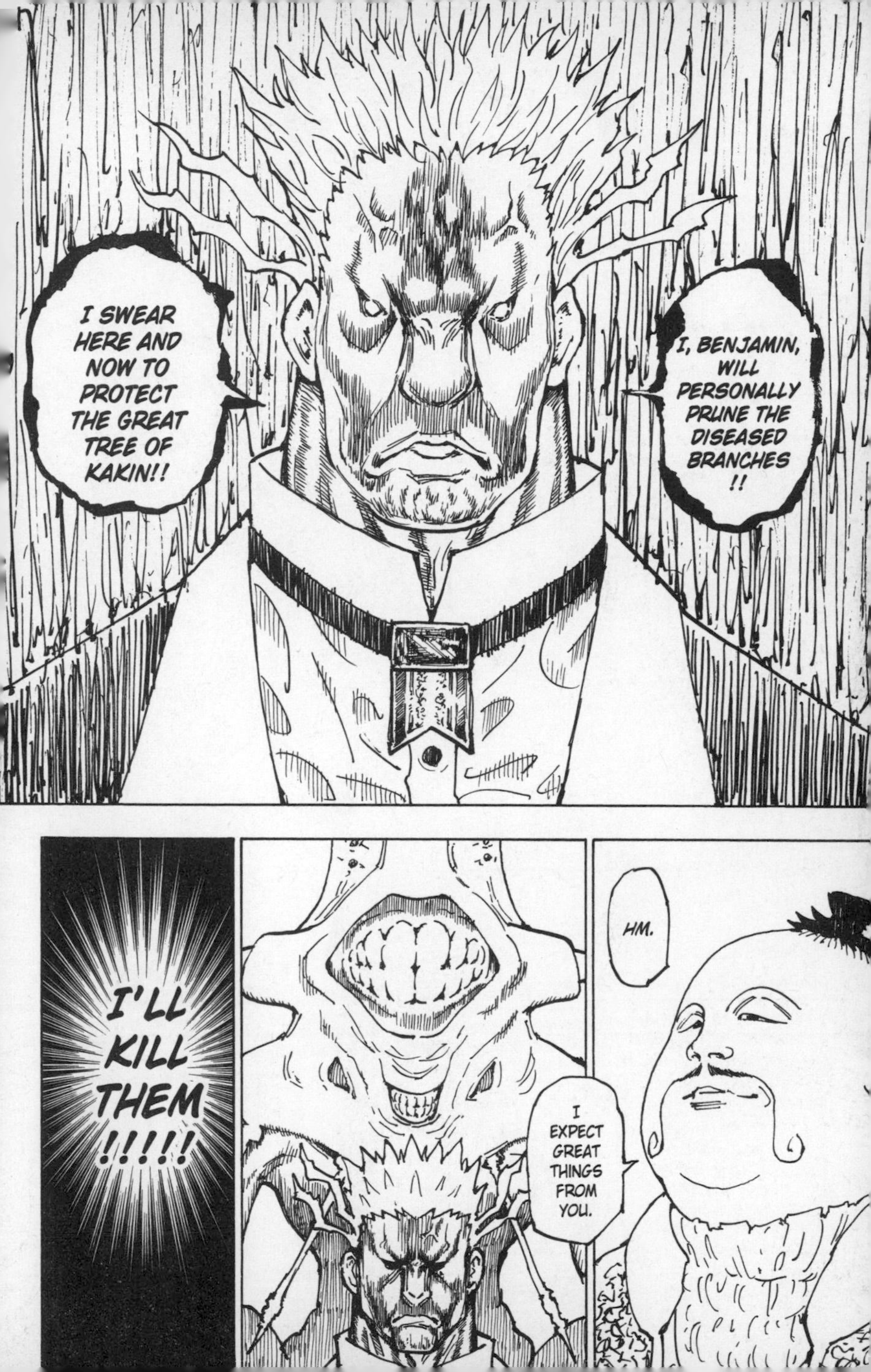
I, BENJAMIN, WILL PERSONALLY PRUNE THE DISEASED BRANCHES !!
I SWEAR HERE AND NOW TO PROTECT THE GREAT TREE OF KAKIN!!
HM.
I EXPECT GREAT THINGS FROM YOU.
I'LL KILL THEM !!!!!

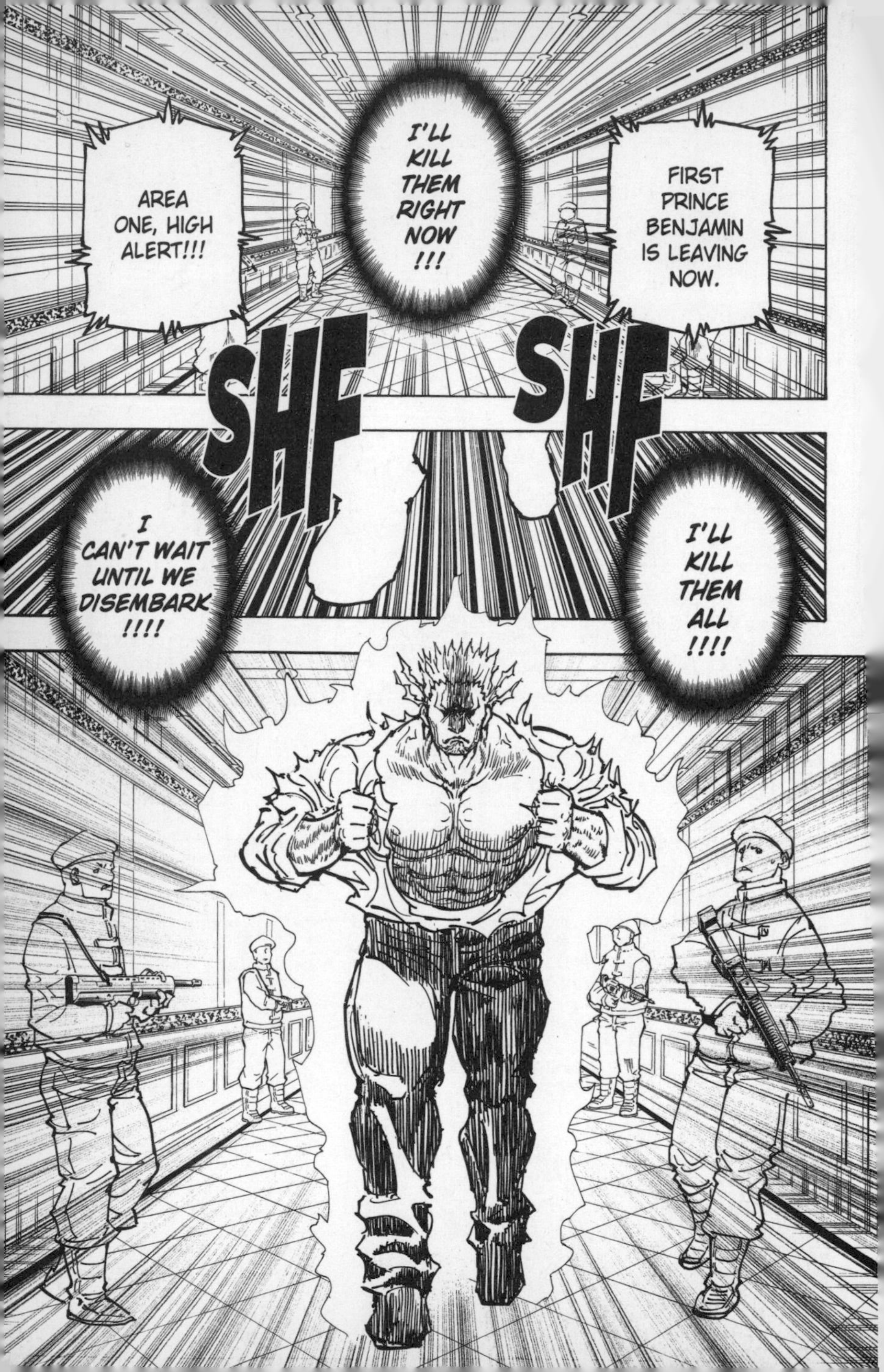
FIRST PRINCE BENJAMIN IS LEAVING NOW.
I'LL KILL THEM RIGHT NOW!!!
AREA ONE, HIGH ALERT!!!
SHF
SHF
I'LL KILL THEM ALL!!!!
I CAN'T WAIT UNTIL WE DISEMBARK!!!!

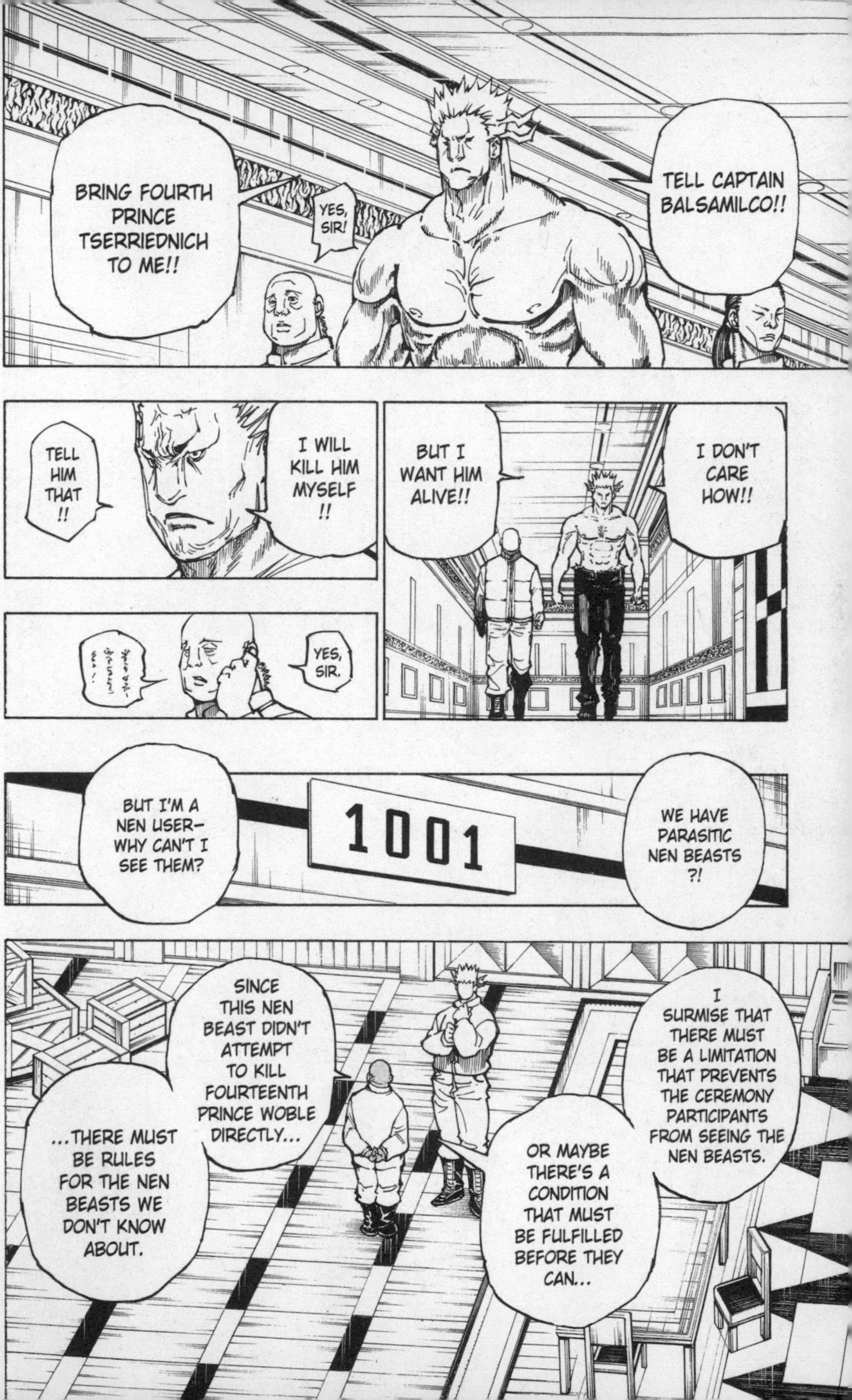
TELL CAPTAIN BALSAMILCO!!
BRING FOURTH PRINCE TSERRIEDNICH TO ME!!
YES, SIR!
I DON'T CARE HOW!!
BUT I WANT HIM ALIVE!!
I WILL KILL HIM MYSELF!!
TELL HIM THAT!!
YES, SIR.
WE HAVE PARASITIC NEN BEASTS?!
1001
BUT I'M A NEN USER—WHY CAN'T I SEE THEM?
I SURMISE THAT THERE MUST BE A LIMITATION THAT PREVENTS THE CEREMONY PARTICIPANTS FROM SEEING THE NEN BEASTS.
OR MAYBE THERE'S A CONDITION THAT MUST BE FULFILLED BEFORE THEY CAN...
SINCE THIS NEN BEAST DIDN'T ATTEMPT TO KILL FOURTEENTH PRINCE WOBLE DIRECTLY...
...THERE MUST BE RULES FOR THE NEN BEASTS WE DON'T KNOW ABOUT.

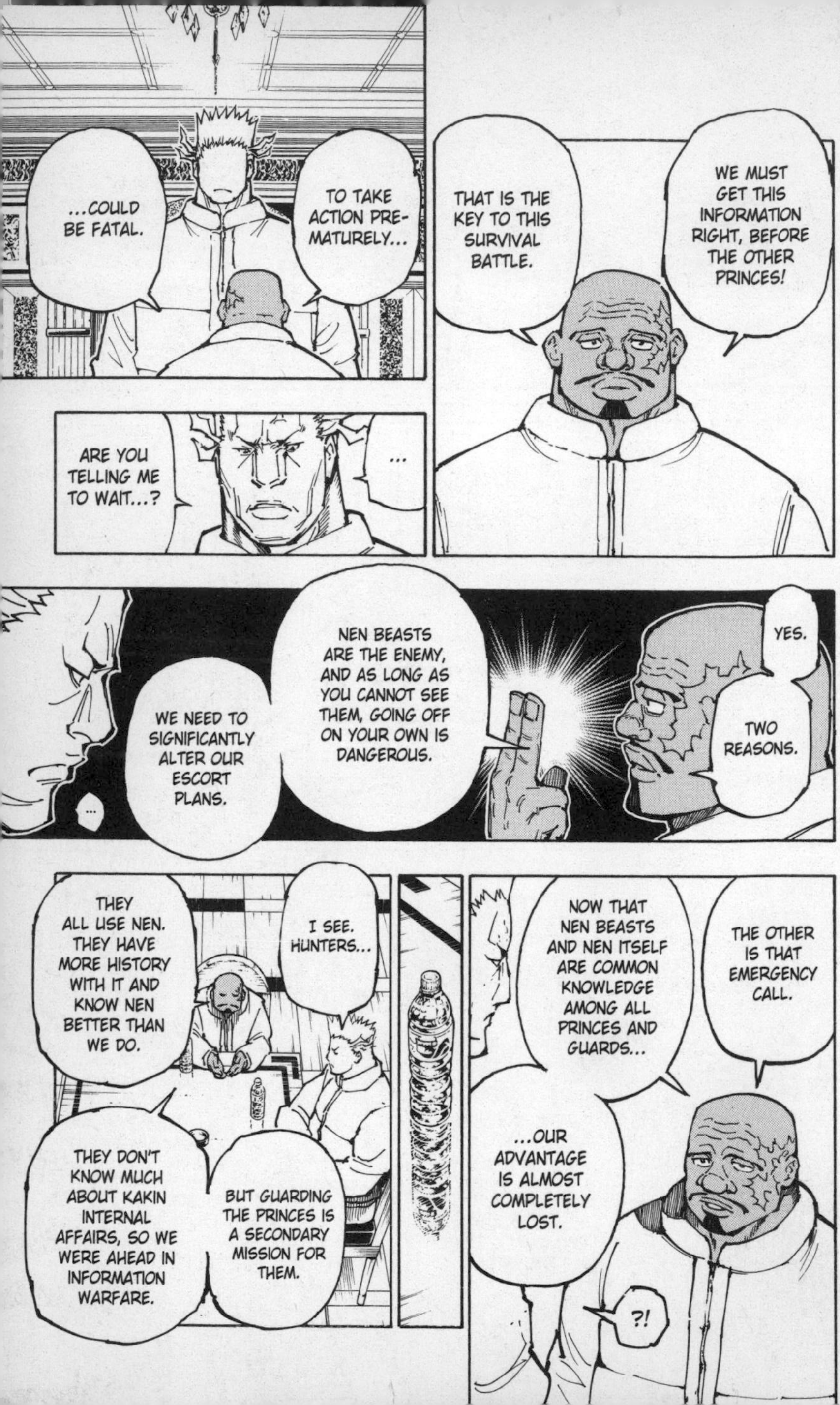
WE MUST GET THIS INFORMATION RIGHT, BEFORE THE OTHER PRINCES!
THAT IS THE KEY TO THIS SURVIVAL BATTLE.
TO TAKE ACTION PRE-MATURELY...
...COULD BE FATAL.
...
ARE YOU TELLING ME TO WAIT...?
YES.
TWO REASONS.
NEN BEASTS ARE THE ENEMY, AND AS LONG AS YOU CANNOT SEE THEM, GOING OFF ON YOUR OWN IS DANGEROUS.
WE NEED TO SIGNIFICANTLY ALTER OUR ESCORT PLANS.
...
THE OTHER IS THAT EMERGENCY CALL.
NOW THAT NEN BEASTS AND NEN ITSELF ARE COMMON KNOWLEDGE AMONG ALL PRINCES AND GUARDS...
...OUR ADVANTAGE IS ALMOST COMPLETELY LOST.
?!
I SEE. HUNTERS...
THEY ALL USE NEN. THEY HAVE MORE HISTORY WITH IT AND KNOW NEN BETTER THAN WE DO.
BUT GUARDING THE PRINCES IS A SECONDARY MISSION FOR THEM.
THEY DON'T KNOW MUCH ABOUT KAKIN INTERNAL AFFAIRS, SO WE WERE AHEAD IN INFORMATION WARFARE.

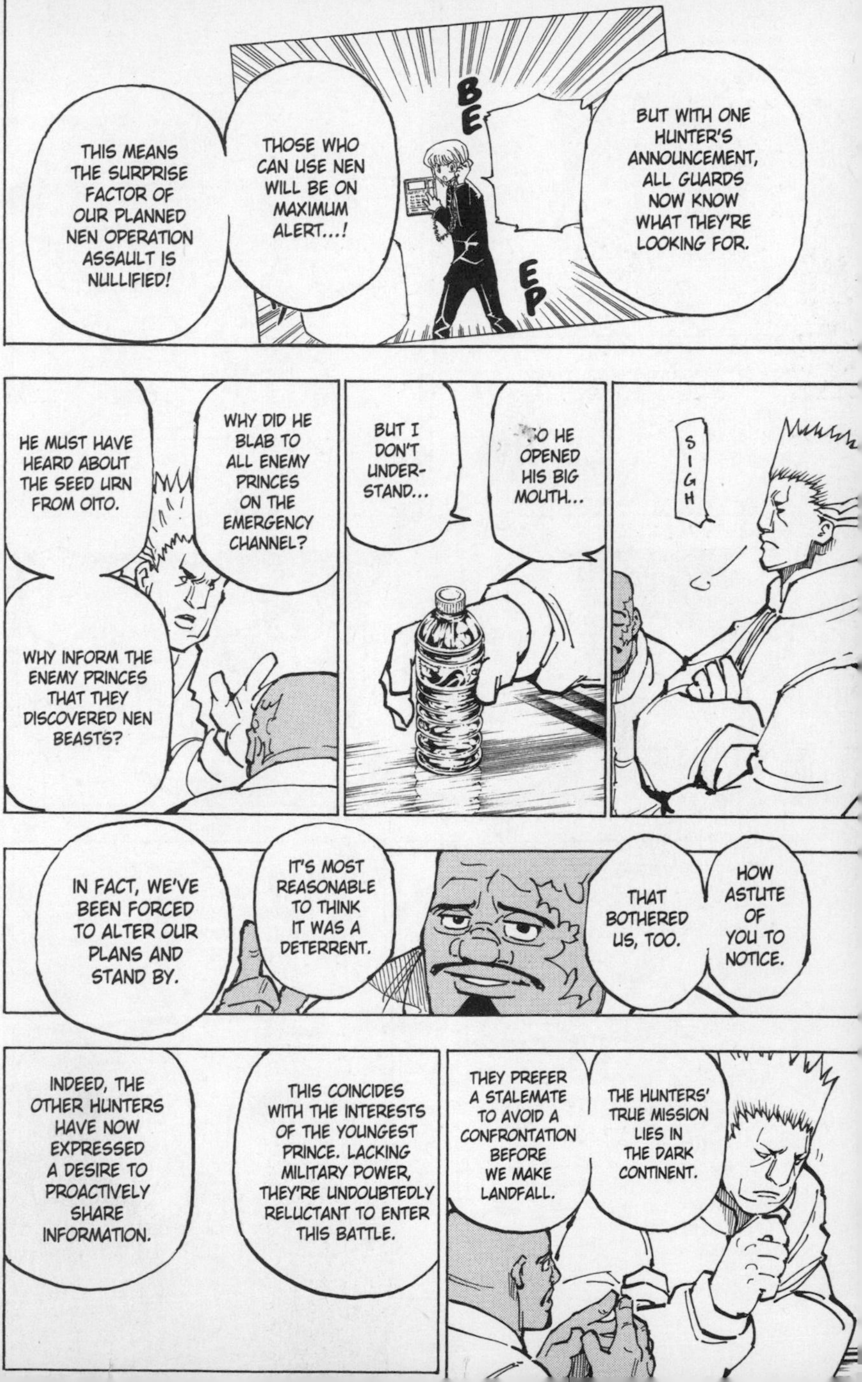
BUT WITH ONE HUNTER'S ANNOUNCEMENT, ALL GUARDS NOW KNOW WHAT THEY'RE LOOKING FOR.
BE
EP
THOSE WHO CAN USE NEN WILL BE ON MAXIMUM ALERT...!
THIS MEANS THE SURPRISE FACTOR OF OUR PLANNED NEN OPERATION ASSAULT IS NULLIFIED!
SIGH
SO HE OPENED HIS BIG MOUTH...
BUT I DON'T UNDER-STAND...
WHY DID HE BLAB TO ALL ENEMY PRINCES ON THE EMERGENCY CHANNEL?
HE MUST HAVE HEARD ABOUT THE SEED URN FROM OITO.
WHY INFORM THE ENEMY PRINCES THAT THEY DISCOVERED NEN BEASTS?
HOW ASTUTE OF YOU TO NOTICE.
THAT BOTHERED US, TOO.
IT'S MOST REASONABLE TO THINK IT WAS A DETERRENT.
IN FACT, WE'VE BEEN FORCED TO ALTER OUR PLANS AND STAND BY.
THE HUNTERS' TRUE MISSION LIES IN THE DARK CONTINENT.
THEY PREFER A STALEMATE TO AVOID A CONFRONTATION BEFORE WE MAKE LANDFALL.
THIS COINCIDES WITH THE INTERESTS OF THE YOUNGEST PRINCE. LACKING MILITARY POWER, THEY'RE UNDOUBTEDLY RELUCTANT TO ENTER THIS BATTLE.
INDEED, THE OTHER HUNTERS HAVE NOW EXPRESSED A DESIRE TO PROACTIVELY SHARE INFORMATION.

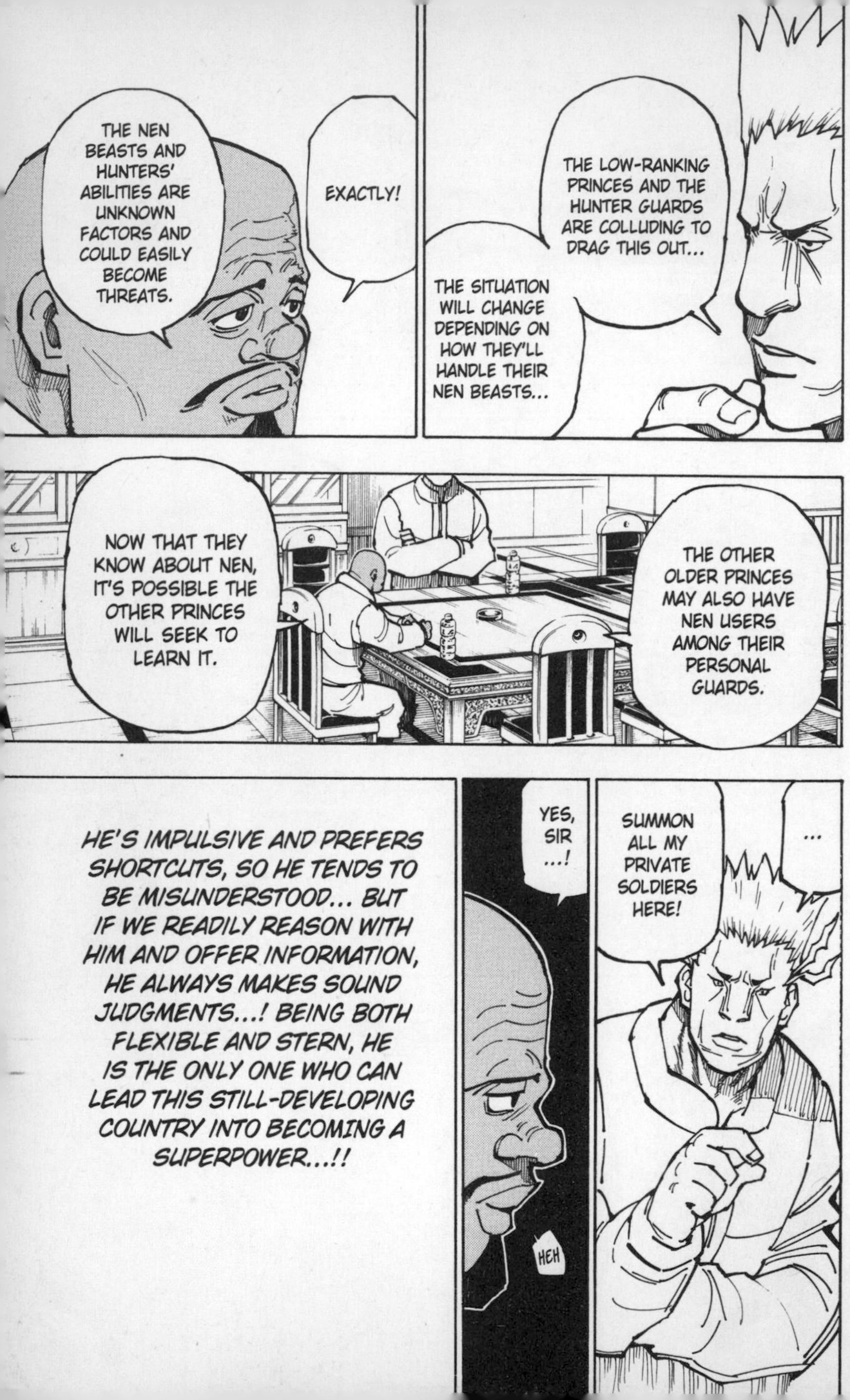
THE LOW-RANKING PRINCES AND THE HUNTER GUARDS ARE COLLUDING TO DRAG THIS OUT...
THE SITUATION WILL CHANGE DEPENDING ON HOW THEY'LL HANDLE THEIR NEN BEASTS...
EXACTLY!
THE NEN BEASTS AND HUNTERS' ABILITIES ARE UNKNOWN FACTORS AND COULD EASILY BECOME THREATS.
THE OTHER OLDER PRINCES MAY ALSO HAVE NEN USERS AMONG THEIR PERSONAL GUARDS.
NOW THAT THEY KNOW ABOUT NEN, IT'S POSSIBLE THE OTHER PRINCES WILL SEEK TO LEARN IT.
...
SUMMON ALL MY PRIVATE SOLDIERS HERE!
YES, SIR ...!
HEH
HE'S IMPULSIVE AND PREFERS SHORTCUTS, SO HE TENDS TO BE MISUNDERSTOOD... BUT IF WE READILY REASON WITH HIM AND OFFER INFORMATION, HE ALWAYS MAKES SOUND JUDGMENTS...! BEING BOTH FLEXIBLE AND STERN, HE IS THE ONLY ONE WHO CAN LEAD THIS STILL-DEVELOPING COUNTRY INTO BECOMING A SUPERPOWER...!!

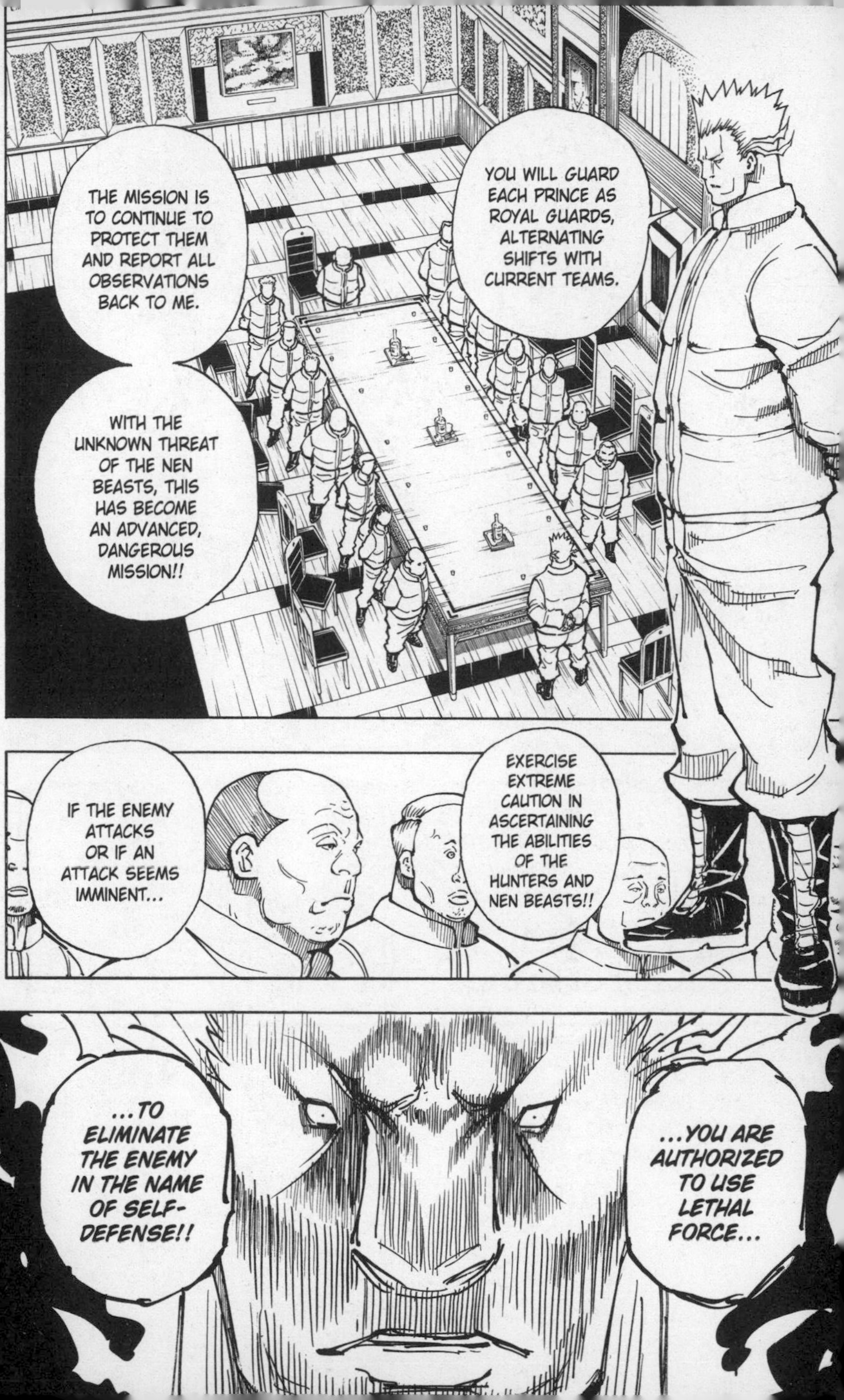
YOU WILL GUARD EACH PRINCE AS ROYAL GUARDS, ALTERNATING SHIFTS WITH CURRENT TEAMS.
THE MISSION IS TO CONTINUE TO PROTECT THEM AND REPORT ALL OBSERVATIONS BACK TO ME.
WITH THE UNKNOWN THREAT OF THE NEN BEASTS, THIS HAS BECOME AN ADVANCED, DANGEROUS MISSION!!
EXERCISE EXTREME CAUTION IN ASCERTAINING THE ABILITIES OF THE HUNTERS AND NEN BEASTS!!
IF THE ENEMY ATTACKS OR IF AN ATTACK SEEMS IMMINENT...
...YOU ARE AUTHORIZED TO USE LETHAL FORCE...
...TO ELIMINATE THE ENEMY IN THE NAME OF SELF-DEFENSE!!

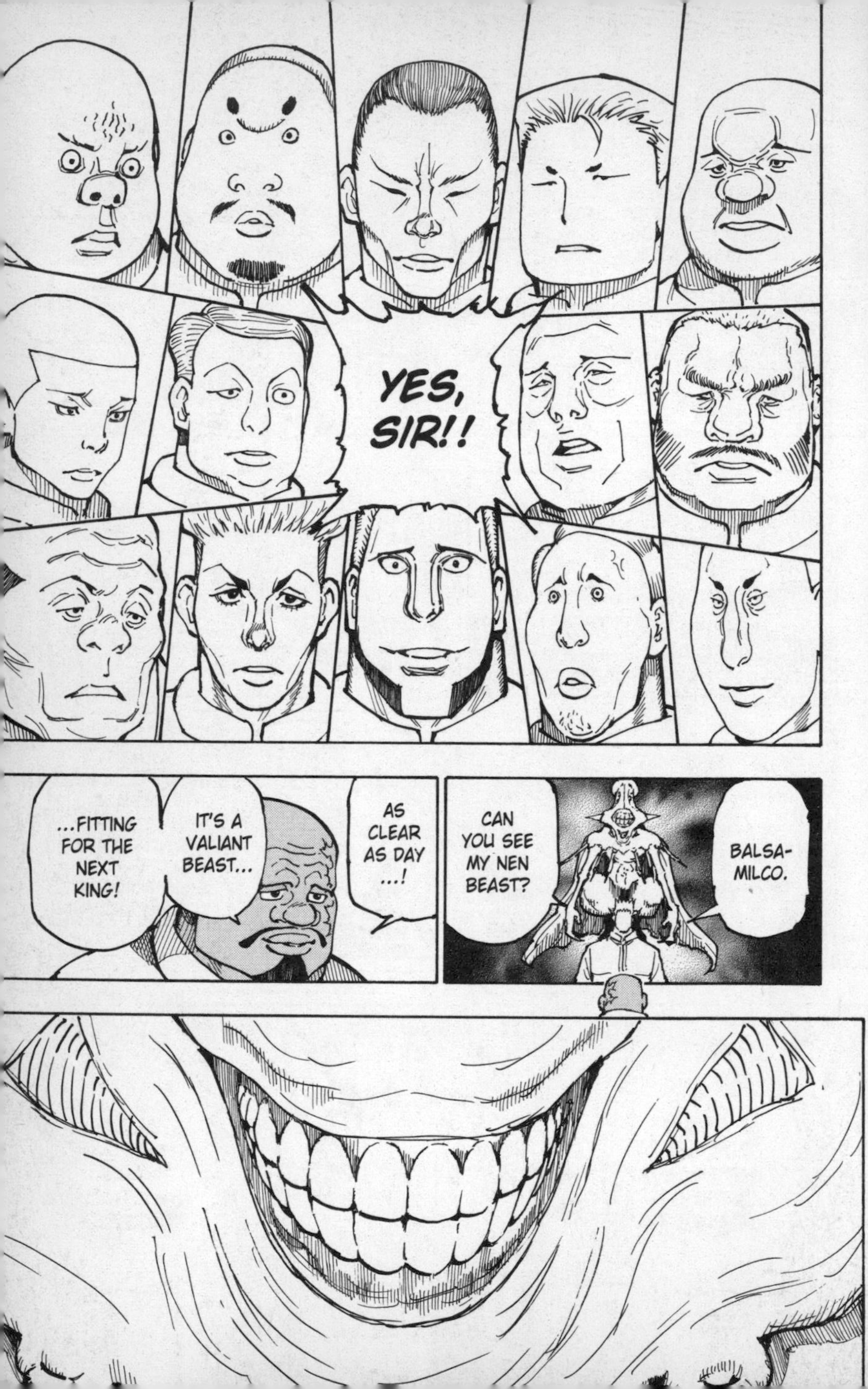
YES, SIR!!
BALSA-MILCO.
CAN YOU SEE MY NEN BEAST?
AS CLEAR AS DAY ...!
IT'S A VALIANT BEAST...
...FITTING FOR THE NEXT KING!

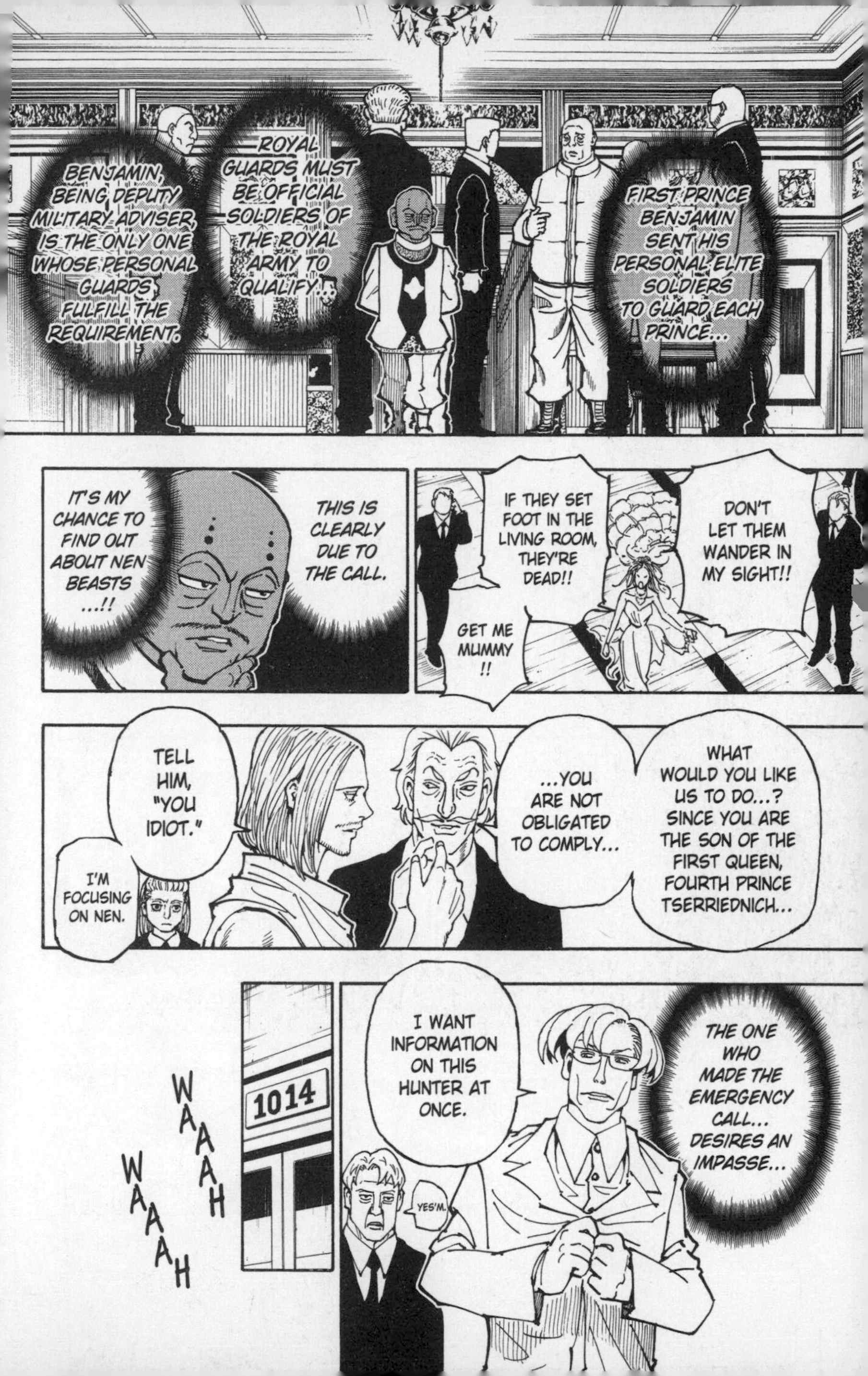
FIRST PRINCE BENJAMIN SENT HIS PERSONAL ELITE SOLDIERS TO GUARD EACH PRINCE...
ROYAL GUARDS MUST BE OFFICIAL SOLDIERS OF THE ROYAL ARMY TO QUALIFY!!
BENJAMIN, BEING DEPUTY MILITARY ADVISER, IS THE ONLY ONE WHOSE PERSONAL GUARDS FULFILL THE REQUIREMENT.
DON'T LET THEM WANDER IN MY SIGHT!!
IF THEY SET FOOT IN THE LIVING ROOM, THEY'RE DEAD!!
GET ME MUMMY !!
THIS IS CLEARLY DUE TO THE CALL.
IT'S MY CHANCE TO FIND OUT ABOUT NEN BEASTS ...!!
WHAT WOULD YOU LIKE US TO DO...? SINCE YOU ARE THE SON OF THE FIRST QUEEN, FOURTH PRINCE TSERRIEDNICH...
...YOU ARE NOT OBLIGATED TO COMPLY...
TELL HIM, "YOU IDIOT."
I'M FOCUSING ON NEN.
THE ONE WHO MADE THE EMERGENCY CALL... DESIRES AN IMPASSE...
I WANT INFORMATION ON THIS HUNTER AT ONCE.
YES'M.
1014
WAAAH
WAAAAH

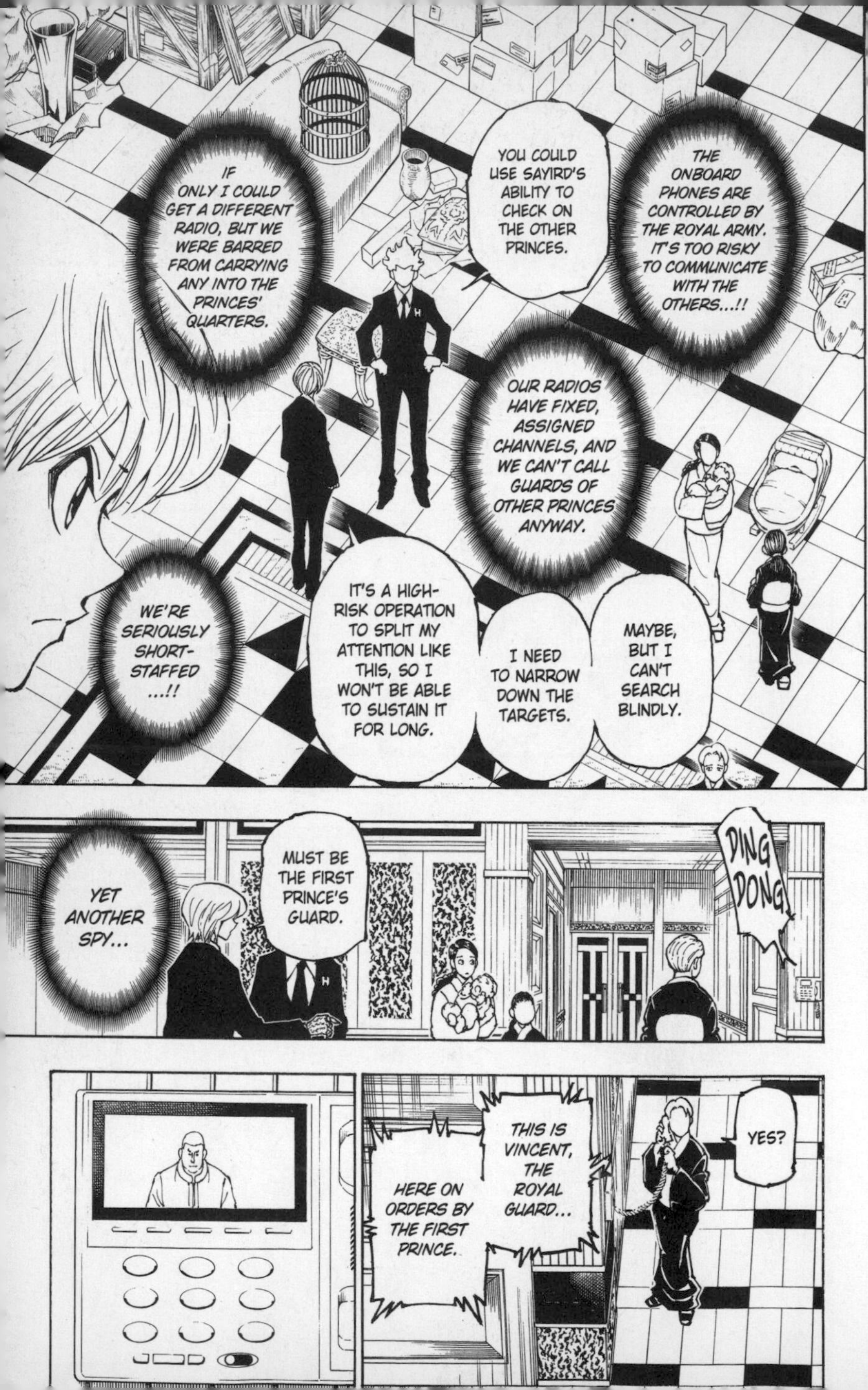

THE ONBOARD PHONES ARE CONTROLLED BY THE ROYAL ARMY. IT'S TOO RISKY TO COMMUNICATE WITH THE OTHERS...!!
YOU COULD USE SAYIRD'S ABILITY TO CHECK ON THE OTHER PRINCES.
IF ONLY I COULD GET A DIFFERENT RADIO, BUT WE WERE BARRED FROM CARRYING ANY INTO THE PRINCES' QUARTERS.
OUR RADIOS HAVE FIXED, ASSIGNED CHANNELS, AND WE CAN'T CALL GUARDS OF OTHER PRINCES ANYWAY.
MAYBE, BUT I CAN'T SEARCH BLINDLY.
I NEED TO NARROW DOWN THE TARGETS.
IT'S A HIGH-RISK OPERATION TO SPLIT MY ATTENTION LIKE THIS, SO I WON'T BE ABLE TO SUSTAIN IT FOR LONG.
WE'RE SERIOUSLY SHORT-STAFFED ...!!
DING DONG
MUST BE THE FIRST PRINCE'S GUARD.
YET ANOTHER SPY...
YES?
THIS IS VINCENT, THE ROYAL GUARD...
HERE ON ORDERS BY THE FIRST PRINCE.

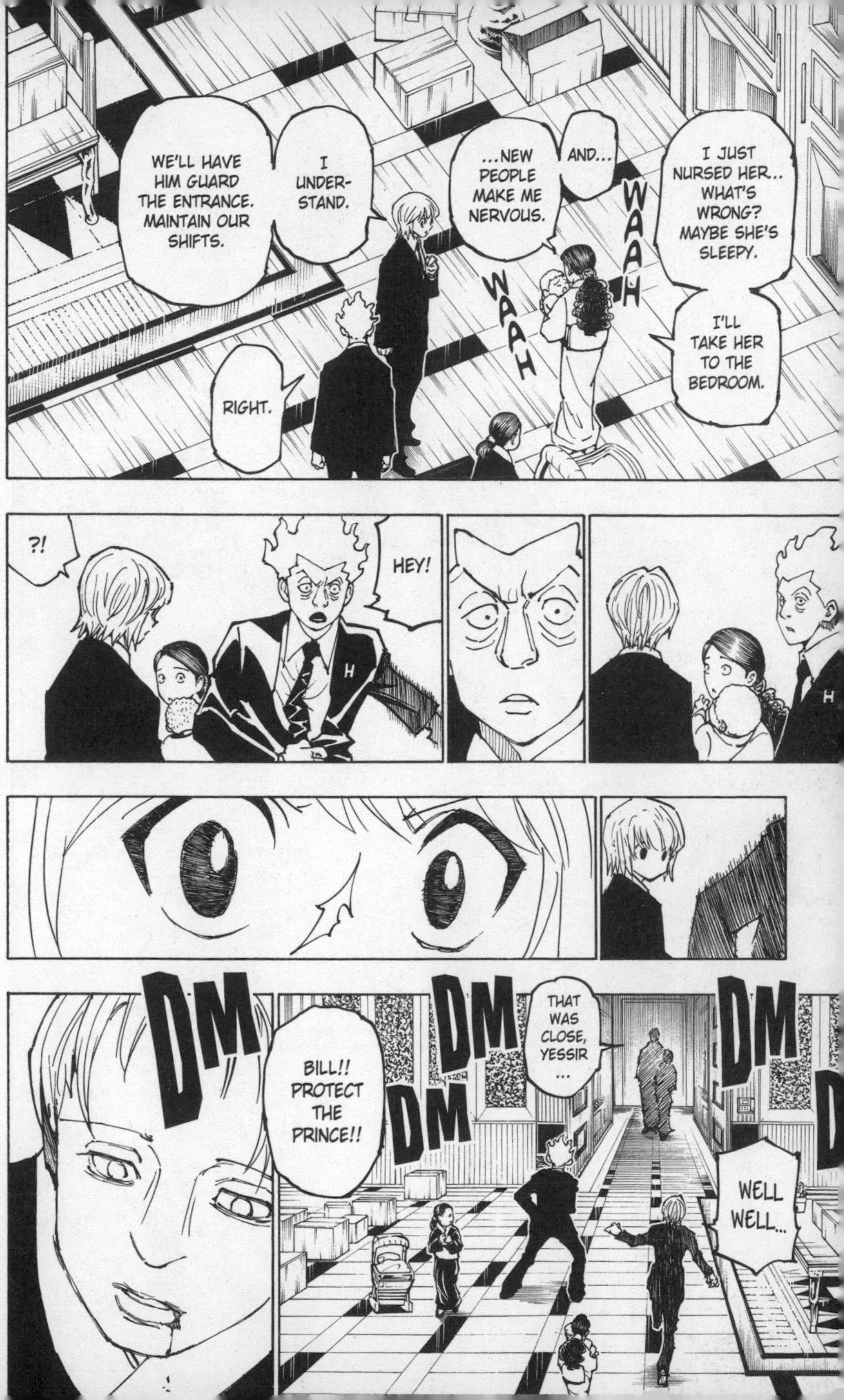
I JUST NURSED HER... WHAT'S WRONG? MAYBE SHE'S SLEEPY.
I'LL TAKE HER TO THE BEDROOM.
WAAH
AND...
...NEW PEOPLE MAKE ME NERVOUS.
WAAH
I UNDER-STAND.
WE'LL HAVE HIM GUARD THE ENTRANCE. MAINTAIN OUR SHIFTS.
RIGHT.
HEY!
?!
DM
WELL WELL...
THAT WAS CLOSE, YESSIR ...
DM
DM
BILL!! PROTECT THE PRINCE!!
DM

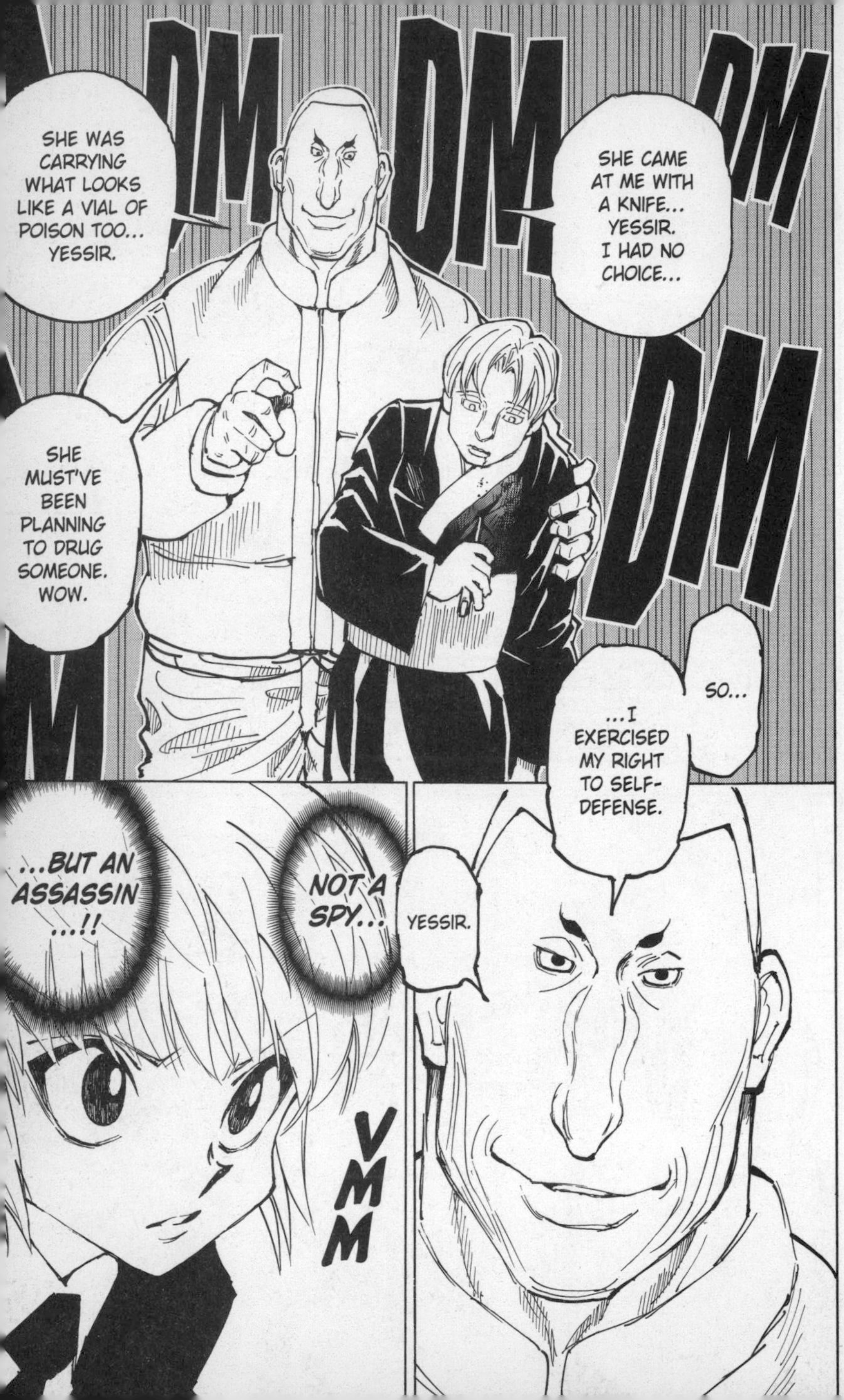
DM DM DM DM
SHE CAME AT ME WITH A KNIFE... YESSIR. I HAD NO CHOICE...
SHE WAS CARRYING WHAT LOOKS LIKE A VIAL OF POISON TOO... YESSIR.
SHE MUST'VE BEEN PLANNING TO DRUG SOMEONE. WOW.
DM
SO...
...I EXERCISED MY RIGHT TO SELF-DEFENSE.
YESSIR.
NOT A SPY...
...BUT AN ASSASSIN ...!!
VMM

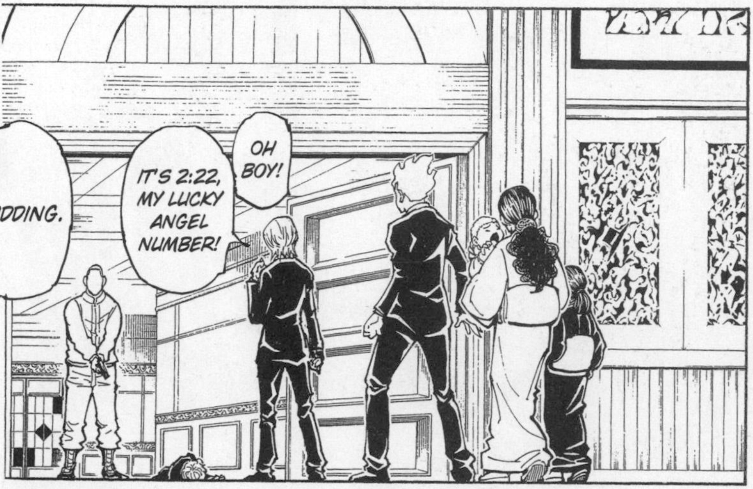
OH BOY!
IT'S 2:22, MY LUCKY ANGEL NUMBER!
KIDDING.
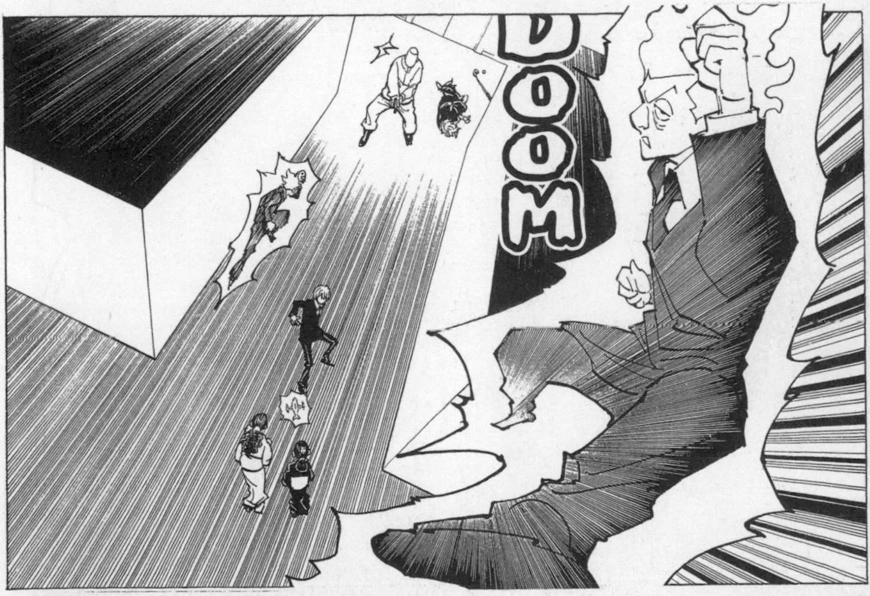
DOOM

Chapter 364: Speculation

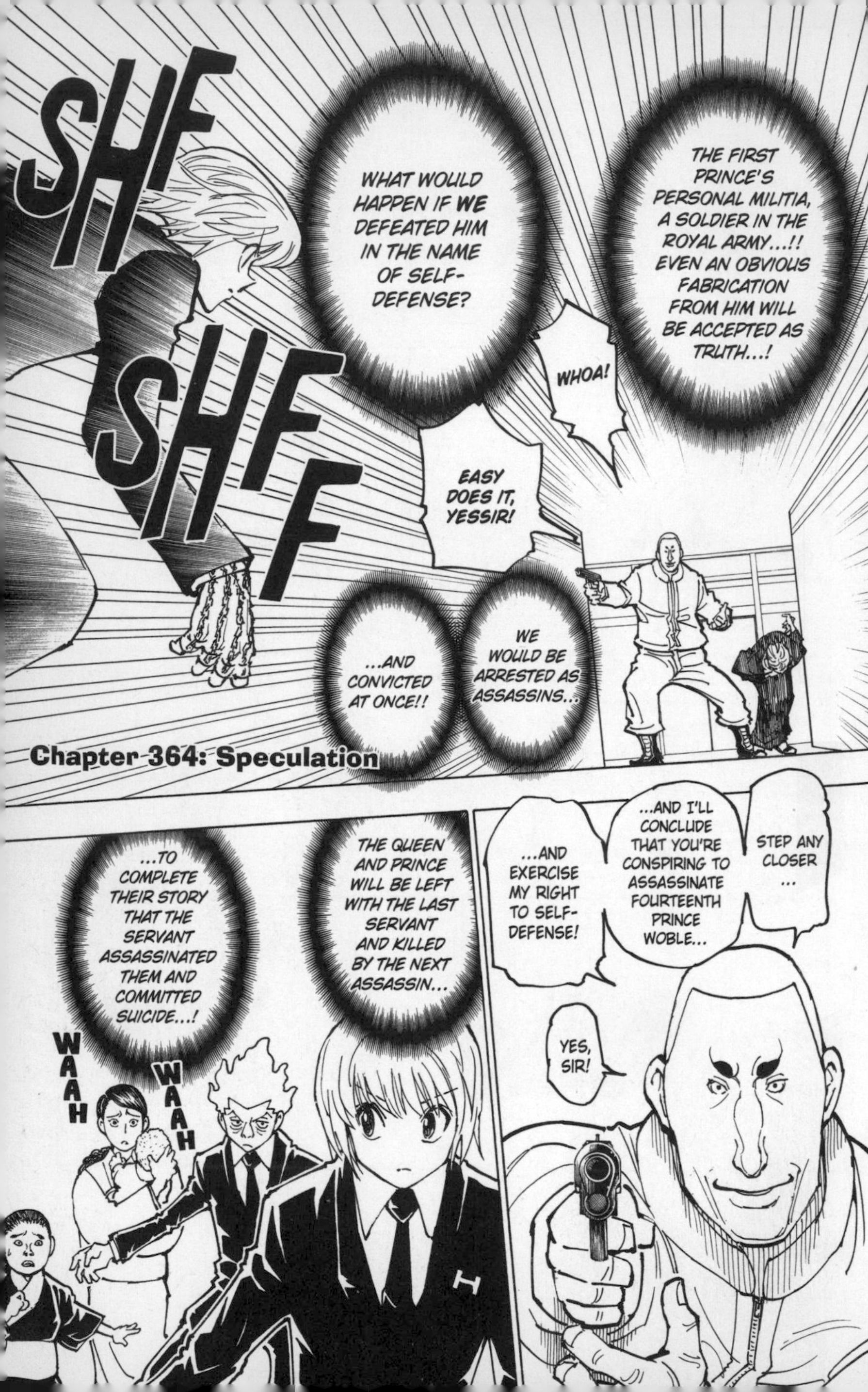
SHF
SHF
SHF
THE FIRST PRINCE'S PERSONAL MILITIA, A SOLDIER IN THE ROYAL ARMY...!! EVEN AN OBVIOUS FABRICATION FROM HIM WILL BE ACCEPTED AS TRUTH...!
WHAT WOULD HAPPEN IF WE DEFEATED HIM IN THE NAME OF SELF-DEFENSE?
WHOA!
EASY DOES IT, YESSIR!
WE WOULD BE ARRESTED AS ASSASSINS...
...AND CONVICTED AT ONCE!!
STEP ANY CLOSER ...
...AND I'LL CONCLUDE THAT YOU'RE CONSPIRING TO ASSASSINATE FOURTEENTH PRINCE WOBLE...
...AND EXERCISE MY RIGHT TO SELF-DEFENSE!
YES, SIR!
THE QUEEN AND PRINCE WILL BE LEFT WITH THE LAST SERVANT AND KILLED BY THE NEXT ASSASSIN...
...TO COMPLETE THEIR STORY THAT THE SERVANT ASSASSINATED THEM AND COMMITTED SUICIDE...!
WAAH
WAAH

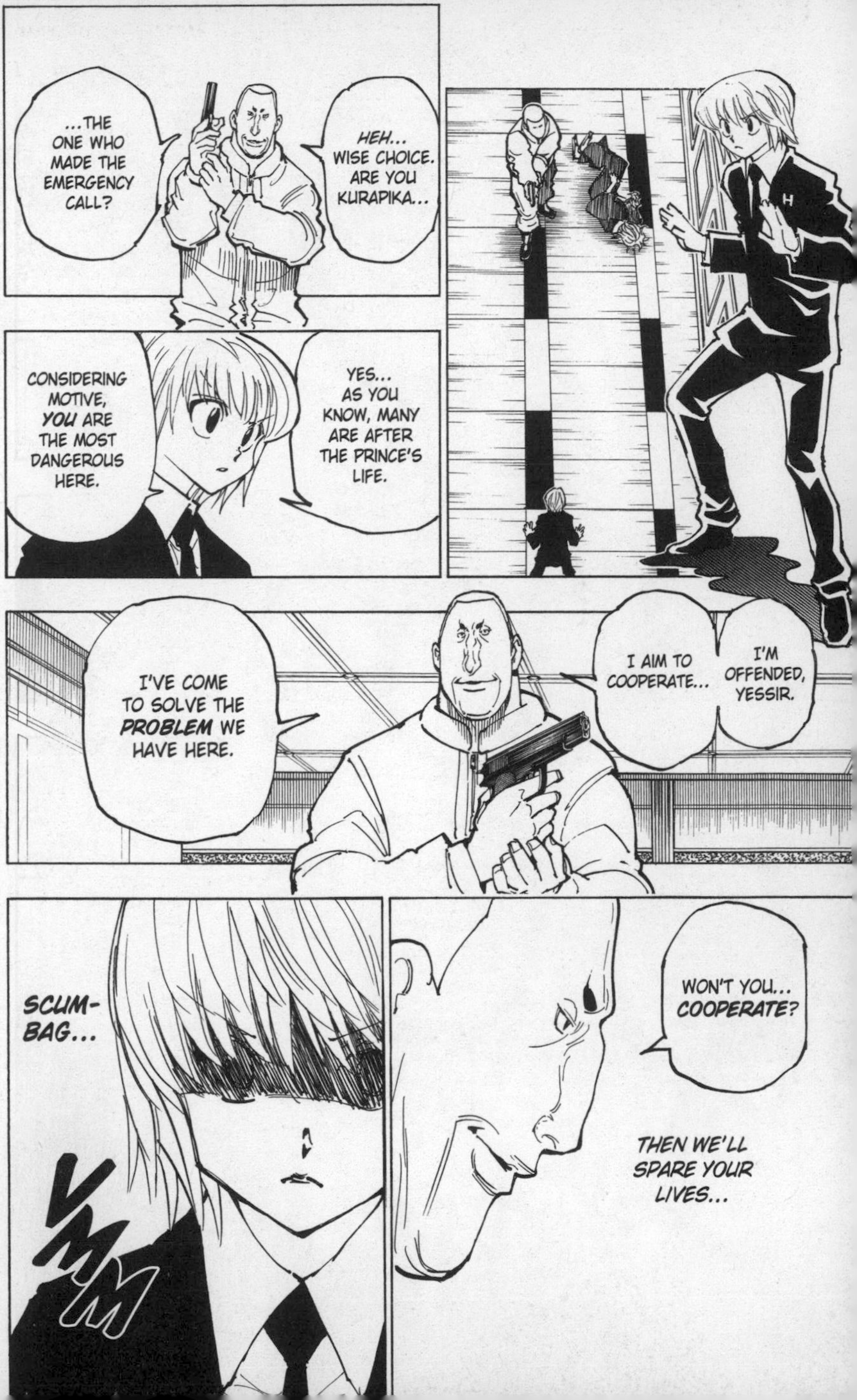
HEH... WISE CHOICE. ARE YOU KURAPIKA...
...THE ONE WHO MADE THE EMERGENCY CALL?
YES... AS YOU KNOW, MANY ARE AFTER THE PRINCE'S LIFE.
CONSIDERING MOTIVE, YOU ARE THE MOST DANGEROUS HERE.
I'M OFFENDED, YESSIR.
I AIM TO COOPERATE...
I'VE COME TO SOLVE THE PROBLEM WE HAVE HERE.
WON'T YOU... COOPERATE?
THEN WE'LL SPARE YOUR LIVES...
SCUM-BAG...
VMMM

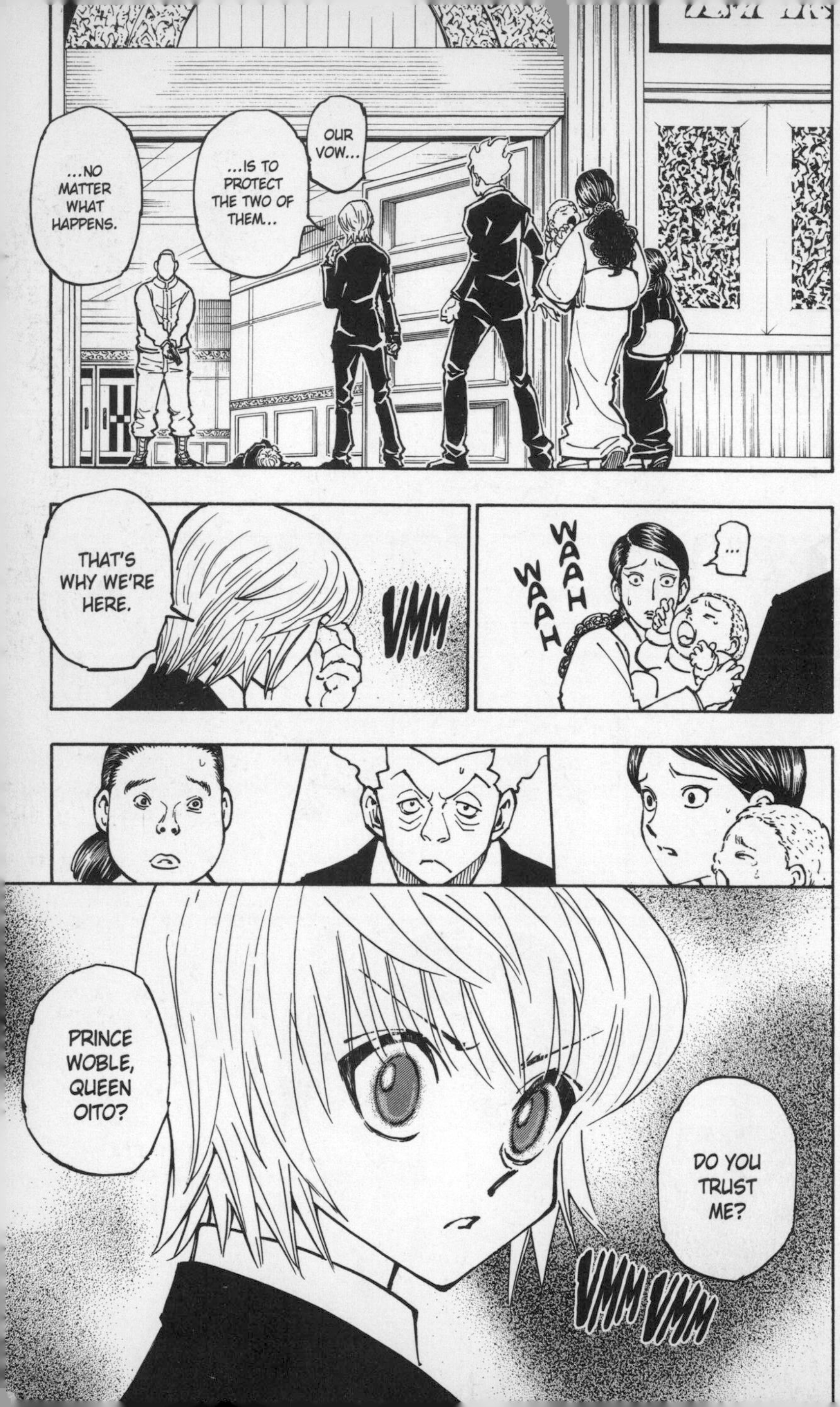
OUR VOW...
...IS TO PROTECT THE TWO OF THEM...
...NO MATTER WHAT HAPPENS.
...
WAAH WAAH
VMM
THAT'S WHY WE'RE HERE.
DO YOU TRUST ME?
PRINCE WOBLE, QUEEN OITO?
VMM VMM

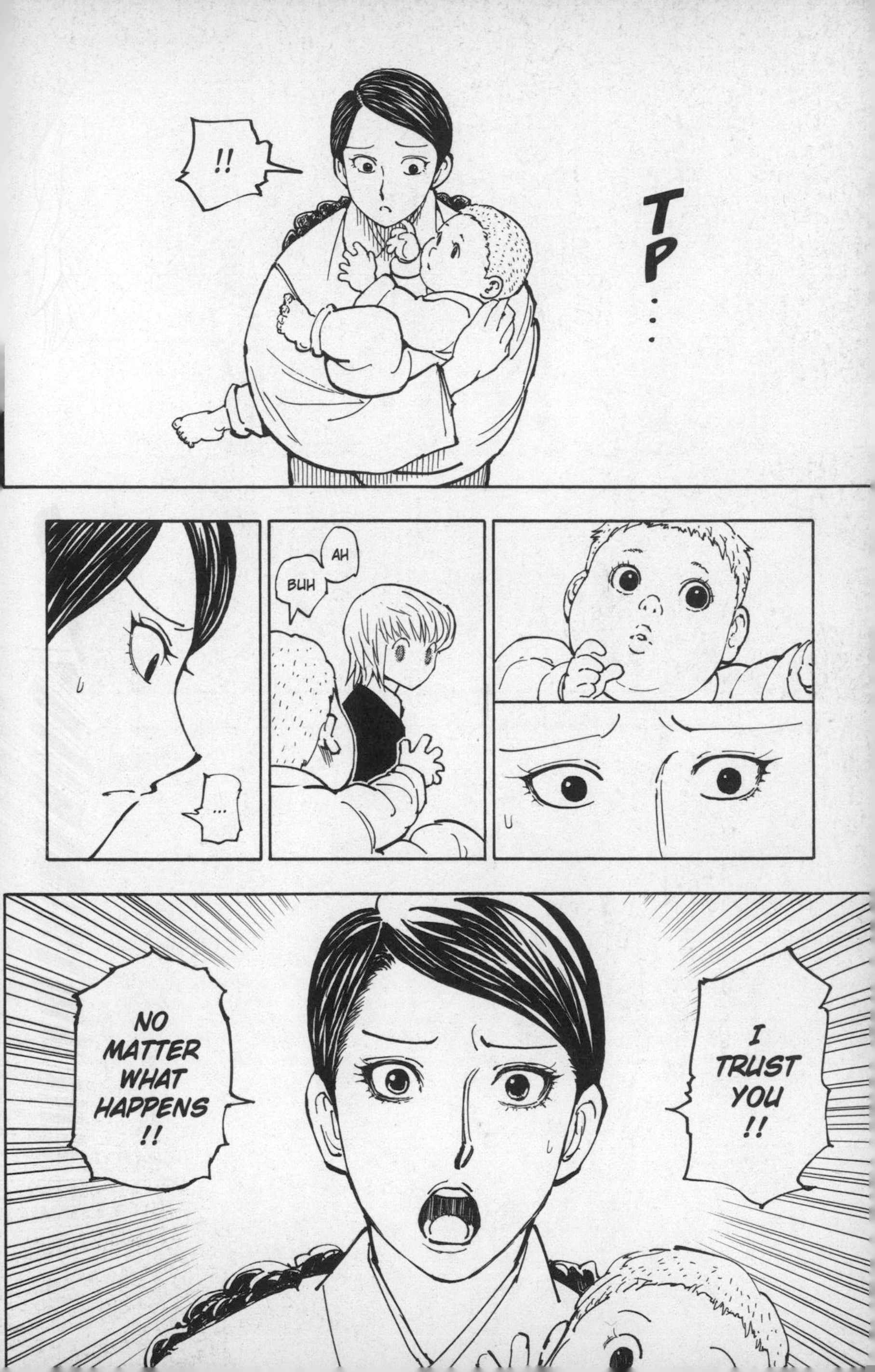
TP...
!!
AH
BUH
...
I TRUST YOU!!
NO MATTER WHAT HAPPENS!!

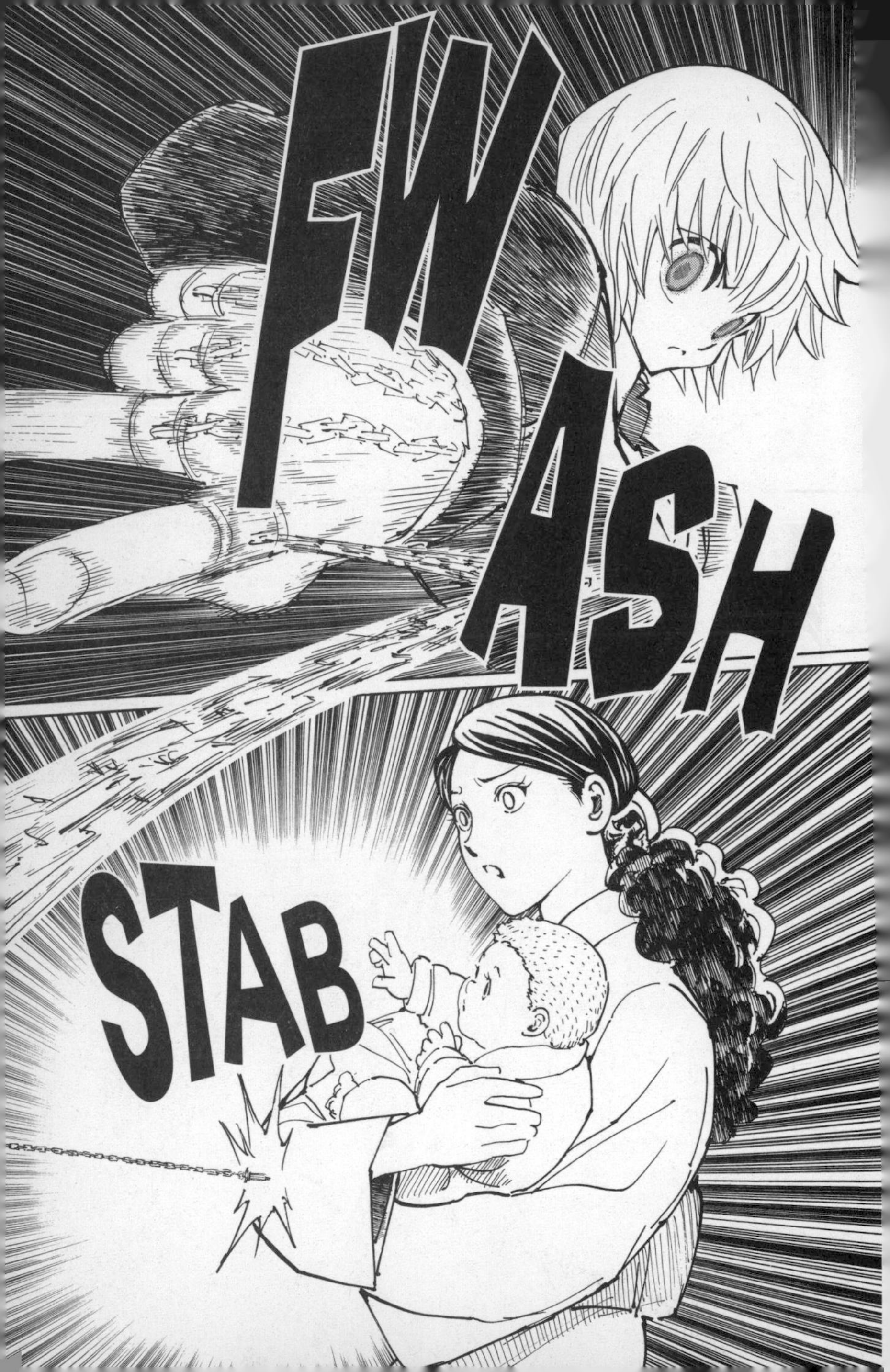
FWASH
STAB

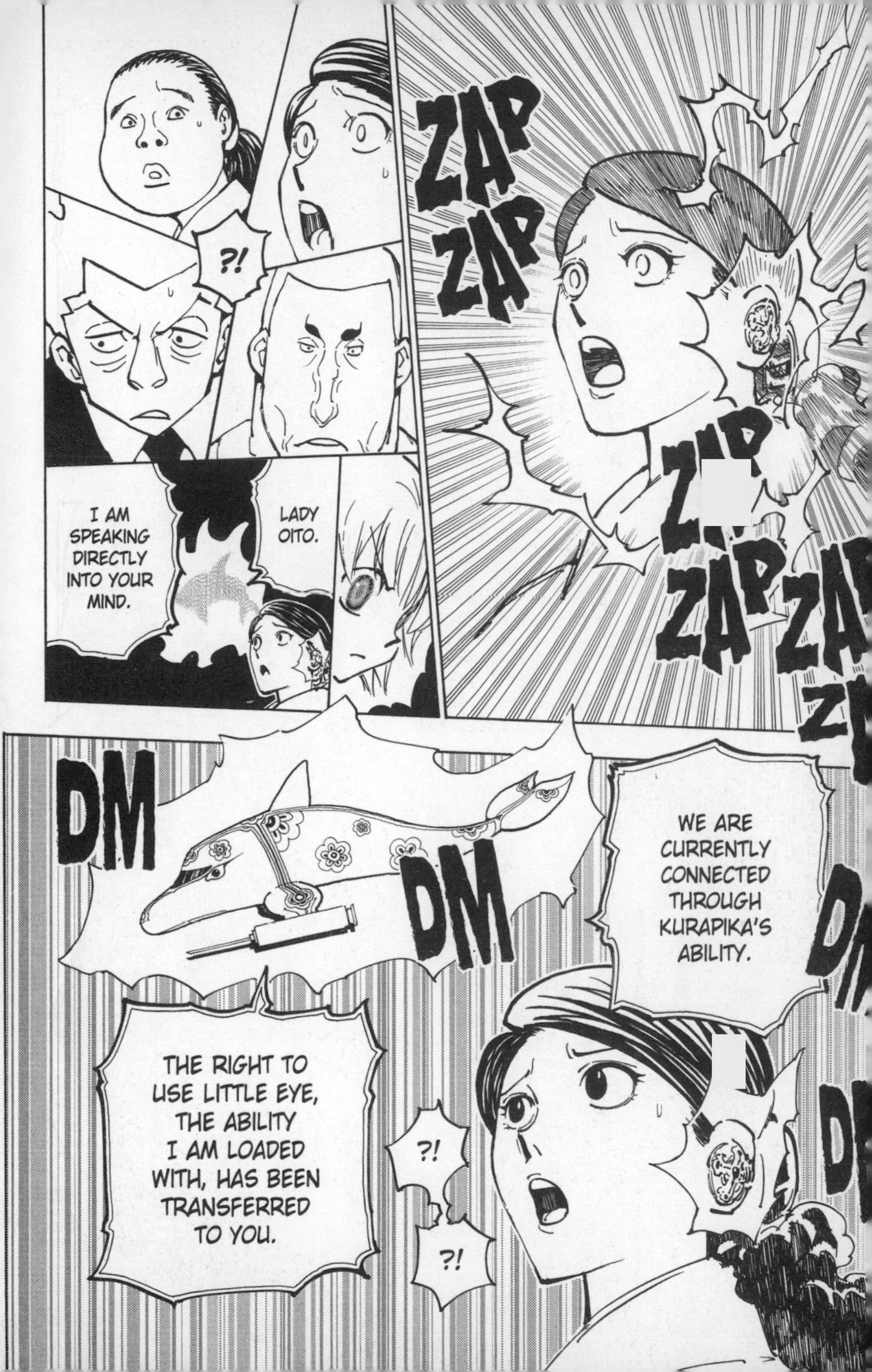
ZAP
ZAP
ZAP
ZAP
?!
LADY OITO.
I AM SPEAKING DIRECTLY INTO YOUR MIND.
WE ARE CURRENTLY CONNECTED THROUGH KURAPIKA'S ABILITY.
?!
?!
DM
DM
THE RIGHT TO USE LITTLE EYE, THE ABILITY I AM LOADED WITH, HAS BEEN TRANSFERRED TO YOU.

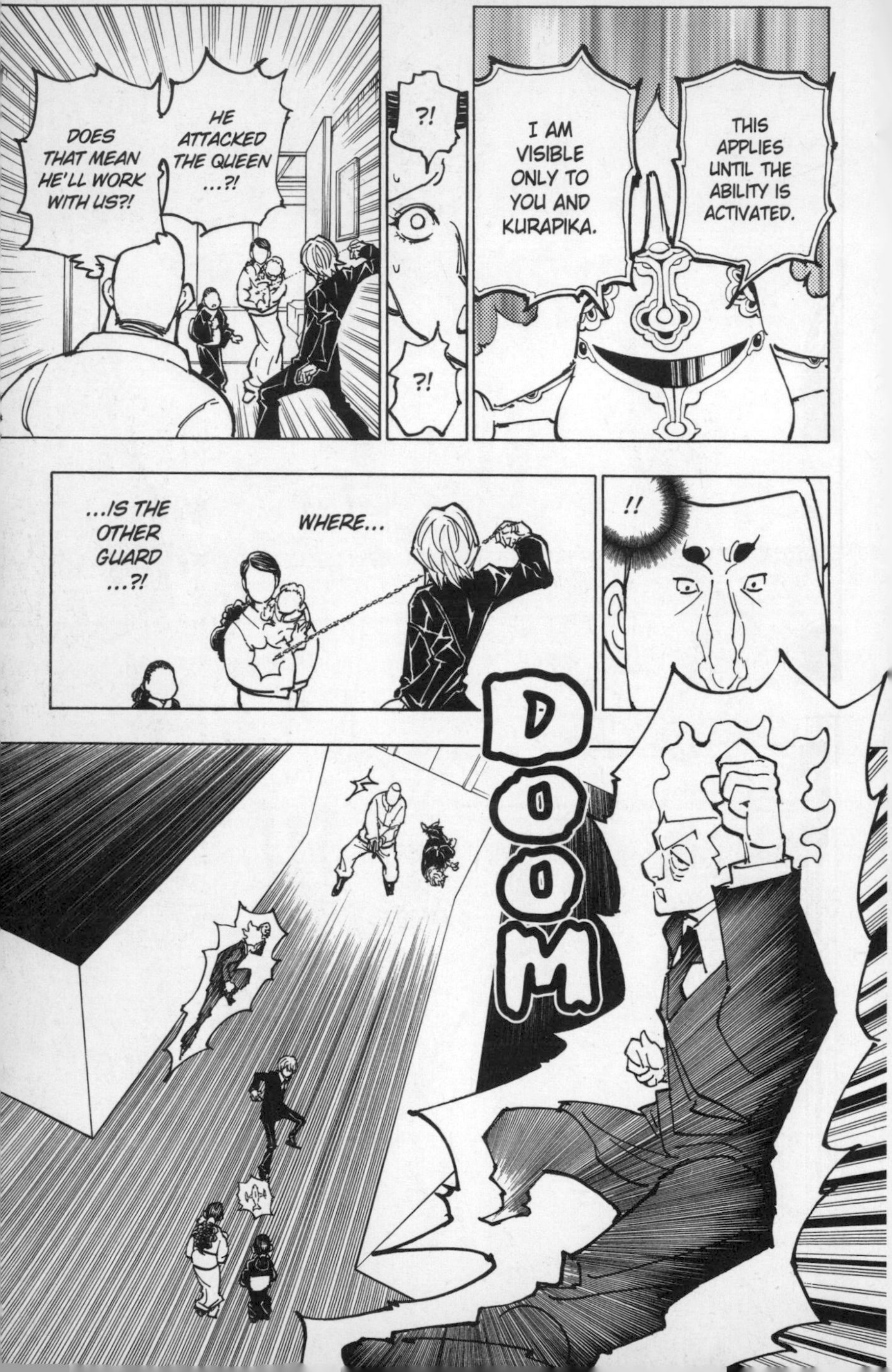
I AM VISIBLE ONLY TO YOU AND KURAPIKA.
THIS APPLIES UNTIL THE ABILITY IS ACTIVATED.
?!
?!
HE ATTACKED THE QUEEN ...?!
DOES THAT MEAN HE'LL WORK WITH US?!
!!
WHERE...
...IS THE OTHER GUARD ...?!
DOOM

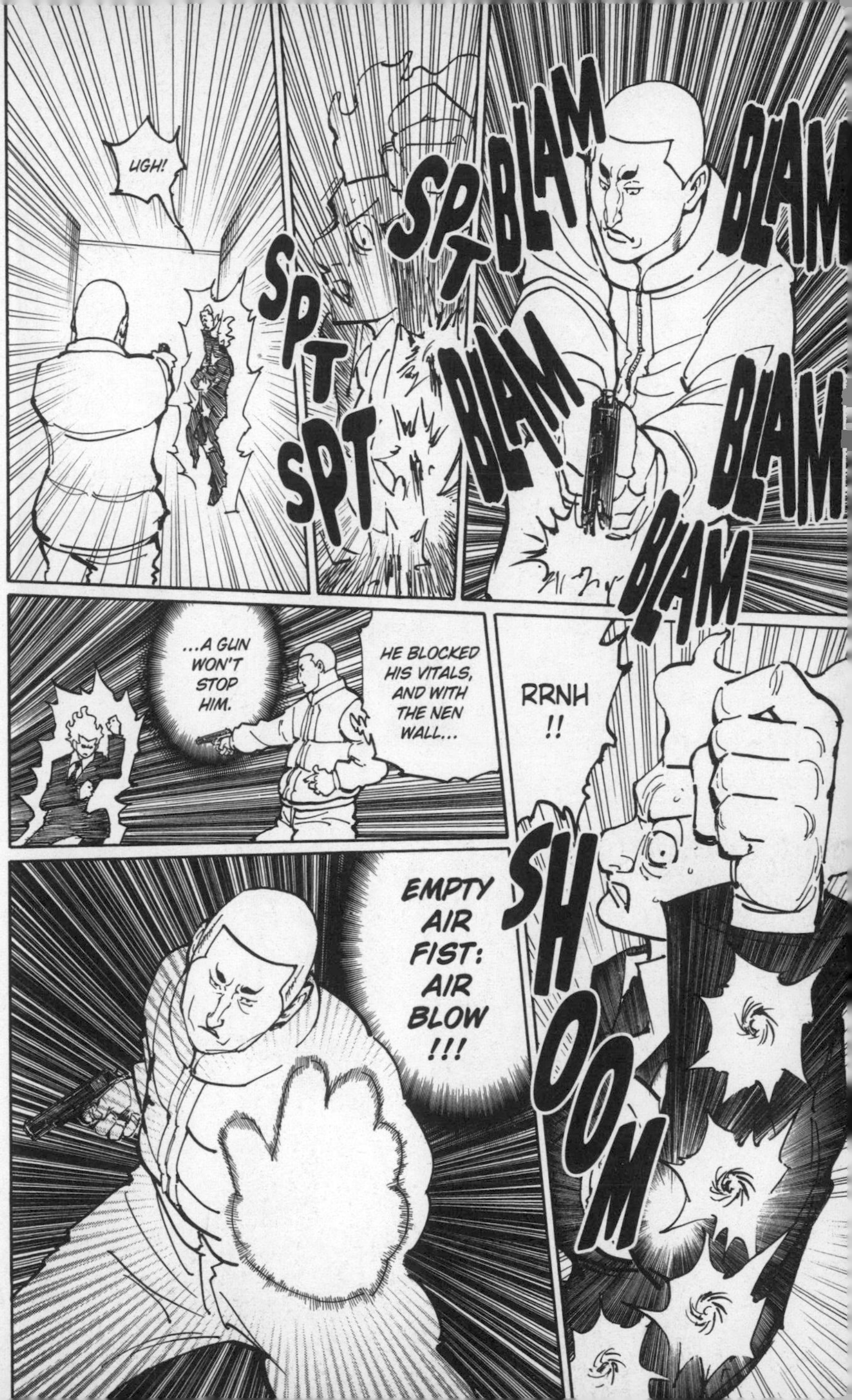
BLAM
BLAM
BLAM
BLAM
BLAM
SPT
SPT
SPT
UGH!
RRNH !!
SHOOOM
HE BLOCKED HIS VITALS, AND WITH THE NEN WALL...
...A GUN WON'T STOP HIM.
EMPTY AIR FIST: AIR BLOW !!!

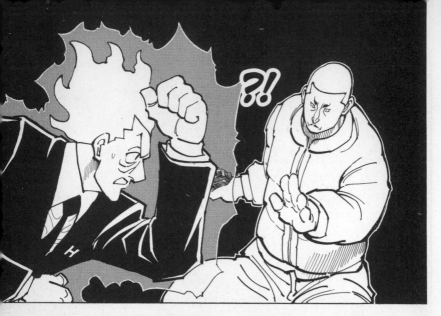

?!

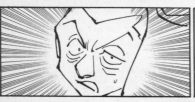

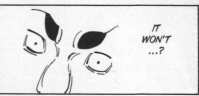

IT WON'T ...?

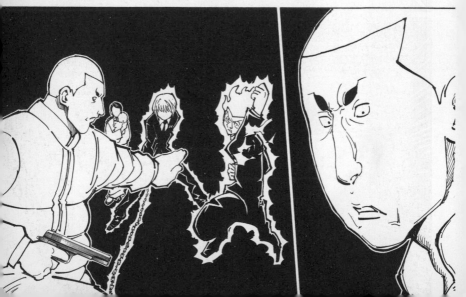

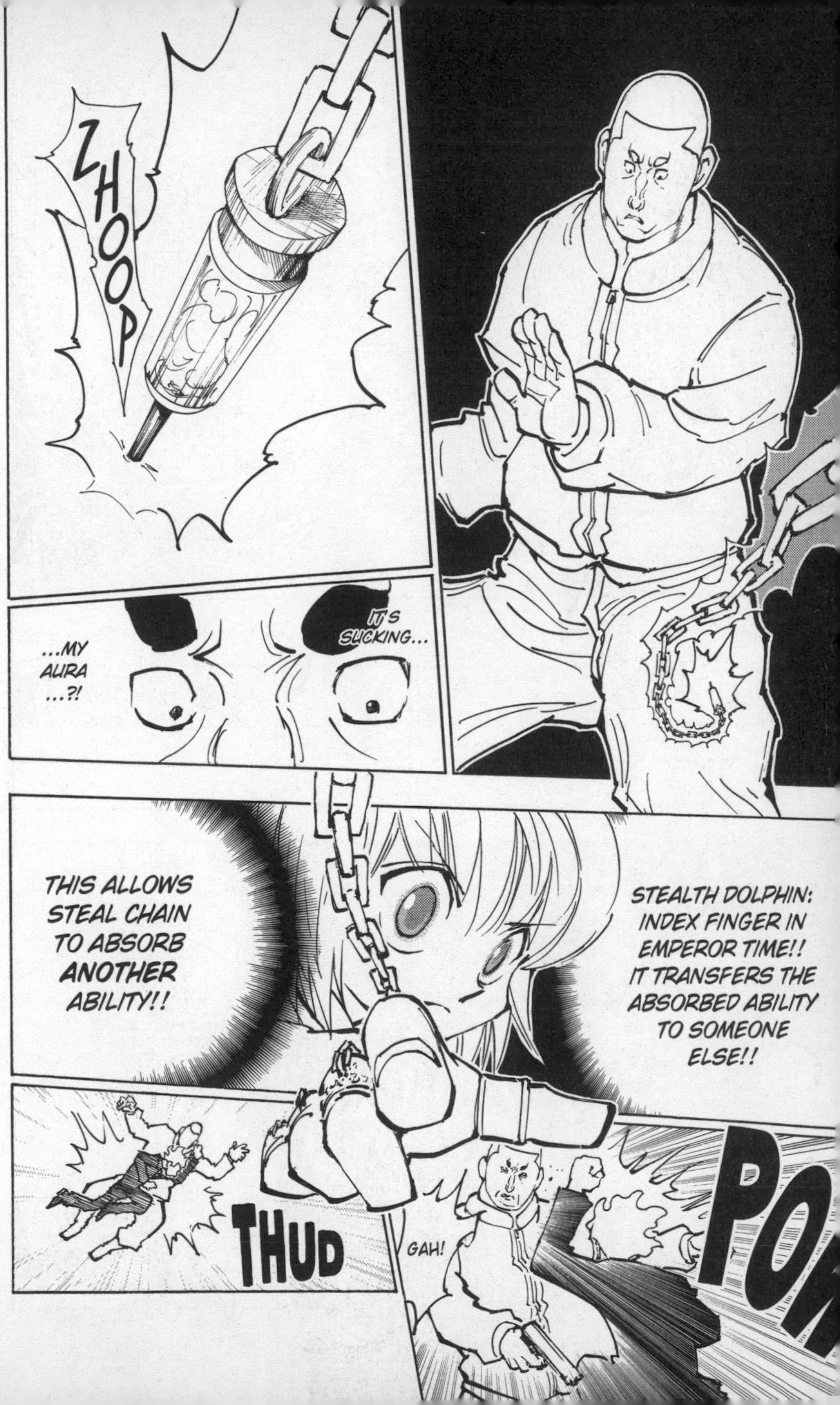
ZHOOP
IT'S SUCKING...
...MY AURA ...?!
STEALTH DOLPHIN: INDEX FINGER IN EMPEROR TIME!! IT TRANSFERS THE ABSORBED ABILITY TO SOMEONE ELSE!!
THIS ALLOWS STEAL CHAIN TO ABSORB ANOTHER ABILITY!!
PO
GAH!
THUD

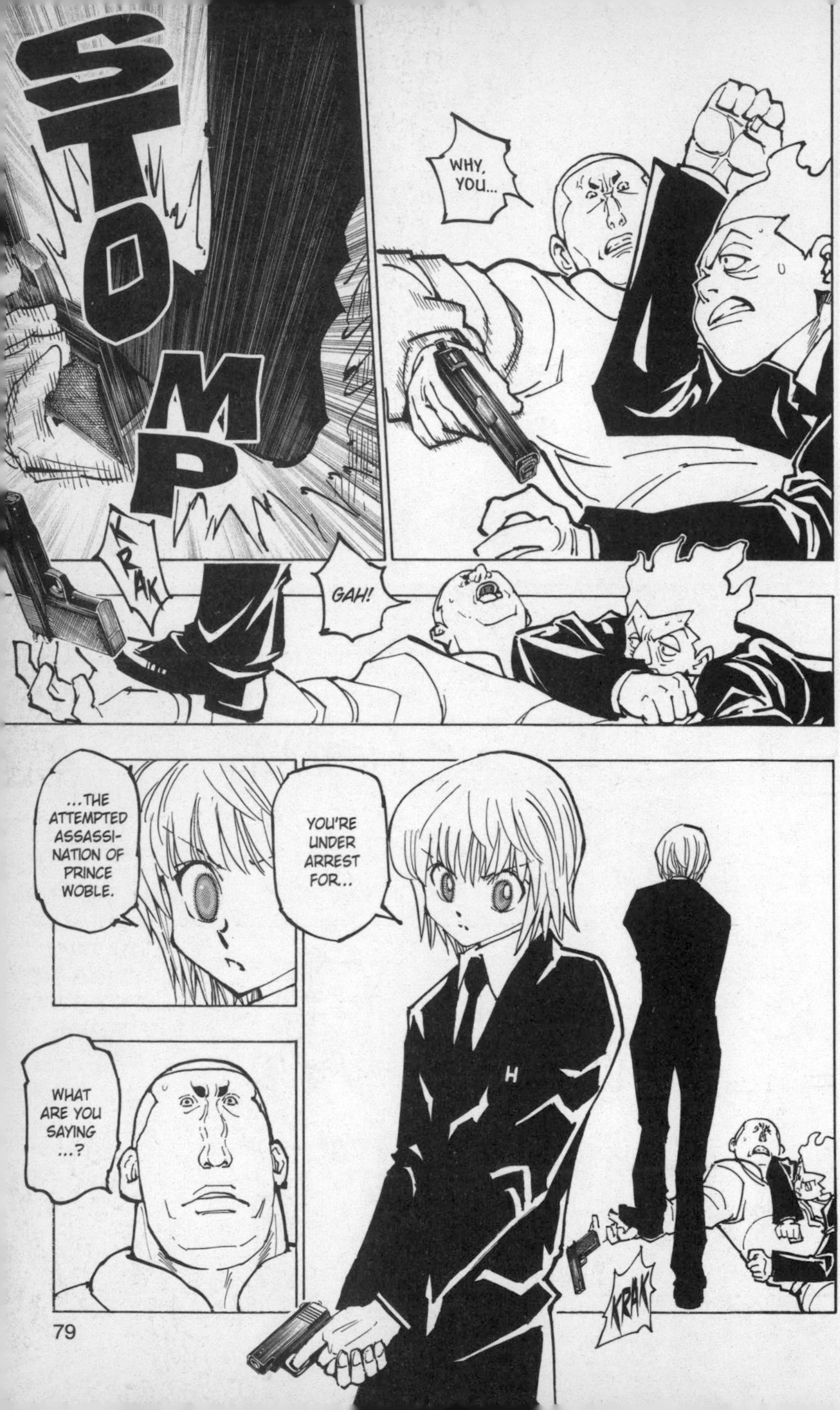
WHY, YOU...
STOMP
KRAK
GAH!
YOU'RE UNDER ARREST FOR...
KRAK
...THE ATTEMPTED ASSASSI- NATION OF PRINCE WOBLE.
WHAT ARE YOU SAYING ...?

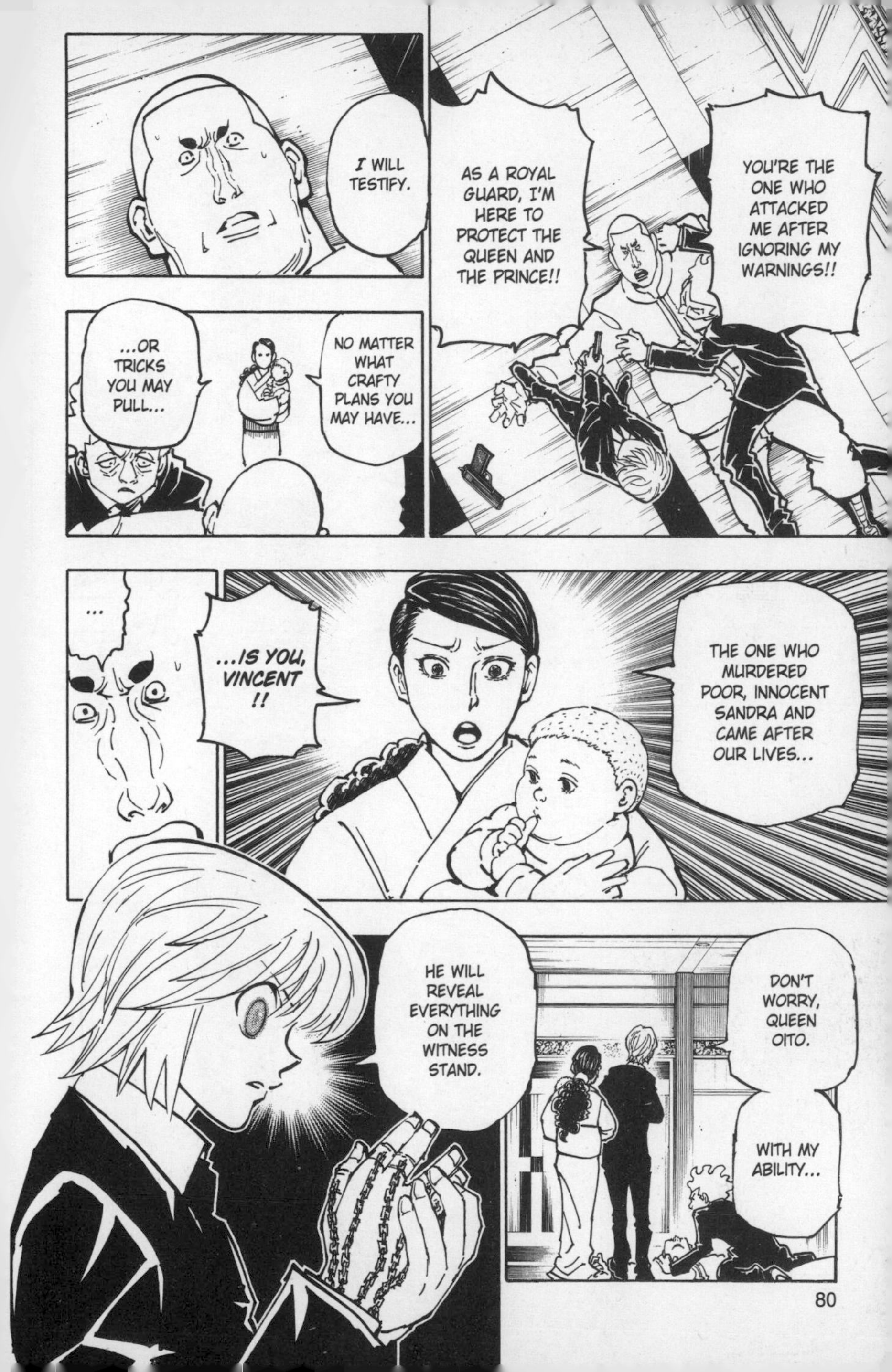
YOU'RE THE ONE WHO ATTACKED ME AFTER IGNORING MY WARNINGS!!
AS A ROYAL GUARD, I'M HERE TO PROTECT THE QUEEN AND THE PRINCE!!
I WILL TESTIFY.
NO MATTER WHAT CRAFTY PLANS YOU MAY HAVE...
...OR TRICKS YOU MAY PULL...
THE ONE WHO MURDERED POOR, INNOCENT SANDRA AND CAME AFTER OUR LIVES...
...IS YOU, VINCENT!!
...
DON'T WORRY, QUEEN OITO.
WITH MY ABILITY...
HE WILL REVEAL EVERYTHING ON THE WITNESS STAND.

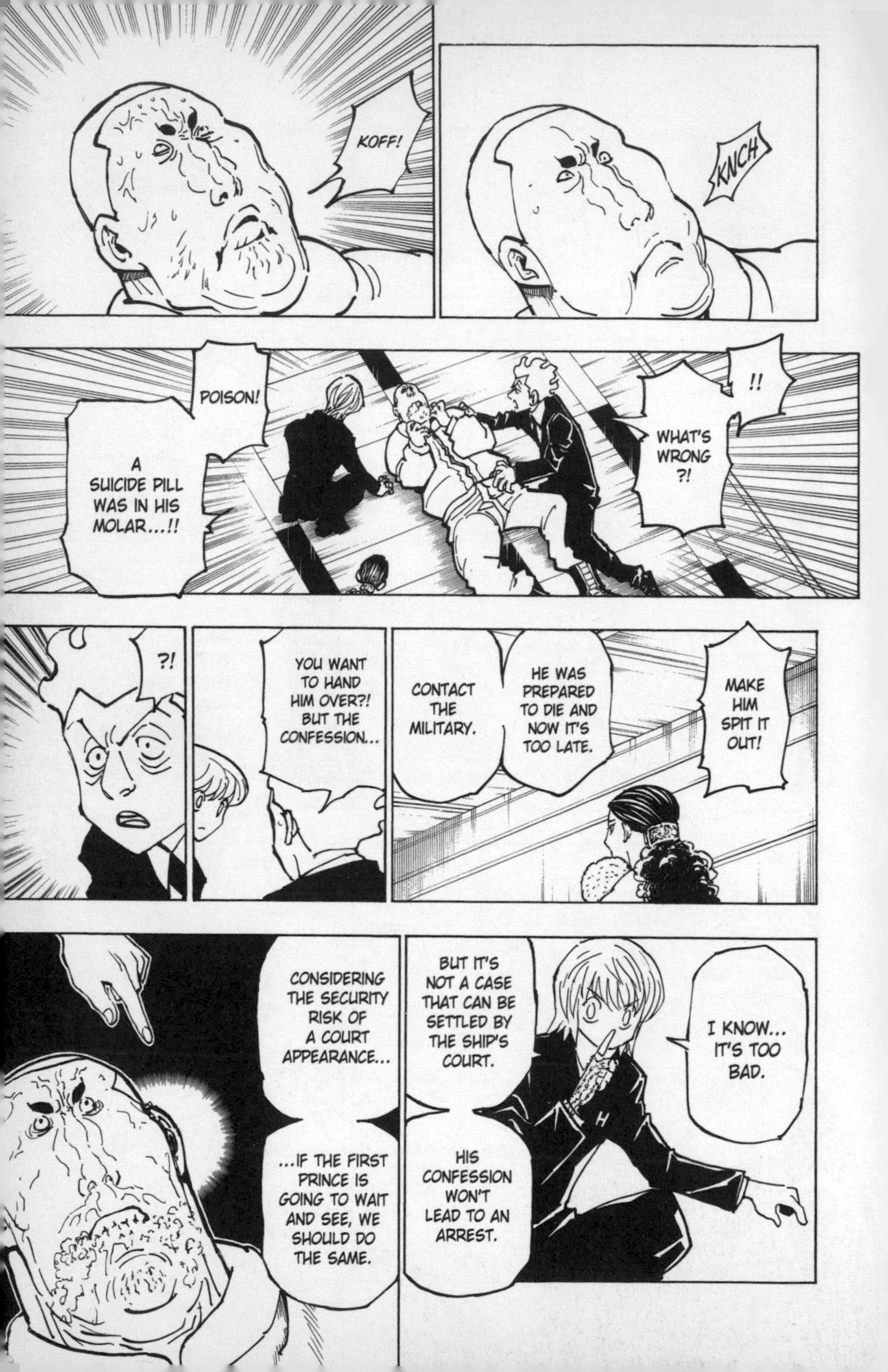
KNCH
KOFF!
!!
WHAT'S WRONG ?!
POISON!
A SUICIDE PILL WAS IN HIS MOLAR...!!
MAKE HIM SPIT IT OUT!
HE WAS PREPARED TO DIE AND NOW IT'S TOO LATE.
CONTACT THE MILITARY.
YOU WANT TO HAND HIM OVER?! BUT THE CONFESSION...
?!
I KNOW... IT'S TOO BAD.
BUT IT'S NOT A CASE THAT CAN BE SETTLED BY THE SHIP'S COURT.
HIS CONFESSION WON'T LEAD TO AN ARREST.
CONSIDERING THE SECURITY RISK OF A COURT APPEARANCE...
...IF THE FIRST PRINCE IS GOING TO WAIT AND SEE, WE SHOULD DO THE SAME.

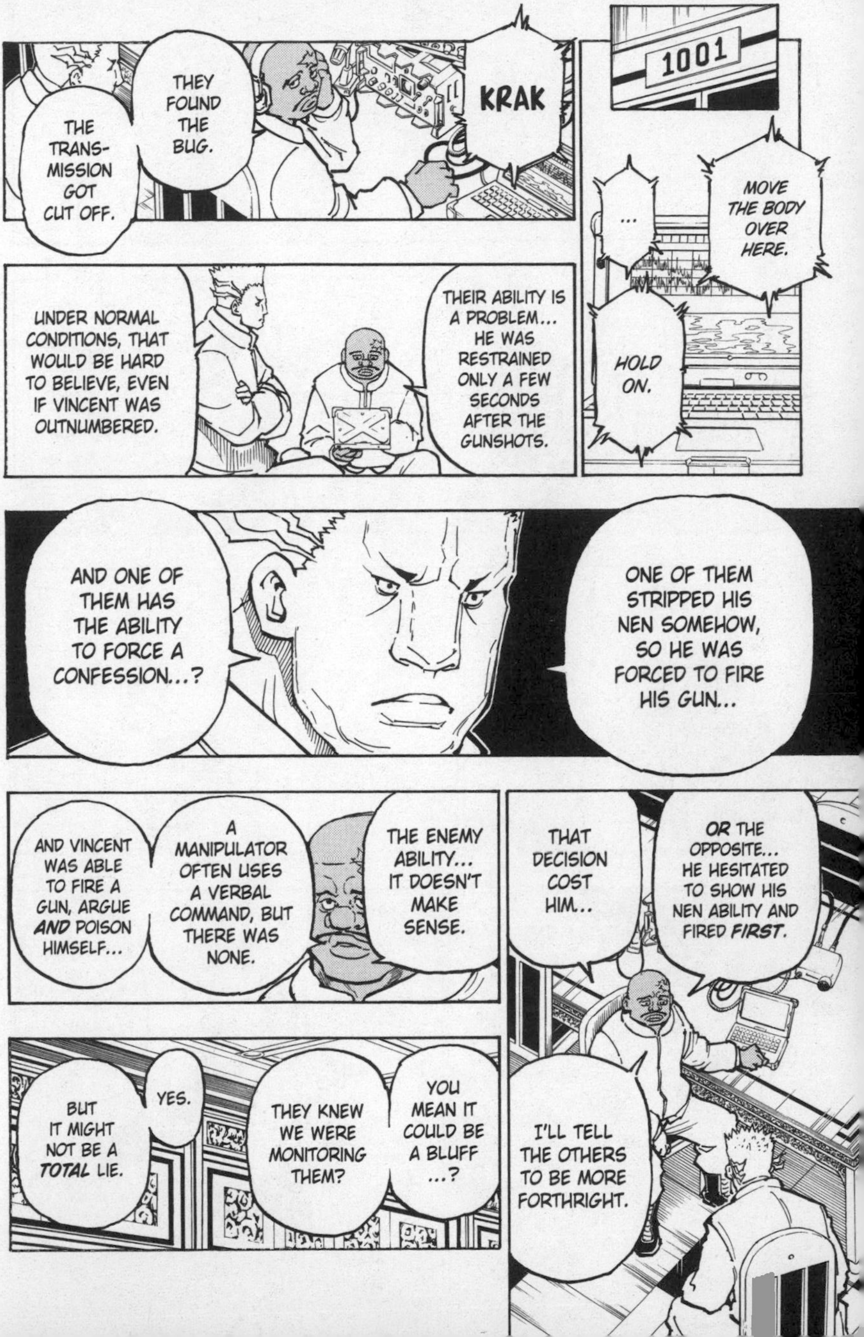
1001
MOVE THE BODY OVER HERE.
...
HOLD ON.
KRAK
THEY FOUND THE BUG.
THE TRANSMISSION GOT CUT OFF.
THEIR ABILITY IS A PROBLEM... HE WAS RESTRAINED ONLY A FEW SECONDS AFTER THE GUNSHOTS.
UNDER NORMAL CONDITIONS, THAT WOULD BE HARD TO BELIEVE, EVEN IF VINCENT WAS OUTNUMBERED.
ONE OF THEM STRIPPED HIS NEN SOMEHOW, SO HE WAS FORCED TO FIRE HIS GUN...
AND ONE OF THEM HAS THE ABILITY TO FORCE A CONFESSION...?
OR THE OPPOSITE... HE HESITATED TO SHOW HIS NEN ABILITY AND FIRED FIRST.
THAT DECISION COST HIM...
I'LL TELL THE OTHERS TO BE MORE FORTHRIGHT.
THE ENEMY ABILITY... IT DOESN'T MAKE SENSE.
A MANIPULATOR OFTEN USES A VERBAL COMMAND, BUT THERE WAS NONE.
AND VINCENT WAS ABLE TO FIRE A GUN, ARGUE AND POISON HIMSELF...
YOU MEAN IT COULD BE A BLUFF ...?
THEY KNEW WE WERE MONITORING THEM?
YES.
BUT IT MIGHT NOT BE A TOTAL LIE.

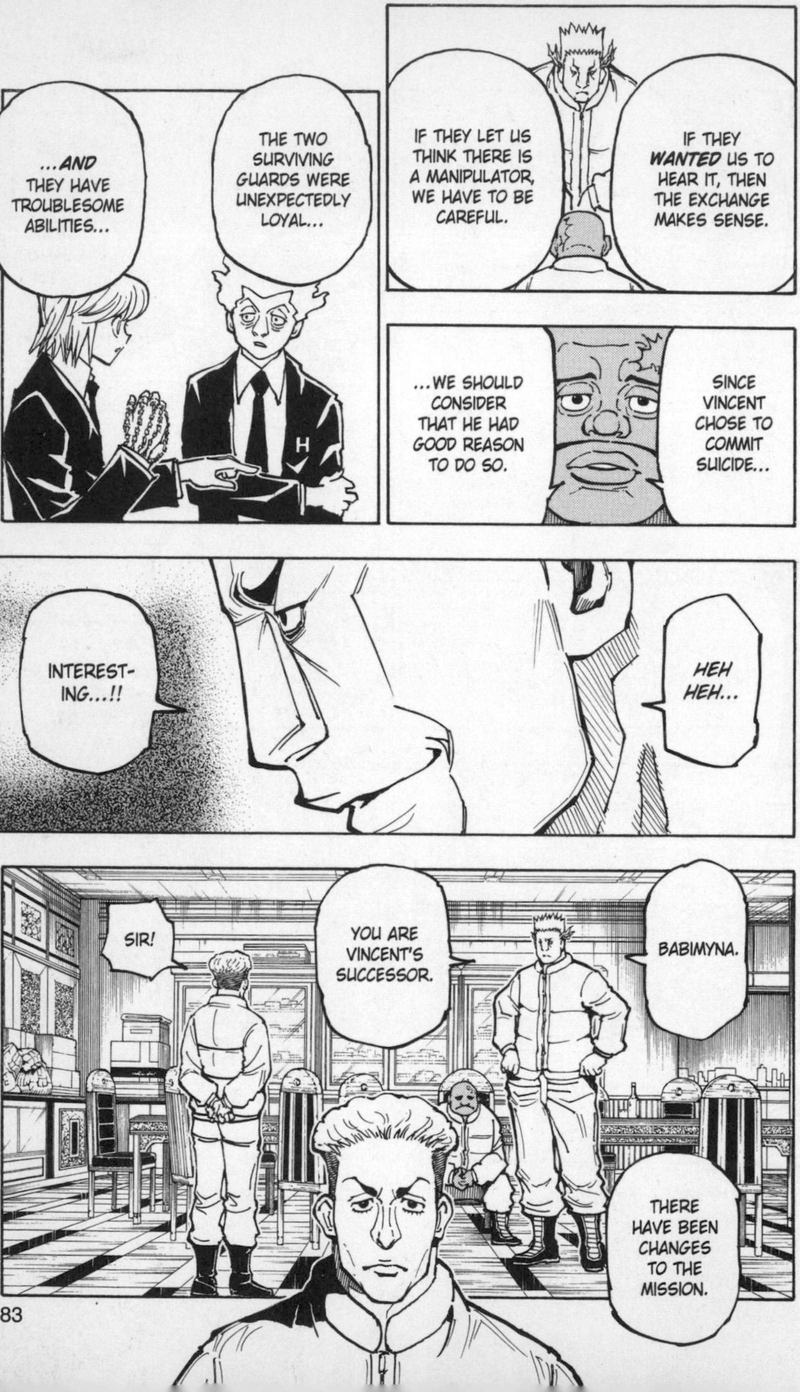
IF THEY *WANTED* US TO HEAR IT, THEN THE EXCHANGE MAKES SENSE.
IF THEY LET US THINK THERE IS A MANIPULATOR, WE HAVE TO BE CAREFUL.
SINCE VINCENT CHOSE TO COMMIT SUICIDE...
...WE SHOULD CONSIDER THAT HE HAD GOOD REASON TO DO SO.
THE TWO SURVIVING GUARDS WERE UNEXPECTEDLY LOYAL...
...AND THEY HAVE TROUBLESOME ABILITIES...
HEH HEH...
INTEREST-ING...!!
BABIMYNA.
YOU ARE VINCENT'S SUCCESSOR.
SIR!
THERE HAVE BEEN CHANGES TO THE MISSION.

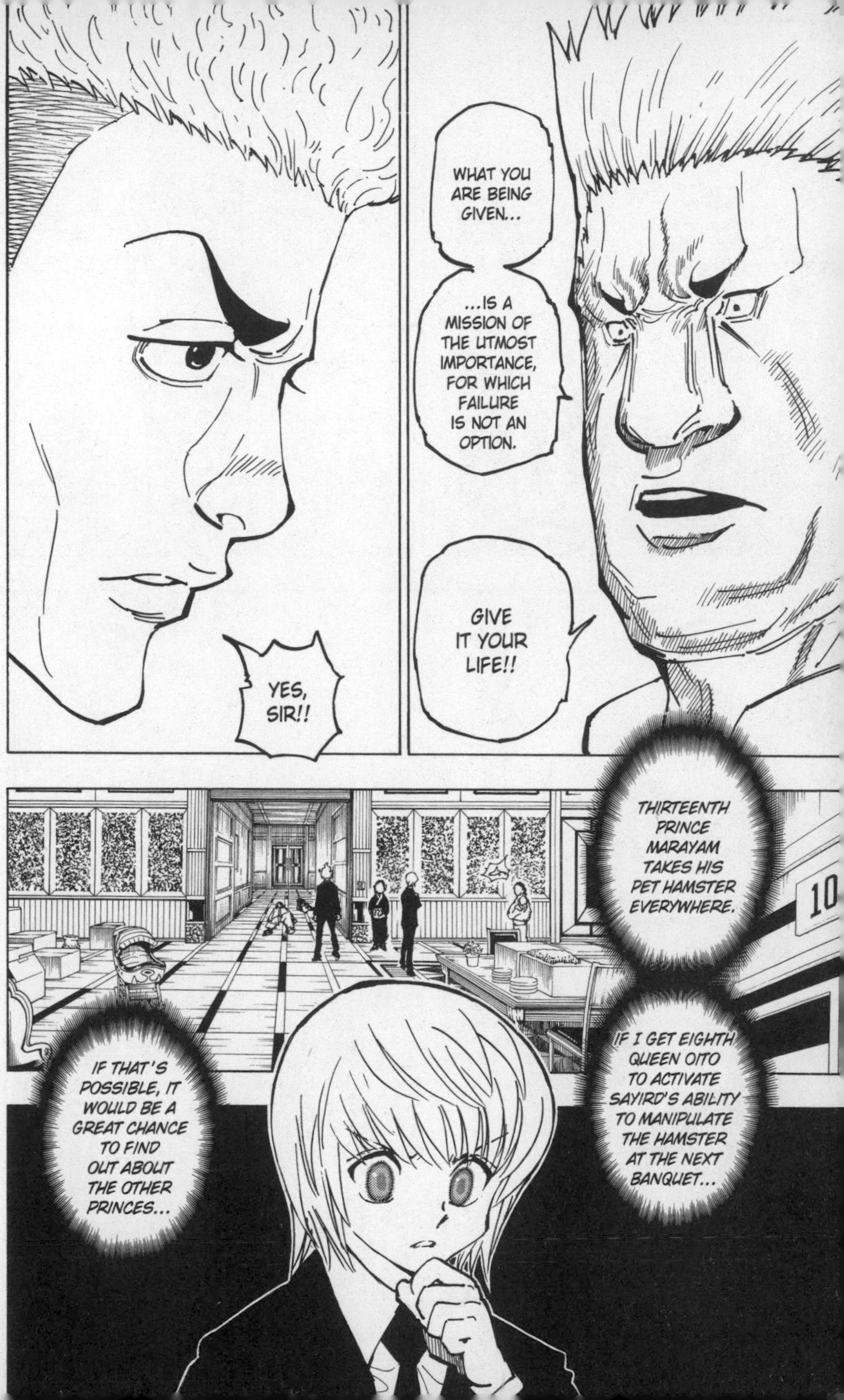
WHAT YOU ARE BEING GIVEN...
...IS A MISSION OF THE UTMOST IMPORTANCE, FOR WHICH FAILURE IS NOT AN OPTION.
GIVE IT YOUR LIFE!!
YES, SIR!!
THIRTEENTH PRINCE MARAYAM TAKES HIS PET HAMSTER EVERYWHERE.
10
IF I GET EIGHTH QUEEN OITO TO ACTIVATE SAYIRD'S ABILITY TO MANIPULATE THE HAMSTER AT THE NEXT BANQUET...
IF THAT'S POSSIBLE, IT WOULD BE A GREAT CHANCE TO FIND OUT ABOUT THE OTHER PRINCES...

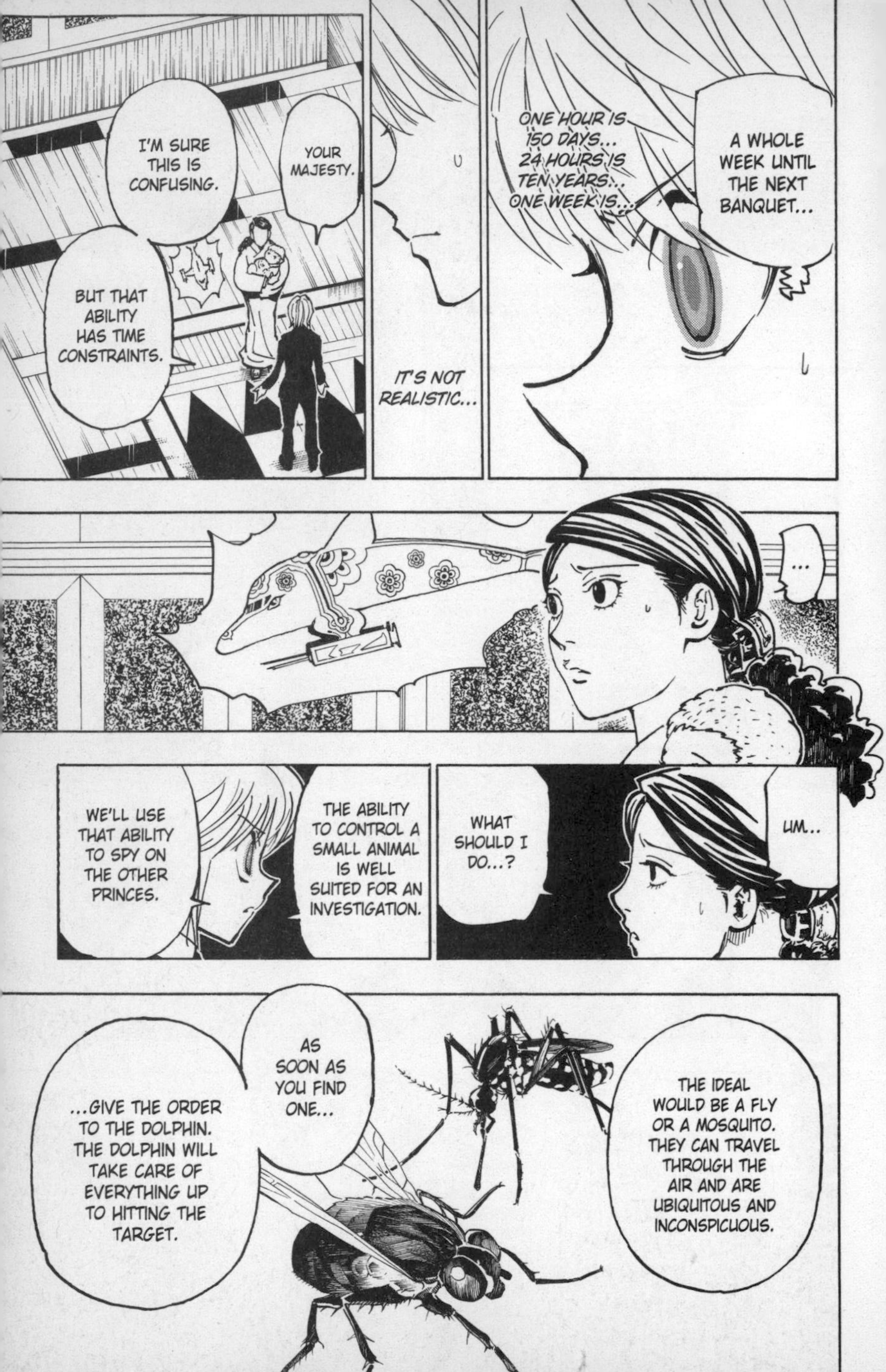
A WHOLE WEEK UNTIL THE NEXT BANQUET...
ONE HOUR IS 150 DAYS... 24 HOURS IS TEN YEARS... ONE WEEK IS...
IT'S NOT REALISTIC...
YOUR MAJESTY.
I'M SURE THIS IS CONFUSING.
BUT THAT ABILITY HAS TIME CONSTRAINTS.
...
UM...
WHAT SHOULD I DO...?
THE ABILITY TO CONTROL A SMALL ANIMAL IS WELL SUITED FOR AN INVESTIGATION.
WE'LL USE THAT ABILITY TO SPY ON THE OTHER PRINCES.
THE IDEAL WOULD BE A FLY OR A MOSQUITO. THEY CAN TRAVEL THROUGH THE AIR AND ARE UBIQUITOUS AND INCONSPICUOUS.
AS SOON AS YOU FIND ONE...
...GIVE THE ORDER TO THE DOLPHIN. THE DOLPHIN WILL TAKE CARE OF EVERYTHING UP TO HITTING THE TARGET.

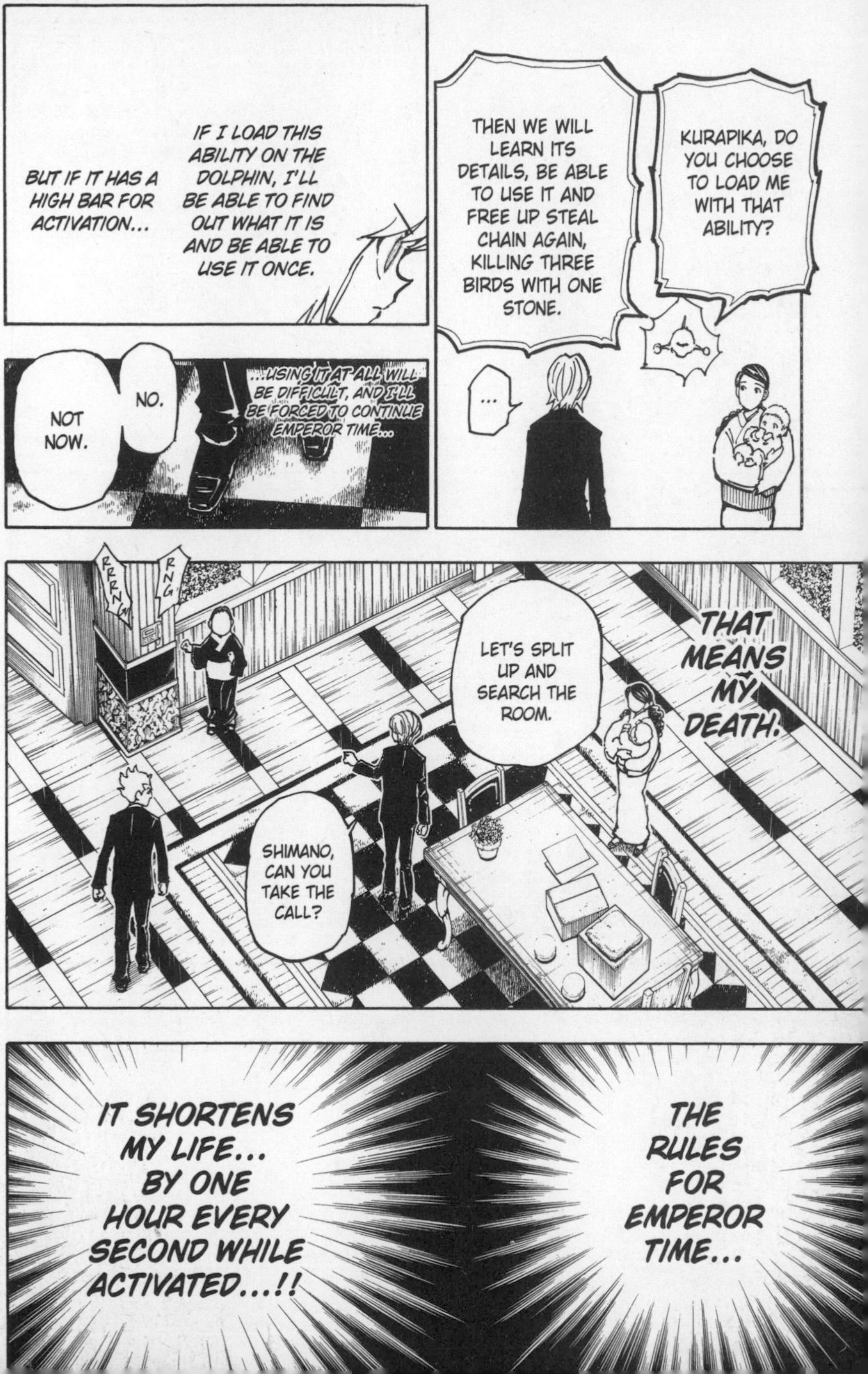

KURAPIKA, DO YOU CHOOSE TO LOAD ME WITH THAT ABILITY?
THEN WE WILL LEARN ITS DETAILS, BE ABLE TO USE IT AND FREE UP STEAL CHAIN AGAIN, KILLING THREE BIRDS WITH ONE STONE.
...
IF I LOAD THIS ABILITY ON THE DOLPHIN, I'LL BE ABLE TO FIND OUT WHAT IT IS AND BE ABLE TO USE IT ONCE.
BUT IF IT HAS A HIGH BAR FOR ACTIVATION...
...USING IT AT ALL WILL BE DIFFICULT, AND I'LL BE FORCED TO CONTINUE EMPEROR TIME...
NO.
NOT NOW.
THAT MEANS MY DEATH.
LET'S SPLIT UP AND SEARCH THE ROOM.
RNG
RRRN
SHIMANO, CAN YOU TAKE THE CALL?
THE RULES FOR EMPEROR TIME...
IT SHORTENS MY LIFE... BY ONE HOUR EVERY SECOND WHILE ACTIVATED...!!

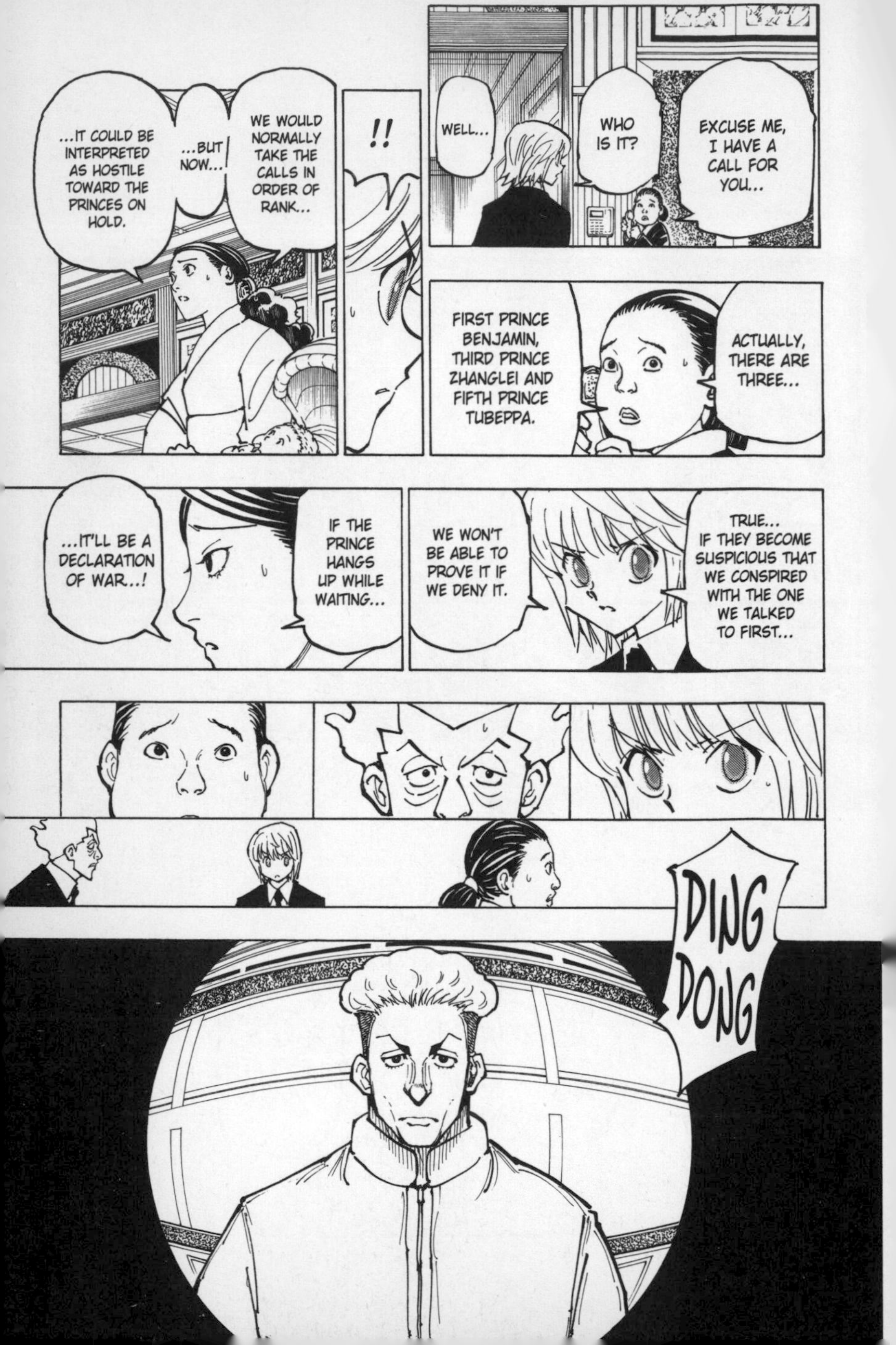
EXCUSE ME, I HAVE A CALL FOR YOU...
WHO IS IT?
WELL...
ACTUALLY, THERE ARE THREE...
FIRST PRINCE BENJAMIN, THIRD PRINCE ZHANGLEI AND FIFTH PRINCE TUBEPPA.
!!
WE WOULD NORMALLY TAKE THE CALLS IN ORDER OF RANK...
...BUT NOW...
...IT COULD BE INTERPRETED AS HOSTILE TOWARD THE PRINCES ON HOLD.
TRUE... IF THEY BECOME SUSPICIOUS THAT WE CONSPIRED WITH THE ONE WE TALKED TO FIRST...
WE WON'T BE ABLE TO PROVE IT IF WE DENY IT.
IF THE PRINCE HANGS UP WHILE WAITING...
...IT'LL BE A DECLARATION OF WAR...!
DING DONG

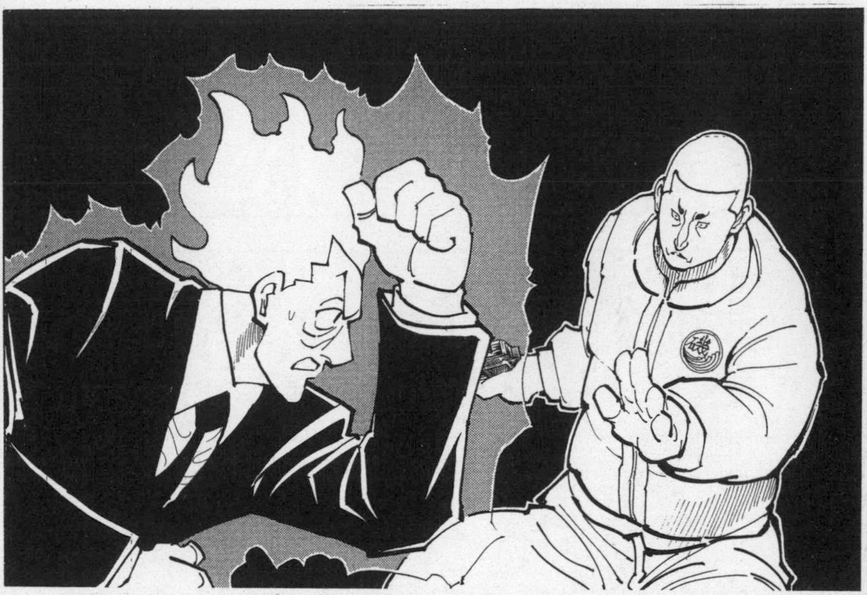

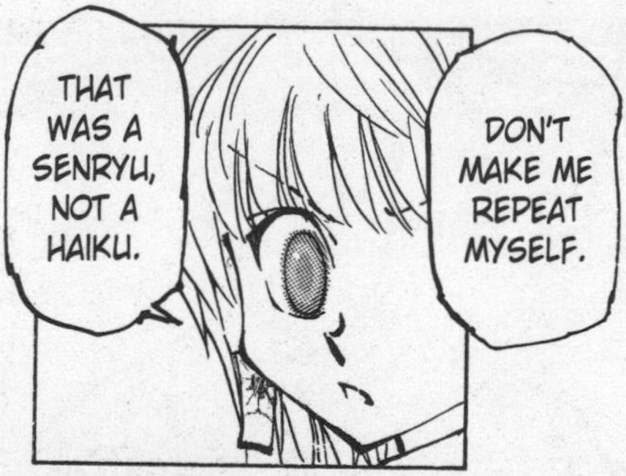
DON'T MAKE ME REPEAT MYSELF.
THAT WAS A SENRYU, NOT A HAIKU.

Chapter 365: Choice

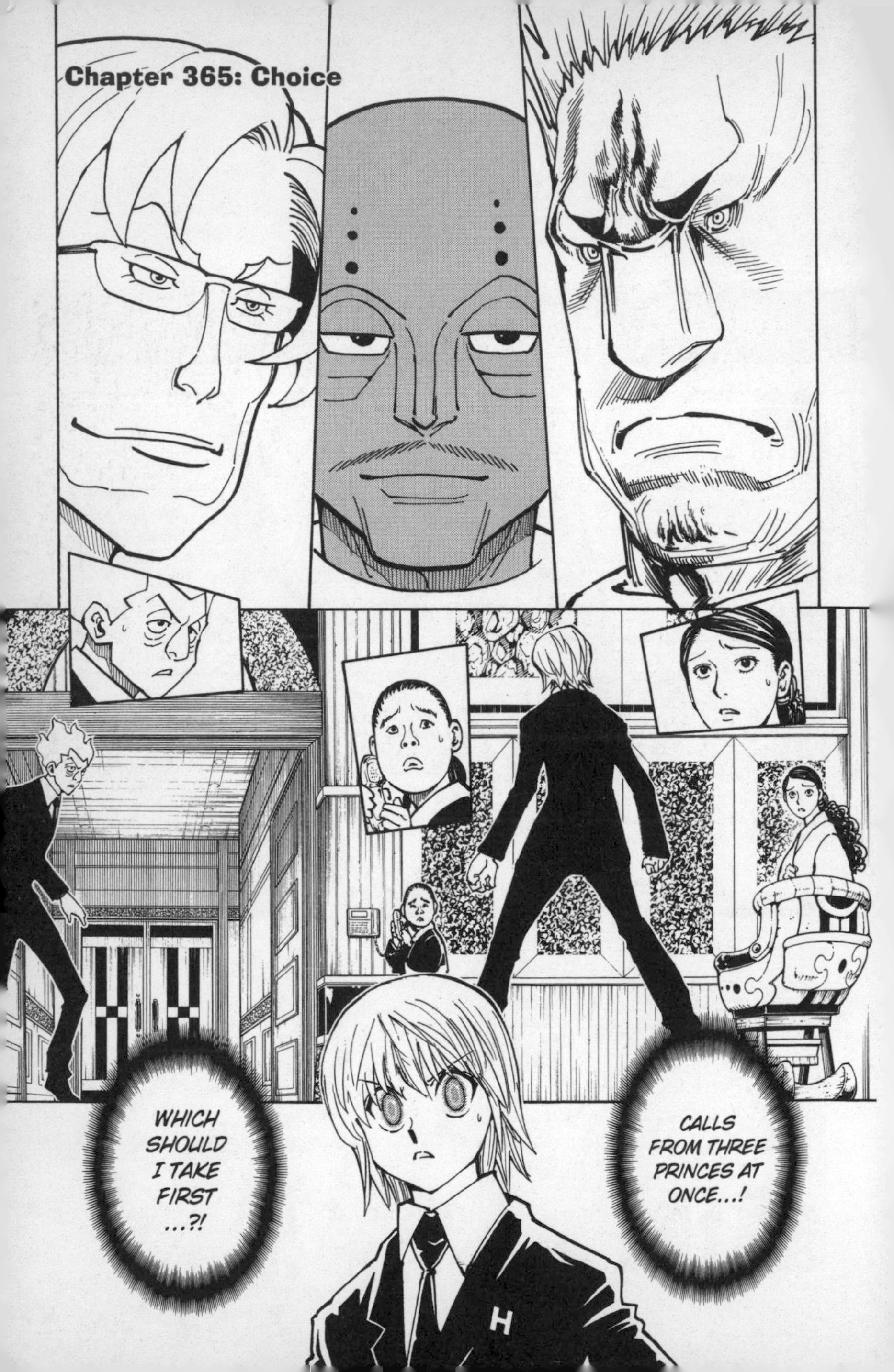
CALLS FROM THREE PRINCES AT ONCE...!
WHICH SHOULD I TAKE FIRST ...?!

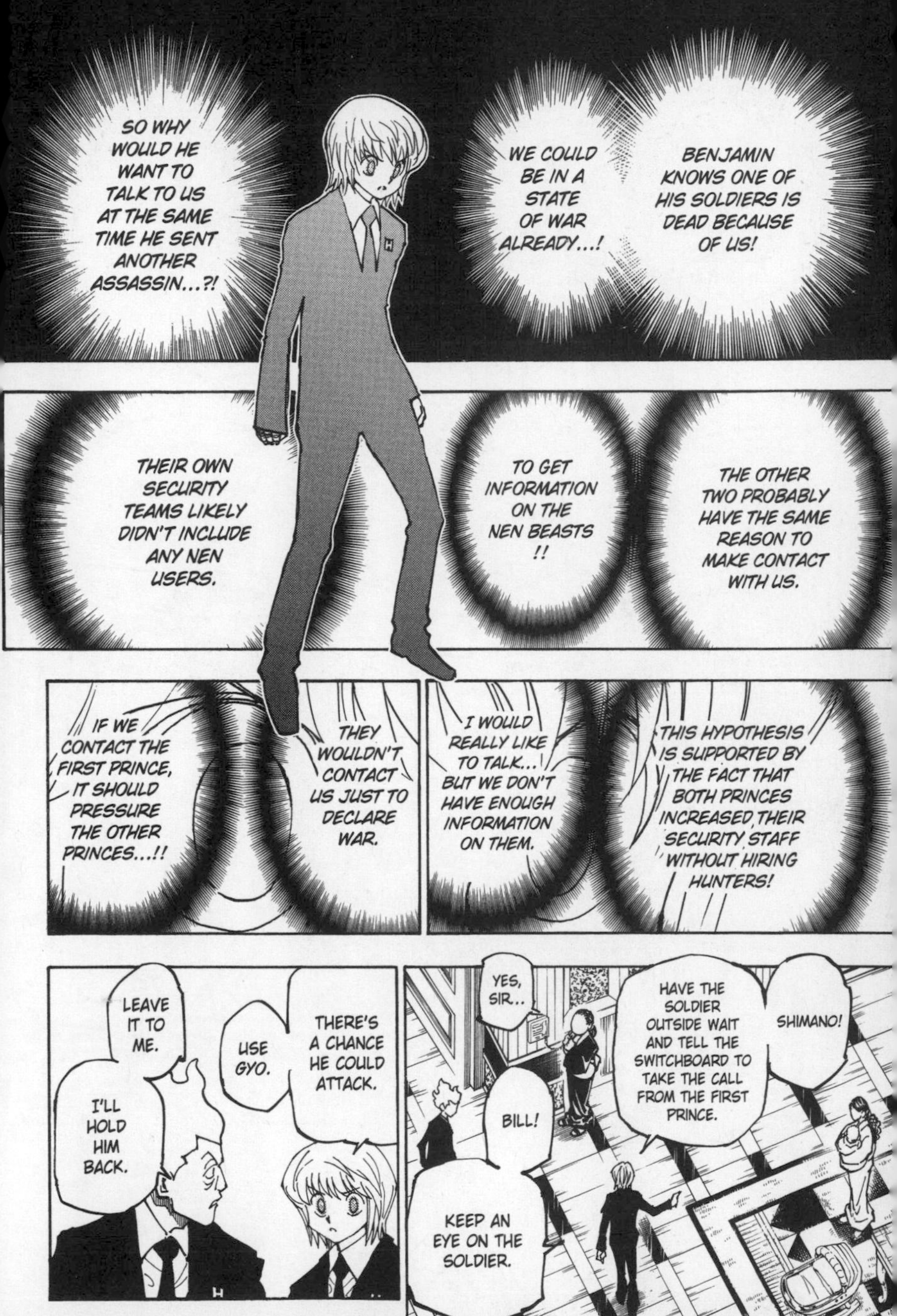
BENJAMIN KNOWS ONE OF HIS SOLDIERS IS DEAD BECAUSE OF US!
WE COULD BE IN A STATE OF WAR ALREADY...!
SO WHY WOULD HE WANT TO TALK TO US AT THE SAME TIME HE SENT ANOTHER ASSASSIN...?!
THE OTHER TWO PROBABLY HAVE THE SAME REASON TO MAKE CONTACT WITH US.
TO GET INFORMATION ON THE NEN BEASTS !!
THEIR OWN SECURITY TEAMS LIKELY DIDN'T INCLUDE ANY NEN USERS.
THIS HYPOTHESIS IS SUPPORTED BY THE FACT THAT BOTH PRINCES INCREASED THEIR SECURITY STAFF WITHOUT HIRING HUNTERS!
I WOULD REALLY LIKE TO TALK... BUT WE DON'T HAVE ENOUGH INFORMATION ON THEM.
THEY WOULDN'T CONTACT US JUST TO DECLARE WAR.
IF WE CONTACT THE FIRST PRINCE, IT SHOULD PRESSURE THE OTHER PRINCES...!!
SHIMANO!
HAVE THE SOLDIER OUTSIDE WAIT AND TELL THE SWITCHBOARD TO TAKE THE CALL FROM THE FIRST PRINCE.
YES, SIR..
BILL!
KEEP AN EYE ON THE SOLDIER.
THERE'S A CHANCE HE COULD ATTACK.
USE GYO.
LEAVE IT TO ME.
I'LL HOLD HIM BACK.

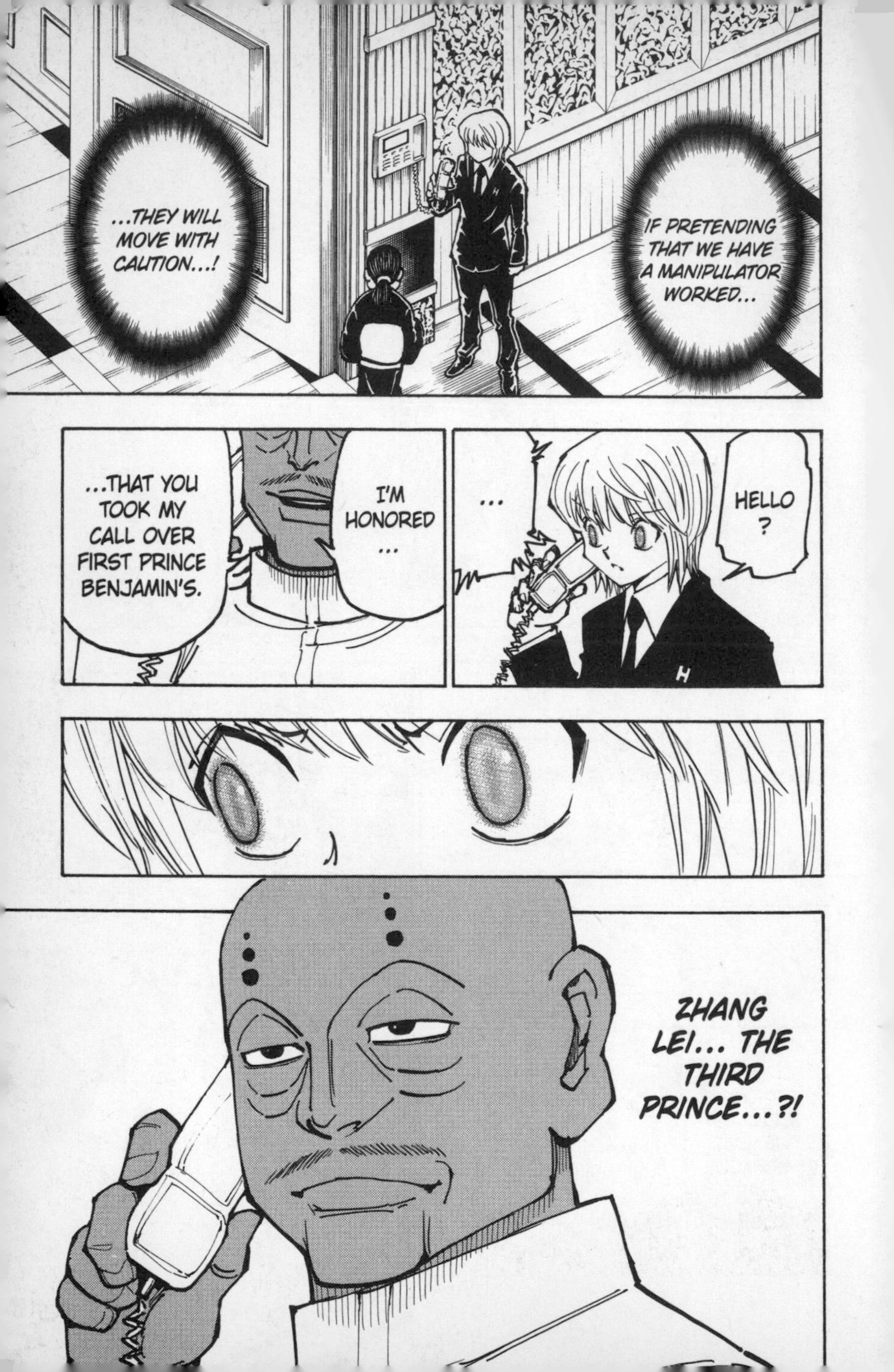
IF PRETENDING THAT WE HAVE A MANIPULATOR WORKED...
...THEY WILL MOVE WITH CAUTION...!
HELLO?
...
I'M HONORED...
...THAT YOU TOOK MY CALL OVER FIRST PRINCE BENJAMIN'S.
ZHANG LEI... THE THIRD PRINCE...?!

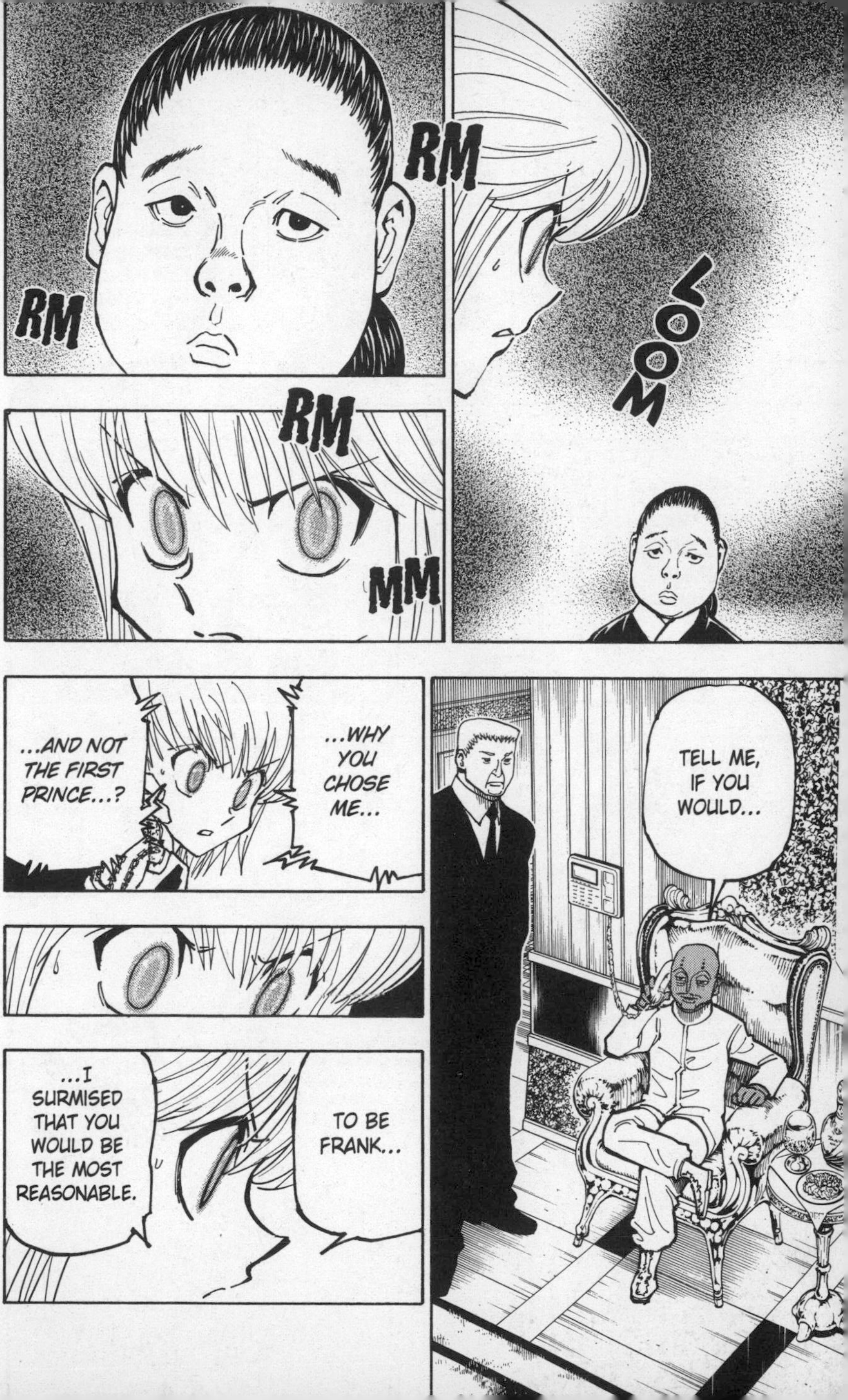
LOOM
RM
RM
RM
MM
TELL ME, IF YOU WOULD...
...WHY YOU CHOSE ME...
...AND NOT THE FIRST PRINCE...?
TO BE FRANK...
...I SURMISED THAT YOU WOULD BE THE MOST REASONABLE.

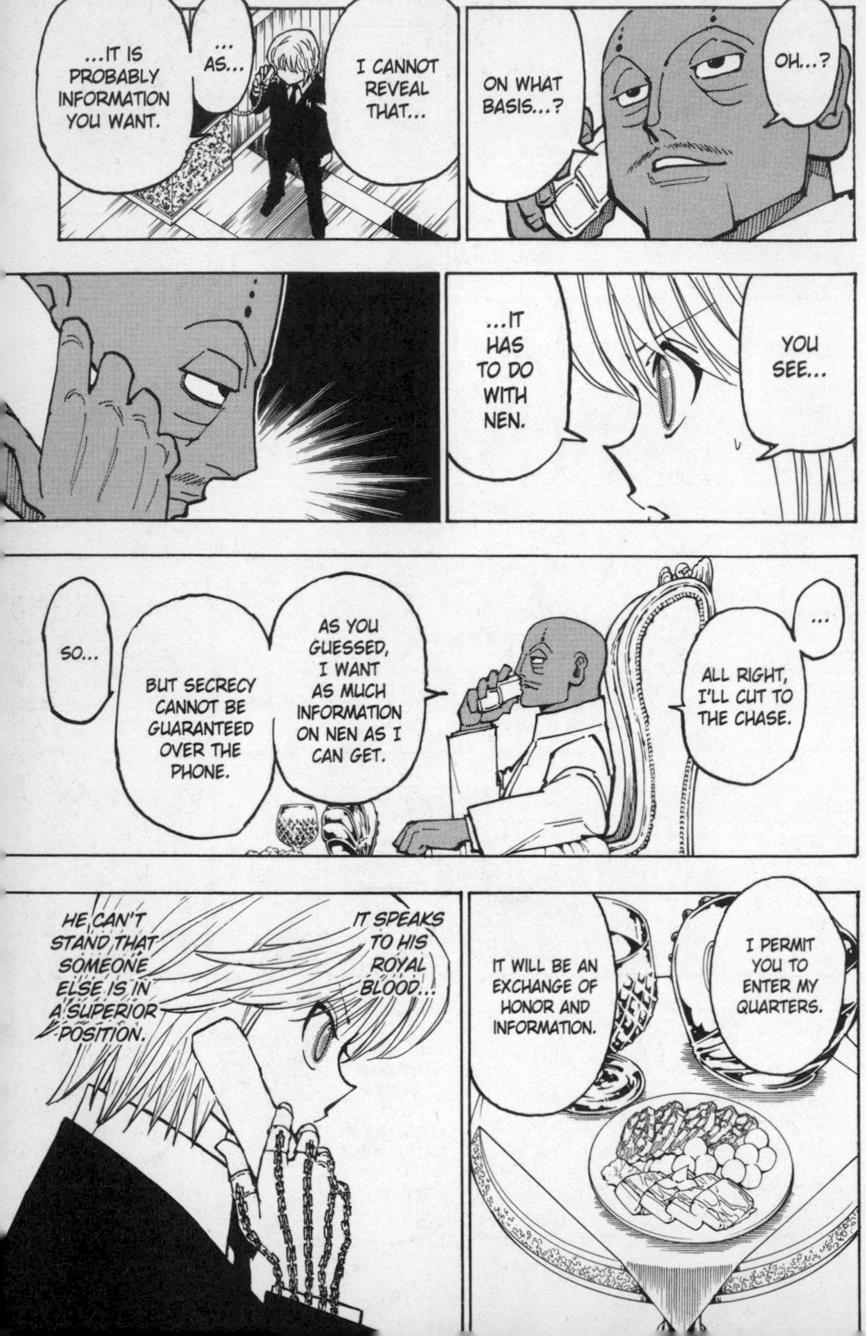
OH...?
ON WHAT BASIS...?
I CANNOT REVEAL THAT...
... AS...
...IT IS PROBABLY INFORMATION YOU WANT.
YOU SEE...
...IT HAS TO DO WITH NEN.
...
ALL RIGHT, I'LL CUT TO THE CHASE.
AS YOU GUESSED, I WANT AS MUCH INFORMATION ON NEN AS I CAN GET.
BUT SECRECY CANNOT BE GUARANTEED OVER THE PHONE.
SO...
I PERMIT YOU TO ENTER MY QUARTERS.
IT WILL BE AN EXCHANGE OF HONOR AND INFORMATION.
IT SPEAKS TO HIS ROYAL BLOOD...
HE CAN'T STAND THAT SOMEONE ELSE IS IN A SUPERIOR POSITION.

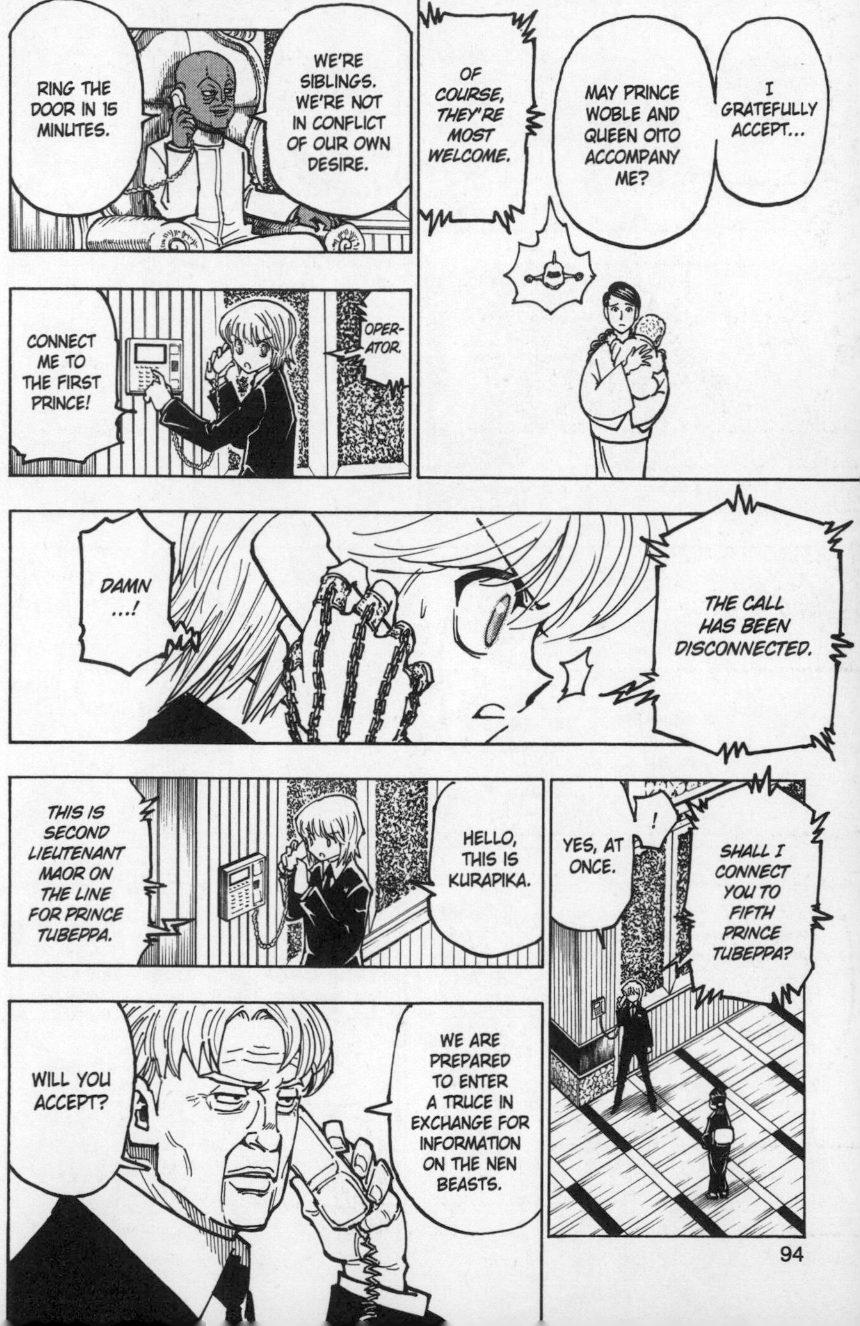
I GRATEFULLY ACCEPT...
MAY PRINCE WOBLE AND QUEEN OITO ACCOMPANY ME?
OF COURSE, THEY'RE MOST WELCOME.
WE'RE SIBLINGS. WE'RE NOT IN CONFLICT OF OUR OWN DESIRE.
RING THE DOOR IN 15 MINUTES.
OPERATOR.
CONNECT ME TO THE FIRST PRINCE!
THE CALL HAS BEEN DISCONNECTED.
DAMN ...!
SHALL I CONNECT YOU TO FIFTH PRINCE TUBEPPA?
!
YES, AT ONCE.
HELLO, THIS IS KURAPIKA.
THIS IS SECOND LIEUTENANT MAOR ON THE LINE FOR PRINCE TUBEPPA.
WE ARE PREPARED TO ENTER A TRUCE IN EXCHANGE FOR INFORMATION ON THE NEN BEASTS.
WILL YOU ACCEPT?

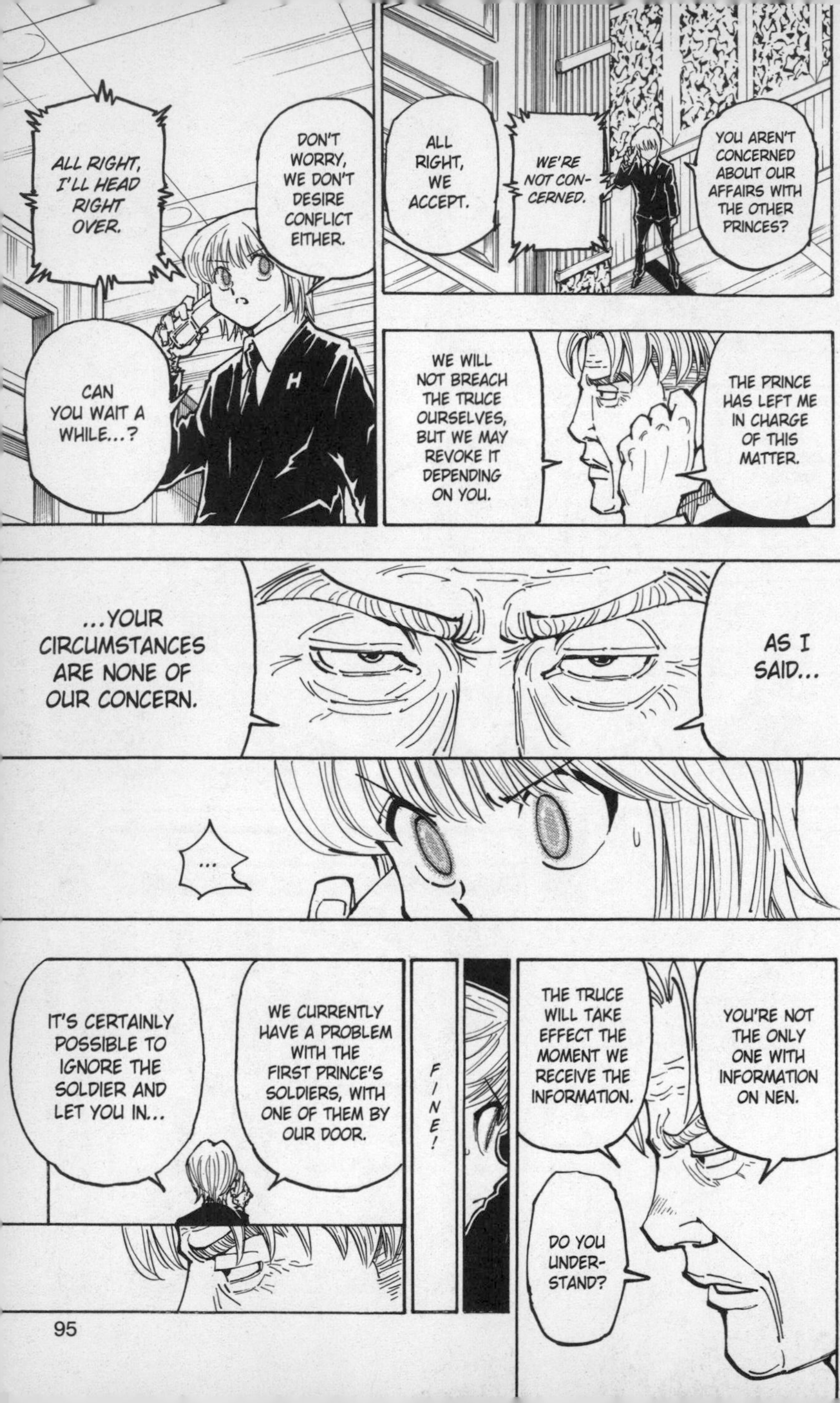

YOU AREN'T CONCERNED ABOUT OUR AFFAIRS WITH THE OTHER PRINCES?
WE'RE NOT CONCERNED.
ALL RIGHT, WE ACCEPT.
THE PRINCE HAS LEFT ME IN CHARGE OF THIS MATTER.
WE WILL NOT BREACH THE TRUCE OURSELVES, BUT WE MAY REVOKE IT DEPENDING ON YOU.
DON'T WORRY, WE DON'T DESIRE CONFLICT EITHER.
ALL RIGHT, I'LL HEAD RIGHT OVER.
CAN YOU WAIT A WHILE...?
AS I SAID...
...YOUR CIRCUMSTANCES ARE NONE OF OUR CONCERN.
...
YOU'RE NOT THE ONLY ONE WITH INFORMATION ON NEN.
THE TRUCE WILL TAKE EFFECT THE MOMENT WE RECEIVE THE INFORMATION.
DO YOU UNDERSTAND?
FINE!
WE CURRENTLY HAVE A PROBLEM WITH THE FIRST PRINCE'S SOLDIERS, WITH ONE OF THEM BY OUR DOOR.
IT'S CERTAINLY POSSIBLE TO IGNORE THE SOLDIER AND LET YOU IN...

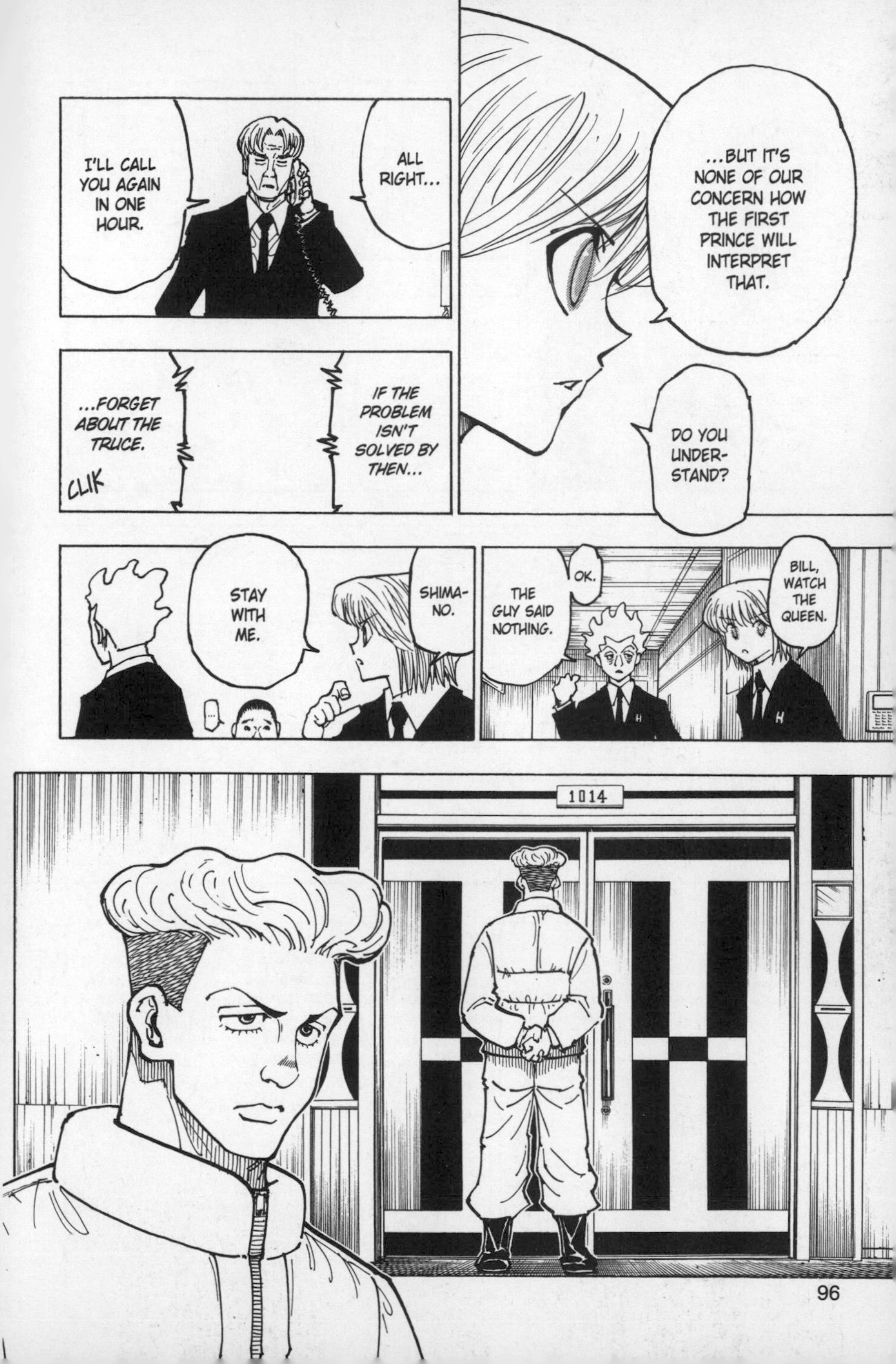

...BUT IT'S NONE OF OUR CONCERN HOW THE FIRST PRINCE WILL INTERPRET THAT.
DO YOU UNDER-STAND?
ALL RIGHT...
I'LL CALL YOU AGAIN IN ONE HOUR.
IF THE PROBLEM ISN'T SOLVED BY THEN...
...FORGET ABOUT THE TRUCE.
CLIK
BILL, WATCH THE QUEEN.
OK.
THE GUY SAID NOTHING.
SHIMA-NO.
STAY WITH ME.
...
1014

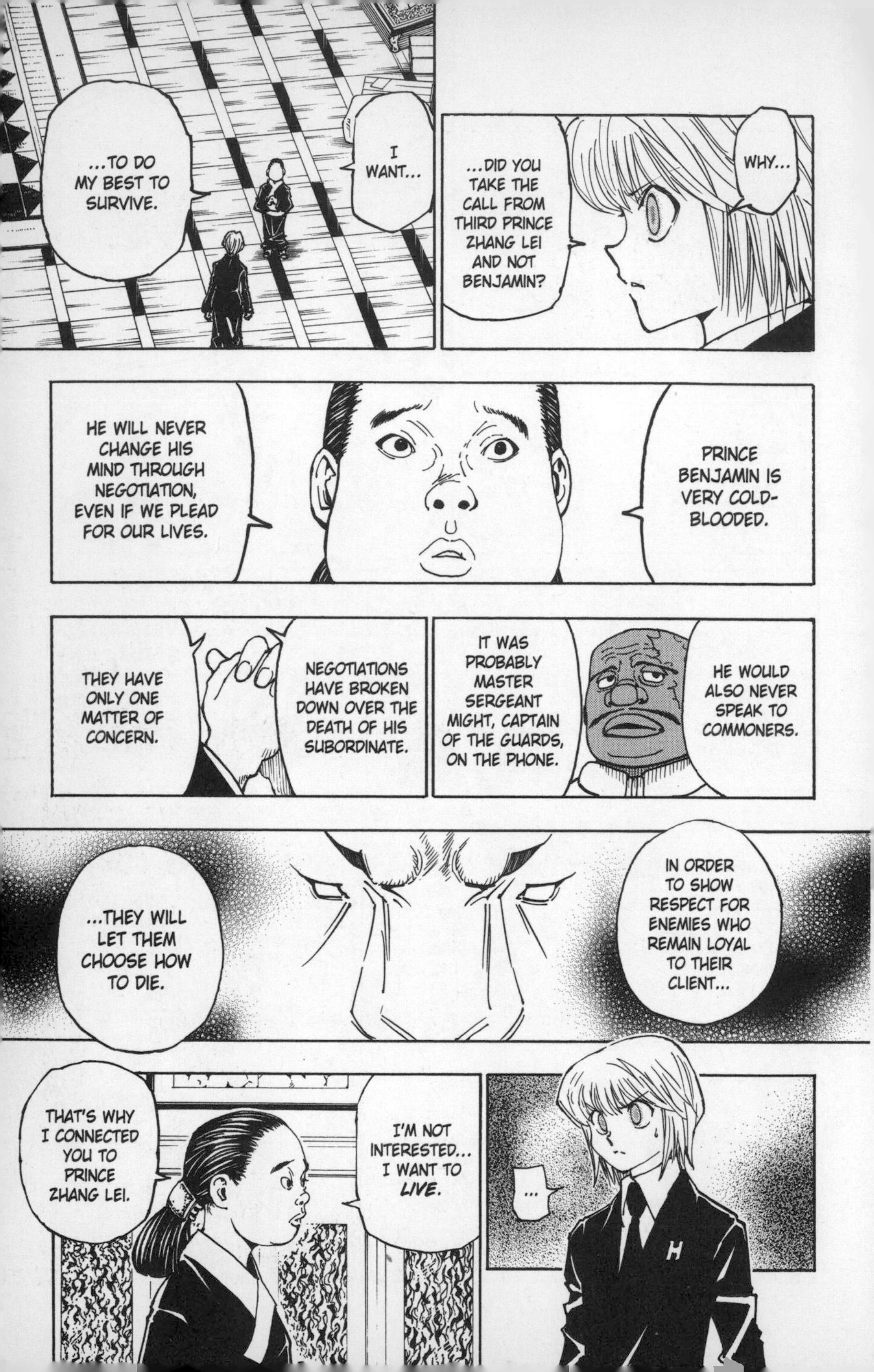
WHY...
...DID YOU TAKE THE CALL FROM THIRD PRINCE ZHANG LEI AND NOT BENJAMIN?
I WANT...
...TO DO MY BEST TO SURVIVE.
PRINCE BENJAMIN IS VERY COLD-BLOODED.
HE WILL NEVER CHANGE HIS MIND THROUGH NEGOTIATION, EVEN IF WE PLEAD FOR OUR LIVES.
HE WOULD ALSO NEVER SPEAK TO COMMONERS.
IT WAS PROBABLY MASTER SERGEANT MIGHT, CAPTAIN OF THE GUARDS, ON THE PHONE.
NEGOTIATIONS HAVE BROKEN DOWN OVER THE DEATH OF HIS SUBORDINATE.
THEY HAVE ONLY ONE MATTER OF CONCERN.
IN ORDER TO SHOW RESPECT FOR ENEMIES WHO REMAIN LOYAL TO THEIR CLIENT...
...THEY WILL LET THEM CHOOSE HOW TO DIE.
...
I'M NOT INTERESTED... I WANT TO *LIVE*.
THAT'S WHY I CONNECTED YOU TO PRINCE ZHANG LEI.

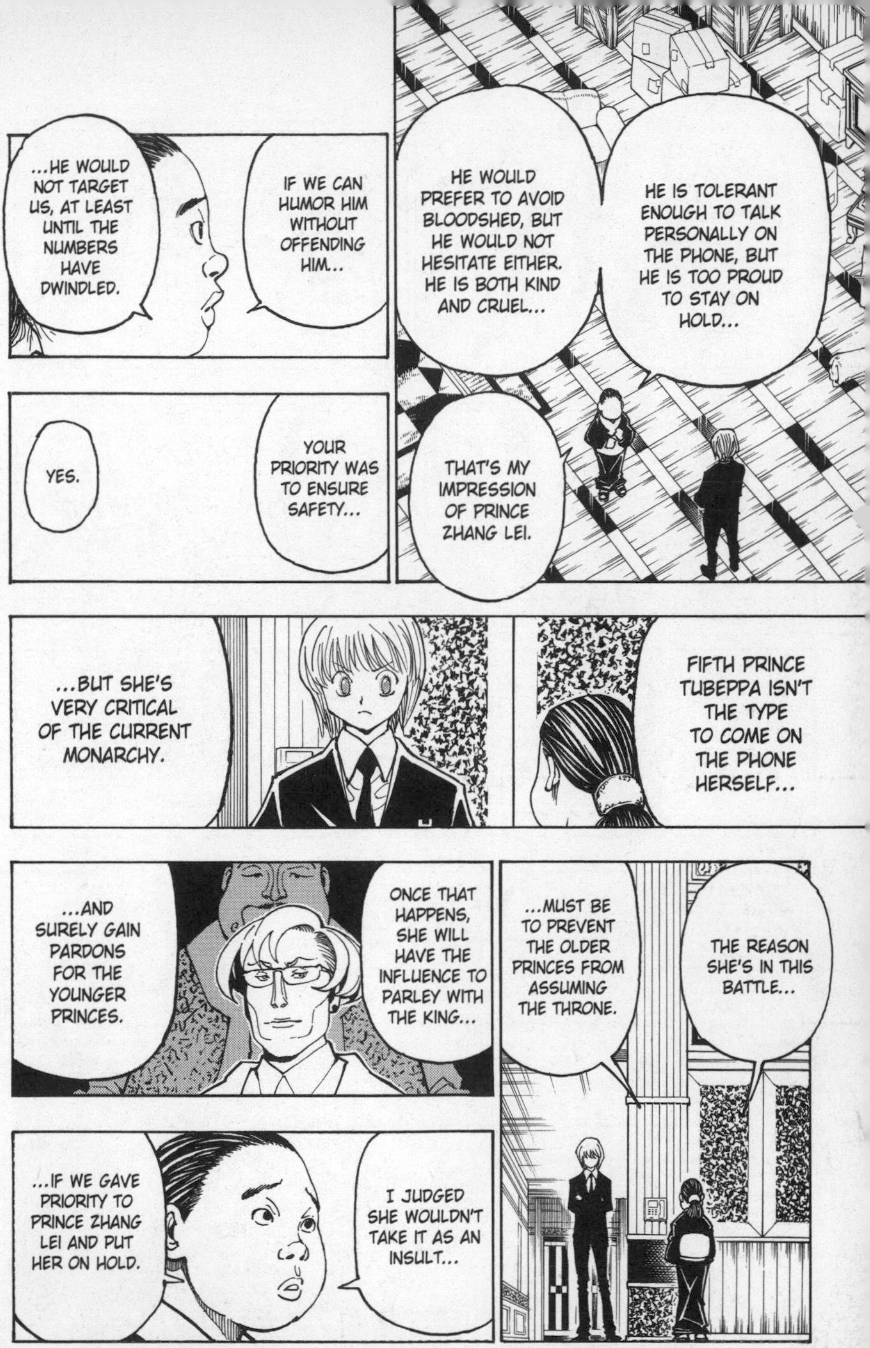
HE IS TOLERANT ENOUGH TO TALK PERSONALLY ON THE PHONE, BUT HE IS TOO PROUD TO STAY ON HOLD...
HE WOULD PREFER TO AVOID BLOODSHED, BUT HE WOULD NOT HESITATE EITHER. HE IS BOTH KIND AND CRUEL...
THAT'S MY IMPRESSION OF PRINCE ZHANG LEI.
IF WE CAN HUMOR HIM WITHOUT OFFENDING HIM...
...HE WOULD NOT TARGET US, AT LEAST UNTIL THE NUMBERS HAVE DWINDLED.
YOUR PRIORITY WAS TO ENSURE SAFETY...
YES.
FIFTH PRINCE TUBEPPA ISN'T THE TYPE TO COME ON THE PHONE HERSELF...
...BUT SHE'S VERY CRITICAL OF THE CURRENT MONARCHY.
THE REASON SHE'S IN THIS BATTLE...
...MUST BE TO PREVENT THE OLDER PRINCES FROM ASSUMING THE THRONE.
ONCE THAT HAPPENS, SHE WILL HAVE THE INFLUENCE TO PARLEY WITH THE KING...
...AND SURELY GAIN PARDONS FOR THE YOUNGER PRINCES.
I JUDGED SHE WOULDN'T TAKE IT AS AN INSULT...
...IF WE GAVE PRIORITY TO PRINCE ZHANG LEI AND PUT HER ON HOLD.

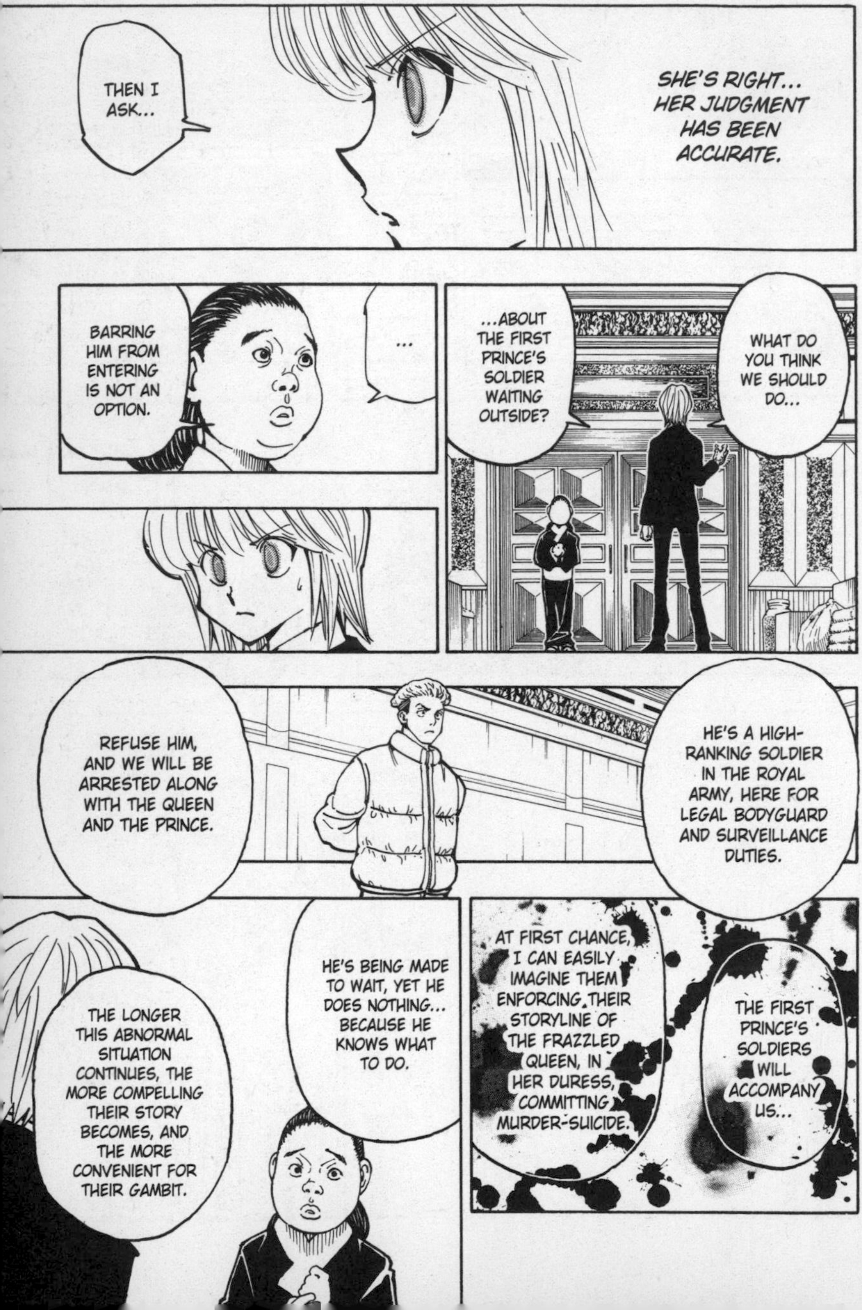
SHE'S RIGHT... HER JUDGMENT HAS BEEN ACCURATE.
THEN I ASK...
WHAT DO YOU THINK WE SHOULD DO...
...ABOUT THE FIRST PRINCE'S SOLDIER WAITING OUTSIDE?
...
BARRING HIM FROM ENTERING IS NOT AN OPTION.
HE'S A HIGH-RANKING SOLDIER IN THE ROYAL ARMY, HERE FOR LEGAL BODYGUARD AND SURVEILLANCE DUTIES.
REFUSE HIM, AND WE WILL BE ARRESTED ALONG WITH THE QUEEN AND THE PRINCE.
THE FIRST PRINCE'S SOLDIERS WILL ACCOMPANY US...
AT FIRST CHANCE, I CAN EASILY IMAGINE THEM ENFORCING THEIR STORYLINE OF THE FRAZZLED QUEEN, IN HER DURESS, COMMITTING MURDER-SUICIDE.
HE'S BEING MADE TO WAIT, YET HE DOES NOTHING... BECAUSE HE KNOWS WHAT TO DO.
THE LONGER THIS ABNORMAL SITUATION CONTINUES, THE MORE COMPELLING THEIR STORY BECOMES, AND THE MORE CONVENIENT FOR THEIR GAMBIT.

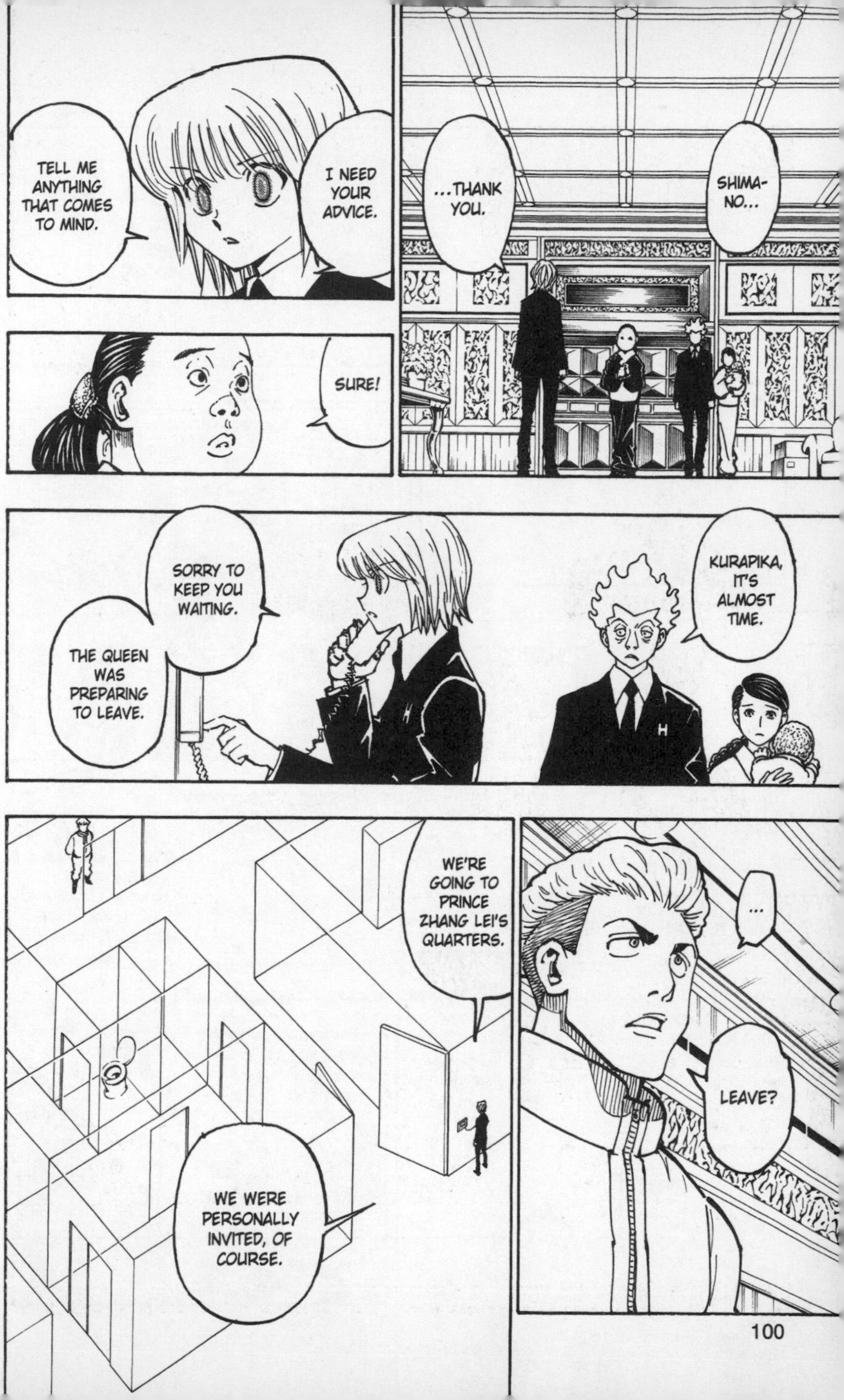
SHIMA-NO...
...THANK YOU.
I NEED YOUR ADVICE.
TELL ME ANYTHING THAT COMES TO MIND.
SURE!
KURAPIKA, IT'S ALMOST TIME.
SORRY TO KEEP YOU WAITING.
THE QUEEN WAS PREPARING TO LEAVE.
...
LEAVE?
WE'RE GOING TO PRINCE ZHANG LEI'S QUARTERS.
WE WERE PERSONALLY INVITED, OF COURSE.

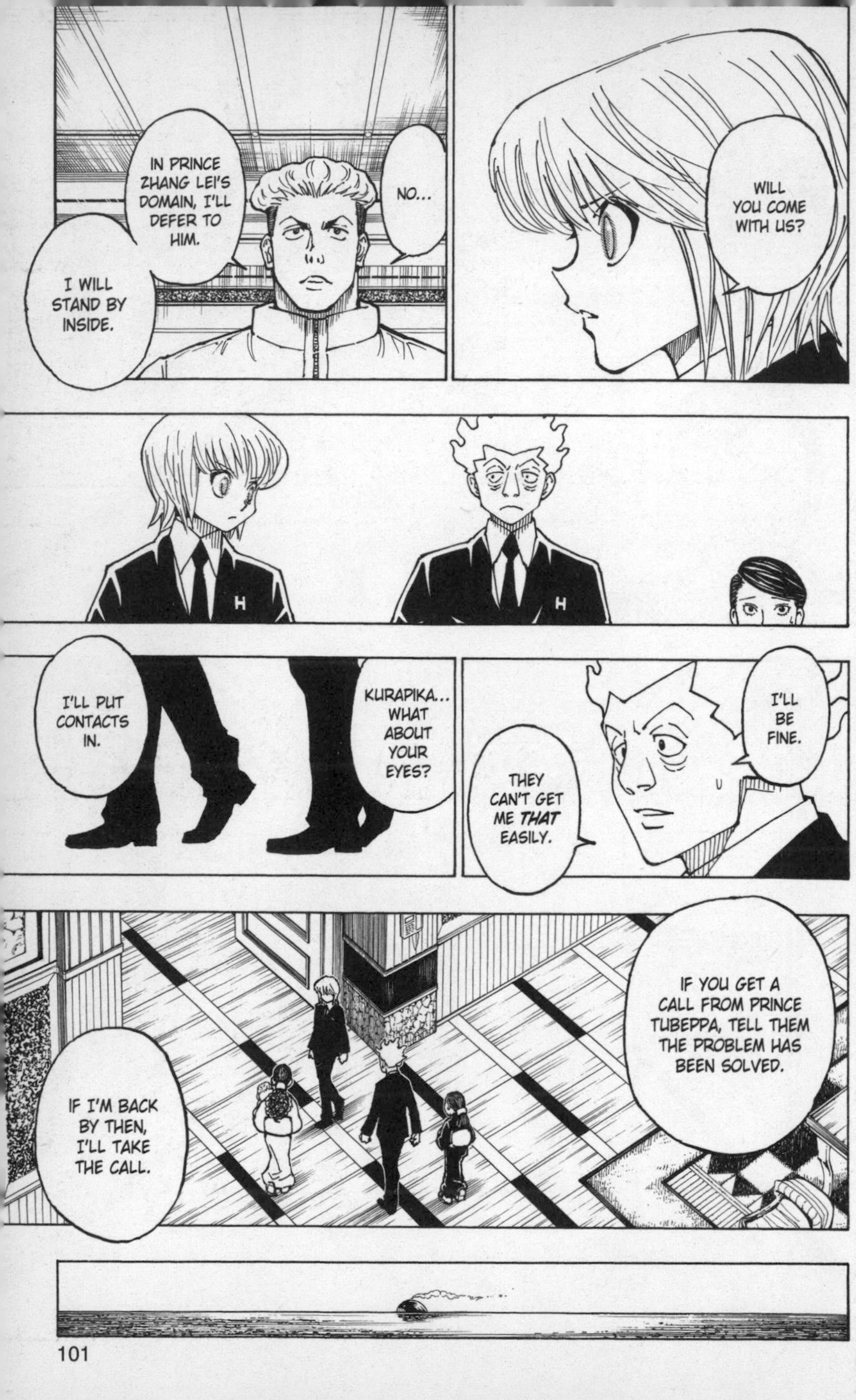
WILL YOU COME WITH US?
NO...
IN PRINCE ZHANG LEI'S DOMAIN, I'LL DEFER TO HIM.
I WILL STAND BY INSIDE.
I'LL BE FINE.
THEY CAN'T GET ME *THAT* EASILY.
KURAPIKA... WHAT ABOUT YOUR EYES?
I'LL PUT CONTACTS IN.
IF YOU GET A CALL FROM PRINCE TUBEPPA, TELL THEM THE PROBLEM HAS BEEN SOLVED.
IF I'M BACK BY THEN, I'LL TAKE THE CALL.

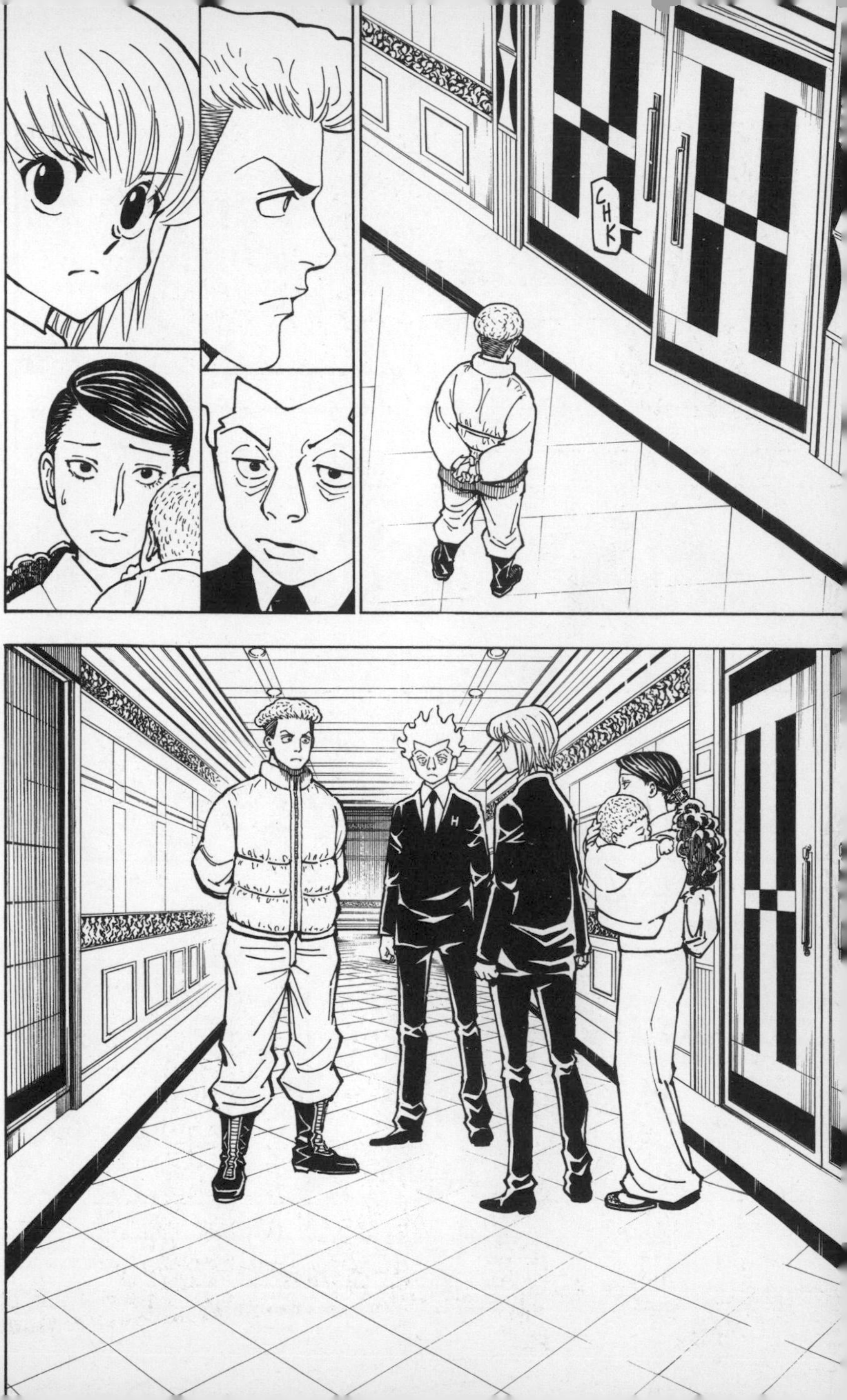
CHK

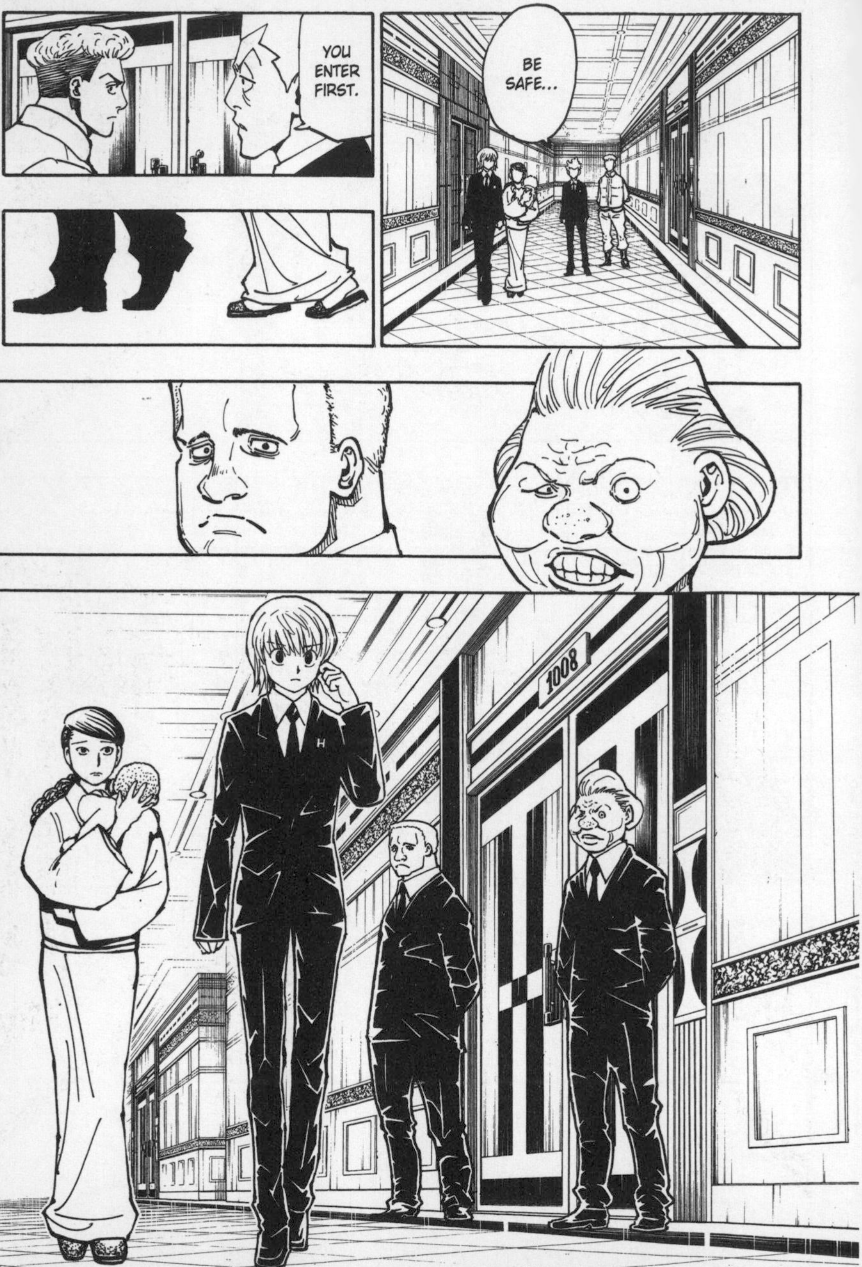
BE SAFE...
YOU ENTER FIRST.

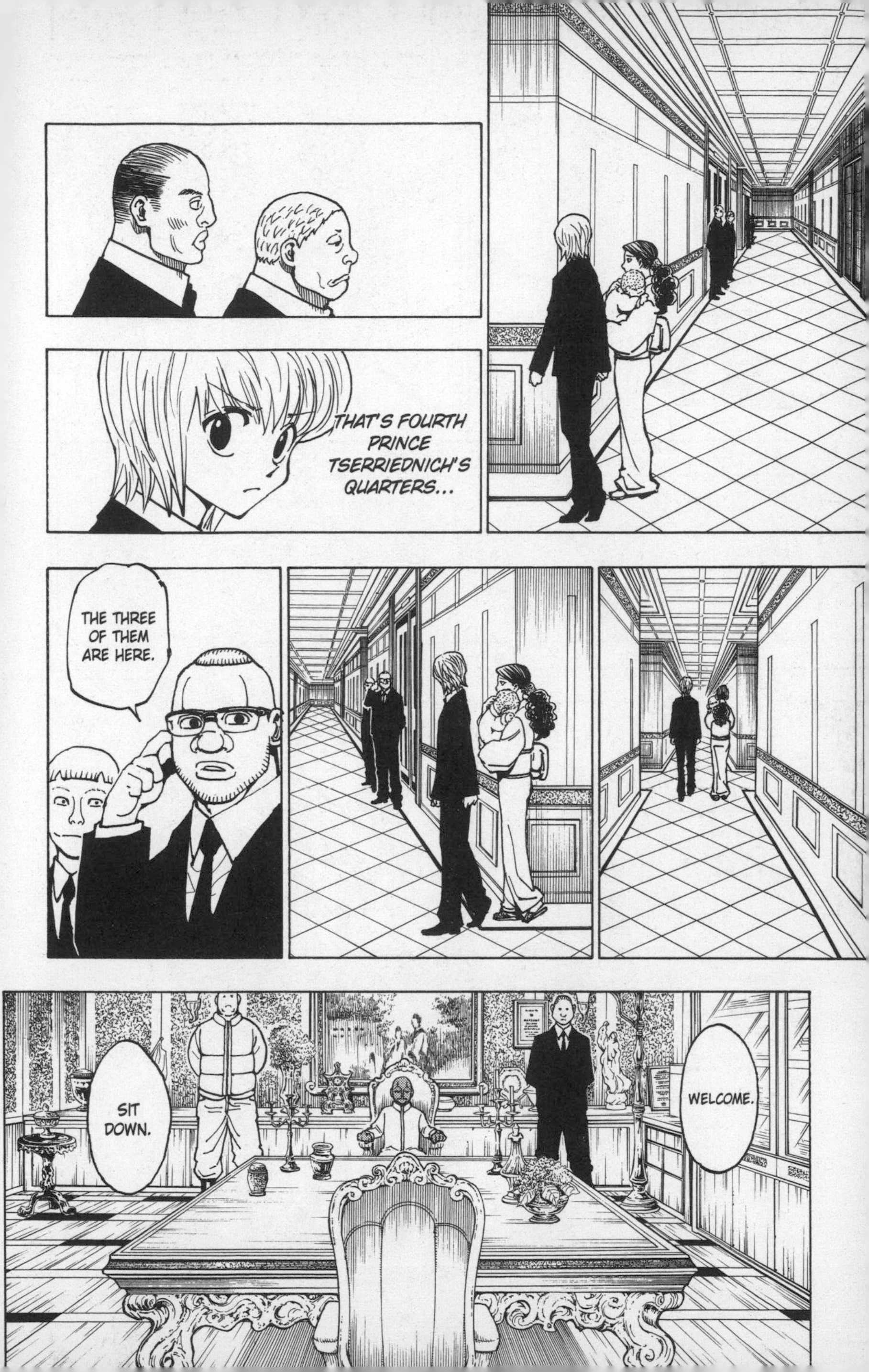
THAT'S FOURTH PRINCE TSERRIEDNICH'S QUARTERS...
THE THREE OF THEM ARE HERE.
WELCOME.
SIT DOWN.

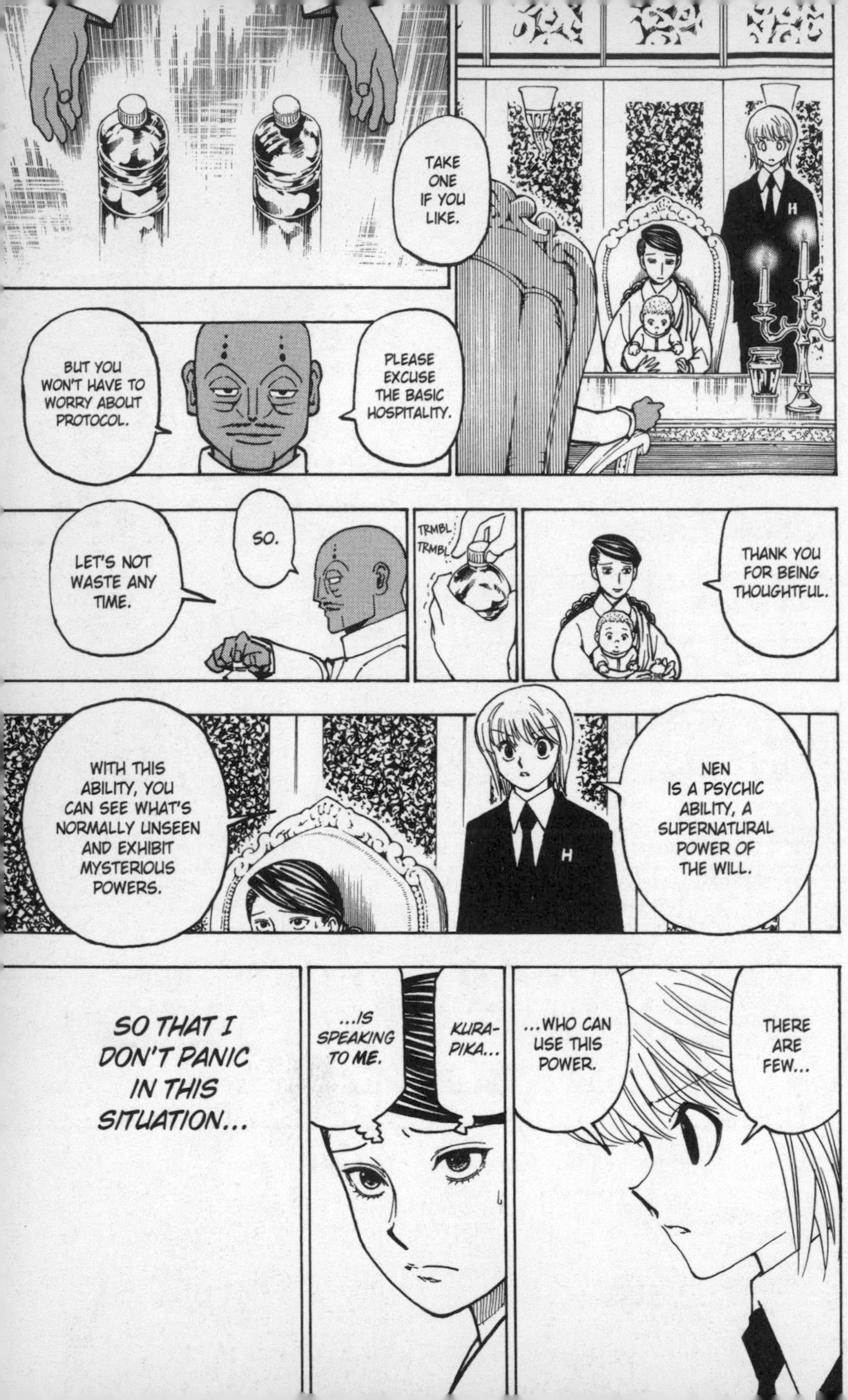
TAKE ONE IF YOU LIKE.
PLEASE EXCUSE THE BASIC HOSPITALITY.
BUT YOU WON'T HAVE TO WORRY ABOUT PROTOCOL.
THANK YOU FOR BEING THOUGHTFUL.
TRMBL TRMBL
SO.
LET'S NOT WASTE ANY TIME.
NEN IS A PSYCHIC ABILITY, A SUPERNATURAL POWER OF THE WILL.
WITH THIS ABILITY, YOU CAN SEE WHAT'S NORMALLY UNSEEN AND EXHIBIT MYSTERIOUS POWERS.
THERE ARE FEW...
...WHO CAN USE THIS POWER.
KURA-PIKA...
...IS SPEAKING TO ME.
SO THAT I DON'T PANIC IN THIS SITUATION...

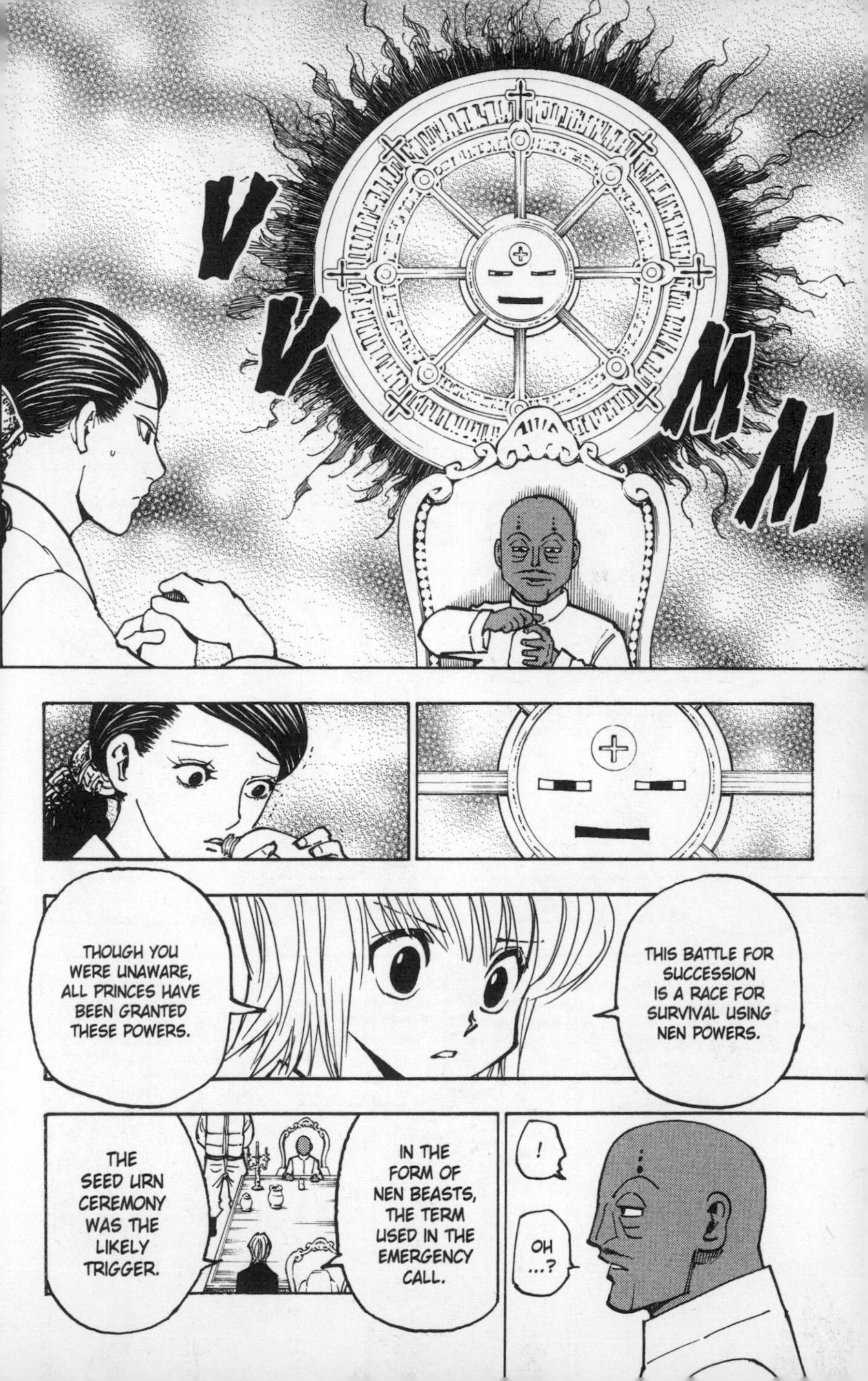
VVMM
THIS BATTLE FOR SUCCESSION IS A RACE FOR SURVIVAL USING NEN POWERS.
THOUGH YOU WERE UNAWARE, ALL PRINCES HAVE BEEN GRANTED THESE POWERS.
!
OH ...?
IN THE FORM OF NEN BEASTS, THE TERM USED IN THE EMERGENCY CALL.
THE SEED URN CEREMONY WAS THE LIKELY TRIGGER.

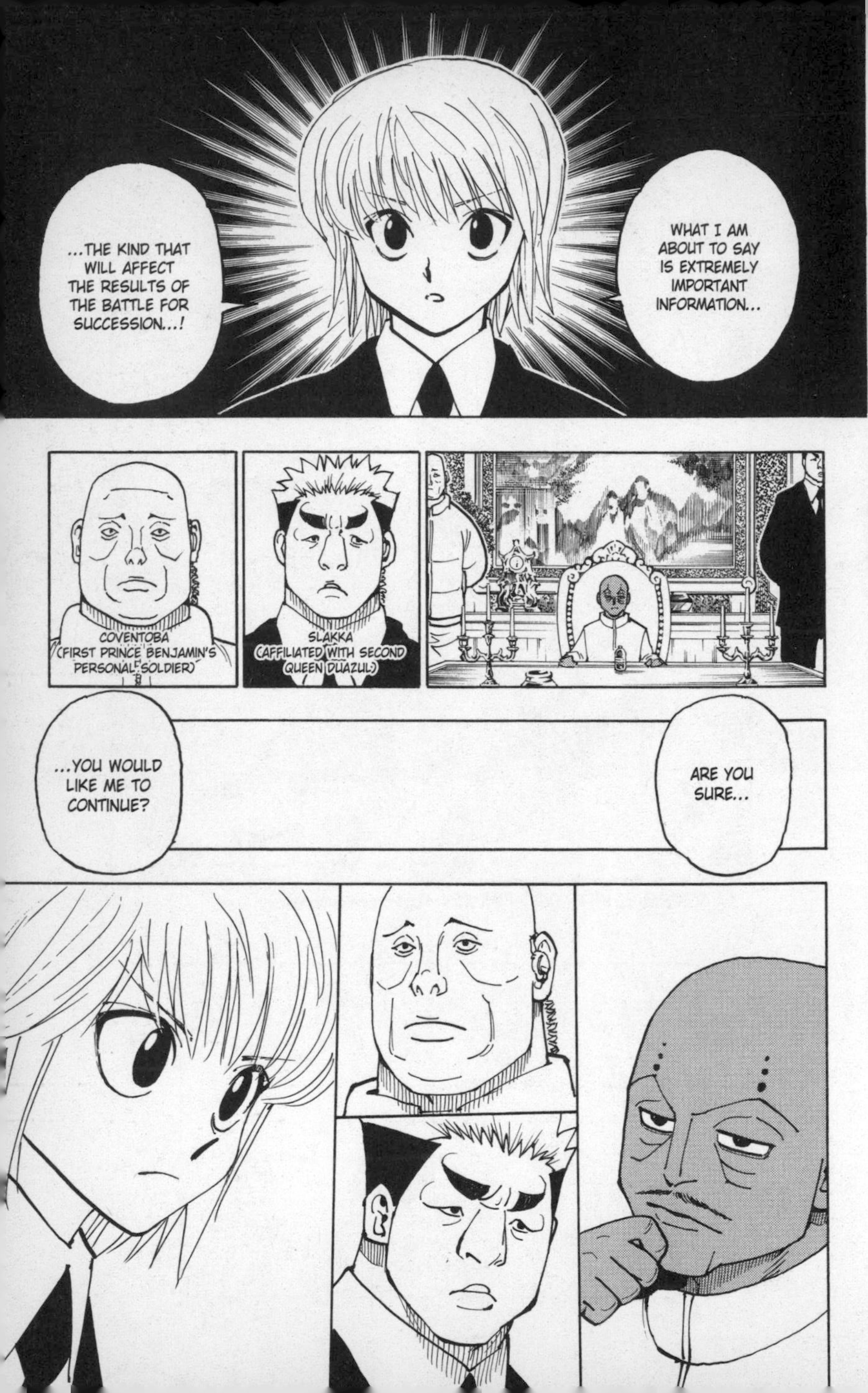
WHAT I AM ABOUT TO SAY IS EXTREMELY IMPORTANT INFORMATION...
...THE KIND THAT WILL AFFECT THE RESULTS OF THE BATTLE FOR SUCCESSION...!
SLAKKA (AFFILIATED WITH SECOND QUEEN DUAZUL)
COVENTOBA (FIRST PRINCE BENJAMIN'S PERSONAL SOLDIER)
ARE YOU SURE...
...YOU WOULD LIKE ME TO CONTINUE?

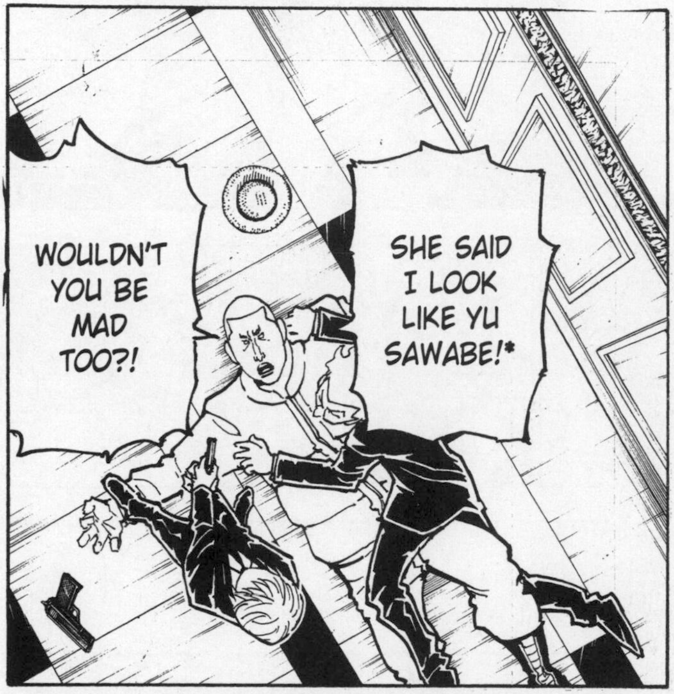
SHE SAID I LOOK LIKE YU SAWABE!*
WOULDN'T YOU BE MAD TOO?!

*A COMEDIAN WHO DOES INDEED RESEMBLE VINCENT.

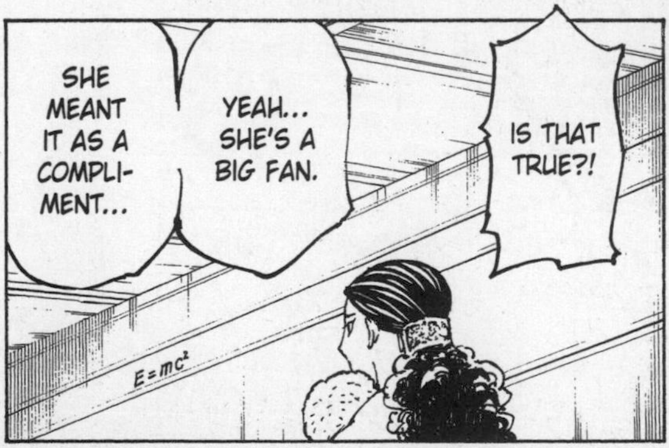
IS THAT TRUE?!
YEAH... SHE'S A BIG FAN.
SHE MEANT IT AS A COMPLIMENT...
$E=mc^2$

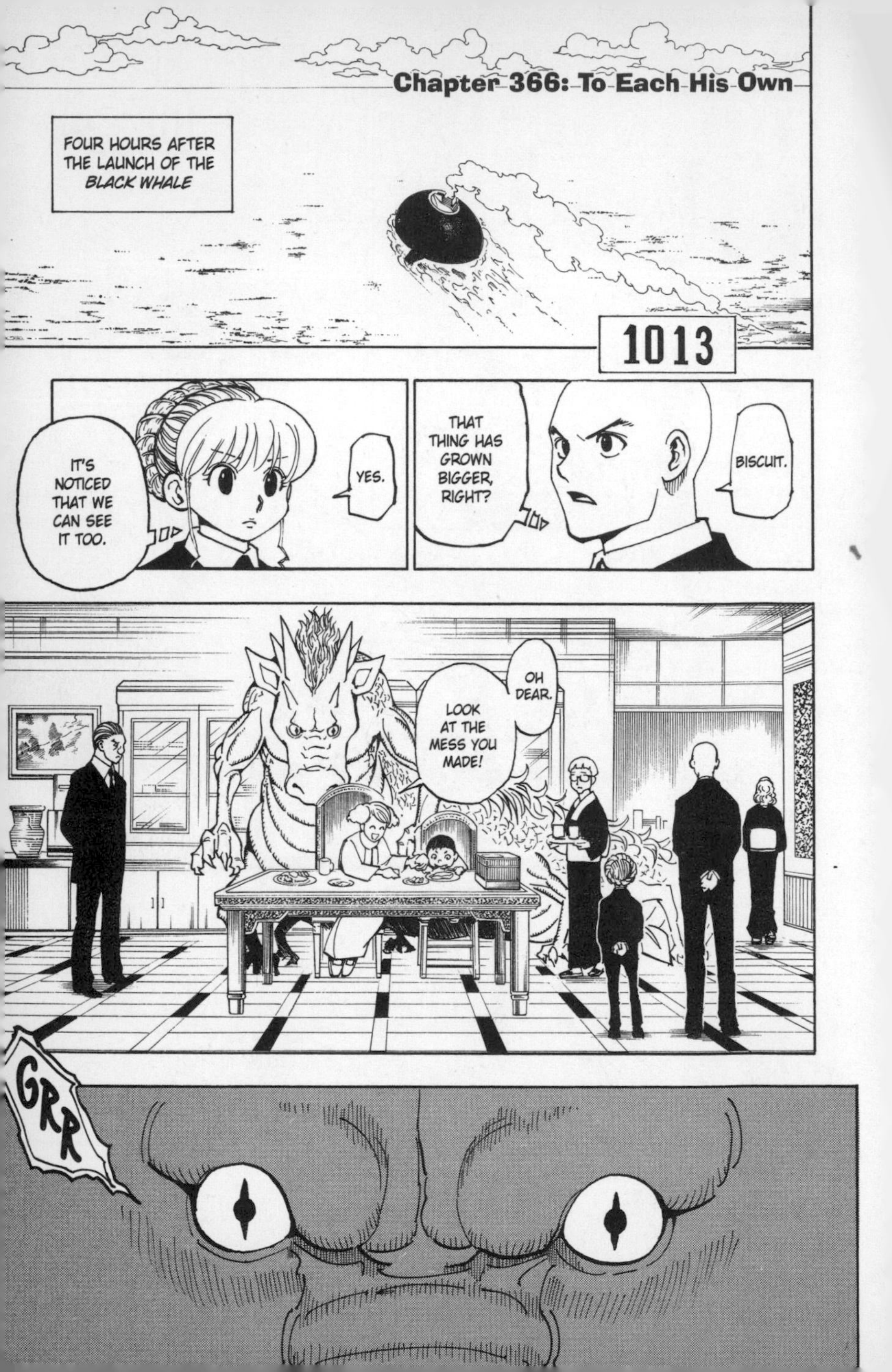

Chapter 366: To Each His Own
FOUR HOURS AFTER THE LAUNCH OF THE *BLACK WHALE*
1013
BISCUIT.
THAT THING HAS GROWN BIGGER, RIGHT?
YES.
IT'S NOTICED THAT WE CAN SEE IT TOO.
OH DEAR.
LOOK AT THE MESS YOU MADE!
GRR

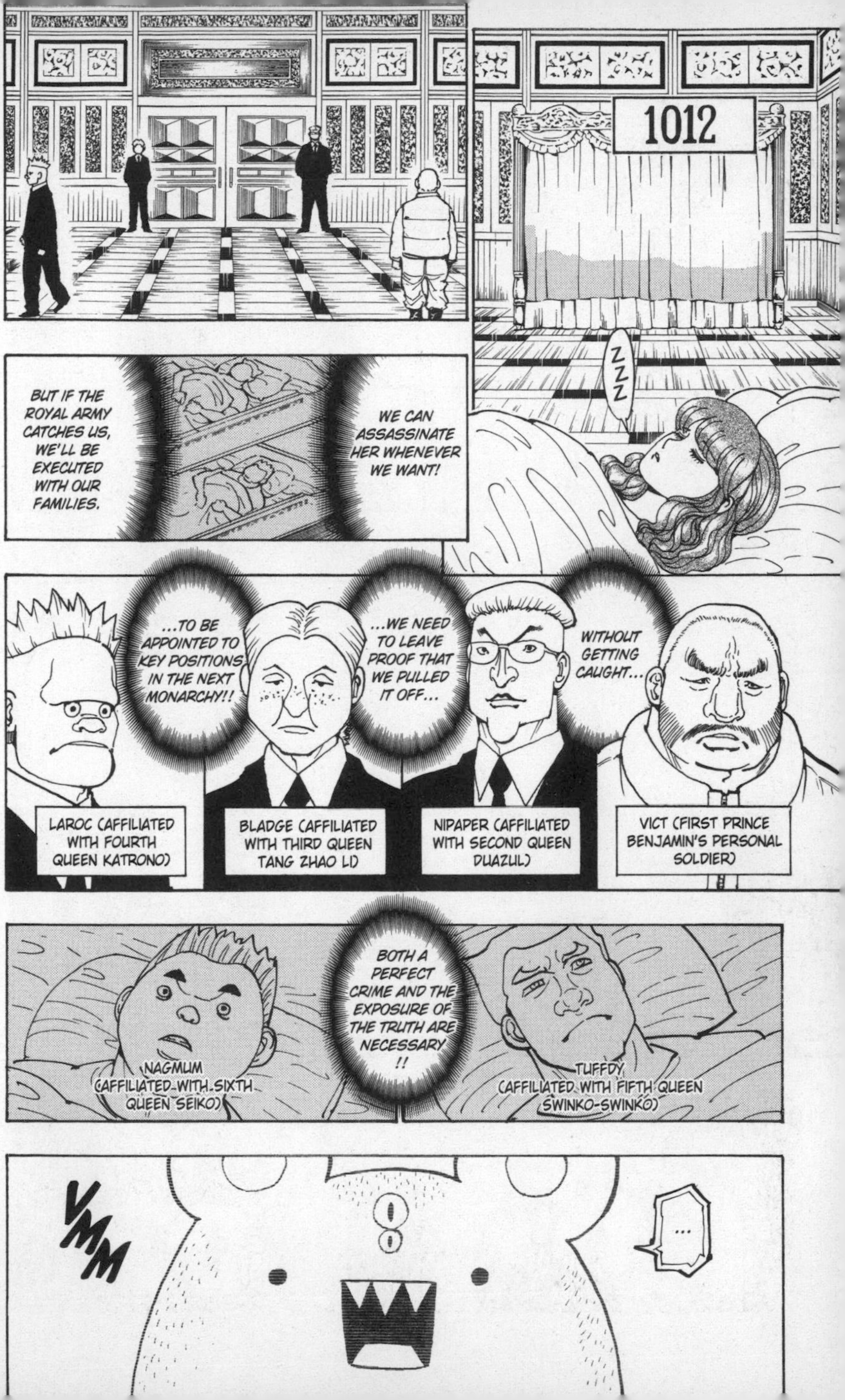
1012
ZZZ
WE CAN ASSASSINATE HER WHENEVER WE WANT!
BUT IF THE ROYAL ARMY CATCHES US, WE'LL BE EXECUTED WITH OUR FAMILIES.
WITHOUT GETTING CAUGHT...
VICT (FIRST PRINCE BENJAMIN'S PERSONAL SOLDIER)
...WE NEED TO LEAVE PROOF THAT WE PULLED IT OFF...
NIPAPER (AFFILIATED WITH SECOND QUEEN DUAZUL)
...TO BE APPOINTED TO KEY POSITIONS IN THE NEXT MONARCHY!!
BLADGE (AFFILIATED WITH THIRD QUEEN TANG ZHAO LI)
LAROC (AFFILIATED WITH FOURTH QUEEN KATRONO)
TUFFDY (AFFILIATED WITH FIFTH QUEEN SWINKO-SWINKO)
BOTH A PERFECT CRIME AND THE EXPOSURE OF THE TRUTH ARE NECESSARY!!
NAGMUM (AFFILIATED WITH SIXTH QUEEN SEIKO)
...
VMM

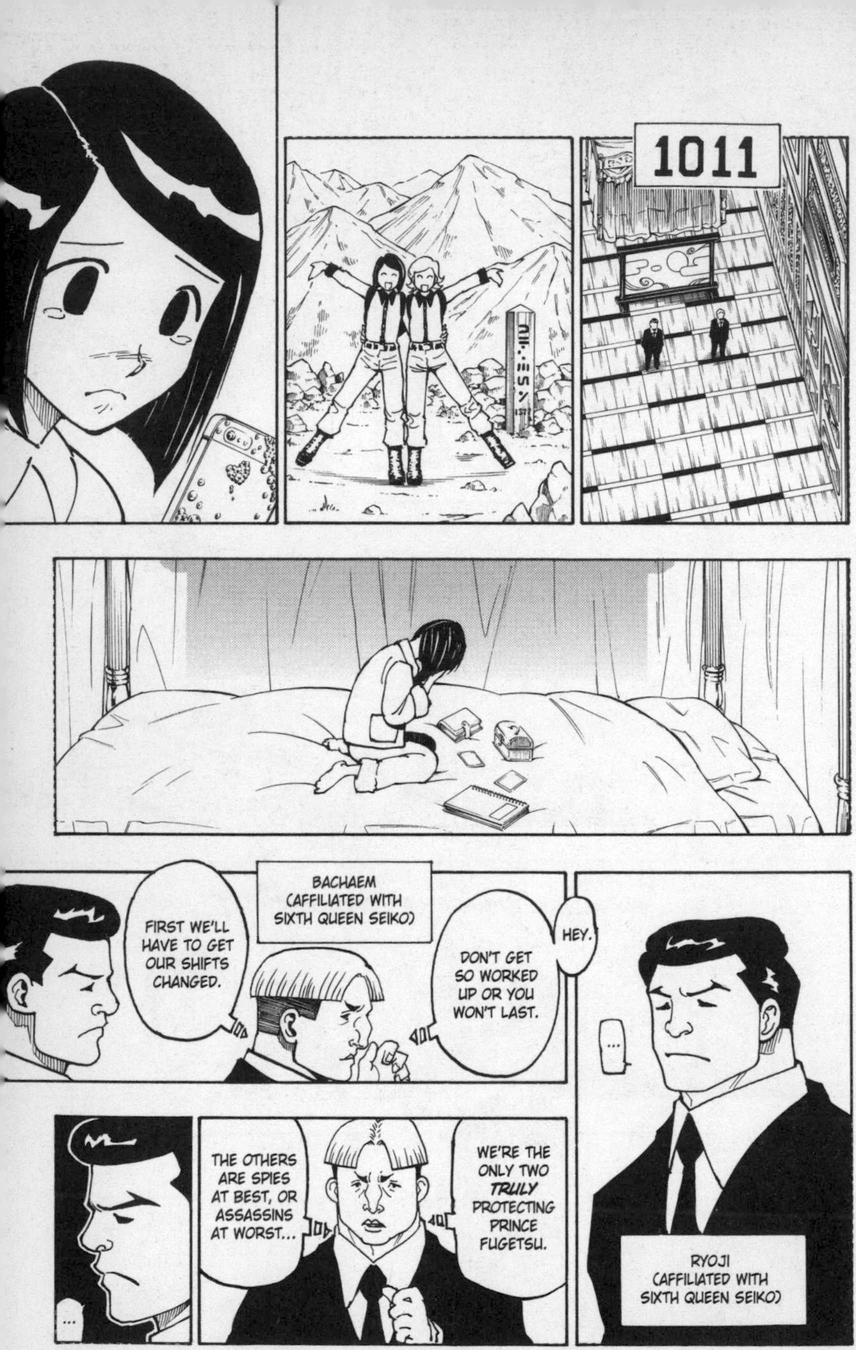

1011
HEY.
...
RYOJI (AFFILIATED WITH SIXTH QUEEN SEIKO)
BACHAEM (AFFILIATED WITH SIXTH QUEEN SEIKO)
DON'T GET SO WORKED UP OR YOU WON'T LAST.
FIRST WE'LL HAVE TO GET OUR SHIFTS CHANGED.
WE'RE THE ONLY TWO *TRULY* PROTECTING PRINCE FUGETSU.
THE OTHERS ARE SPIES AT BEST, OR ASSASSINS AT WORST...
...

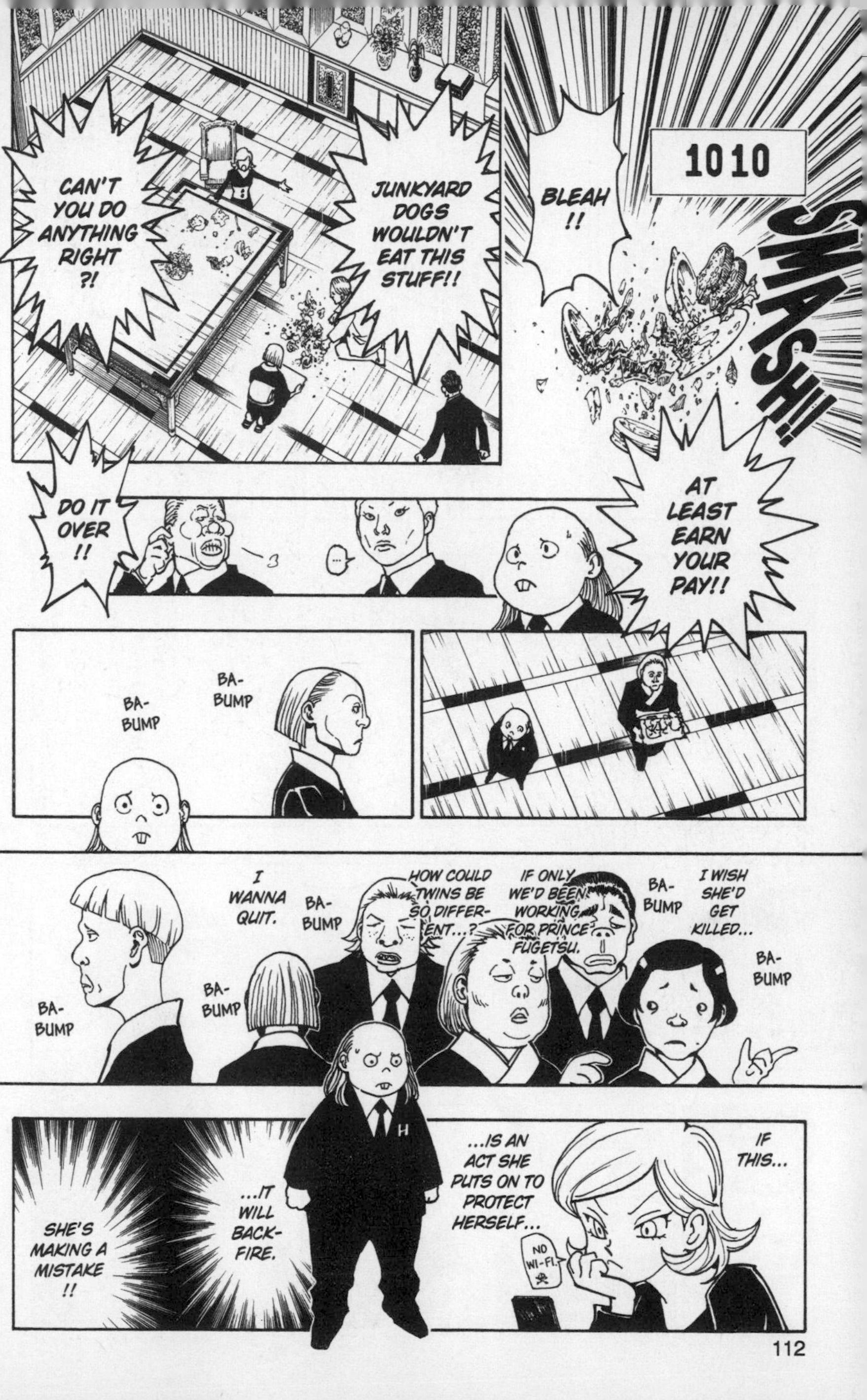
1010
BLEAH !!
SMASH!!
JUNKYARD DOGS WOULDN'T EAT THIS STUFF!!
CAN'T YOU DO ANYTHING RIGHT ?!
AT LEAST EARN YOUR PAY!!
...
DO IT OVER !!
BA-BUMP
BA-BUMP
BA-BUMP
I WISH SHE'D GET KILLED...
BA-BUMP
IF ONLY WE'D BEEN WORKING FOR PRINCE FUGETSU.
HOW COULD TWINS BE SO DIFFERENT...?
BA-BUMP
I WANNA QUIT.
BA-BUMP
BA-BUMP
IF THIS...
...IS AN ACT SHE PUTS ON TO PROTECT HERSELF...
NO WI-FI.
...IT WILL BACKFIRE.
SHE'S MAKING A MISTAKE !!

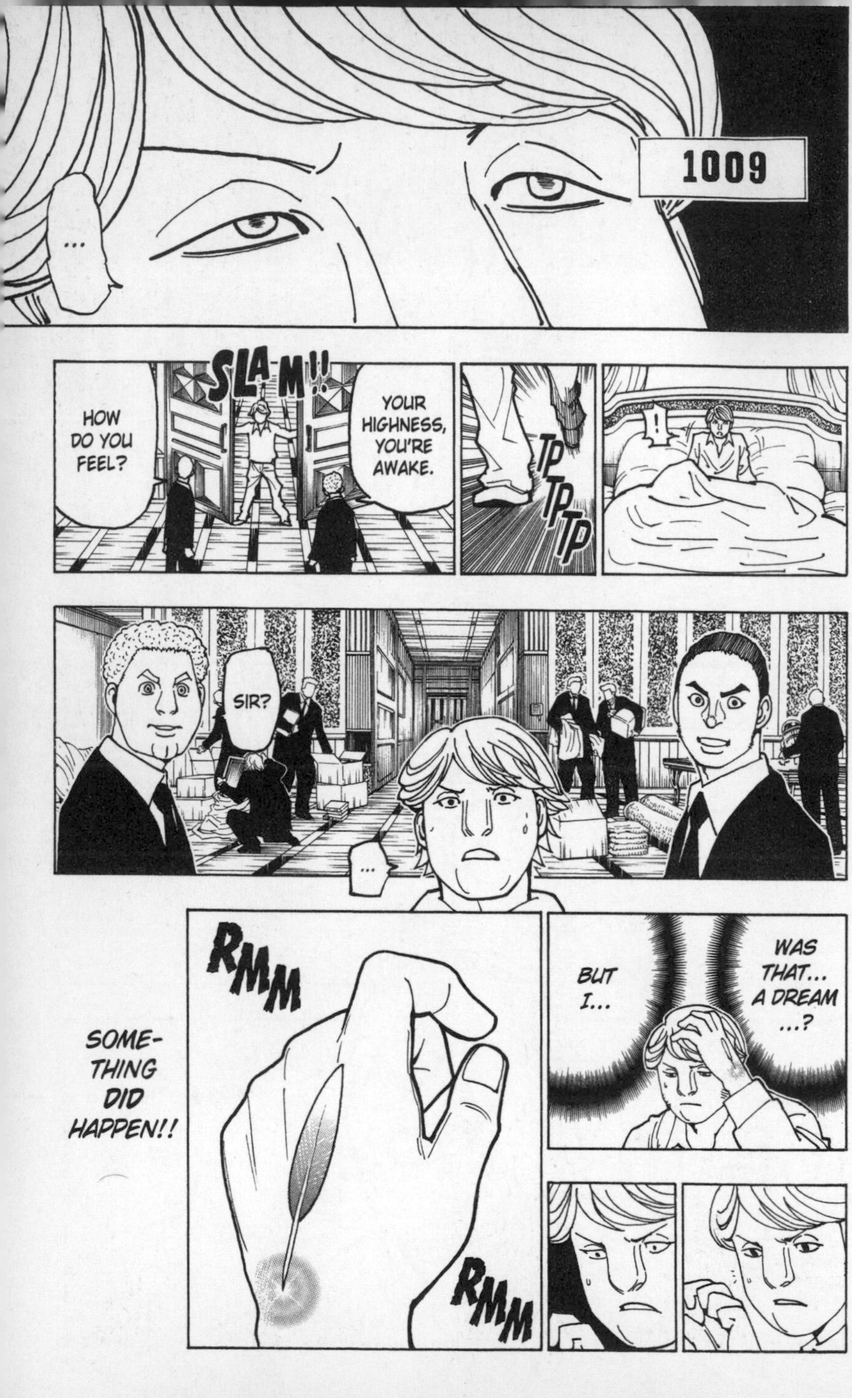

1009
...
!
TP TP TP
YOUR HIGHNESS, YOU'RE AWAKE.
SLAM!!
HOW DO YOU FEEL?
SIR?
...
WAS THAT... A DREAM ...?
BUT I...
RMM
RMM
SOME-THING DID HAPPEN!!

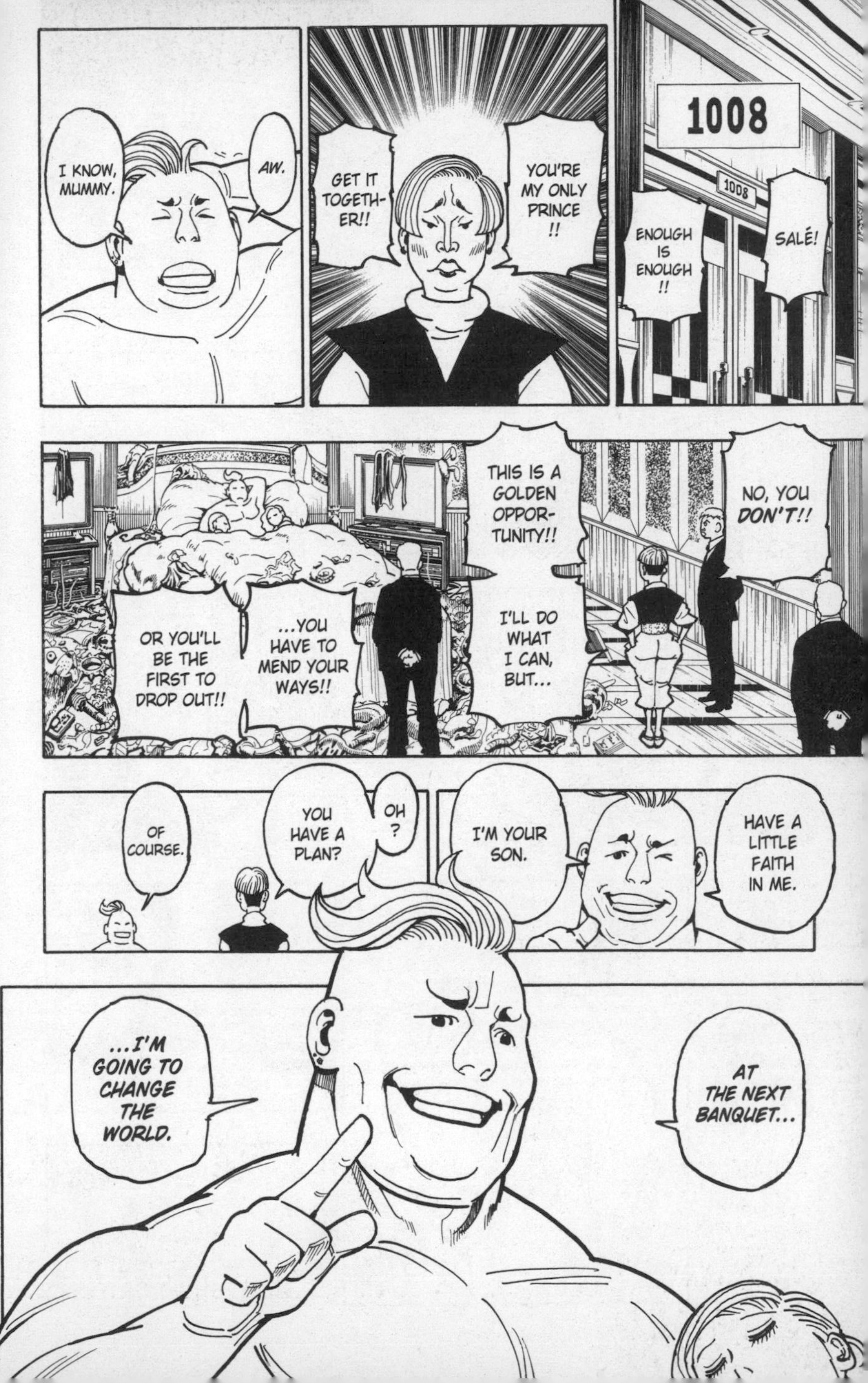
1008
1008
SALÉ!
ENOUGH IS ENOUGH!!
YOU'RE MY ONLY PRINCE!!
GET IT TOGETHER!!
AW.
I KNOW, MUMMY.
NO, YOU DON'T!!
THIS IS A GOLDEN OPPORTUNITY!!
I'LL DO WHAT I CAN, BUT...
...YOU HAVE TO MEND YOUR WAYS!!
OR YOU'LL BE THE FIRST TO DROP OUT!!
HAVE A LITTLE FAITH IN ME.
I'M YOUR SON.
OH?
YOU HAVE A PLAN?
OF COURSE.
AT THE NEXT BANQUET...
...I'M GOING TO CHANGE THE WORLD.

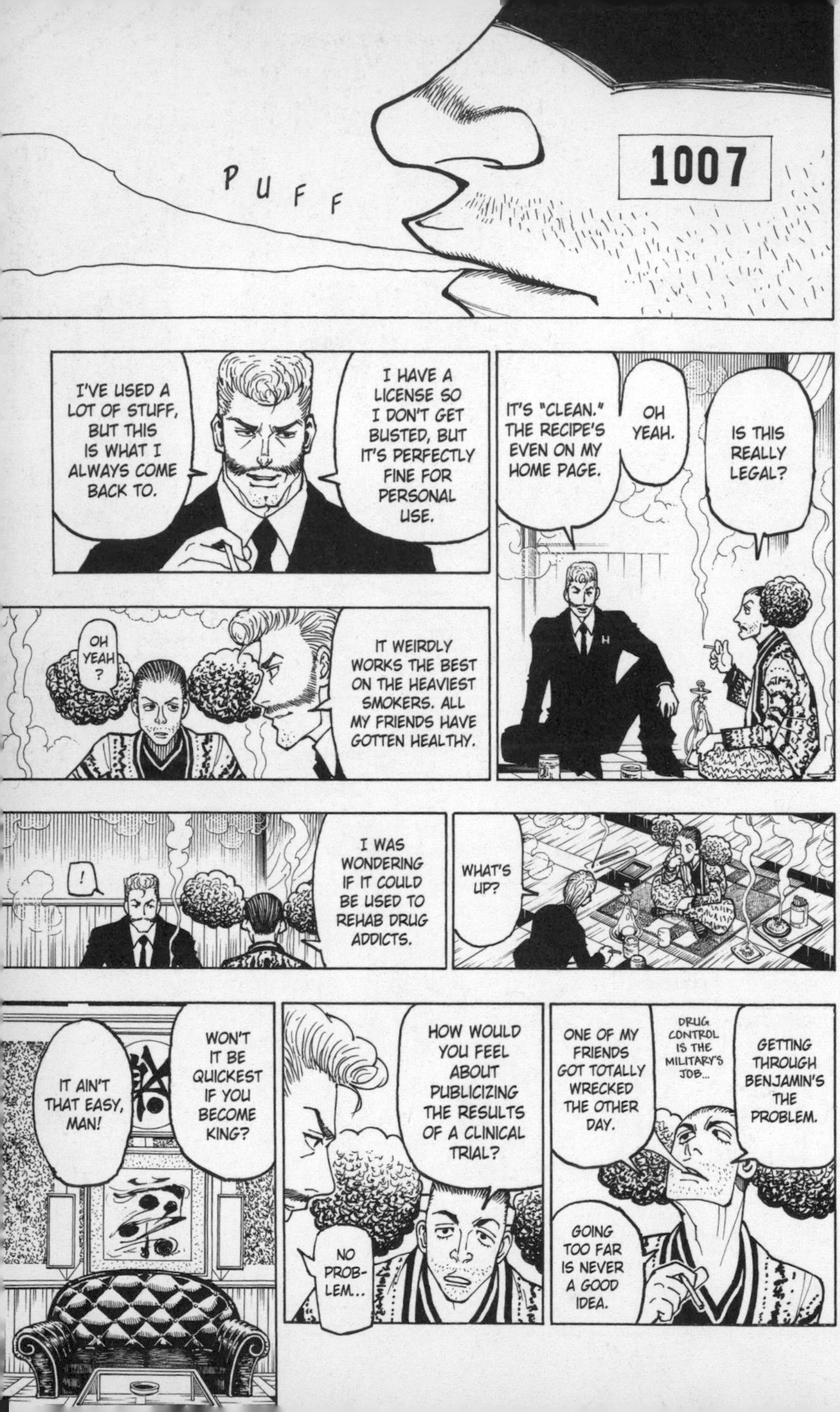
1007
PUFF
IS THIS REALLY LEGAL?
OH YEAH.
IT'S "CLEAN." THE RECIPE'S EVEN ON MY HOME PAGE.
I HAVE A LICENSE SO I DON'T GET BUSTED, BUT IT'S PERFECTLY FINE FOR PERSONAL USE.
I'VE USED A LOT OF STUFF, BUT THIS IS WHAT I ALWAYS COME BACK TO.
IT WEIRDLY WORKS THE BEST ON THE HEAVIEST SMOKERS. ALL MY FRIENDS HAVE GOTTEN HEALTHY.
OH YEAH?
WHAT'S UP?
I WAS WONDERING IF IT COULD BE USED TO REHAB DRUG ADDICTS.
!
GETTING THROUGH BENJAMIN'S THE PROBLEM.
DRUG CONTROL IS THE MILITARY'S JOB...
ONE OF MY FRIENDS GOT TOTALLY WRECKED THE OTHER DAY.
GOING TOO FAR IS NEVER A GOOD IDEA.
HOW WOULD YOU FEEL ABOUT PUBLICIZING THE RESULTS OF A CLINICAL TRIAL?
NO PROBLEM...
WON'T IT BE QUICKEST IF YOU BECOME KING?
IT AIN'T THAT EASY, MAN!

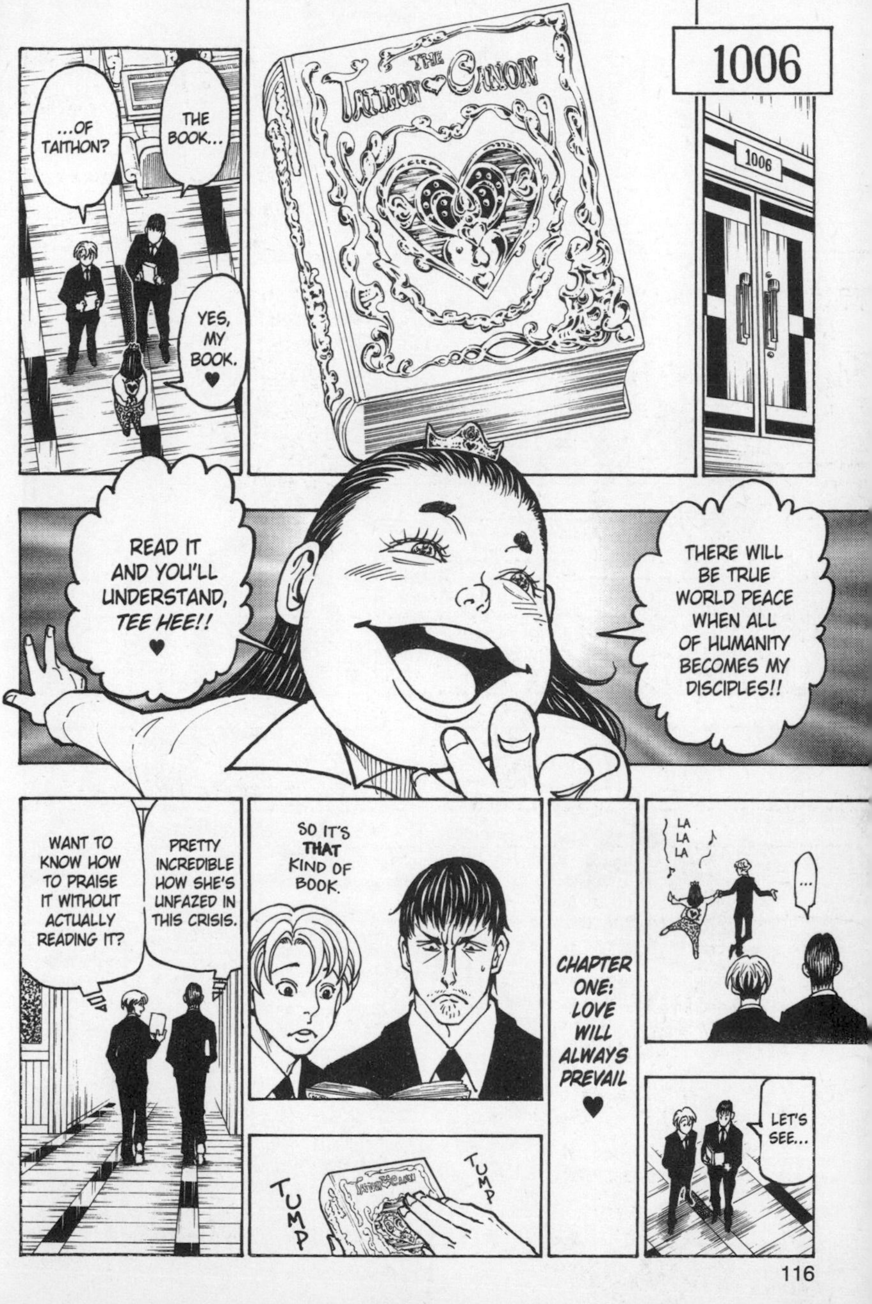

1006
1006
THE TAITHON♥CANON
THE BOOK...
...OF TAITHON?
YES, MY BOOK. ♥
THERE WILL BE TRUE WORLD PEACE WHEN ALL OF HUMANITY BECOMES MY DISCIPLES!!
READ IT AND YOU'LL UNDERSTAND, *TEE HEE!!* ♥
LA LA LA
...
LET'S SEE...
CHAPTER ONE: LOVE WILL ALWAYS PREVAIL ♥
SO IT'S **THAT** KIND OF BOOK.
TUMP
TUMP
PRETTY INCREDIBLE HOW SHE'S UNFAZED IN THIS CRISIS.
WANT TO KNOW HOW TO PRAISE IT WITHOUT ACTUALLY READING IT?

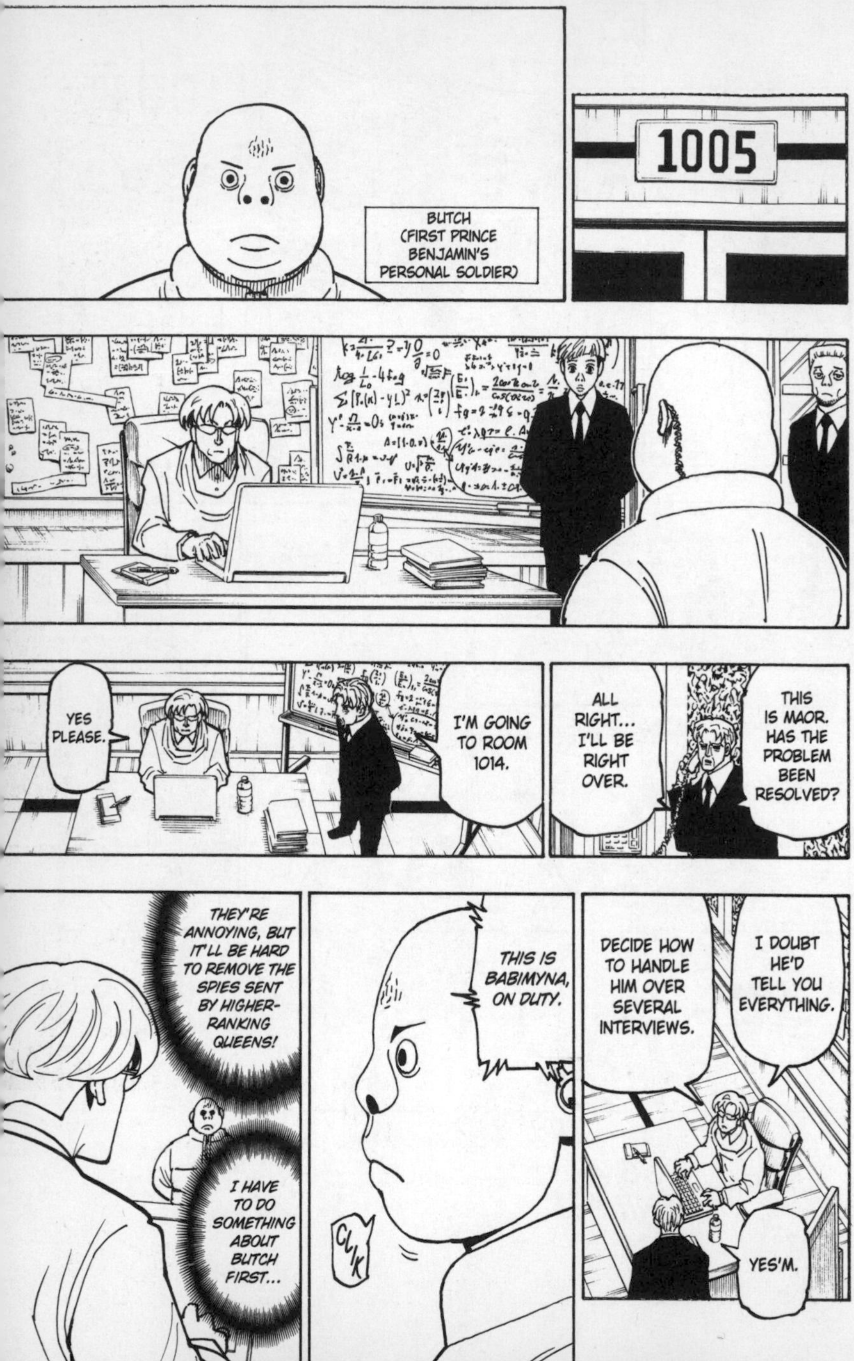
1005
BUTCH (FIRST PRINCE BENJAMIN'S PERSONAL SOLDIER)
THIS IS MAOR. HAS THE PROBLEM BEEN RESOLVED?
ALL RIGHT... I'LL BE RIGHT OVER.
I'M GOING TO ROOM 1014.
YES PLEASE.
I DOUBT HE'D TELL YOU EVERYTHING.
DECIDE HOW TO HANDLE HIM OVER SEVERAL INTERVIEWS.
YES'M.
THIS IS BABIMYNA, ON DUTY.
CLIK
THEY'RE ANNOYING, BUT IT'LL BE HARD TO REMOVE THE SPIES SENT BY HIGHER-RANKING QUEENS!
I HAVE TO DO SOMETHING ABOUT BUTCH FIRST...

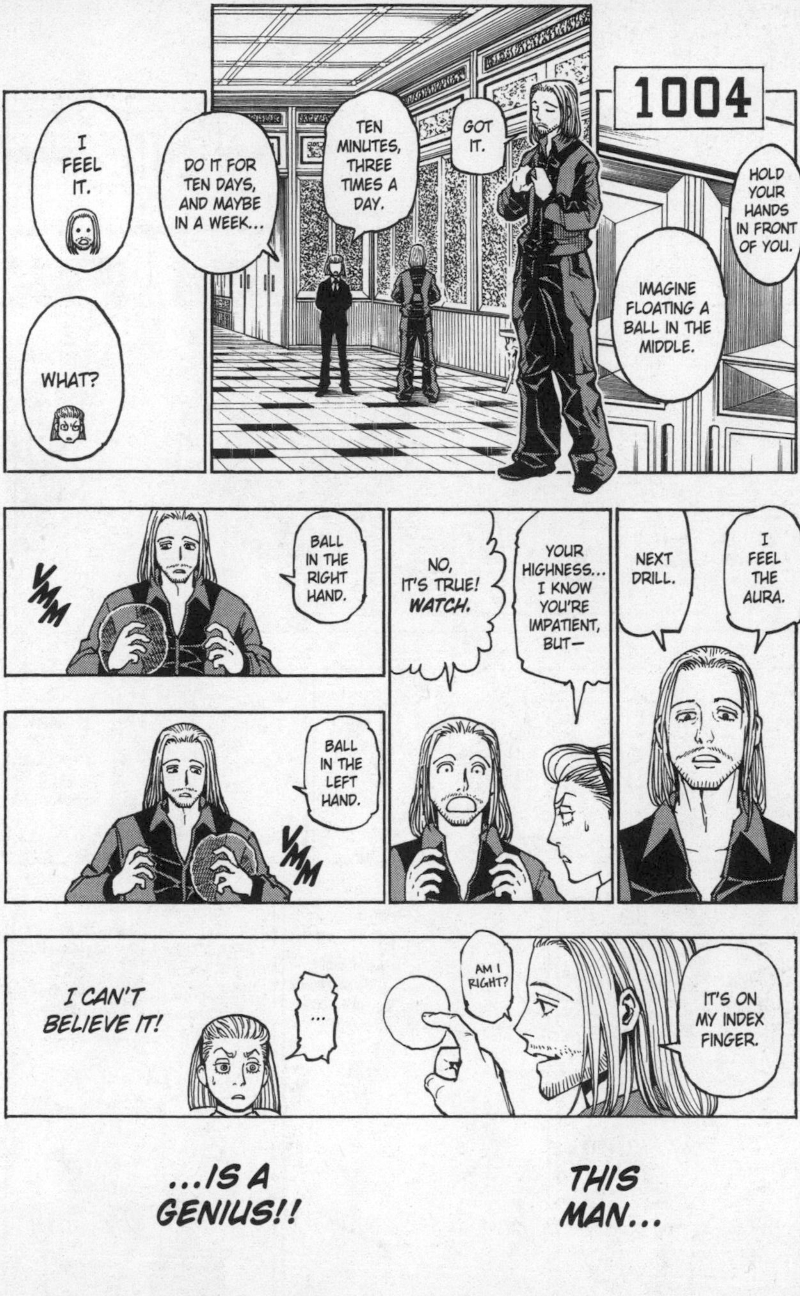
1004
HOLD YOUR HANDS IN FRONT OF YOU.
IMAGINE FLOATING A BALL IN THE MIDDLE.
GOT IT.
TEN MINUTES, THREE TIMES A DAY.
DO IT FOR TEN DAYS, AND MAYBE IN A WEEK...
I FEEL IT.
WHAT?
I FEEL THE AURA.
NEXT DRILL.
YOUR HIGHNESS... I KNOW YOU'RE IMPATIENT, BUT—
NO, IT'S TRUE! WATCH.
BALL IN THE RIGHT HAND.
VMM
BALL IN THE LEFT HAND.
VMM
IT'S ON MY INDEX FINGER.
AM I RIGHT?
...
I CAN'T BELIEVE IT!
THIS MAN...
...IS A GENIUS!!

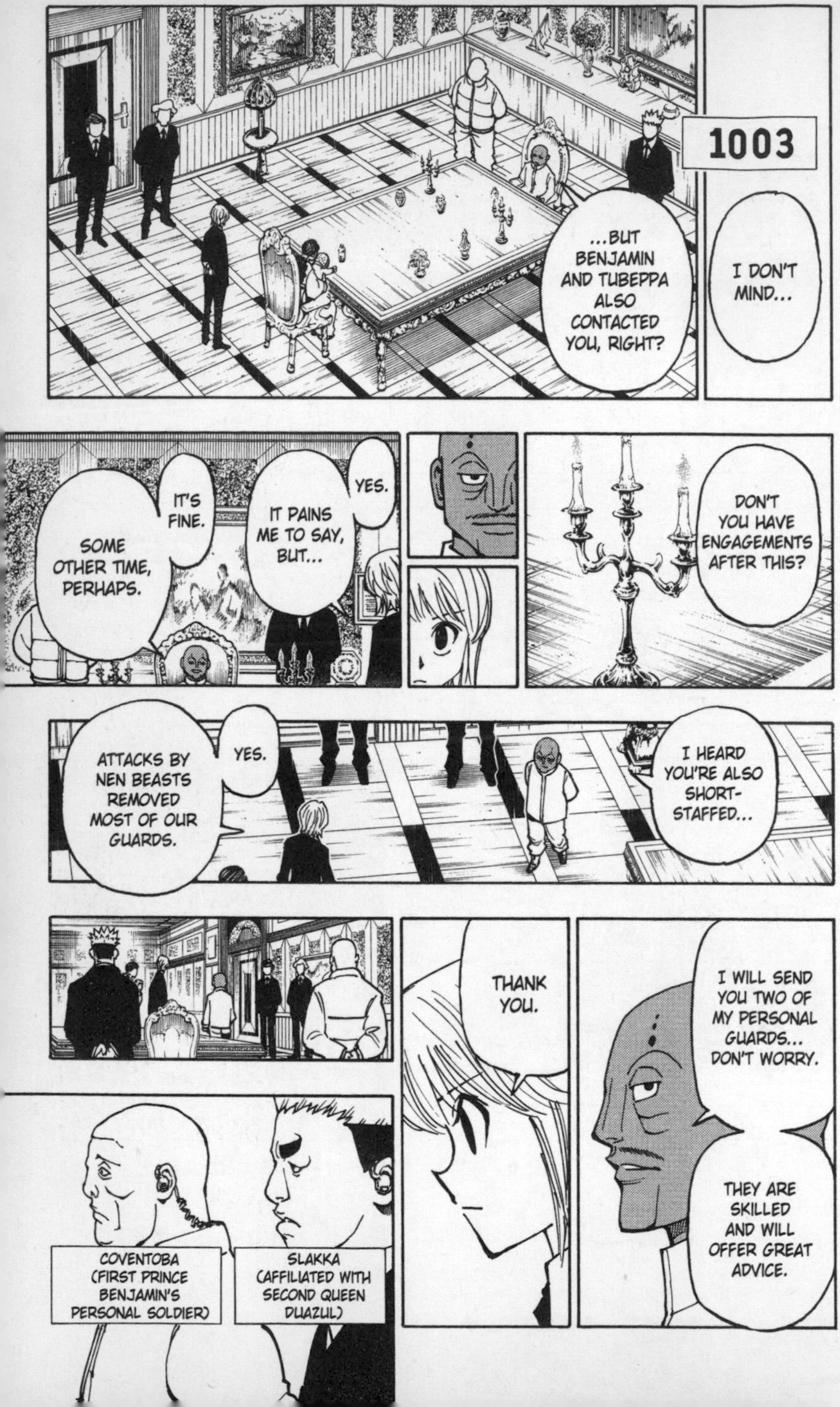
1003
I DON'T MIND...
...BUT BENJAMIN AND TUBEPPA ALSO CONTACTED YOU, RIGHT?
DON'T YOU HAVE ENGAGEMENTS AFTER THIS?
YES.
IT PAINS ME TO SAY, BUT...
IT'S FINE.
SOME OTHER TIME, PERHAPS.
I HEARD YOU'RE ALSO SHORT-STAFFED...
YES.
ATTACKS BY NEN BEASTS REMOVED MOST OF OUR GUARDS.
I WILL SEND YOU TWO OF MY PERSONAL GUARDS... DON'T WORRY.
THEY ARE SKILLED AND WILL OFFER GREAT ADVICE.
THANK YOU.
SLAKKA (AFFILIATED WITH SECOND QUEEN DUAZUL)
COVENTOBA (FIRST PRINCE BENJAMIN'S PERSONAL SOLDIER)

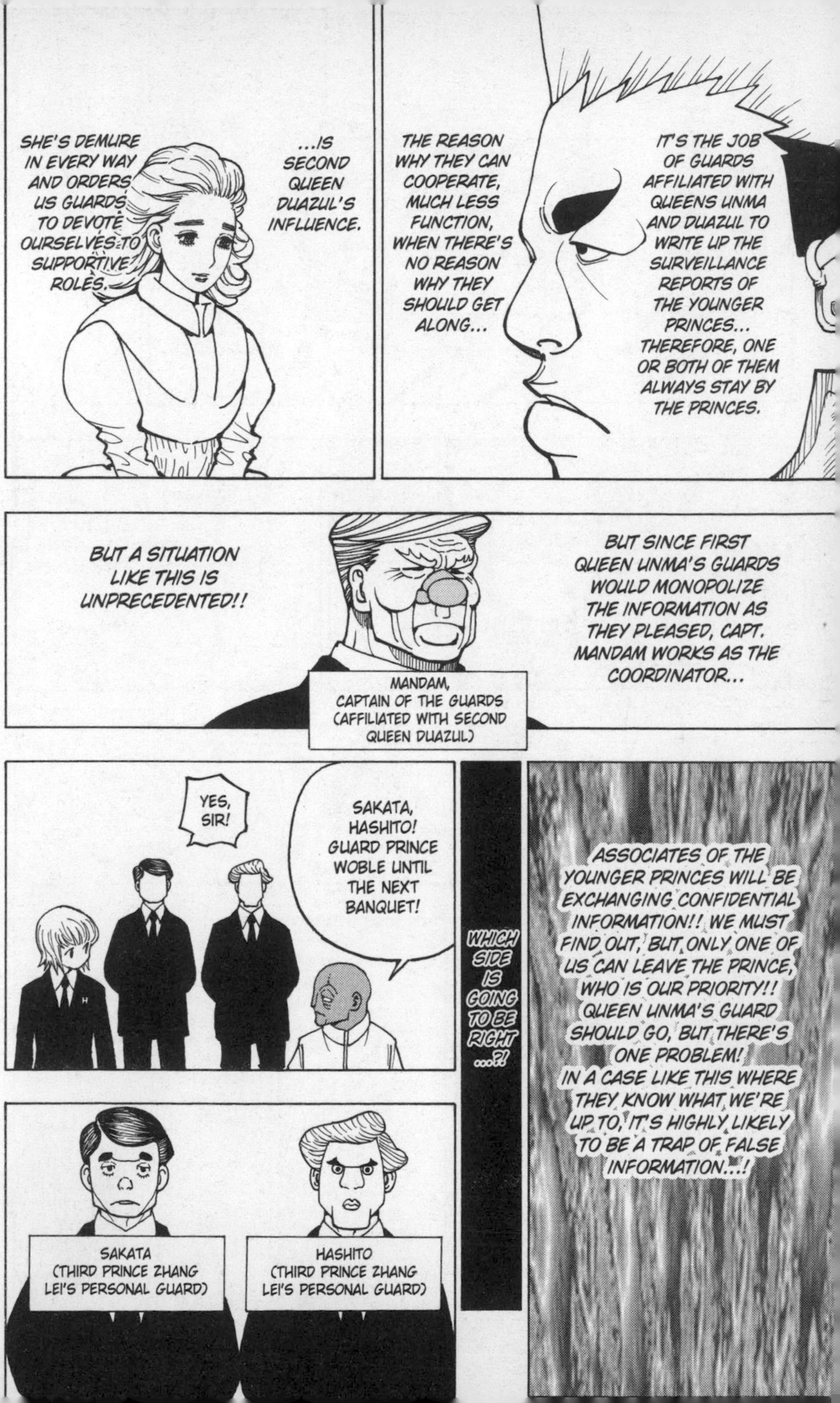
IT'S THE JOB OF GUARDS AFFILIATED WITH QUEENS UNMA AND DUAZUL TO WRITE UP THE SURVEILLANCE REPORTS OF THE YOUNGER PRINCES... THEREFORE, ONE OR BOTH OF THEM ALWAYS STAY BY THE PRINCES.
THE REASON WHY THEY CAN COOPERATE, MUCH LESS FUNCTION, WHEN THERE'S NO REASON WHY THEY SHOULD GET ALONG...
...IS SECOND QUEEN DUAZUL'S INFLUENCE.
SHE'S DEMURE IN EVERY WAY AND ORDERS US GUARDS TO DEVOTE OURSELVES TO SUPPORTIVE ROLES.
BUT SINCE FIRST QUEEN UNMA'S GUARDS WOULD MONOPOLIZE THE INFORMATION AS THEY PLEASED, CAPT. MANDAM WORKS AS THE COORDINATOR...
MANDAM, CAPTAIN OF THE GUARDS (AFFILIATED WITH SECOND QUEEN DUAZUL)
BUT A SITUATION LIKE THIS IS UNPRECEDENTED!!
ASSOCIATES OF THE YOUNGER PRINCES WILL BE EXCHANGING CONFIDENTIAL INFORMATION!! WE MUST FIND OUT, BUT ONLY ONE OF US CAN LEAVE THE PRINCE, WHO IS OUR PRIORITY!! QUEEN UNMA'S GUARD SHOULD GO, BUT THERE'S ONE PROBLEM! IN A CASE LIKE THIS WHERE THEY KNOW WHAT WE'RE UP TO, IT'S HIGHLY LIKELY TO BE A TRAP OF FALSE INFORMATION...!
WHICH SIDE IS GOING TO BE RIGHT...?!
SAKATA, HASHITO! GUARD PRINCE WOBLE UNTIL THE NEXT BANQUET!
YES, SIR!
HASHITO (THIRD PRINCE ZHANG LEI'S PERSONAL GUARD)
SAKATA (THIRD PRINCE ZHANG LEI'S PERSONAL GUARD)

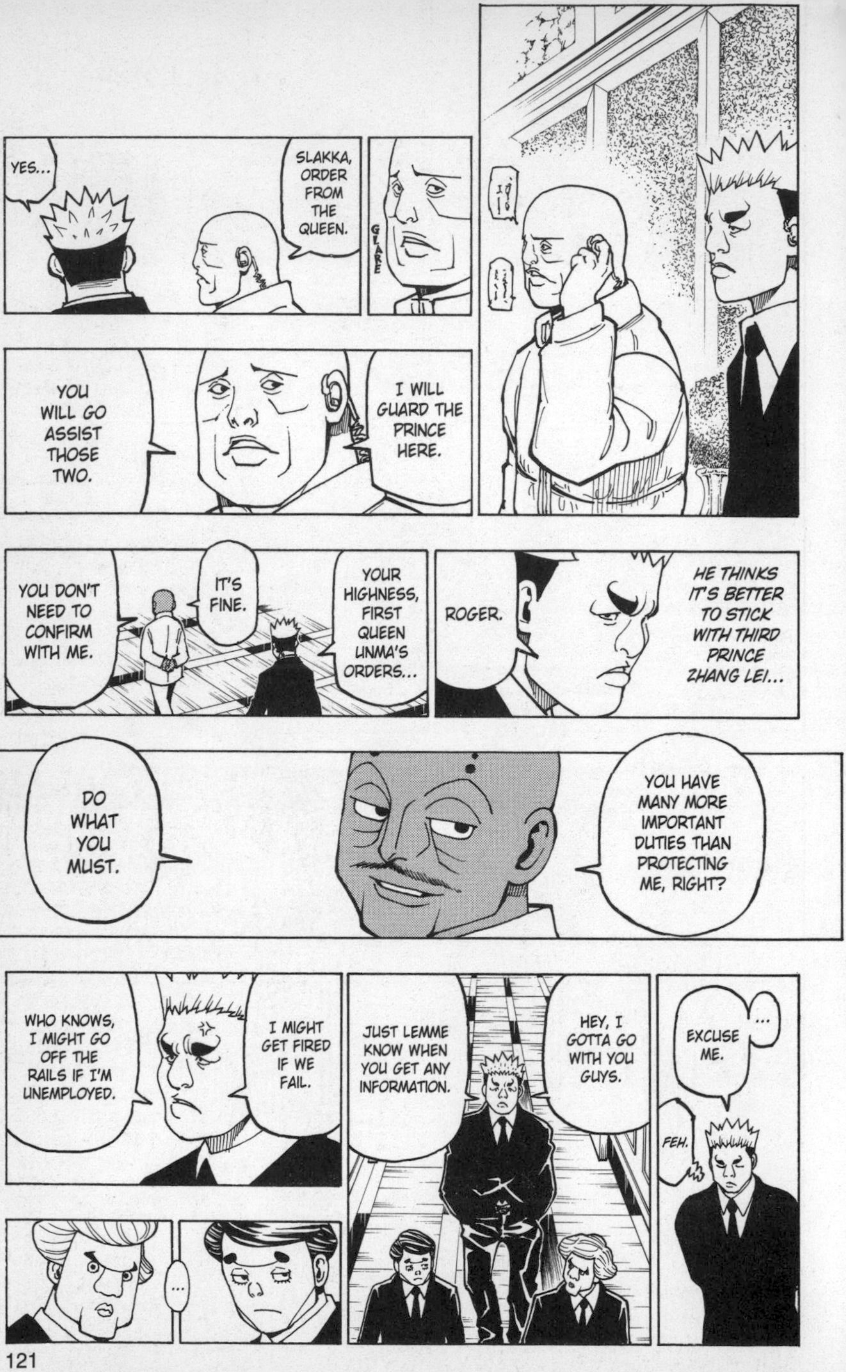
GLARE
SLAKKA, ORDER FROM THE QUEEN.
YES...
I WILL GUARD THE PRINCE HERE.
YOU WILL GO ASSIST THOSE TWO.
HE THINKS IT'S BETTER TO STICK WITH THIRD PRINCE ZHANG LEI...
ROGER.
YOUR HIGHNESS, FIRST QUEEN UNMA'S ORDERS...
IT'S FINE.
YOU DON'T NEED TO CONFIRM WITH ME.
YOU HAVE MANY MORE IMPORTANT DUTIES THAN PROTECTING ME, RIGHT?
DO WHAT YOU MUST.
...
EXCUSE ME.
FEH.
HEY, I GOTTA GO WITH YOU GUYS.
JUST LEMME KNOW WHEN YOU GET ANY INFORMATION.
I MIGHT GET FIRED IF WE FAIL.
WHO KNOWS, I MIGHT GO OFF THE RAILS IF I'M UNEMPLOYED.
...

1002

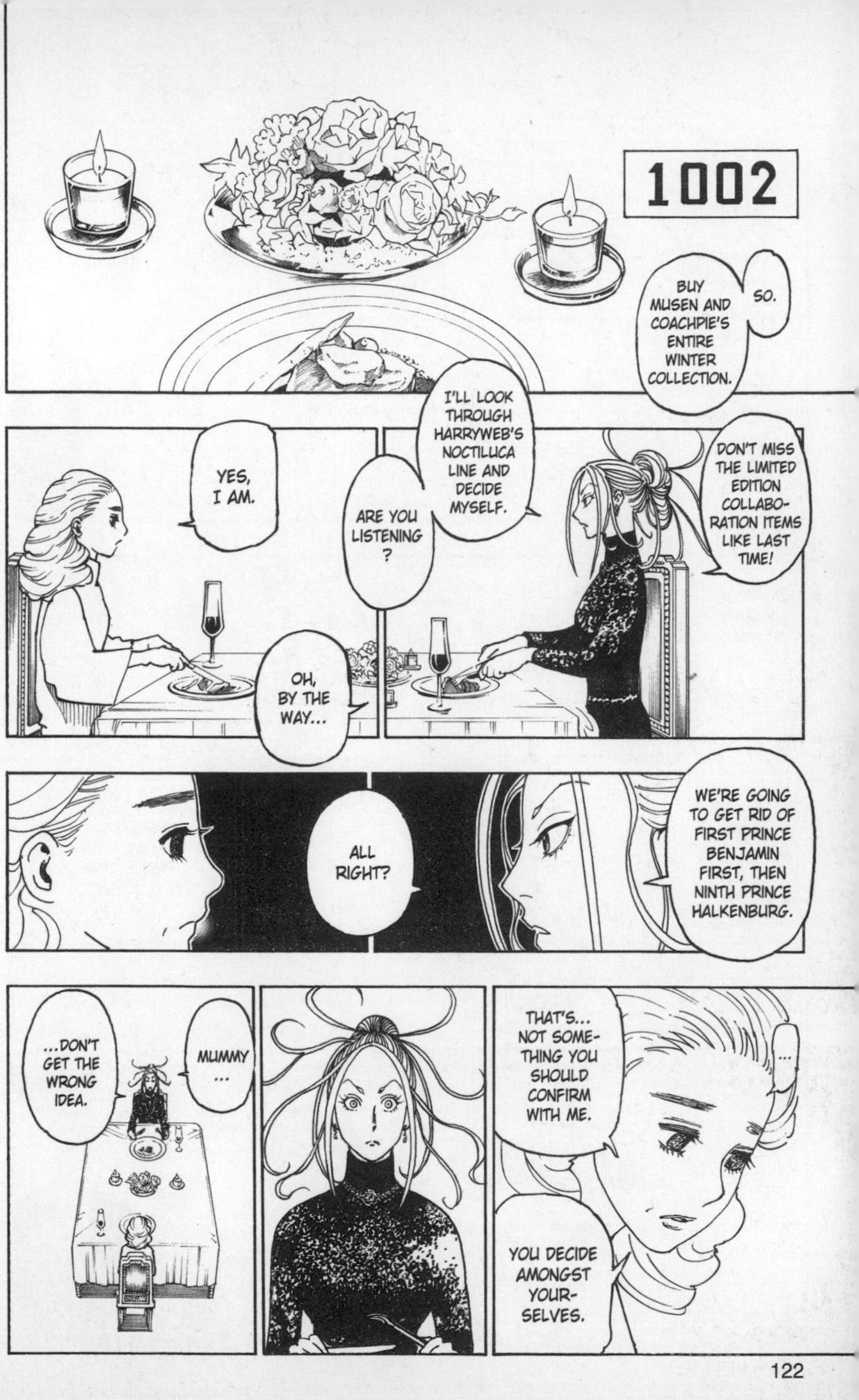
SO.
BUY MUSEN AND COACHPIE'S ENTIRE WINTER COLLECTION.
DON'T MISS THE LIMITED EDITION COLLABO-RATION ITEMS LIKE LAST TIME!
I'LL LOOK THROUGH HARRYWEB'S NOCTILUCA LINE AND DECIDE MYSELF.
ARE YOU LISTENING?
YES, I AM.
OH, BY THE WAY...
WE'RE GOING TO GET RID OF FIRST PRINCE BENJAMIN FIRST, THEN NINTH PRINCE HALKENBURG.
ALL RIGHT?
...
THAT'S... NOT SOME-THING YOU SHOULD CONFIRM WITH ME.
YOU DECIDE AMONGST YOUR-SELVES.
MUMMY...
...DON'T GET THE WRONG IDEA.

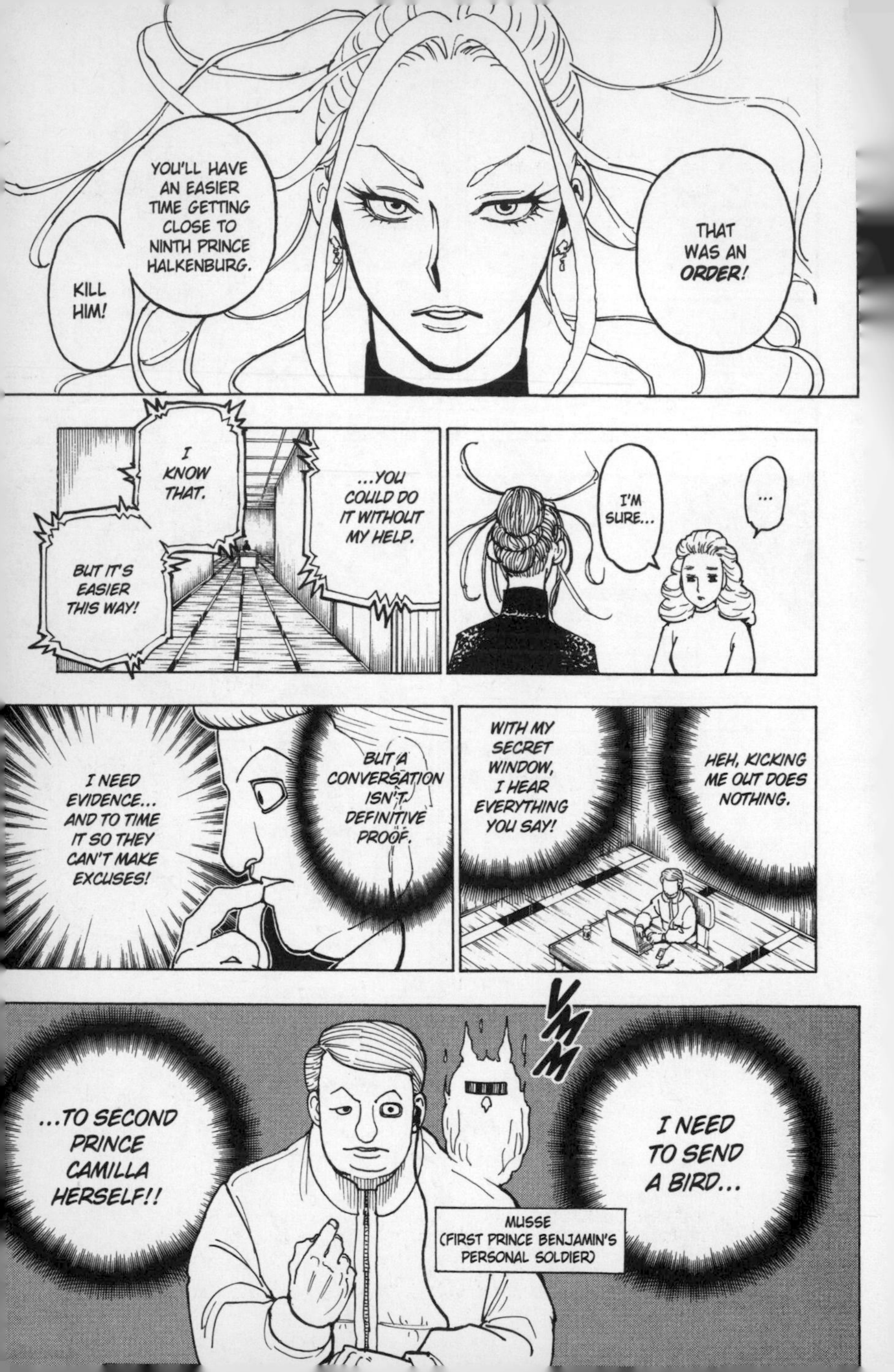
THAT WAS AN ORDER!
YOU'LL HAVE AN EASIER TIME GETTING CLOSE TO NINTH PRINCE HALKENBURG.
KILL HIM!
...
I'M SURE...
...YOU COULD DO IT WITHOUT MY HELP.
I KNOW THAT.
BUT IT'S EASIER THIS WAY!
HEH, KICKING ME OUT DOES NOTHING.
WITH MY SECRET WINDOW, I HEAR EVERYTHING YOU SAY!
BUT A CONVERSATION ISN'T DEFINITIVE PROOF.
I NEED EVIDENCE... AND TO TIME IT SO THEY CAN'T MAKE EXCUSES!
VMM
I NEED TO SEND A BIRD...
MUSSE (FIRST PRINCE BENJAMIN'S PERSONAL SOLDIER)
...TO SECOND PRINCE CAMILLA HERSELF!!

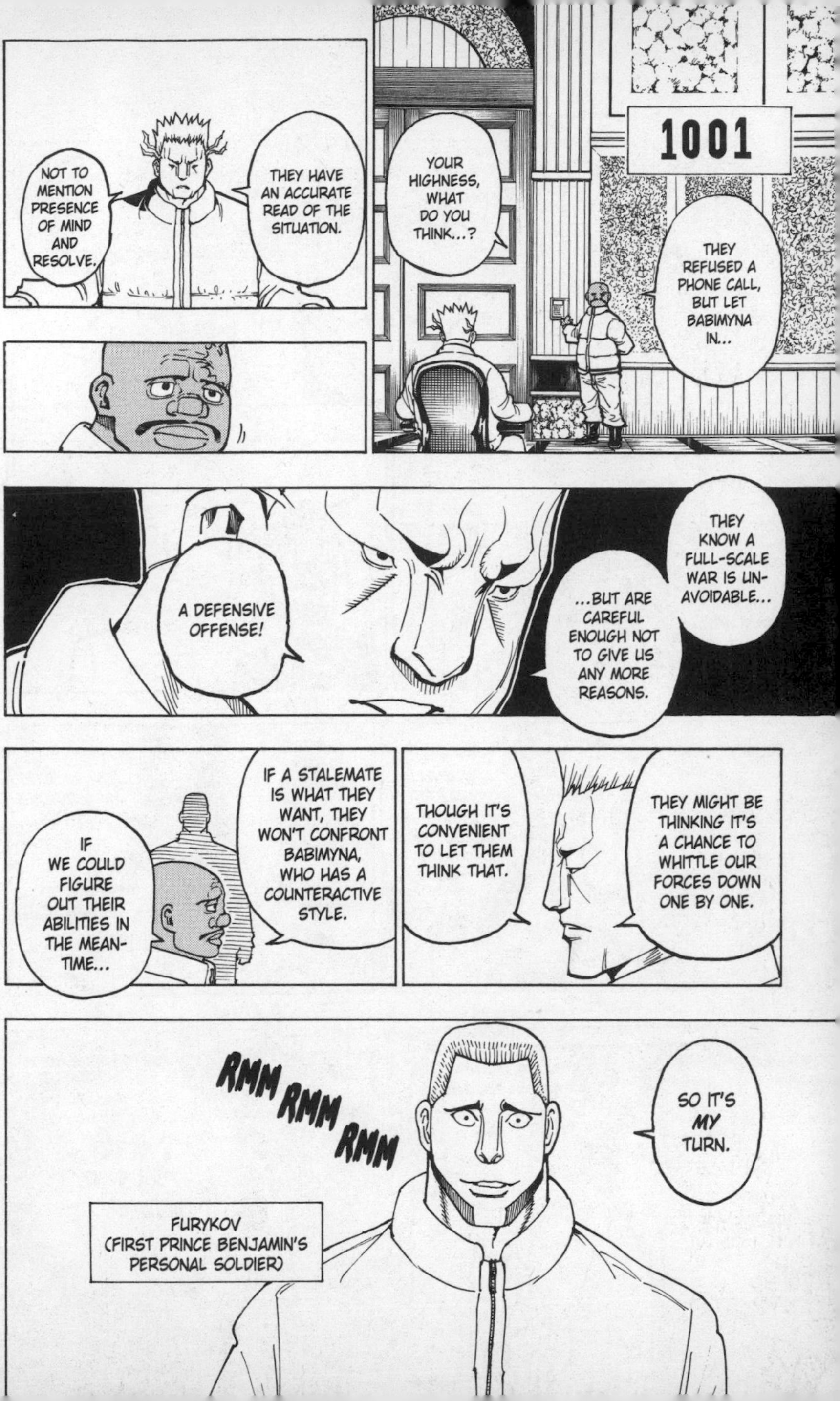
1001
THEY REFUSED A PHONE CALL, BUT LET BABIMYNA IN...
YOUR HIGHNESS, WHAT DO YOU THINK...?
THEY HAVE AN ACCURATE READ OF THE SITUATION.
NOT TO MENTION PRESENCE OF MIND AND RESOLVE.
THEY KNOW A FULL-SCALE WAR IS UN-AVOIDABLE...
...BUT ARE CAREFUL ENOUGH NOT TO GIVE US ANY MORE REASONS.
A DEFENSIVE OFFENSE!
THEY MIGHT BE THINKING IT'S A CHANCE TO WHITTLE OUR FORCES DOWN ONE BY ONE.
THOUGH IT'S CONVENIENT TO LET THEM THINK THAT.
IF A STALEMATE IS WHAT THEY WANT, THEY WON'T CONFRONT BABIMYNA, WHO HAS A COUNTERACTIVE STYLE.
IF WE COULD FIGURE OUT THEIR ABILITIES IN THE MEAN-TIME...
SO IT'S *MY* TURN.
RMM RMM RMM
FURYKOV (FIRST PRINCE BENJAMIN'S PERSONAL SOLDIER)

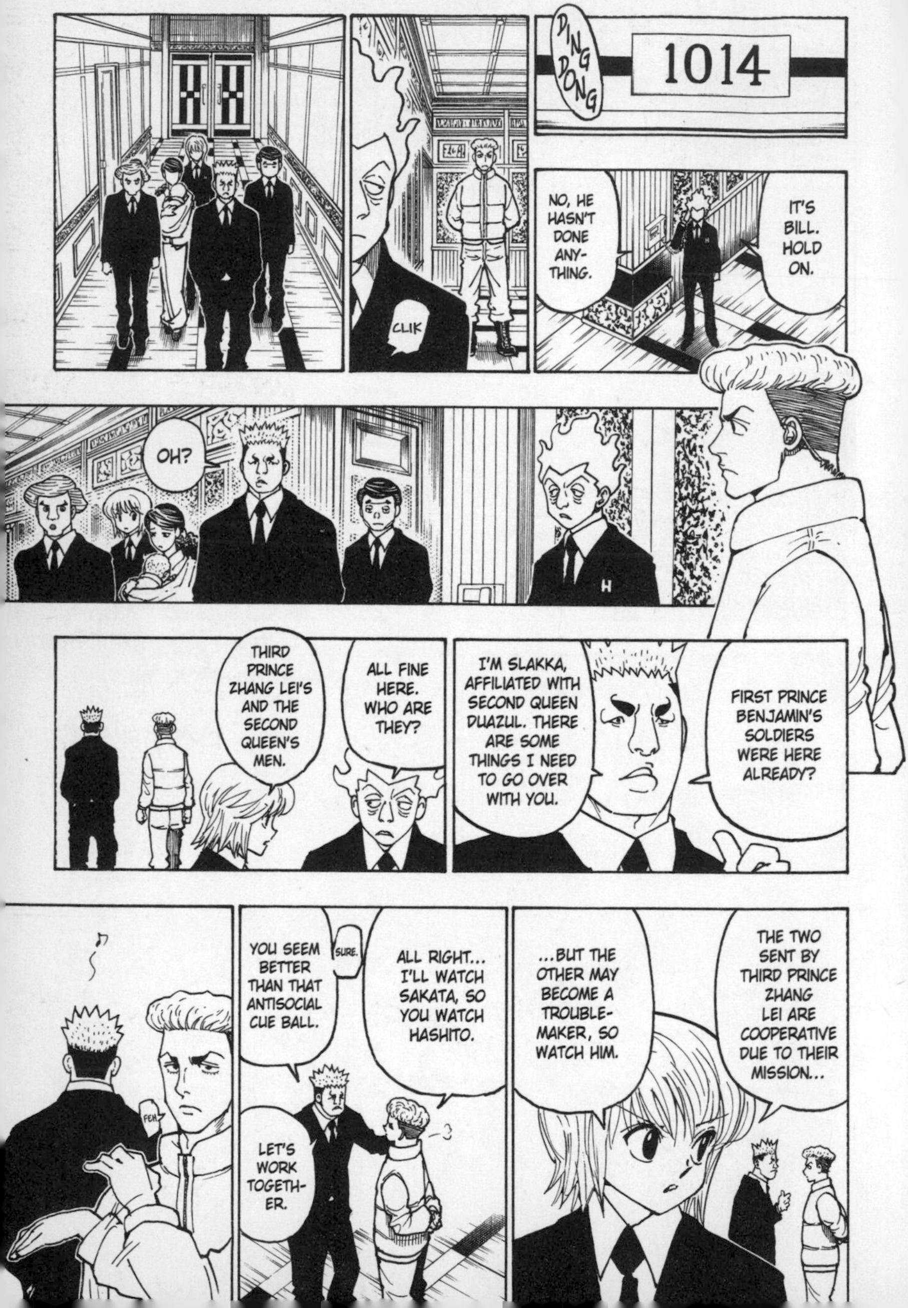
DING DONG
1014
IT'S BILL. HOLD ON.
NO, HE HASN'T DONE ANY-THING.
CLIK
OH?
FIRST PRINCE BENJAMIN'S SOLDIERS WERE HERE ALREADY?
I'M SLAKKA, AFFILIATED WITH SECOND QUEEN DUAZUL. THERE ARE SOME THINGS I NEED TO GO OVER WITH YOU.
ALL FINE HERE. WHO ARE THEY?
THIRD PRINCE ZHANG LEI'S AND THE SECOND QUEEN'S MEN.
THE TWO SENT BY THIRD PRINCE ZHANG LEI ARE COOPERATIVE DUE TO THEIR MISSION...
...BUT THE OTHER MAY BECOME A TROUBLE-MAKER, SO WATCH HIM.
ALL RIGHT... I'LL WATCH SAKATA, SO YOU WATCH HASHITO.
SURE.
YOU SEEM BETTER THAN THAT ANTISOCIAL CUE BALL.
LET'S WORK TOGETH-ER.
FEH

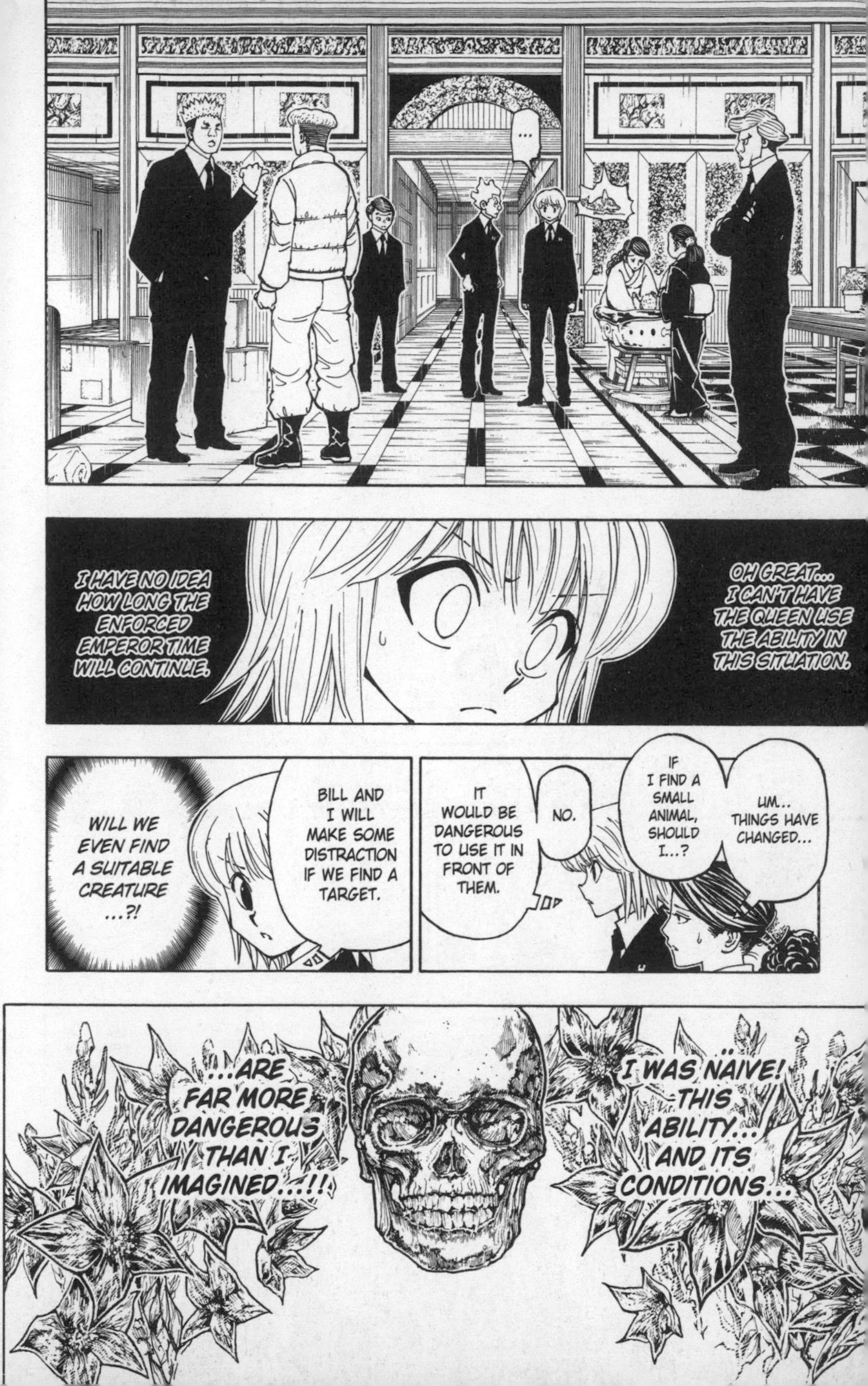
...
OH GREAT... I CAN'T HAVE THE QUEEN USE THE ABILITY IN THIS SITUATION.
I HAVE NO IDEA HOW LONG THE ENFORCED EMPEROR TIME WILL CONTINUE.
UM.. THINGS HAVE CHANGED...
IF I FIND A SMALL ANIMAL, SHOULD I...?
NO.
IT WOULD BE DANGEROUS TO USE IT IN FRONT OF THEM.
BILL AND I WILL MAKE SOME DISTRACTION IF WE FIND A TARGET.
WILL WE EVEN FIND A SUITABLE CREATURE ...?!
I WAS NAIVE! THIS ABILITY... AND ITS CONDITIONS...
...ARE FAR MORE DANGEROUS THAN I IMAGINED...!!

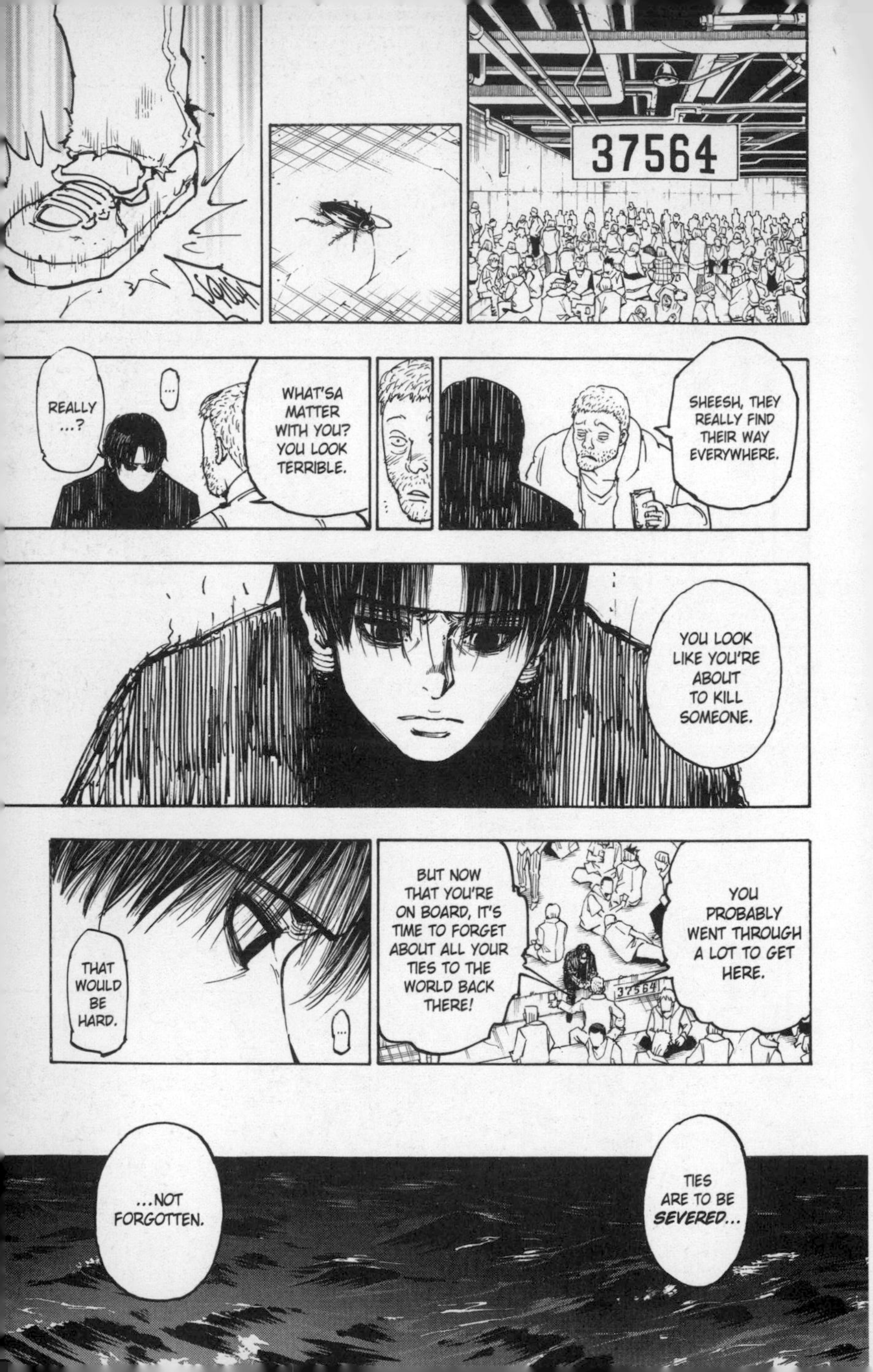
37564
SHEESH, THEY REALLY FIND THEIR WAY EVERYWHERE.
WHAT'SA MATTER WITH YOU? YOU LOOK TERRIBLE.
...
REALLY ...?
YOU LOOK LIKE YOU'RE ABOUT TO KILL SOMEONE.
YOU PROBABLY WENT THROUGH A LOT TO GET HERE.
BUT NOW THAT YOU'RE ON BOARD, IT'S TIME TO FORGET ABOUT ALL YOUR TIES TO THE WORLD BACK THERE!
37564
...
THAT WOULD BE HARD.
TIES ARE TO BE *SEVERED*...
...NOT FORGOTTEN.

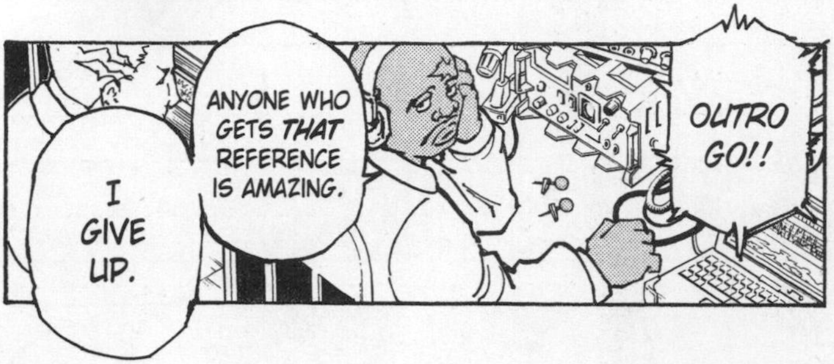
OUTRO GO!!
ANYONE WHO GETS *THAT* REFERENCE IS AMAZING.
I GIVE UP.

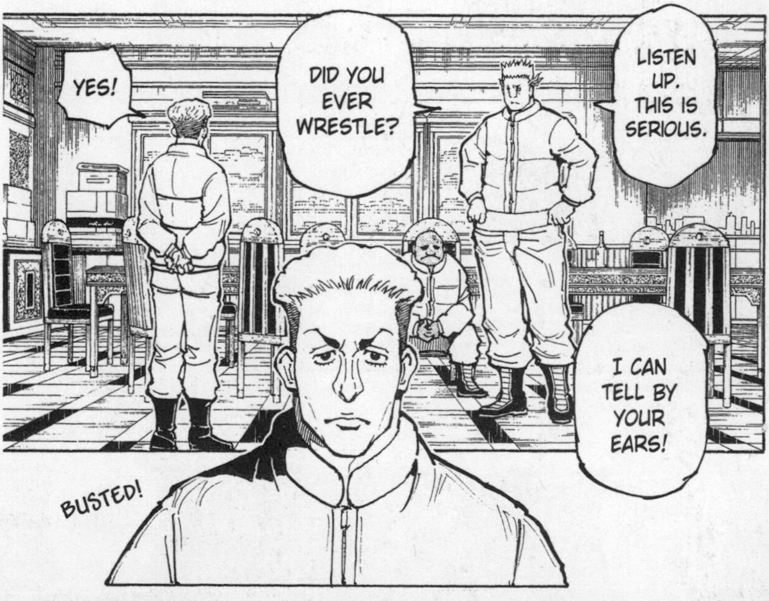
LISTEN UP. THIS IS SERIOUS.
DID YOU EVER WRESTLE?
YES!
I CAN TELL BY YOUR EARS!
BUSTED!

Chapter 367: Synchronization

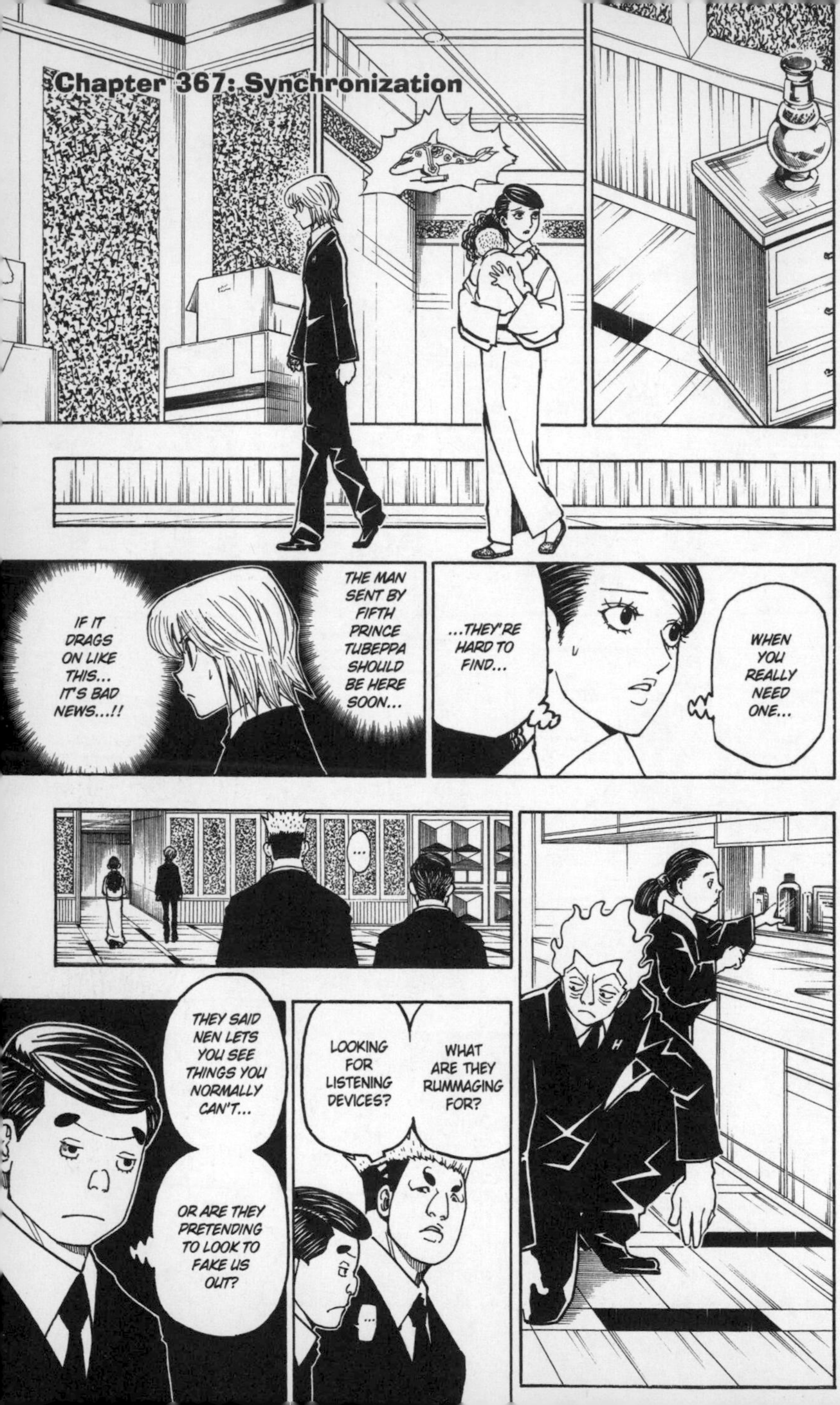

WHEN YOU REALLY NEED ONE...
...THEY'RE HARD TO FIND...
THE MAN SENT BY FIFTH PRINCE TUBEPPA SHOULD BE HERE SOON...
IF IT DRAGS ON LIKE THIS... IT'S BAD NEWS...!!
...
WHAT ARE THEY RUMMAGING FOR?
LOOKING FOR LISTENING DEVICES?
...
THEY SAID NEN LETS YOU SEE THINGS YOU NORMALLY CAN'T...
OR ARE THEY PRETENDING TO LOOK TO FAKE US OUT?

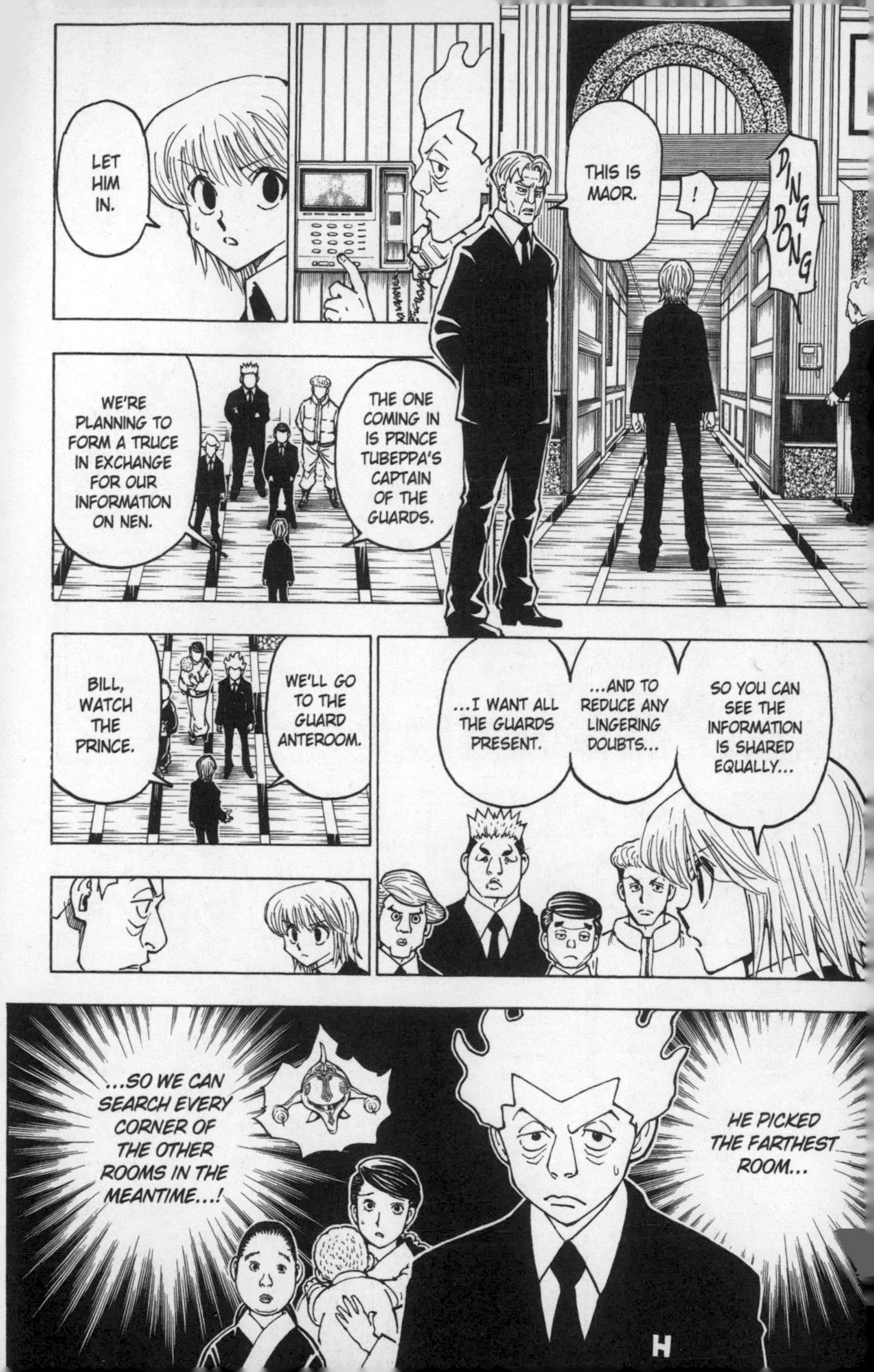
DING DONG
!
THIS IS MAOR.
LET HIM IN.
THE ONE COMING IN IS PRINCE TUBEPPA'S CAPTAIN OF THE GUARDS.
WE'RE PLANNING TO FORM A TRUCE IN EXCHANGE FOR OUR INFORMATION ON NEN.
SO YOU CAN SEE THE INFORMATION IS SHARED EQUALLY...
...AND TO REDUCE ANY LINGERING DOUBTS...
...I WANT ALL THE GUARDS PRESENT.
WE'LL GO TO THE GUARD ANTEROOM.
BILL, WATCH THE PRINCE.
HE PICKED THE FARTHEST ROOM...
...SO WE CAN SEARCH EVERY CORNER OF THE OTHER ROOMS IN THE MEANTIME...!
H

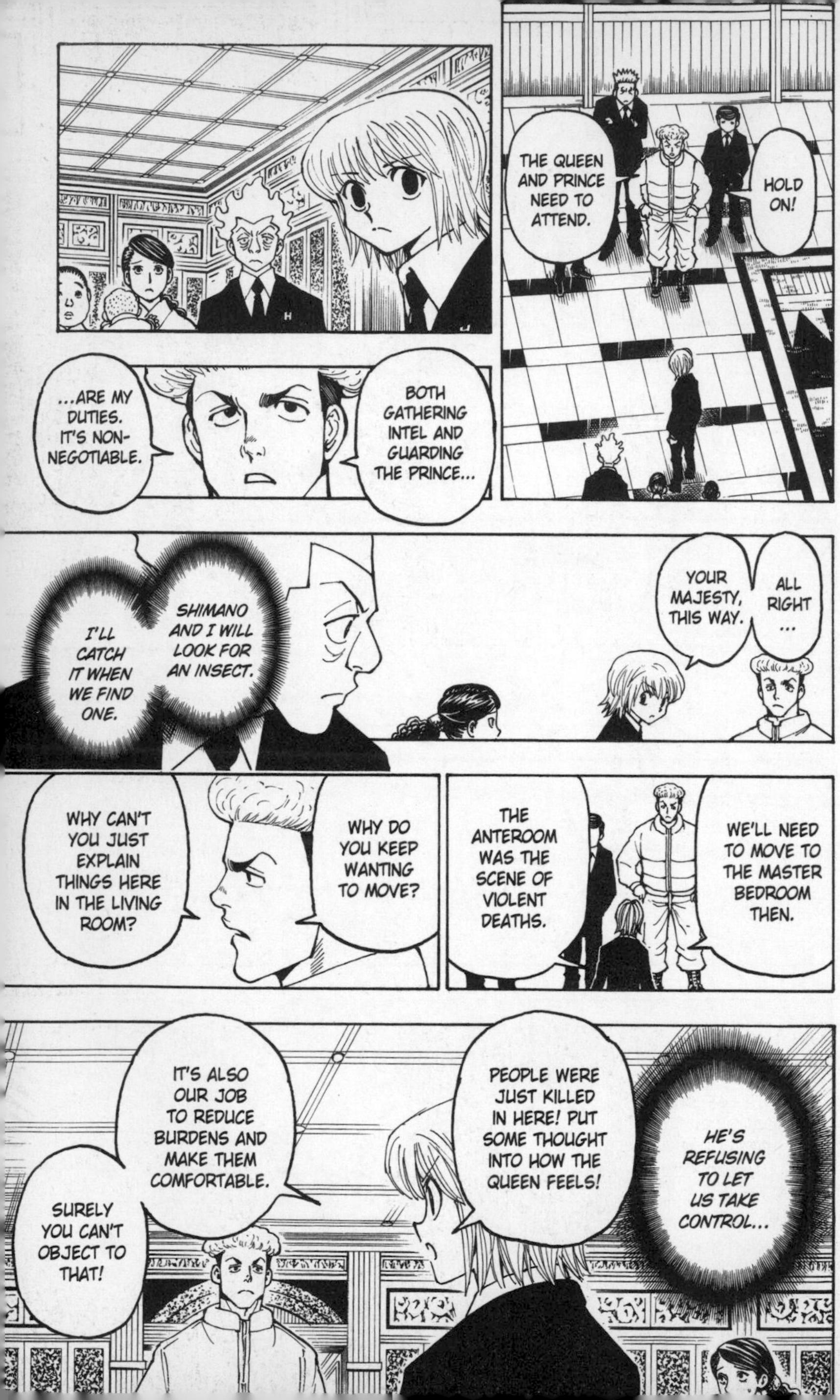
HOLD ON!
THE QUEEN AND PRINCE NEED TO ATTEND.
BOTH GATHERING INTEL AND GUARDING THE PRINCE...
...ARE MY DUTIES. IT'S NON-NEGOTIABLE.
ALL RIGHT ...
YOUR MAJESTY, THIS WAY.
SHIMANO AND I WILL LOOK FOR AN INSECT.
I'LL CATCH IT WHEN WE FIND ONE.
WE'LL NEED TO MOVE TO THE MASTER BEDROOM THEN.
THE ANTEROOM WAS THE SCENE OF VIOLENT DEATHS.
WHY DO YOU KEEP WANTING TO MOVE?
WHY CAN'T YOU JUST EXPLAIN THINGS HERE IN THE LIVING ROOM?
HE'S REFUSING TO LET US TAKE CONTROL...
PEOPLE WERE JUST KILLED IN HERE! PUT SOME THOUGHT INTO HOW THE QUEEN FEELS!
IT'S ALSO OUR JOB TO REDUCE BURDENS AND MAKE THEM COMFORTABLE.
SURELY YOU CAN'T OBJECT TO THAT!

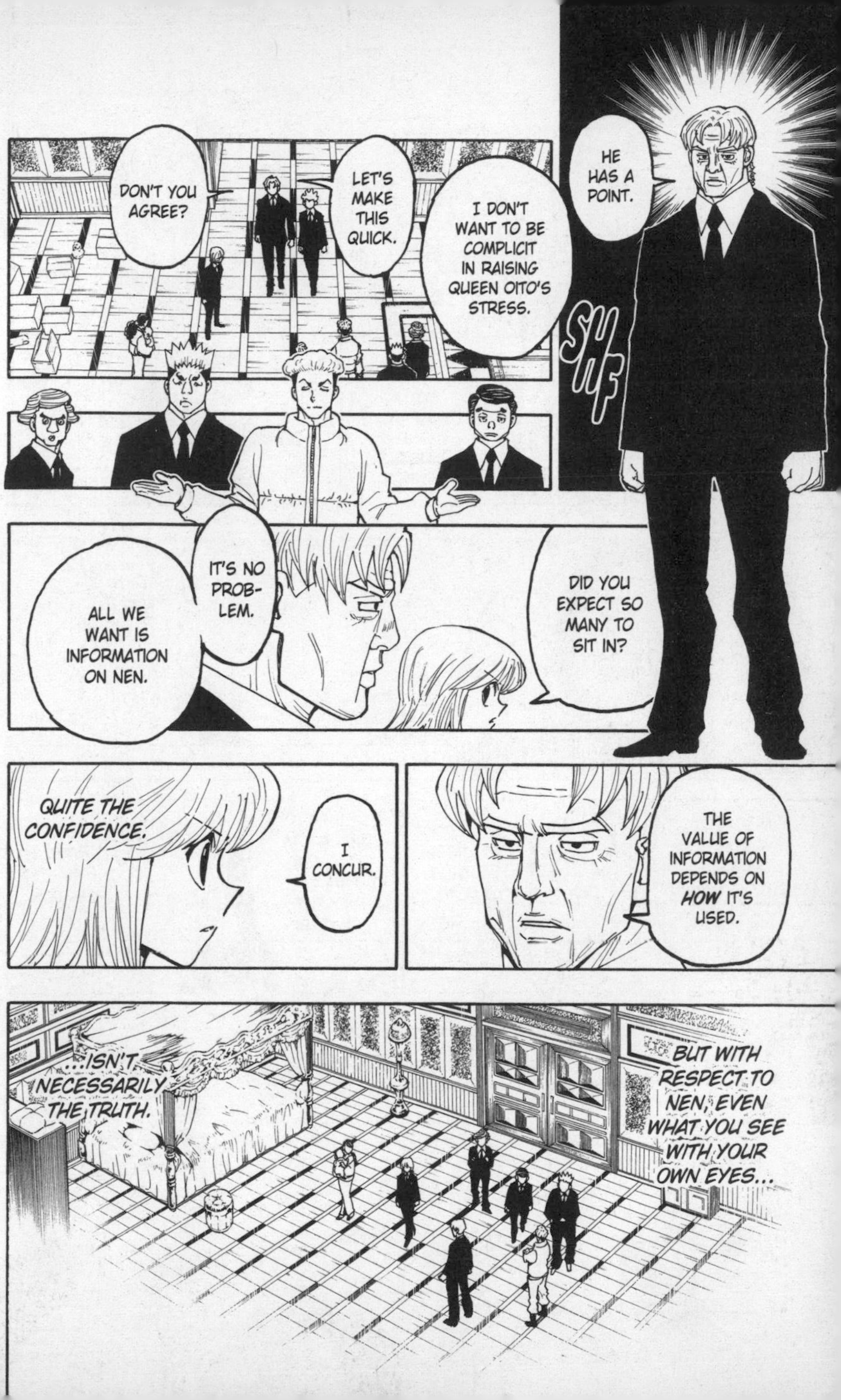
HE HAS A POINT.
I DON'T WANT TO BE COMPLICIT IN RAISING QUEEN OITO'S STRESS.
SHF
LET'S MAKE THIS QUICK.
DON'T YOU AGREE?
DID YOU EXPECT SO MANY TO SIT IN?
IT'S NO PROBLEM.
ALL WE WANT IS INFORMATION ON NEN.
THE VALUE OF INFORMATION DEPENDS ON *HOW* IT'S USED.
I CONCUR.
QUITE THE CONFIDENCE.
BUT WITH RESPECT TO NEN, EVEN WHAT YOU SEE WITH YOUR OWN EYES...
...ISN'T NECESSARILY THE TRUTH.

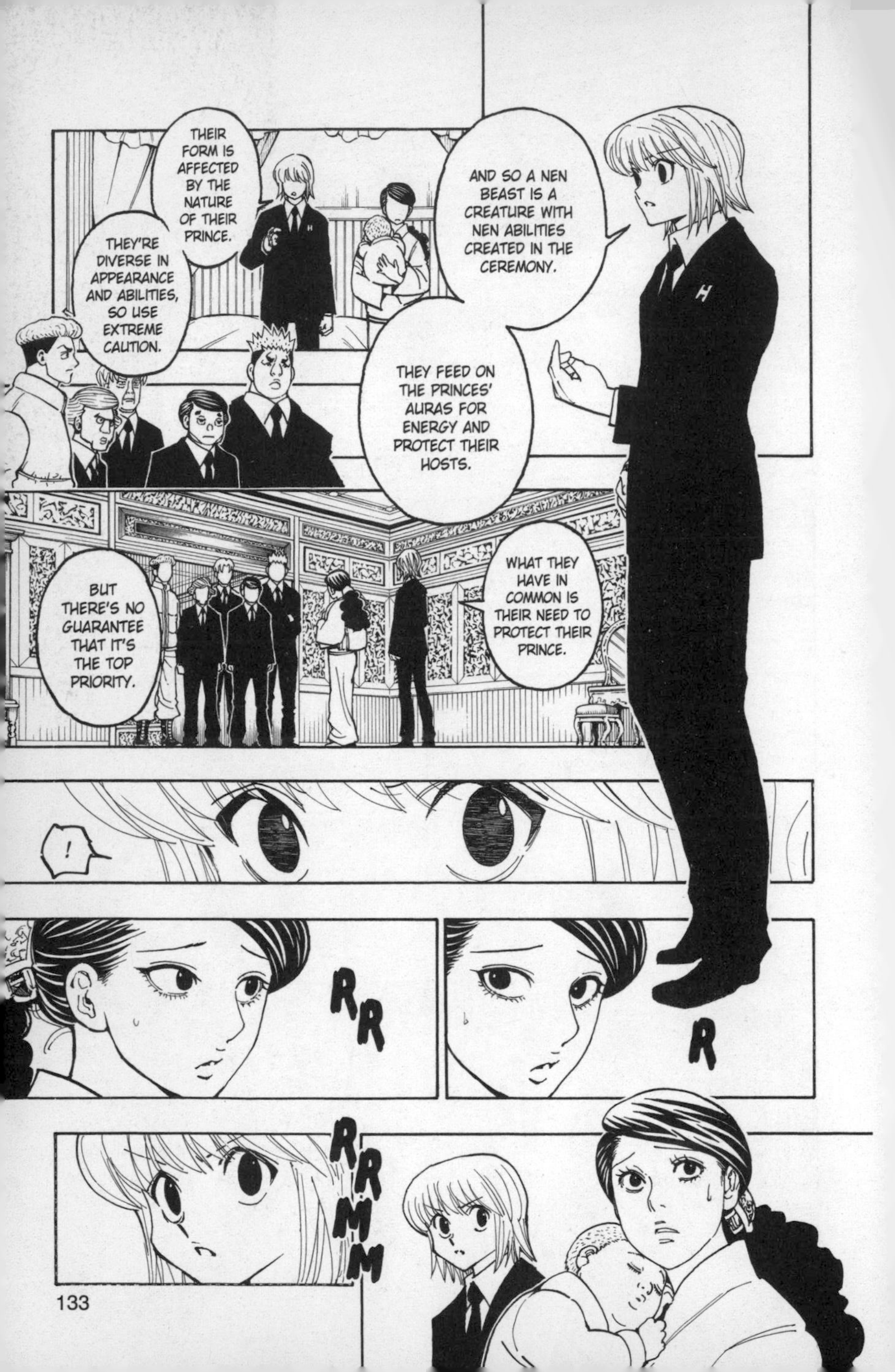
AND SO A NEN BEAST IS A CREATURE WITH NEN ABILITIES CREATED IN THE CEREMONY.
THEY FEED ON THE PRINCES' AURAS FOR ENERGY AND PROTECT THEIR HOSTS.
THEIR FORM IS AFFECTED BY THE NATURE OF THEIR PRINCE.
THEY'RE DIVERSE IN APPEARANCE AND ABILITIES, SO USE EXTREME CAUTION.
WHAT THEY HAVE IN COMMON IS THEIR NEED TO PROTECT THEIR PRINCE.
BUT THERE'S NO GUARANTEE THAT IT'S THE TOP PRIORITY.
!
R
RR
RRRMM

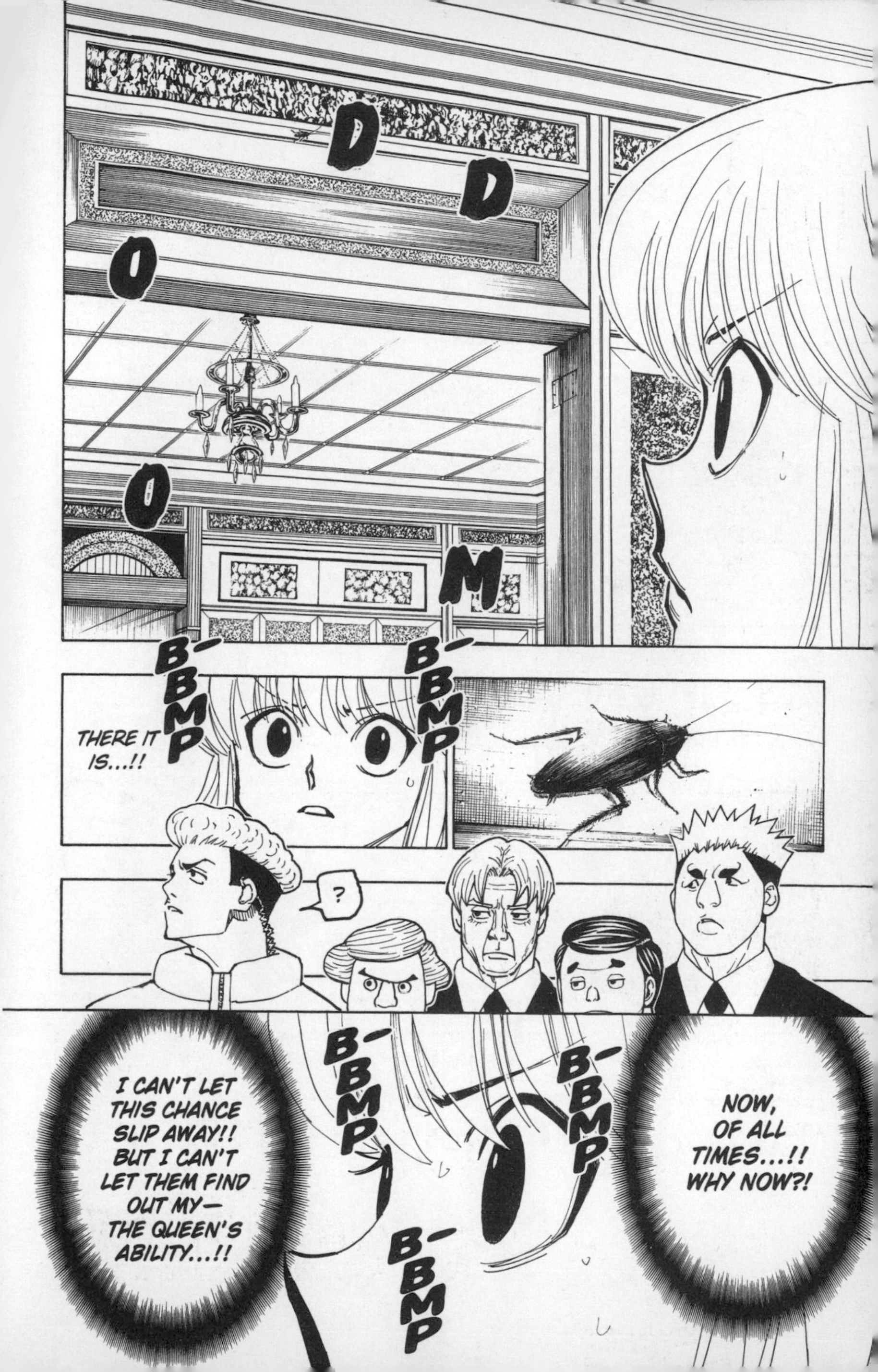

DDOOM
B-BBMP
B-BBMP
THERE IT IS...!!
?
NOW, OF ALL TIMES...!! WHY NOW?!
B-BBMP
B-BBMP
B-BBMP
I CAN'T LET THIS CHANCE SLIP AWAY!! BUT I CAN'T LET THEM FIND OUT MY— THE QUEEN'S ABILITY...!!

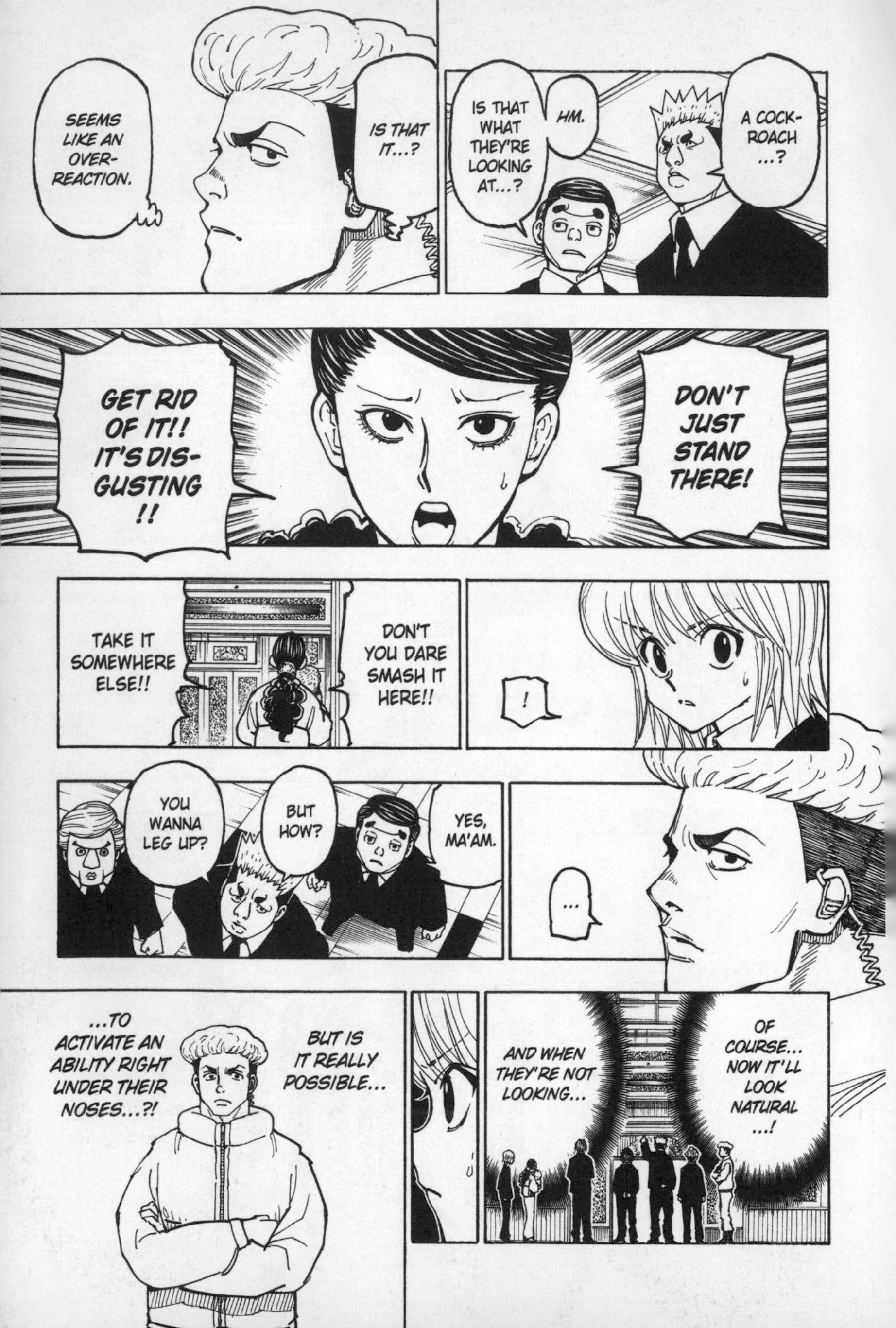
A COCK-ROACH ...?
HM.
IS THAT WHAT THEY'RE LOOKING AT...?
IS THAT IT...?
SEEMS LIKE AN OVER-REACTION.
DON'T JUST STAND THERE!
GET RID OF IT!! IT'S DIS-GUSTING !!
!
DON'T YOU DARE SMASH IT HERE!!
TAKE IT SOMEWHERE ELSE!!
...
YES, MA'AM.
BUT HOW?
YOU WANNA LEG UP?
OF COURSE... NOW IT'LL LOOK NATURAL ...!
AND WHEN THEY'RE NOT LOOKING...
BUT IS IT REALLY POSSIBLE...
...TO ACTIVATE AN ABILITY RIGHT UNDER THEIR NOSES...?!

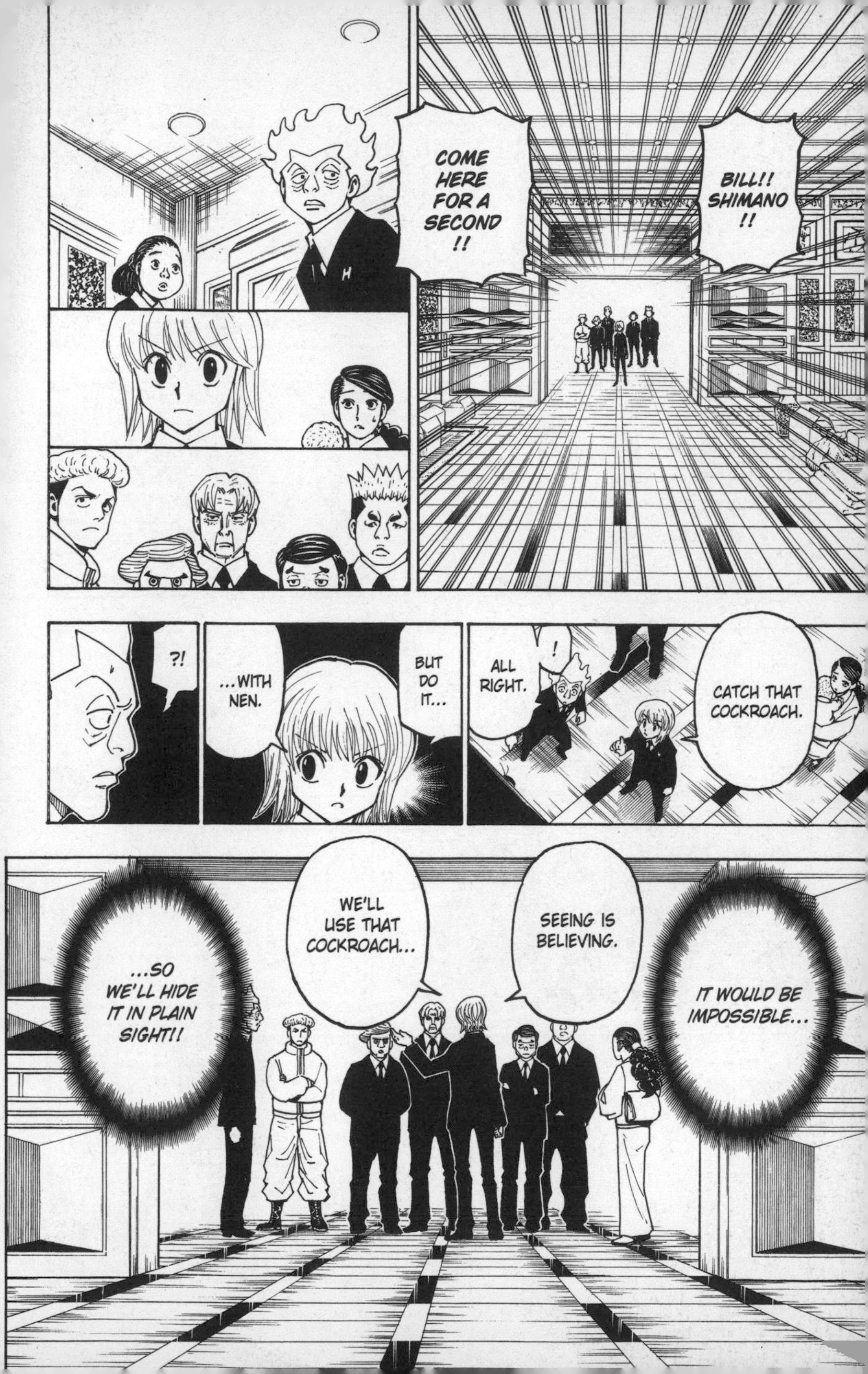
BILL!! SHIMANO !!
COME HERE FOR A SECOND !!
CATCH THAT COCKROACH.
!
ALL RIGHT.
BUT DO IT...
...WITH NEN.
?!
IT WOULD BE IMPOSSIBLE...
SEEING IS BELIEVING.
WE'LL USE THAT COCKROACH...
...SO WE'LL HIDE IT IN PLAIN SIGHT!!

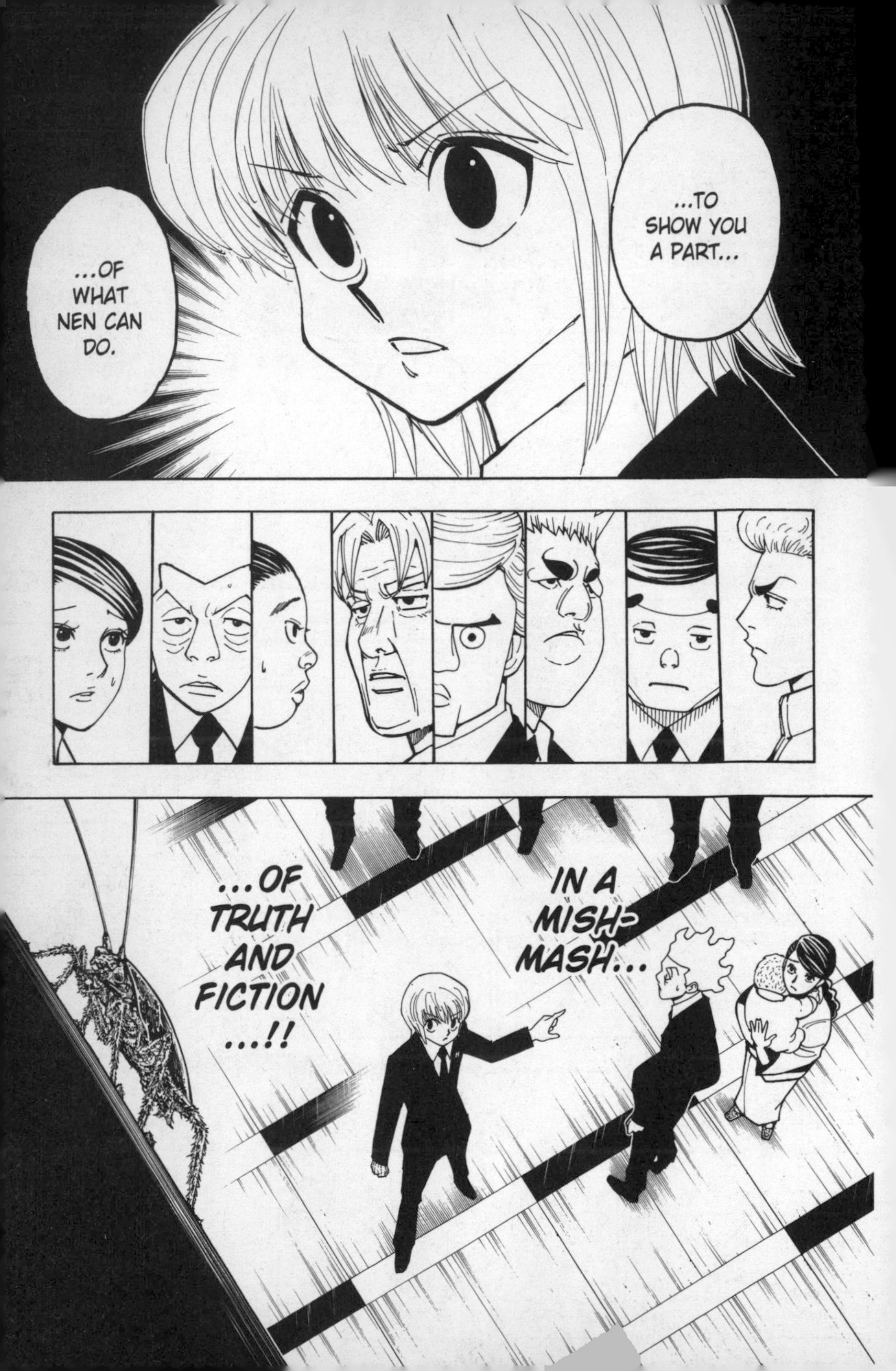
...TO SHOW YOU A PART...
...OF WHAT NEN CAN DO.
IN A MISH-MASH...
...OF TRUTH AND FICTION ...!!

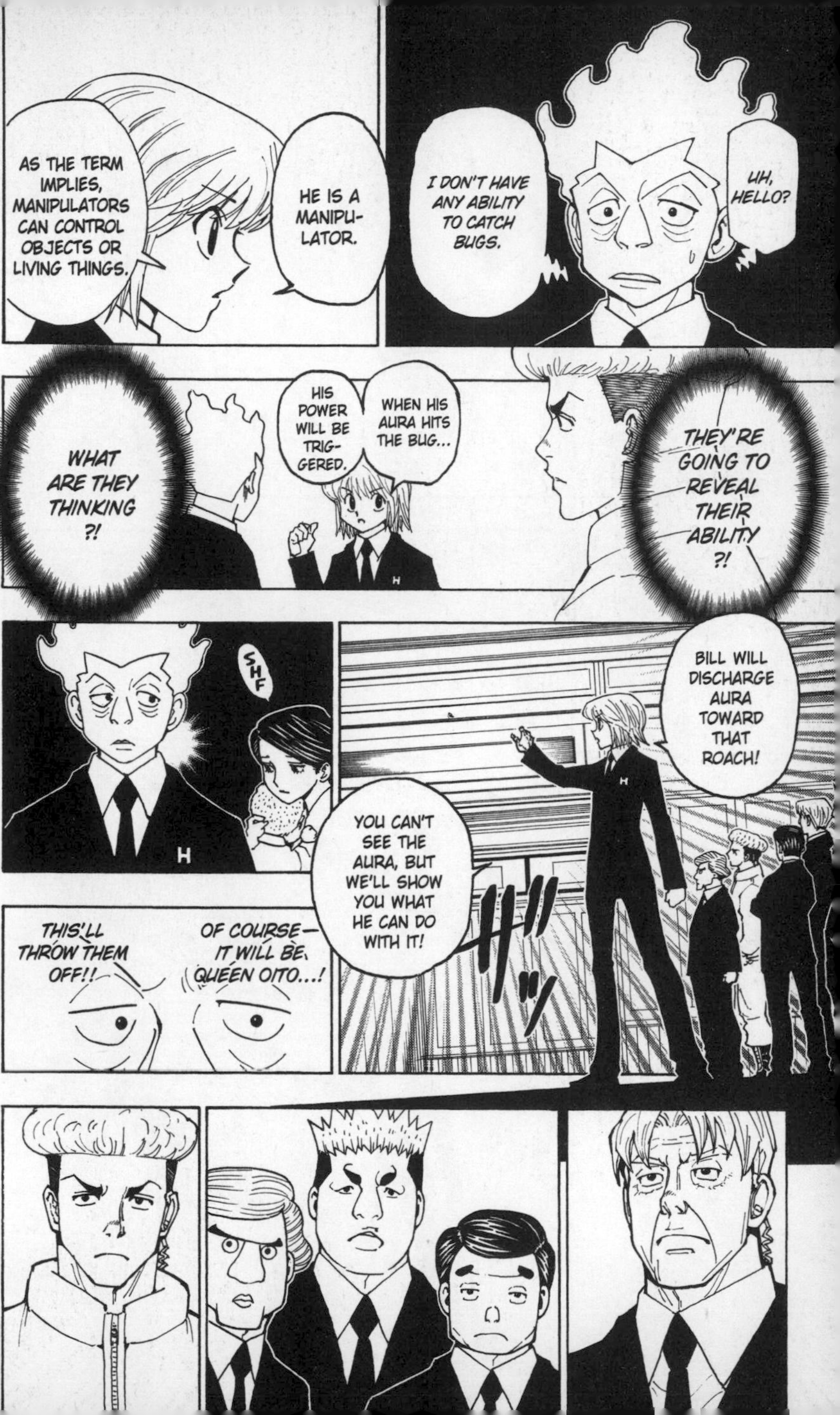
UH, HELLO?
I DON'T HAVE ANY ABILITY TO CATCH BUGS.
HE IS A MANIPU-LATOR.
AS THE TERM IMPLIES, MANIPULATORS CAN CONTROL OBJECTS OR LIVING THINGS.
THEY'RE GOING TO REVEAL THEIR ABILITY ?!
WHEN HIS AURA HITS THE BUG...
HIS POWER WILL BE TRIG-GERED.
WHAT ARE THEY THINKING ?!
BILL WILL DISCHARGE AURA TOWARD THAT ROACH!
YOU CAN'T SEE THE AURA, BUT WE'LL SHOW YOU WHAT HE CAN DO WITH IT!
SHF
OF COURSE— IT WILL BE QUEEN OITO...!
THIS'LL THROW THEM OFF!!

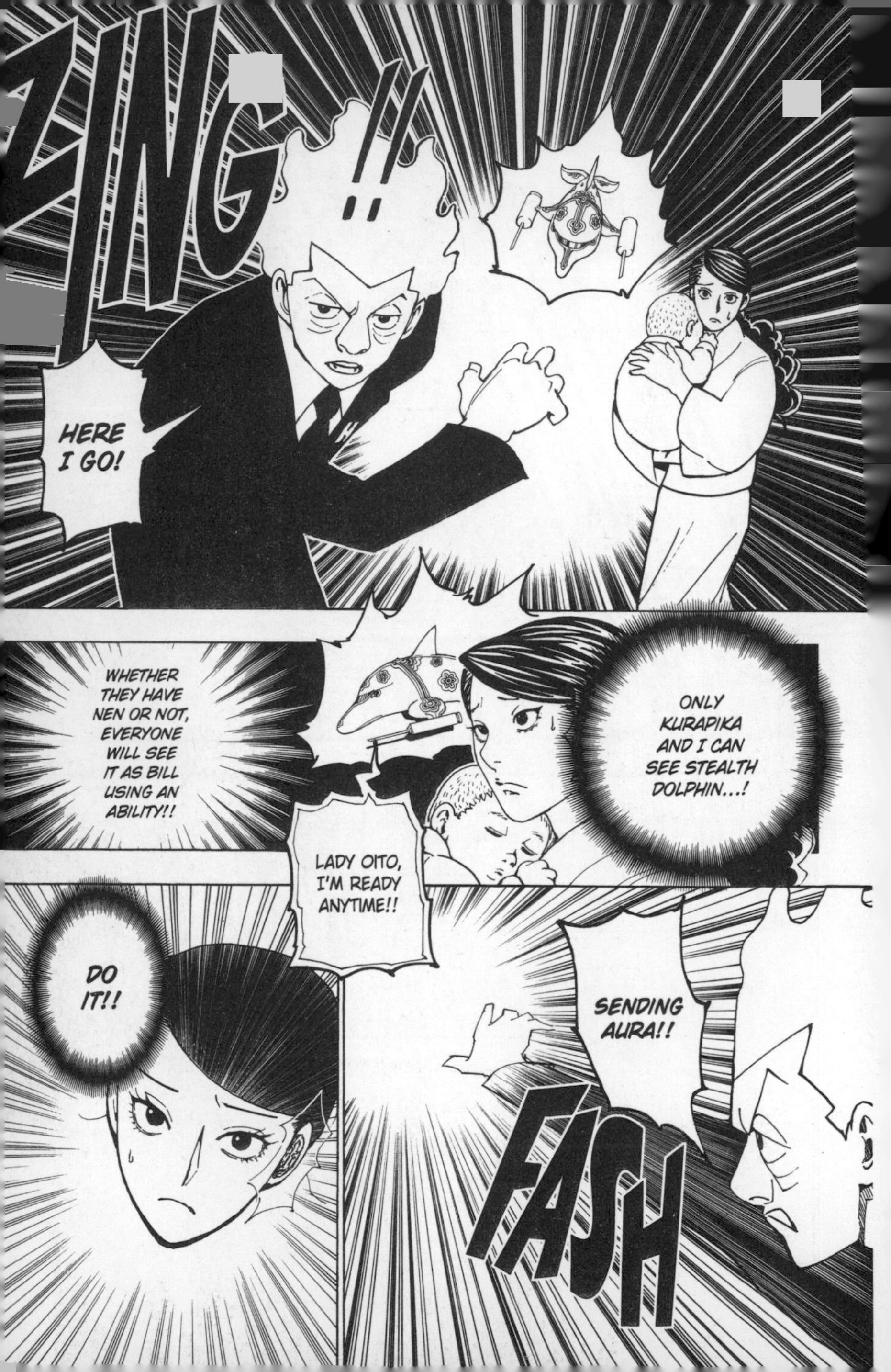
ZING!!
HERE I GO!
ONLY KURAPIKA AND I CAN SEE STEALTH DOLPHIN...!
WHETHER THEY HAVE NEN OR NOT, EVERYONE WILL SEE IT AS BILL USING AN ABILITY!!
LADY OITO, I'M READY ANYTIME!!
SENDING AURA!!
FASH
DO IT!!

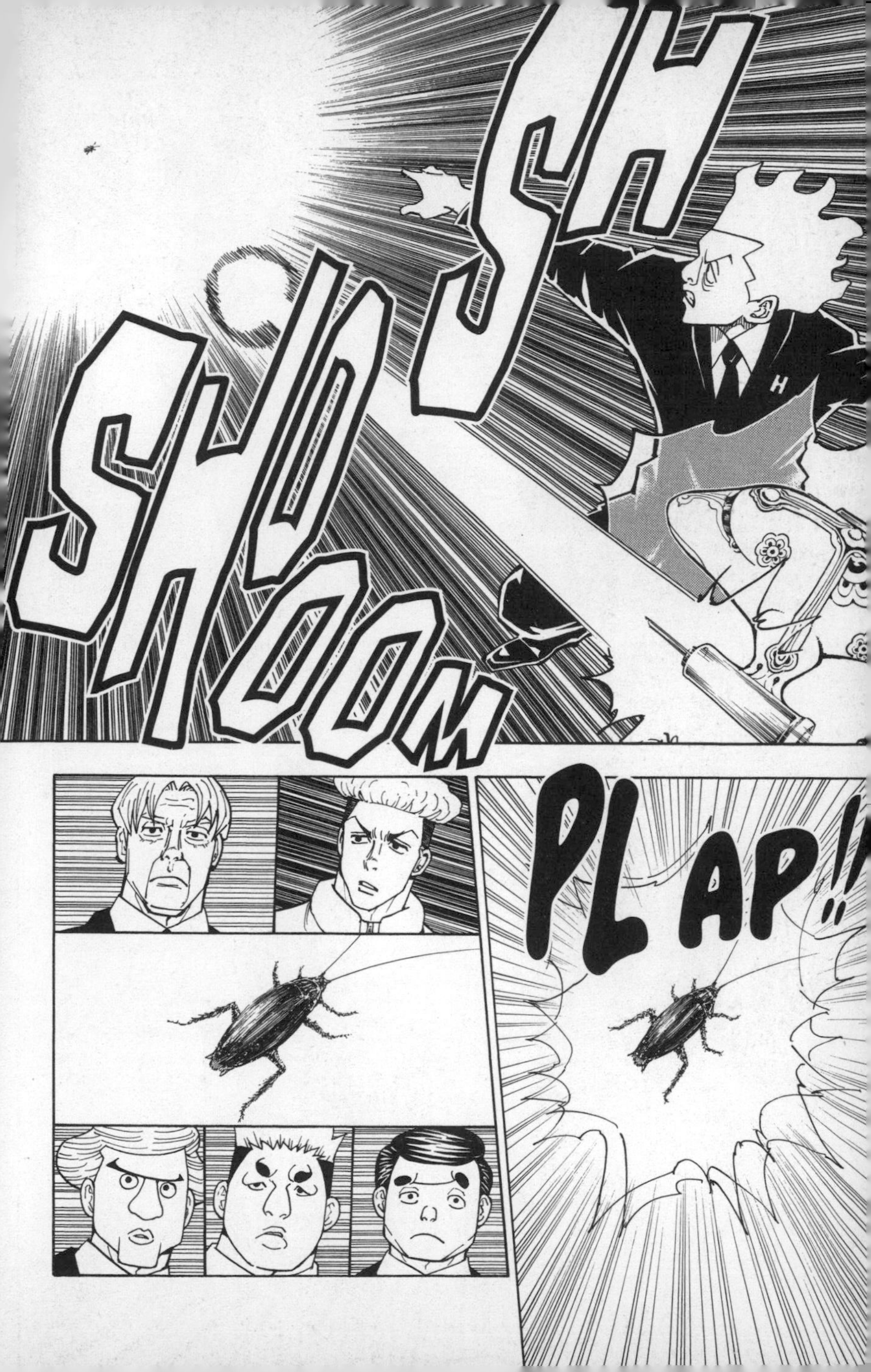
SHOOM
SHOOSH
PLAP!!

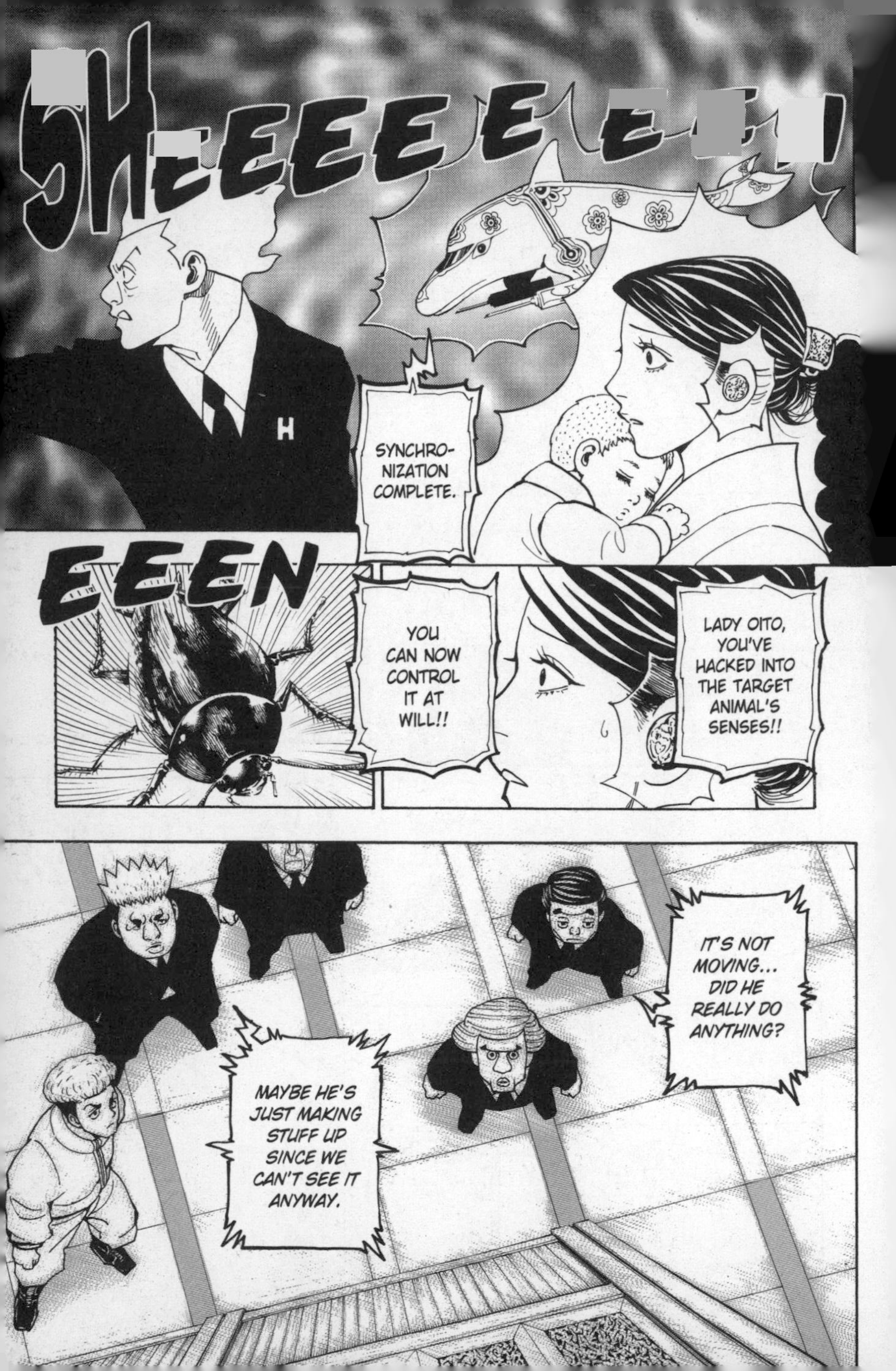
SH-EEEEEEE!
SYNCHRO-NIZATION COMPLETE.
LADY OITO, YOU'VE HACKED INTO THE TARGET ANIMAL'S SENSES!!
YOU CAN NOW CONTROL IT AT WILL!!
EEEN
IT'S NOT MOVING... DID HE REALLY DO ANYTHING?
MAYBE HE'S JUST MAKING STUFF UP SINCE WE CAN'T SEE IT ANYWAY.

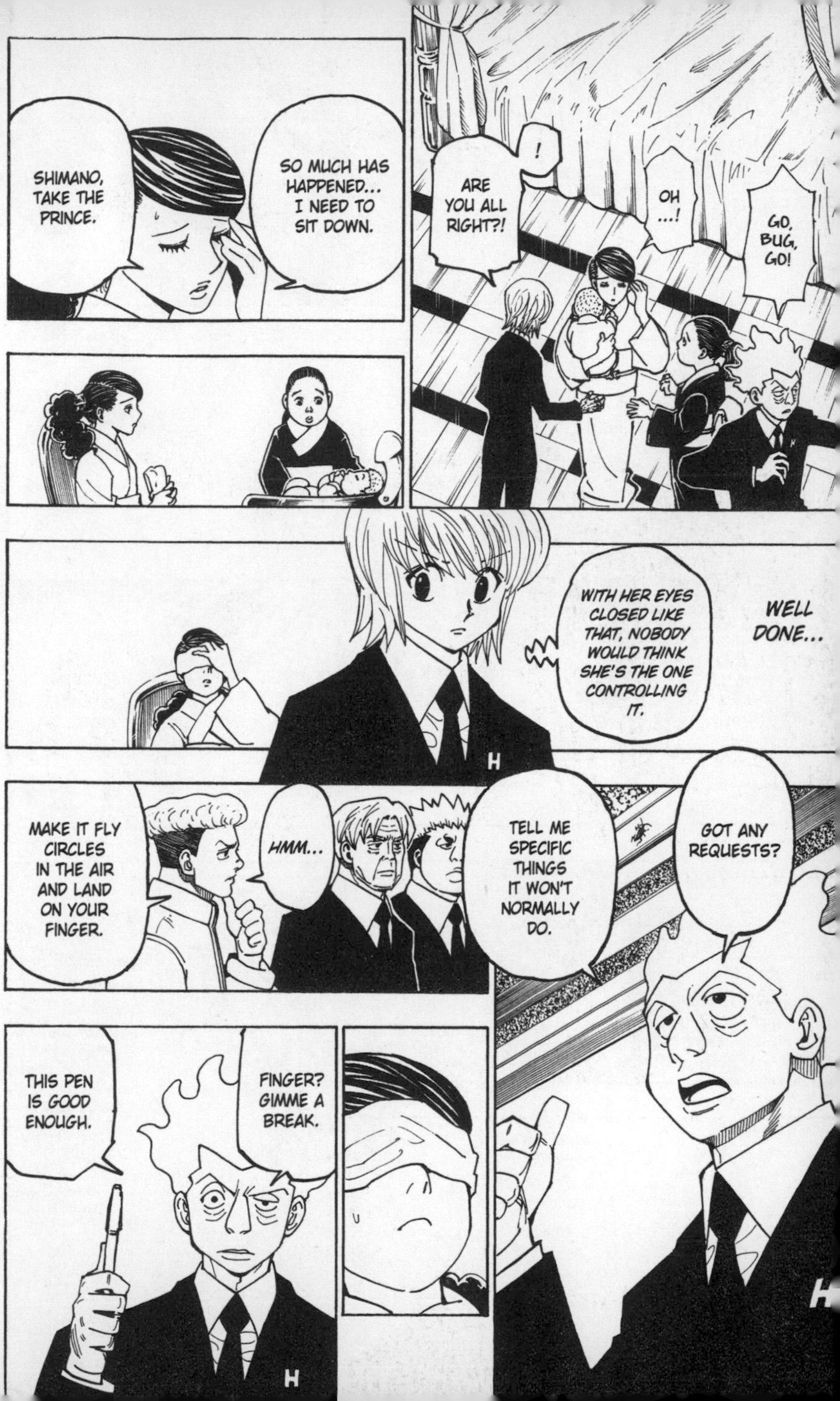
GO, BUG, GO!
OH ...!
!
ARE YOU ALL RIGHT?!
SO MUCH HAS HAPPENED... I NEED TO SIT DOWN.
SHIMANO, TAKE THE PRINCE.
WELL DONE...
WITH HER EYES CLOSED LIKE THAT, NOBODY WOULD THINK SHE'S THE ONE CONTROLLING IT.
GOT ANY REQUESTS?
TELL ME SPECIFIC THINGS IT WON'T NORMALLY DO.
HMM...
MAKE IT FLY CIRCLES IN THE AIR AND LAND ON YOUR FINGER.
FINGER? GIMME A BREAK.
THIS PEN IS GOOD ENOUGH.

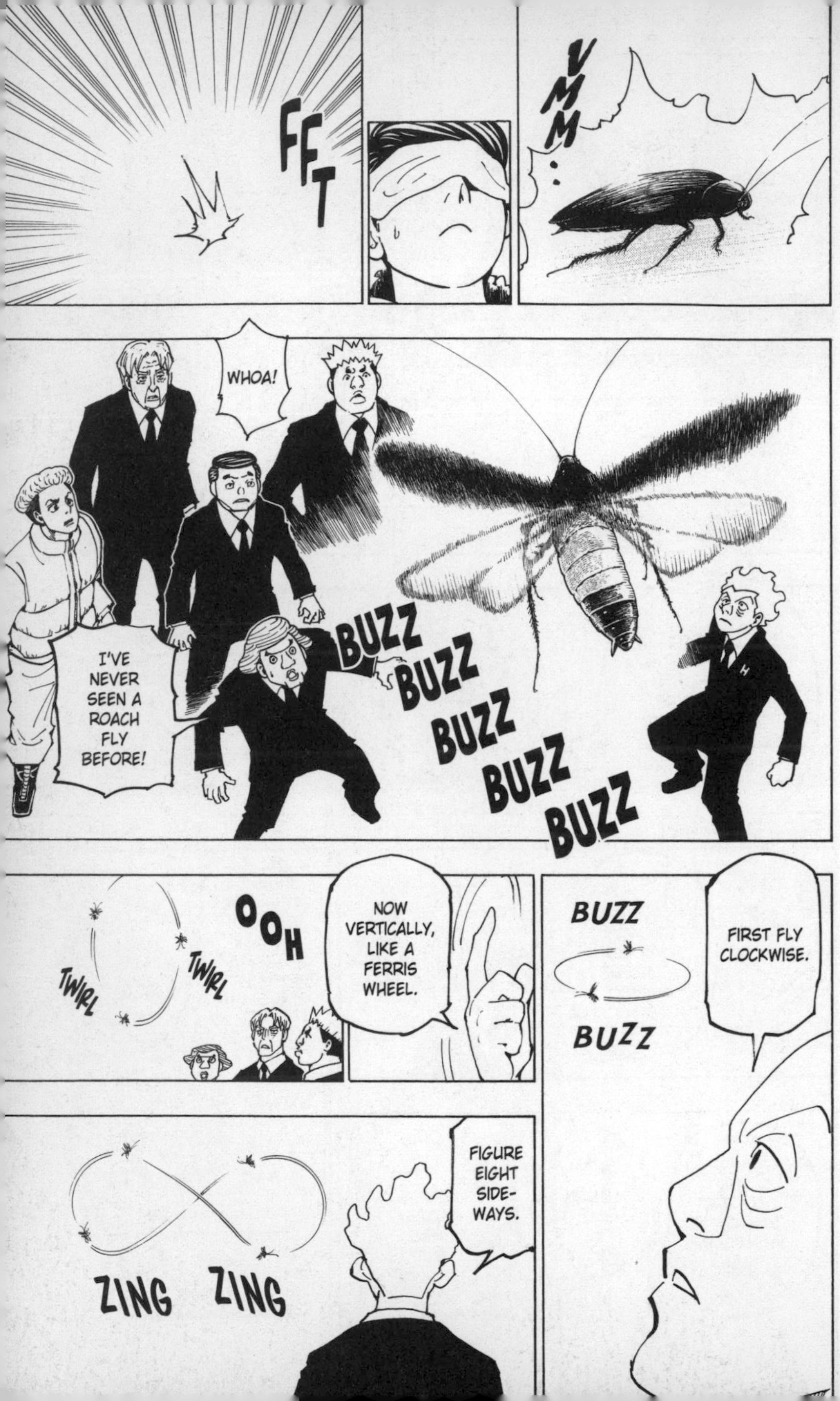
VMM...
FFT
WHOA!
BUZZ BUZZ BUZZ BUZZ BUZZ
I'VE NEVER SEEN A ROACH FLY BEFORE!
BUZZ
FIRST FLY CLOCKWISE.
BUZZ
NOW VERTICALLY, LIKE A FERRIS WHEEL.
OOH
TWIRL
TWIRL
FIGURE EIGHT SIDEWAYS.
ZING ZING

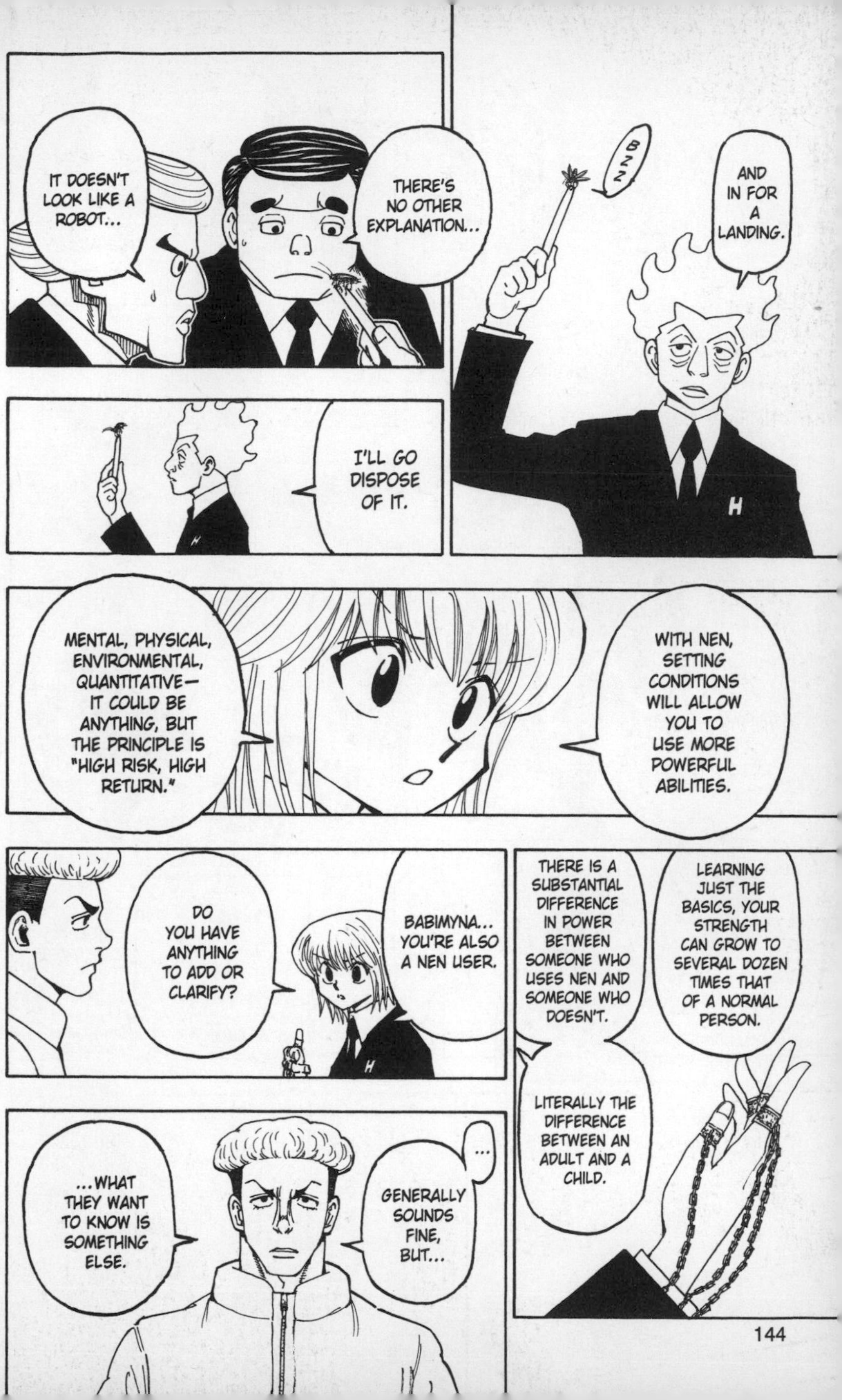
BZZ
AND IN FOR A LANDING.
THERE'S NO OTHER EXPLANATION...
IT DOESN'T LOOK LIKE A ROBOT...
I'LL GO DISPOSE OF IT.
WITH NEN, SETTING CONDITIONS WILL ALLOW YOU TO USE MORE POWERFUL ABILITIES.
MENTAL, PHYSICAL, ENVIRONMENTAL, QUANTITATIVE—IT COULD BE ANYTHING, BUT THE PRINCIPLE IS "HIGH RISK, HIGH RETURN."
LEARNING JUST THE BASICS, YOUR STRENGTH CAN GROW TO SEVERAL DOZEN TIMES THAT OF A NORMAL PERSON.
THERE IS A SUBSTANTIAL DIFFERENCE IN POWER BETWEEN SOMEONE WHO USES NEN AND SOMEONE WHO DOESN'T.
LITERALLY THE DIFFERENCE BETWEEN AN ADULT AND A CHILD.
BABIMYNA... YOU'RE ALSO A NEN USER.
DO YOU HAVE ANYTHING TO ADD OR CLARIFY?
...
GENERALLY SOUNDS FINE, BUT...
...WHAT THEY WANT TO KNOW IS SOMETHING ELSE.

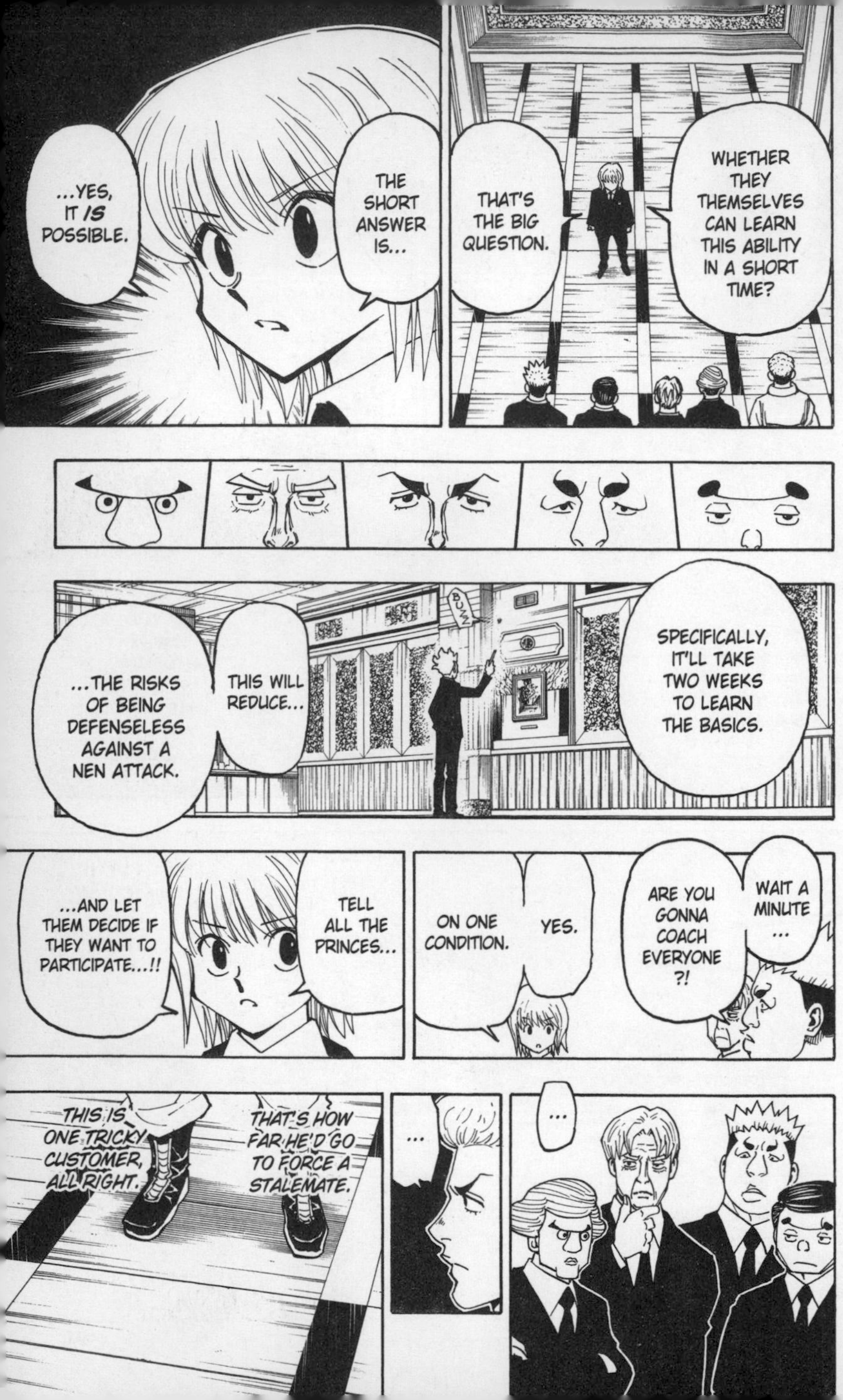

WHETHER THEY THEMSELVES CAN LEARN THIS ABILITY IN A SHORT TIME?
THAT'S THE BIG QUESTION.
THE SHORT ANSWER IS...
...YES, IT *IS* POSSIBLE.
SPECIFICALLY, IT'LL TAKE TWO WEEKS TO LEARN THE BASICS.
BUZZ
THIS WILL REDUCE...
...THE RISKS OF BEING DEFENSELESS AGAINST A NEN ATTACK.
WAIT A MINUTE ...
ARE YOU GONNA COACH EVERYONE ?!
YES.
ON ONE CONDITION.
TELL ALL THE PRINCES...
...AND LET THEM DECIDE IF THEY WANT TO PARTICIPATE...!!
...
...
THAT'S HOW FAR HE'D GO TO FORCE A STALEMATE.
THIS IS ONE TRICKY CUSTOMER, ALL RIGHT.

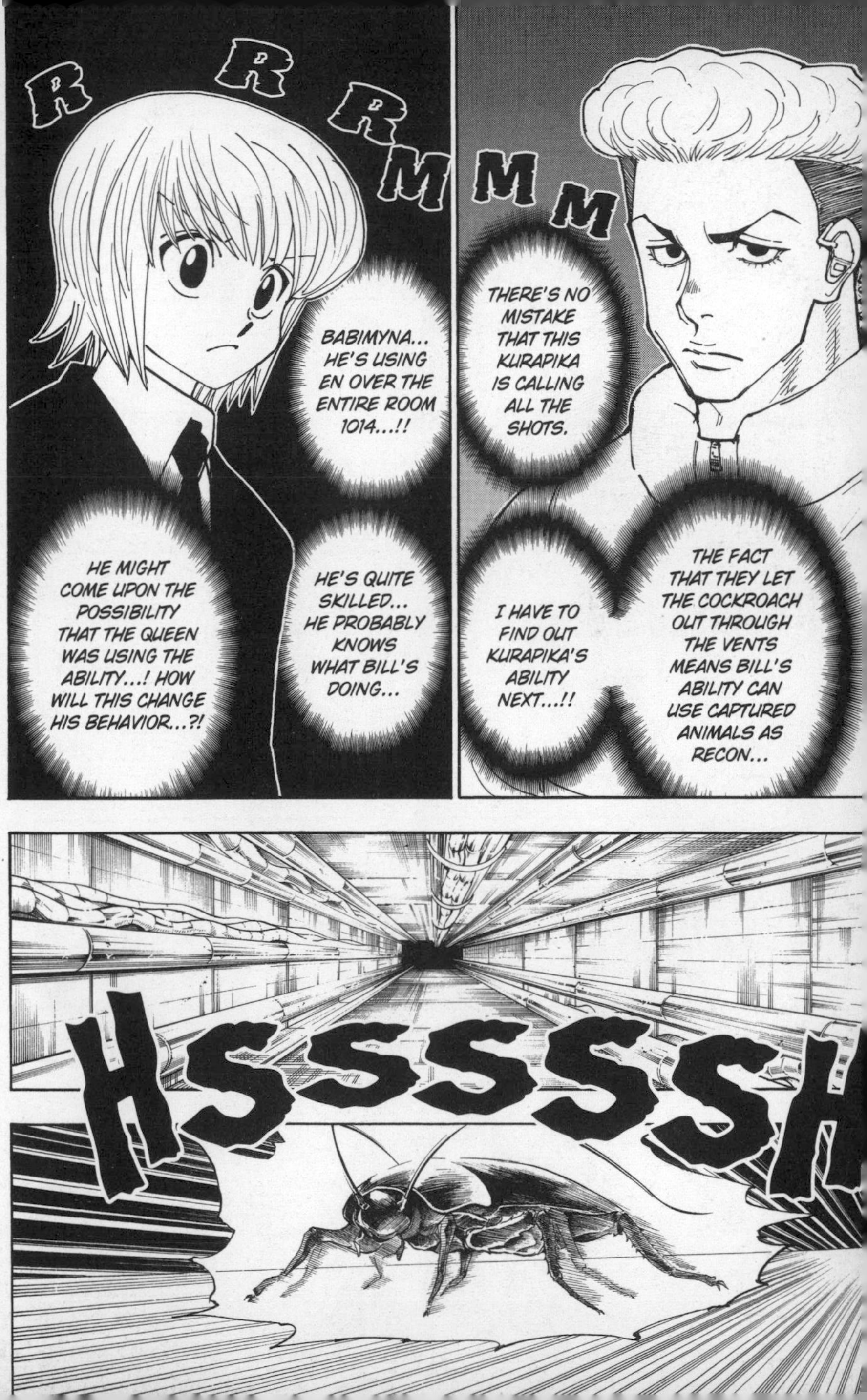

THERE'S NO MISTAKE THAT THIS KURAPIKA IS CALLING ALL THE SHOTS.
THE FACT THAT THEY LET THE COCKROACH OUT THROUGH THE VENTS MEANS BILL'S ABILITY CAN USE CAPTURED ANIMALS AS RECON...
I HAVE TO FIND OUT KURAPIKA'S ABILITY NEXT...!!
RRRRMMMM
BABIMYNA... HE'S USING EN OVER THE ENTIRE ROOM 1014...!!
HE'S QUITE SKILLED... HE PROBABLY KNOWS WHAT BILL'S DOING...
HE MIGHT COME UPON THE POSSIBILITY THAT THE QUEEN WAS USING THE ABILITY...! HOW WILL THIS CHANGE HIS BEHAVIOR...?!
HSSSSH

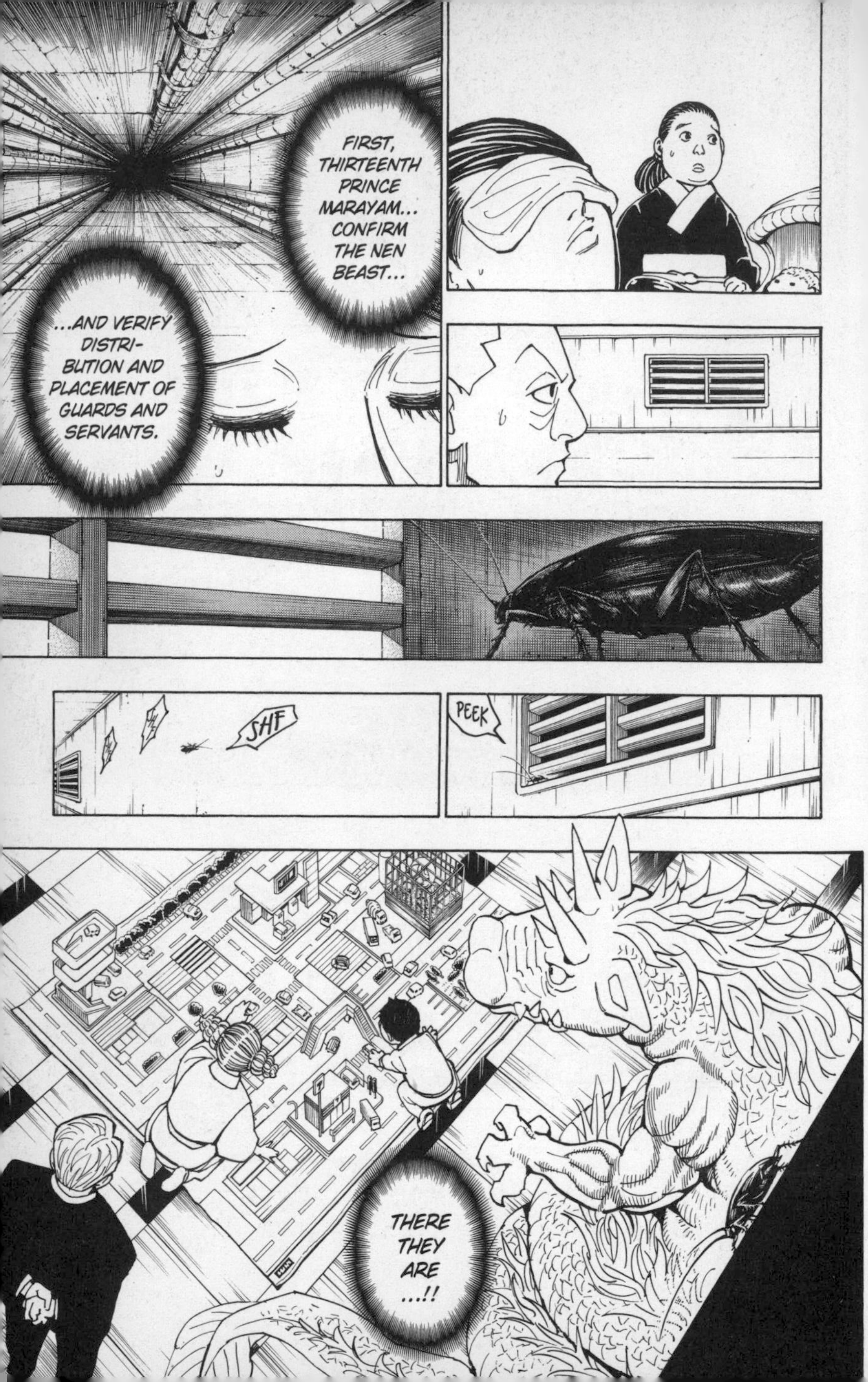
FIRST, THIRTEENTH PRINCE MARAYAM... CONFIRM THE NEN BEAST...
...AND VERIFY DISTRI-BUTION AND PLACEMENT OF GUARDS AND SERVANTS.
PEEK
SHF
THERE THEY ARE ...!!

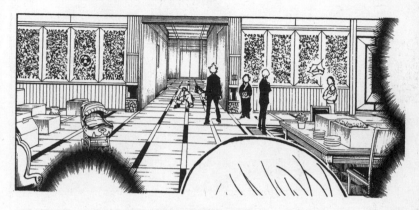

THE MANNEQUIN
CHALLENGE...NOW?!
KINDA LATE TO THE
PARTY...

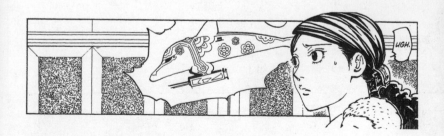

PIGS ARE
CUTE TOO...

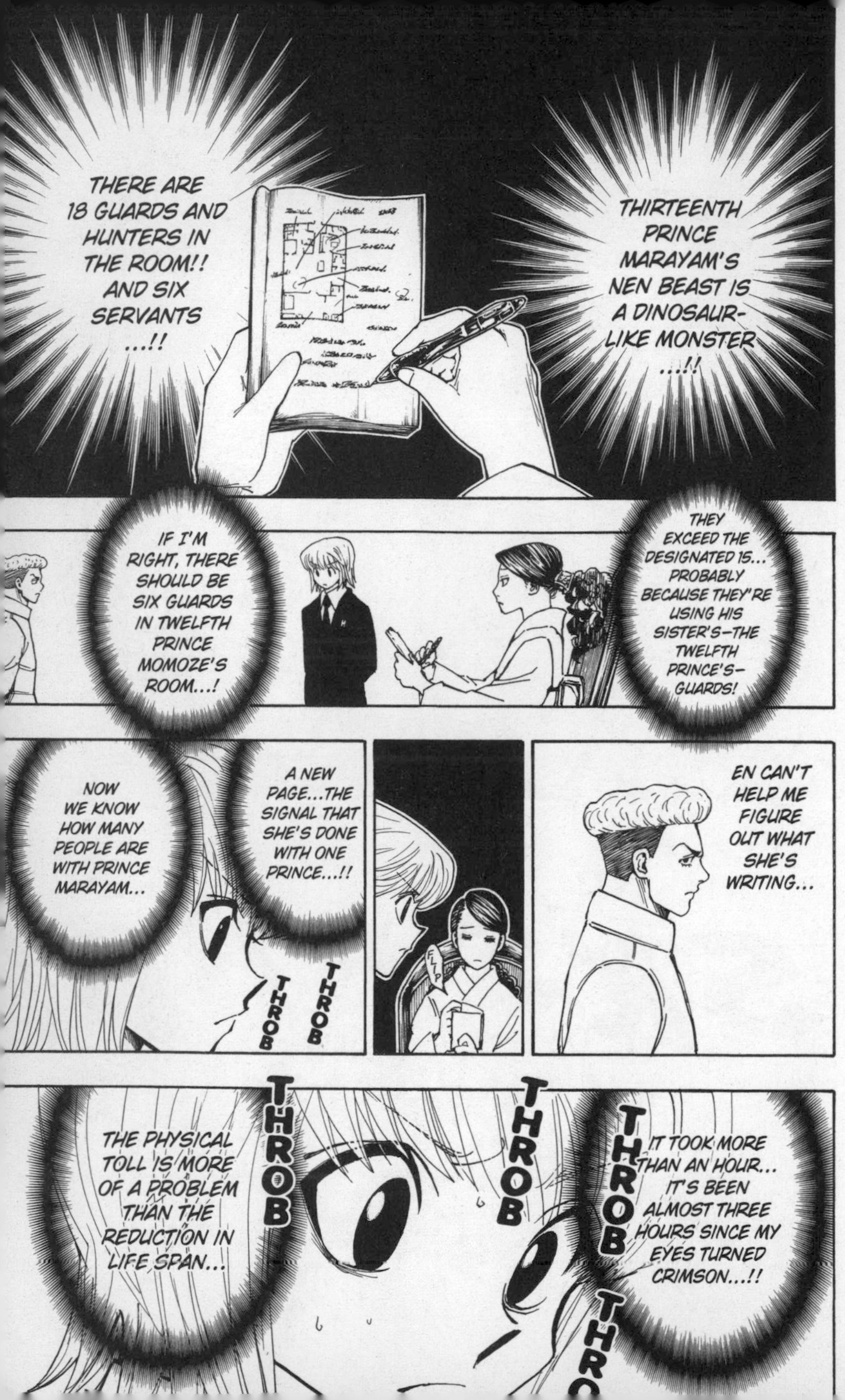
THIRTEENTH PRINCE MARAYAM'S NEN BEAST IS A DINOSAUR-LIKE MONSTER ...!!
THERE ARE 18 GUARDS AND HUNTERS IN THE ROOM!! AND SIX SERVANTS ...!!
THEY EXCEED THE DESIGNATED 15... PROBABLY BECAUSE THEY'RE USING HIS SISTER'S—THE TWELFTH PRINCE'S—GUARDS!
IF I'M RIGHT, THERE SHOULD BE SIX GUARDS IN TWELFTH PRINCE MOMOZE'S ROOM...!
EN CAN'T HELP ME FIGURE OUT WHAT SHE'S WRITING...
FLIP
A NEW PAGE...THE SIGNAL THAT SHE'S DONE WITH ONE PRINCE...!!
NOW WE KNOW HOW MANY PEOPLE ARE WITH PRINCE MARAYAM...
THROB
THROB
IT TOOK MORE THAN AN HOUR... IT'S BEEN ALMOST THREE HOURS SINCE MY EYES TURNED CRIMSON...!!
THROB
THROB
THROB
THE PHYSICAL TOLL IS MORE OF A PROBLEM THAN THE REDUCTION IN LIFE SPAN...

Chapter 368: Foul Play

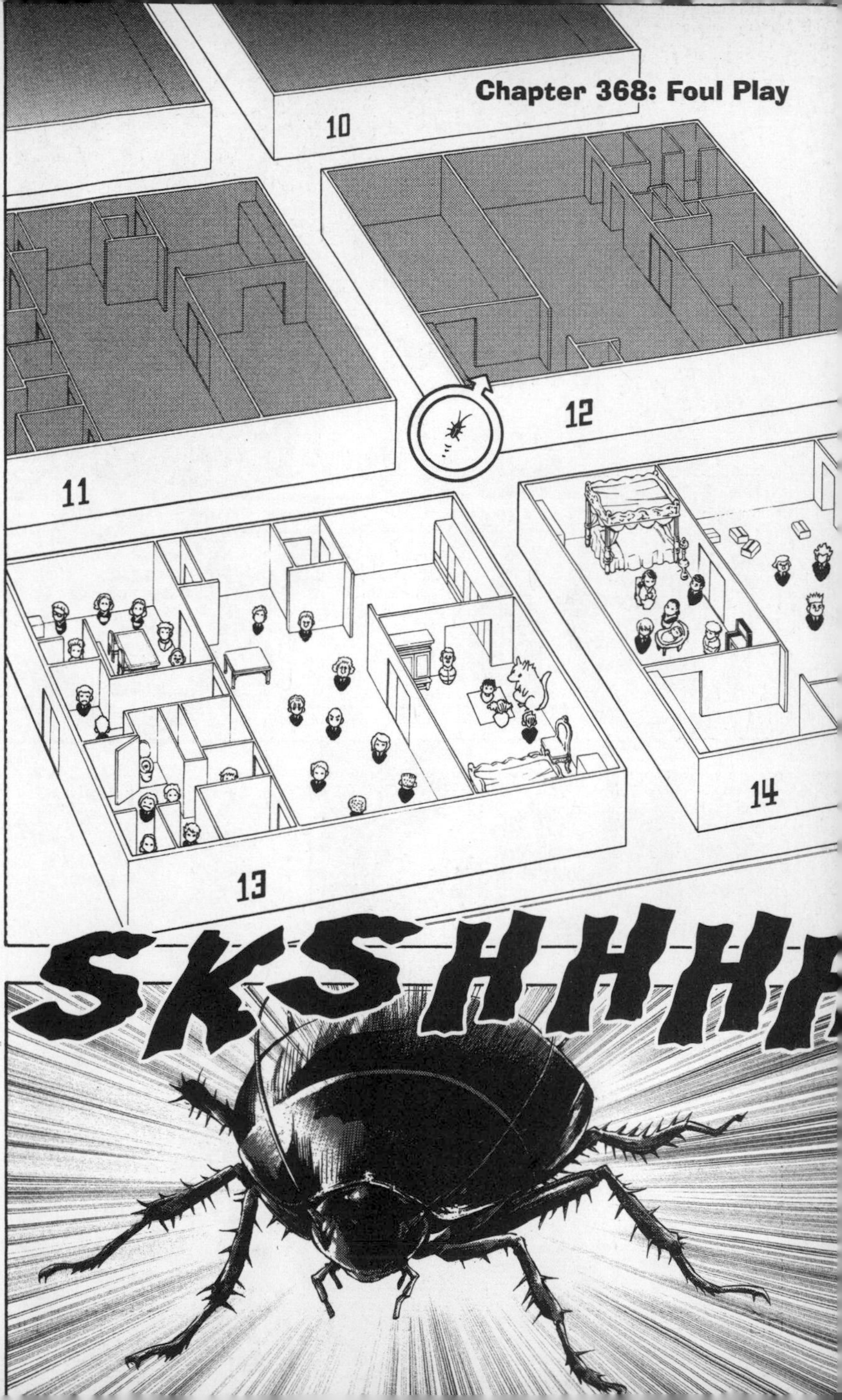
10
12
11
14
13
SKSHHH

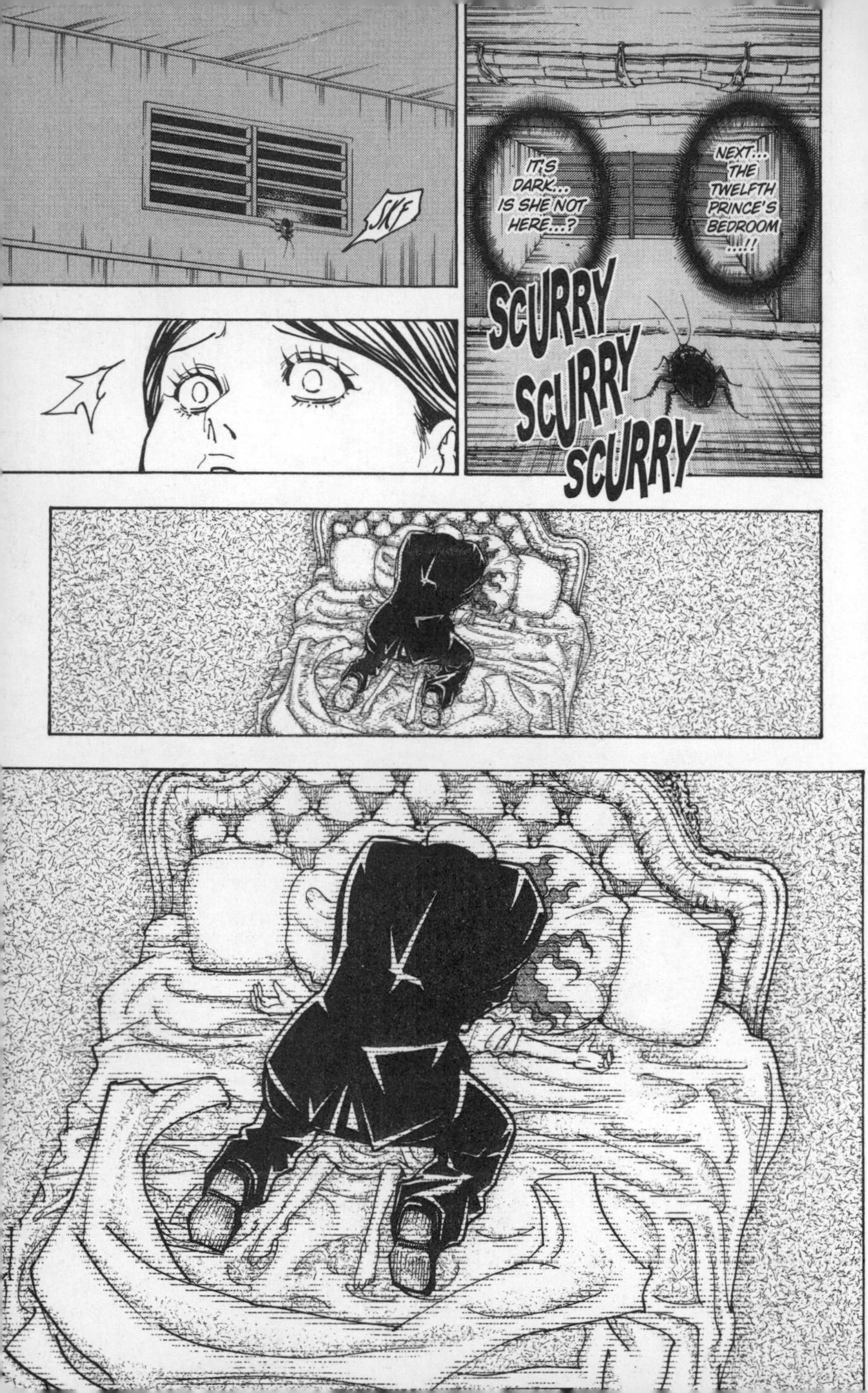
NEXT... THE TWELFTH PRINCE'S BEDROOM ...!!
IT'S DARK... IS SHE NOT HERE...?
SCURRY SCURRY SCURRY
SKF

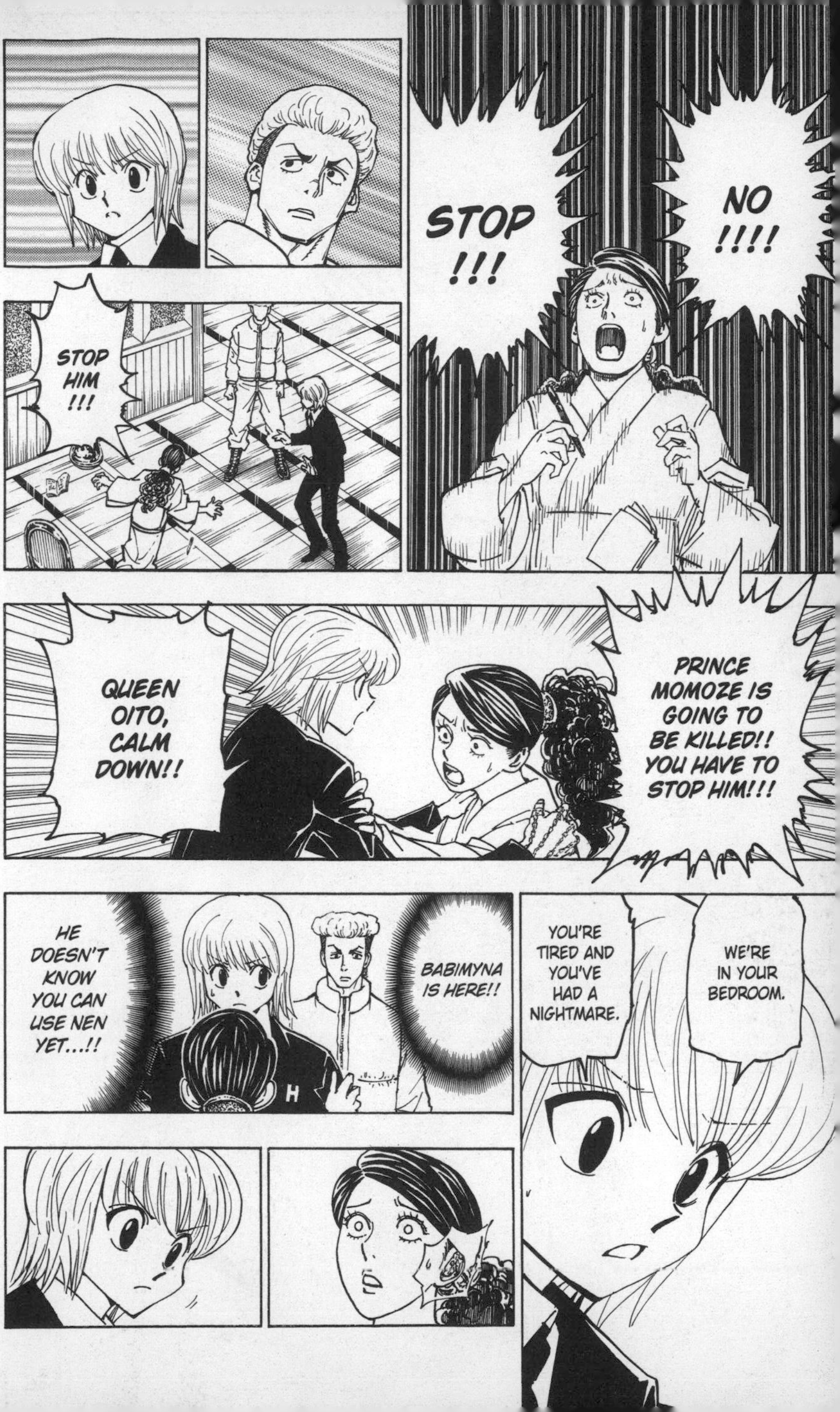
NO !!!!
STOP !!!
STOP HIM !!!
PRINCE MOMOZE IS GOING TO BE KILLED!! YOU HAVE TO STOP HIM!!!
QUEEN OITO, CALM DOWN!!
WE'RE IN YOUR BEDROOM.
YOU'RE TIRED AND YOU'VE HAD A NIGHTMARE.
BABIMYNA IS HERE!!
HE DOESN'T KNOW YOU CAN USE NEN YET...!!

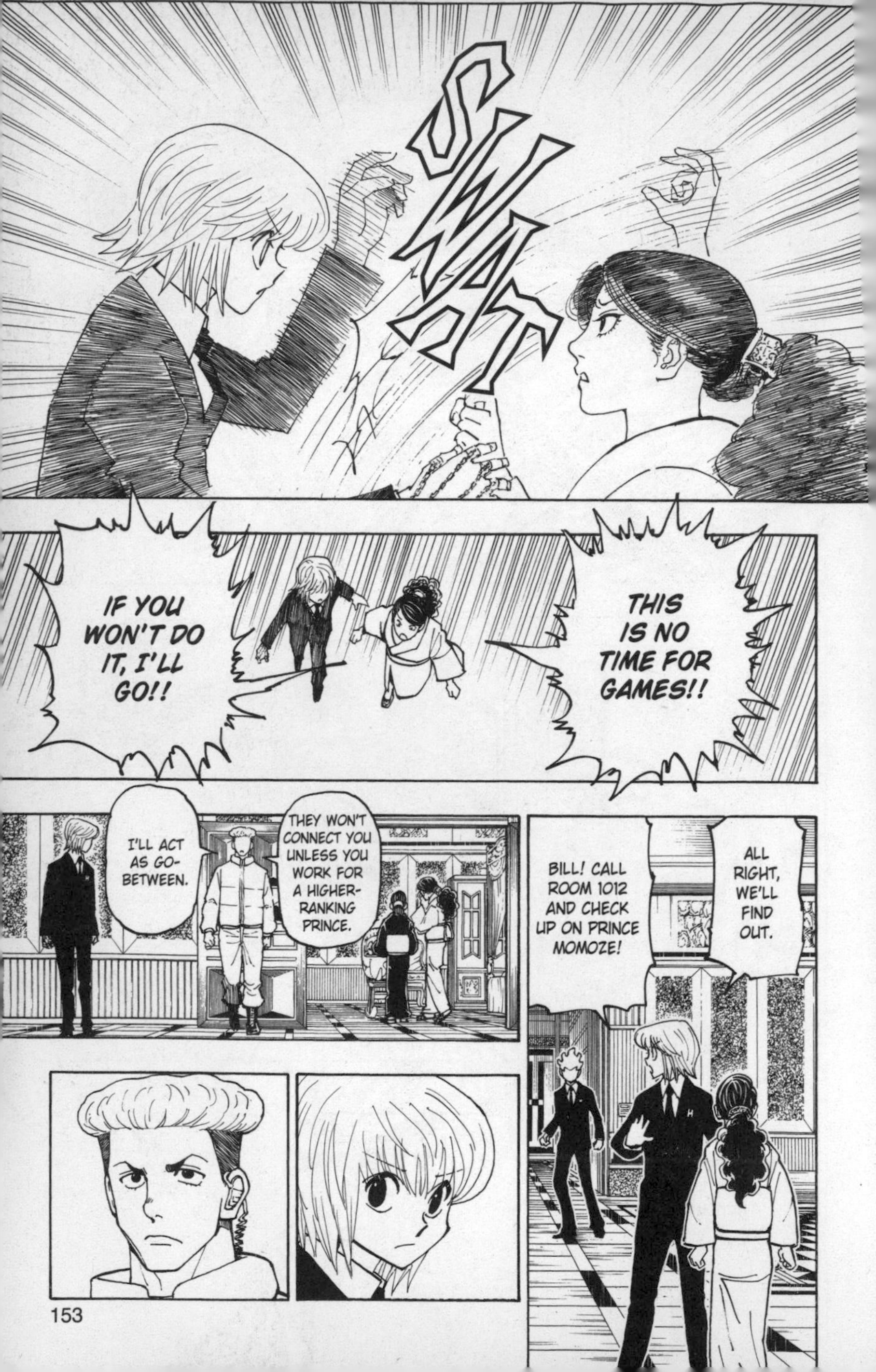
SWAT
THIS IS NO TIME FOR GAMES!!
IF YOU WON'T DO IT, I'LL GO!!
ALL RIGHT, WE'LL FIND OUT.
BILL! CALL ROOM 1012 AND CHECK UP ON PRINCE MOMOZE!
THEY WON'T CONNECT YOU UNLESS YOU WORK FOR A HIGHER-RANKING PRINCE.
I'LL ACT AS GO-BETWEEN.

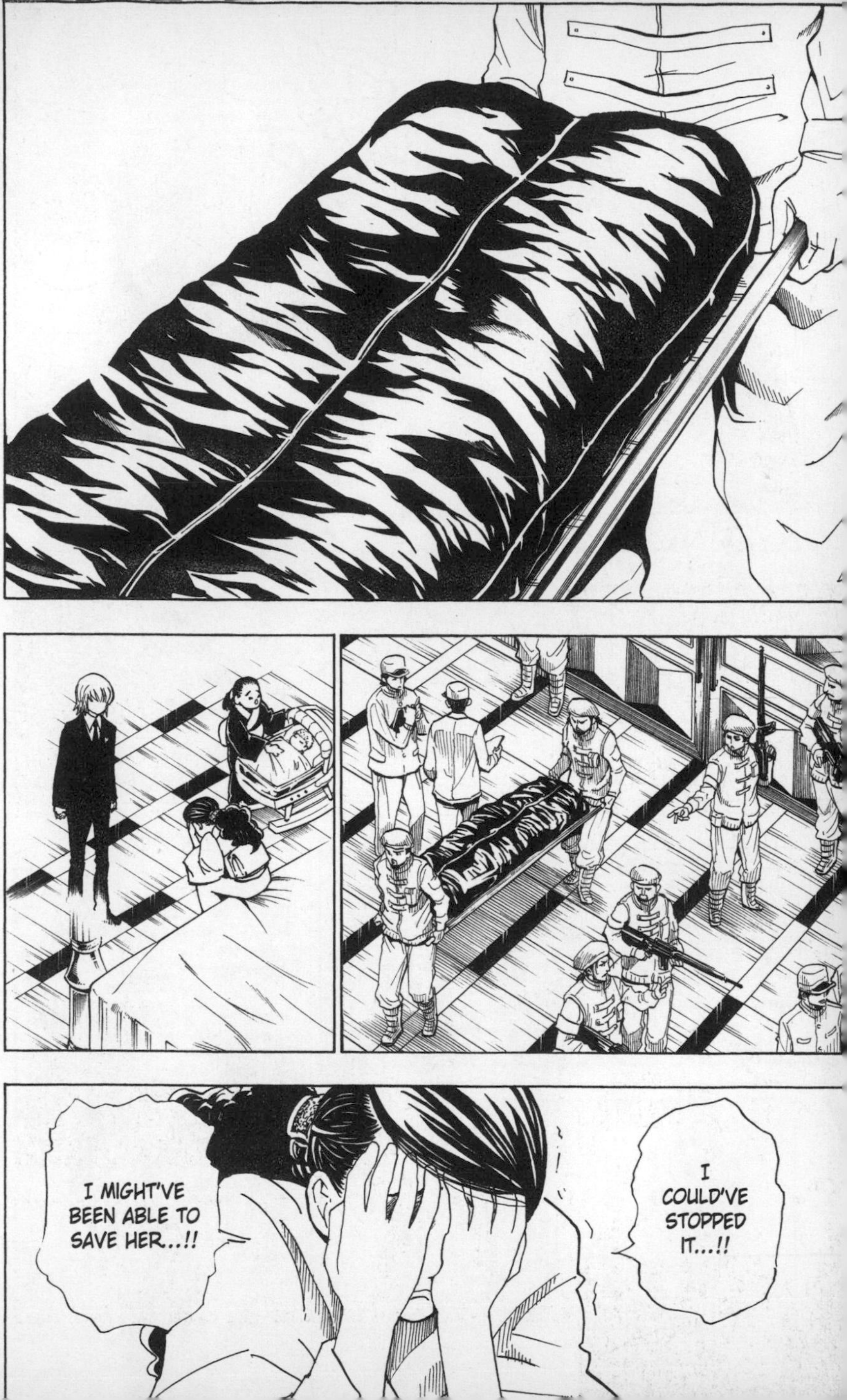
I COULD'VE STOPPED IT...!!
I MIGHT'VE BEEN ABLE TO SAVE HER...!!

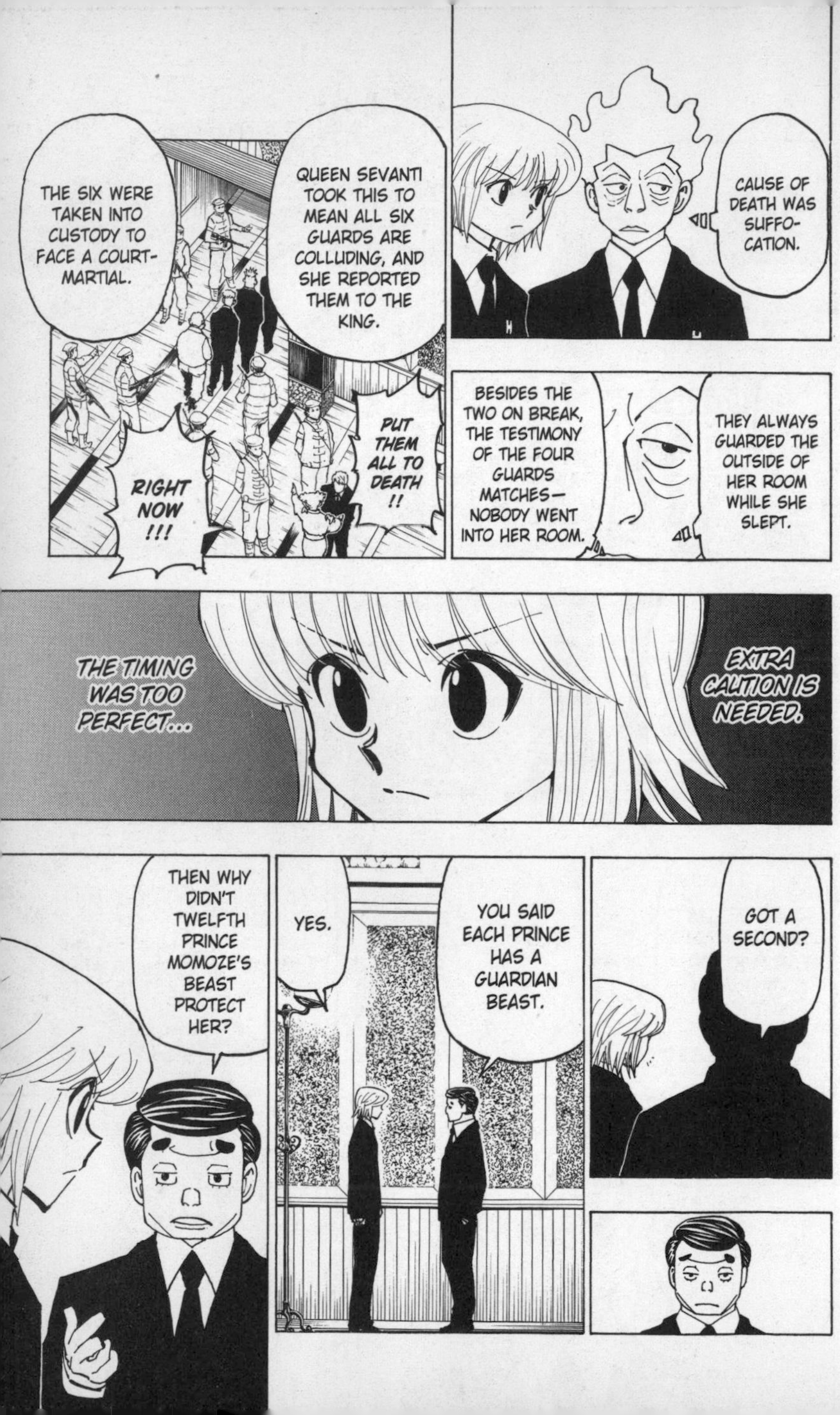

CAUSE OF DEATH WAS SUFFOCATION.
THEY ALWAYS GUARDED THE OUTSIDE OF HER ROOM WHILE SHE SLEPT.
BESIDES THE TWO ON BREAK, THE TESTIMONY OF THE FOUR GUARDS MATCHES— NOBODY WENT INTO HER ROOM.
QUEEN SEVANTI TOOK THIS TO MEAN ALL SIX GUARDS ARE COLLUDING, AND SHE REPORTED THEM TO THE KING.
THE SIX WERE TAKEN INTO CUSTODY TO FACE A COURT-MARTIAL.
PUT THEM ALL TO DEATH !!
RIGHT NOW !!!
EXTRA CAUTION IS NEEDED.
THE TIMING WAS TOO PERFECT...
GOT A SECOND?
YOU SAID EACH PRINCE HAS A GUARDIAN BEAST.
YES.
THEN WHY DIDN'T TWELFTH PRINCE MOMOZE'S BEAST PROTECT HER?

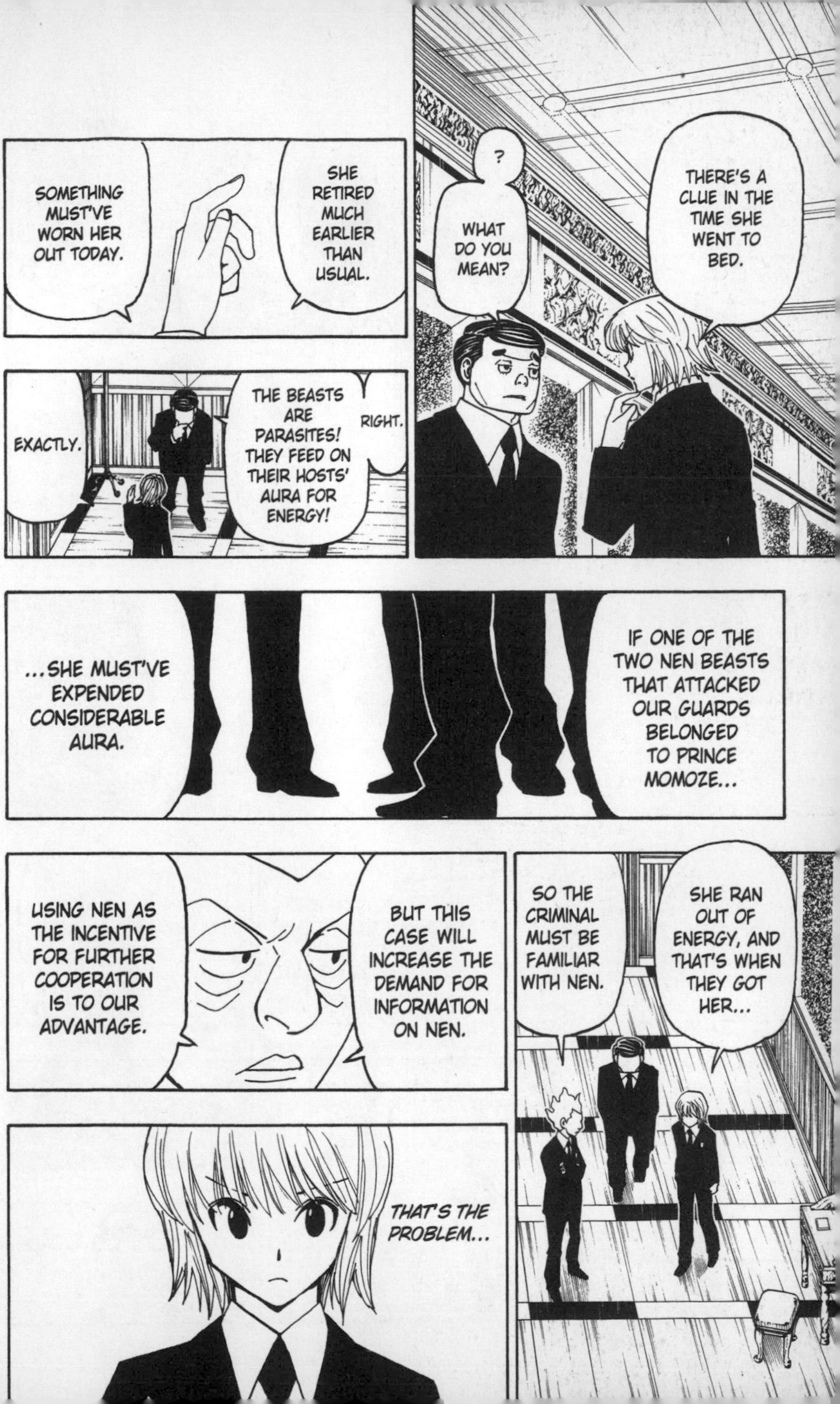
THERE'S A CLUE IN THE TIME SHE WENT TO BED.
?
WHAT DO YOU MEAN?
SHE RETIRED MUCH EARLIER THAN USUAL.
SOMETHING MUST'VE WORN HER OUT TODAY.
RIGHT.
THE BEASTS ARE PARASITES! THEY FEED ON THEIR HOSTS' AURA FOR ENERGY!
EXACTLY.
IF ONE OF THE TWO NEN BEASTS THAT ATTACKED OUR GUARDS BELONGED TO PRINCE MOMOZE...
...SHE MUST'VE EXPENDED CONSIDERABLE AURA.
SHE RAN OUT OF ENERGY, AND THAT'S WHEN THEY GOT HER...
SO THE CRIMINAL MUST BE FAMILIAR WITH NEN.
BUT THIS CASE WILL INCREASE THE DEMAND FOR INFORMATION ON NEN.
USING NEN AS THE INCENTIVE FOR FURTHER COOPERATION IS TO OUR ADVANTAGE.
THAT'S THE PROBLEM...

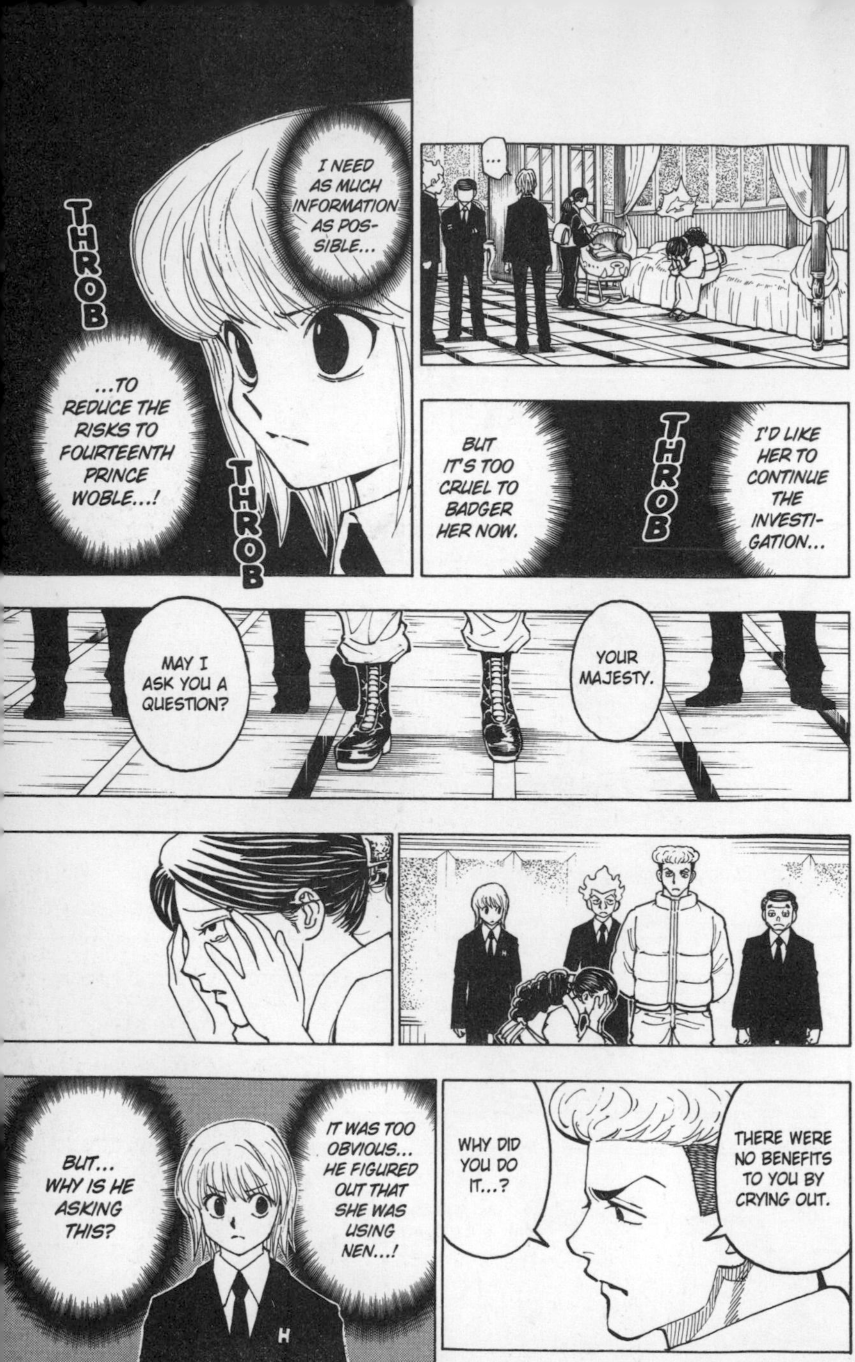
...
I'D LIKE HER TO CONTINUE THE INVESTIGATION...
THROB
BUT IT'S TOO CRUEL TO BADGER HER NOW.
I NEED AS MUCH INFORMATION AS POSSIBLE...
THROB
...TO REDUCE THE RISKS TO FOURTEENTH PRINCE WOBLE...!
THROB
YOUR MAJESTY.
MAY I ASK YOU A QUESTION?
THERE WERE NO BENEFITS TO YOU BY CRYING OUT.
WHY DID YOU DO IT...?
IT WAS TOO OBVIOUS... HE FIGURED OUT THAT SHE WAS USING NEN...!
BUT... WHY IS HE ASKING THIS?

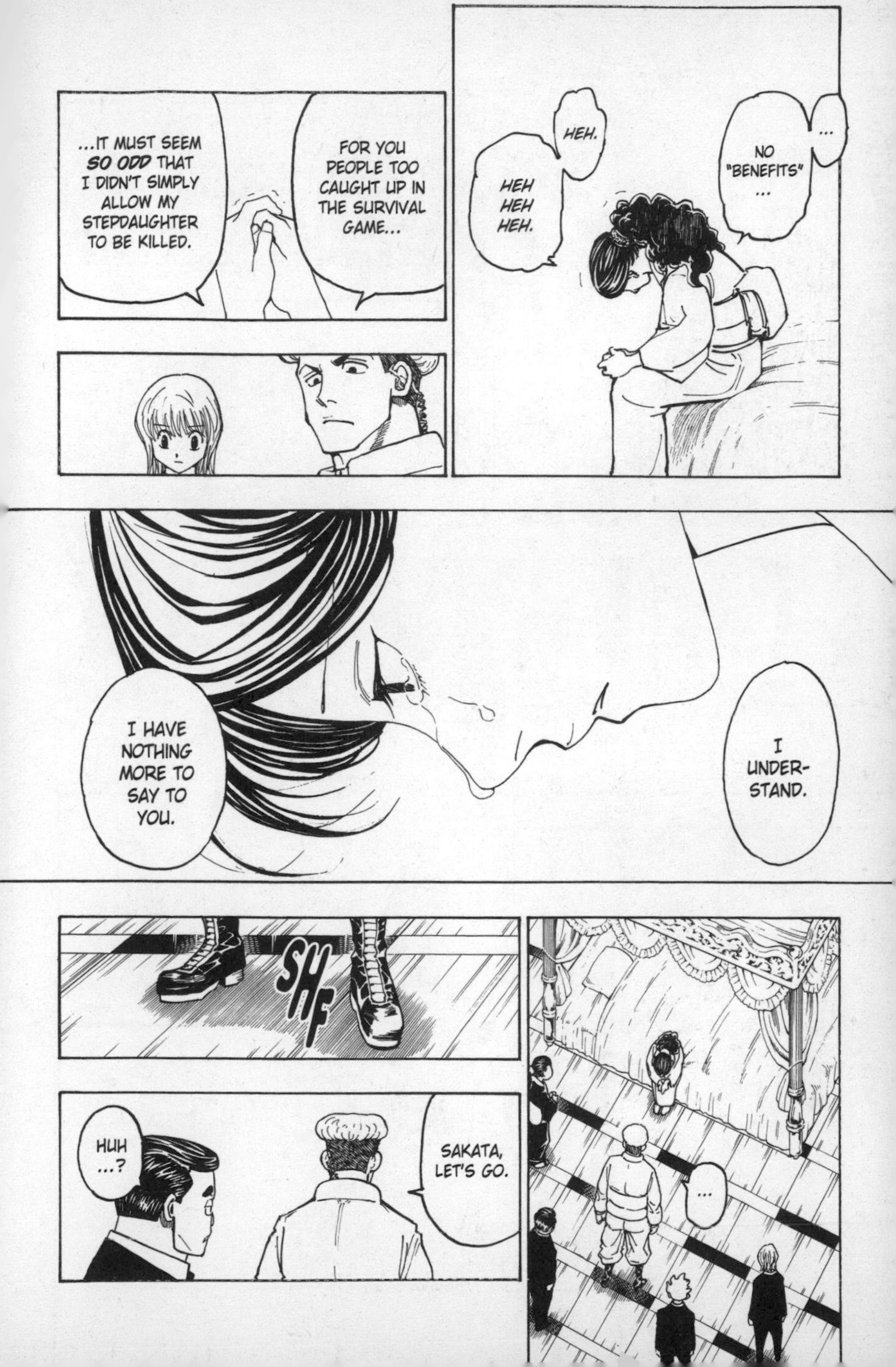
...
NO "BENEFITS" ...
HEH.
HEH HEH HEH.
FOR YOU PEOPLE TOO CAUGHT UP IN THE SURVIVAL GAME...
...IT MUST SEEM *SO ODD* THAT I DIDN'T SIMPLY ALLOW MY STEPDAUGHTER TO BE KILLED.
I UNDER-STAND.
I HAVE NOTHING MORE TO SAY TO YOU.
...
SHF
SAKATA, LET'S GO.
HUH ...?

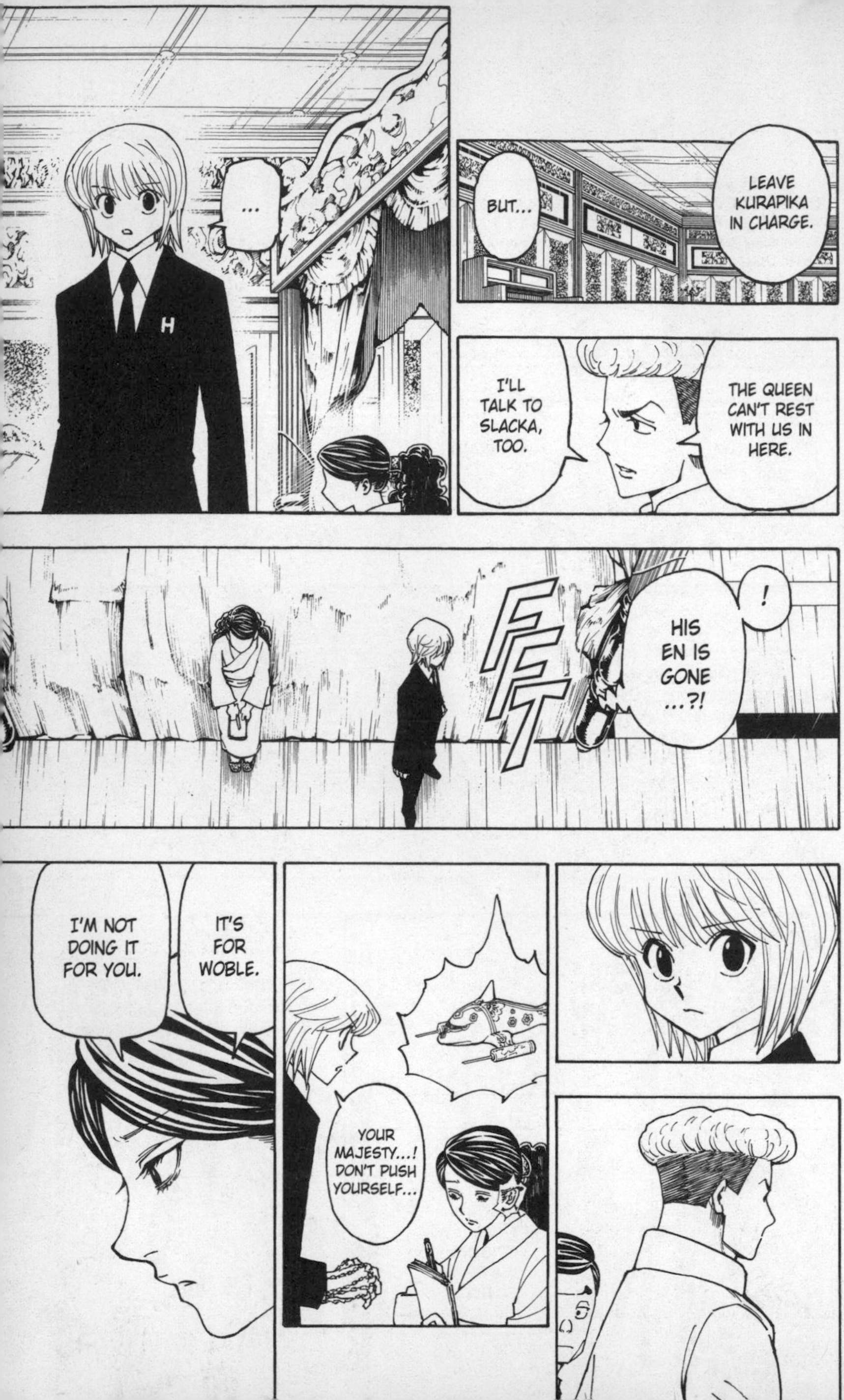
LEAVE KURAPIKA IN CHARGE.
BUT...
THE QUEEN CAN'T REST WITH US IN HERE.
I'LL TALK TO SLACKA, TOO.
...
!
HIS EN IS GONE ...?!
FFT
YOUR MAJESTY...! DON'T PUSH YOURSELF...
IT'S FOR WOBLE.
I'M NOT DOING IT FOR YOU.

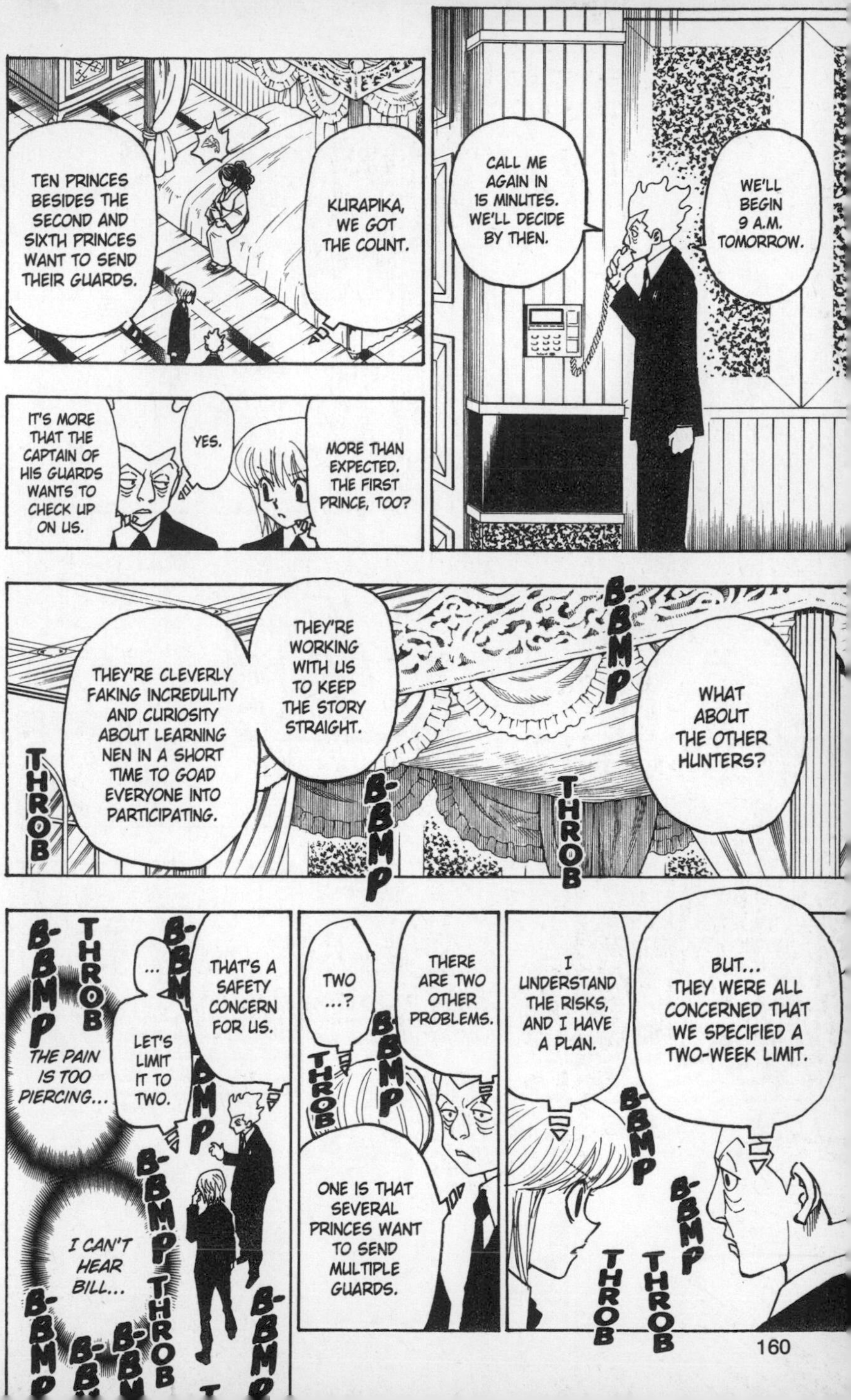
WE'LL BEGIN 9 A.M. TOMORROW.
CALL ME AGAIN IN 15 MINUTES. WE'LL DECIDE BY THEN.
KURAPIKA, WE GOT THE COUNT.
TEN PRINCES BESIDES THE SECOND AND SIXTH PRINCES WANT TO SEND THEIR GUARDS.
MORE THAN EXPECTED. THE FIRST PRINCE, TOO?
YES.
IT'S MORE THAT THE CAPTAIN OF HIS GUARDS WANTS TO CHECK UP ON US.
B-BMP
WHAT ABOUT THE OTHER HUNTERS?
THROB
THEY'RE WORKING WITH US TO KEEP THE STORY STRAIGHT.
B-BMP
THEY'RE CLEVERLY FAKING INCREDULITY AND CURIOSITY ABOUT LEARNING NEN IN A SHORT TIME TO GOAD EVERYONE INTO PARTICIPATING.
THROB
BUT... THEY WERE ALL CONCERNED THAT WE SPECIFIED A TWO-WEEK LIMIT.
I UNDERSTAND THE RISKS, AND I HAVE A PLAN.
B-BMP
THROB
B-BMP
THROB
THERE ARE TWO OTHER PROBLEMS.
TWO ...?
B-BMP
THROB
ONE IS THAT SEVERAL PRINCES WANT TO SEND MULTIPLE GUARDS.
THAT'S A SAFETY CONCERN FOR US.
...
LET'S LIMIT IT TO TWO.
B-BMP
THROB
THE PAIN IS TOO PIERCING...
I CAN'T HEAR BILL...
B-BMP
THROB

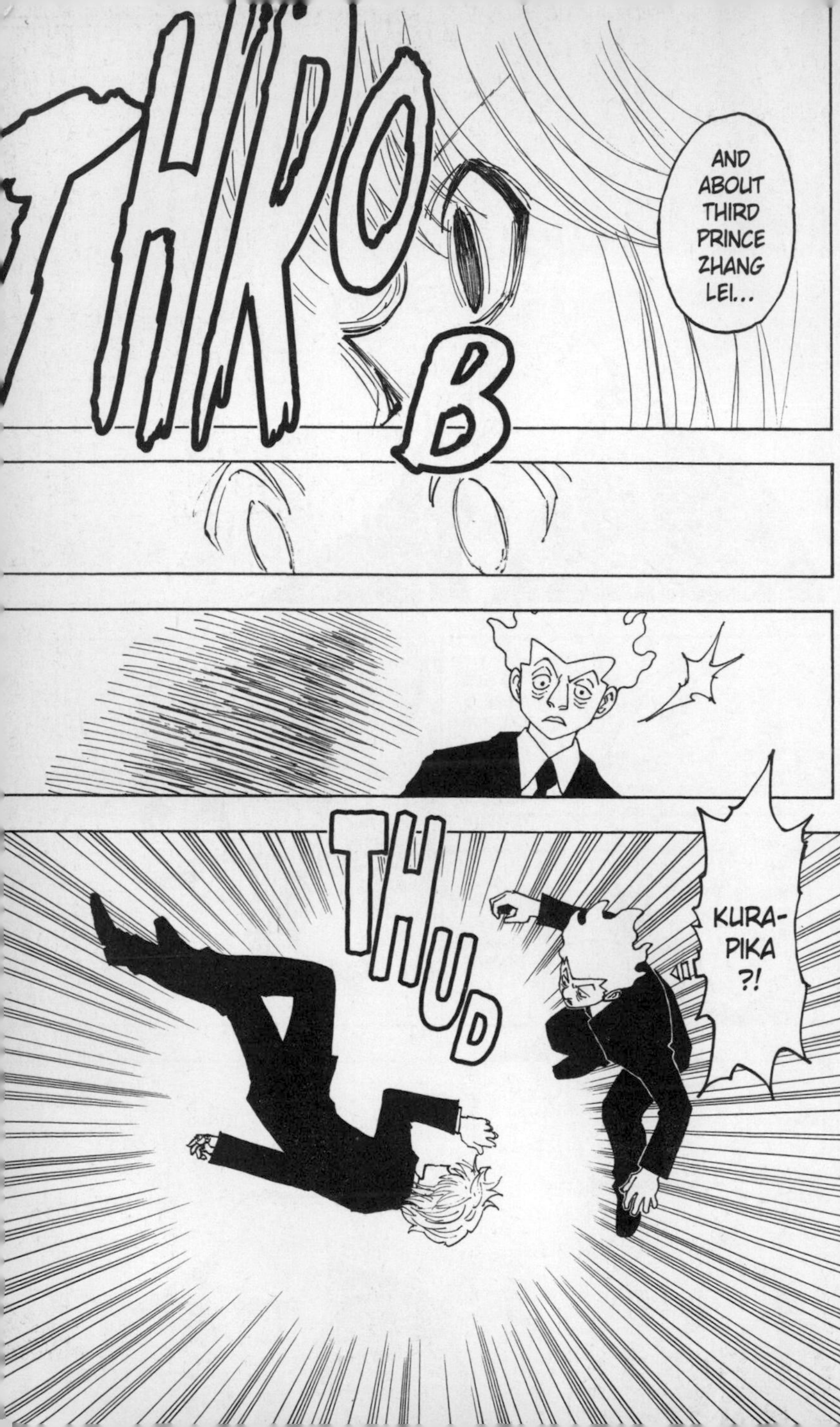
AND ABOUT THIRD PRINCE ZHANG LEI...
THROB
KURA-PIKA?!
THUD

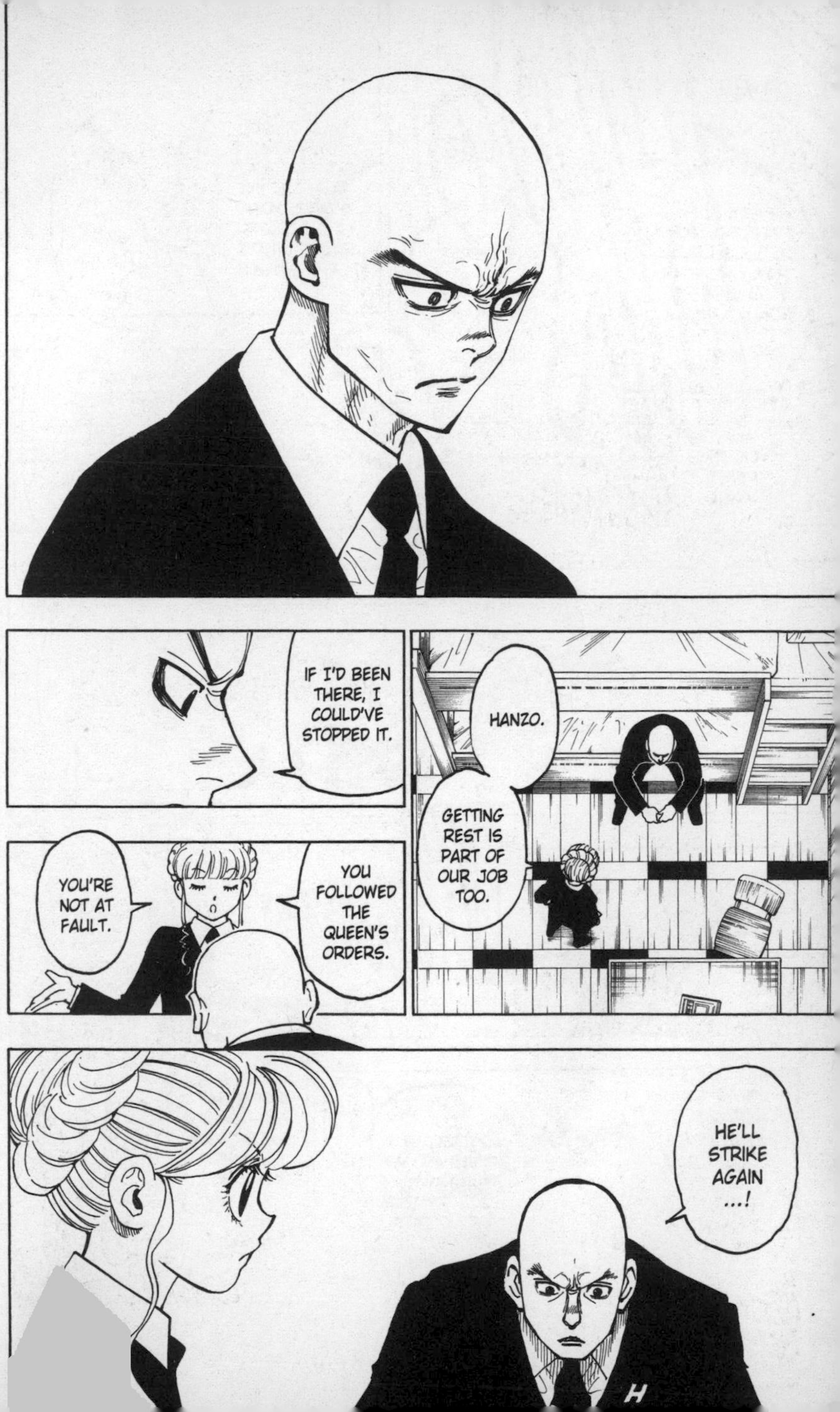
HANZO.
GETTING REST IS PART OF OUR JOB TOO.
IF I'D BEEN THERE, I COULD'VE STOPPED IT.
YOU FOLLOWED THE QUEEN'S ORDERS.
YOU'RE NOT AT FAULT.
HE'LL STRIKE AGAIN ...!

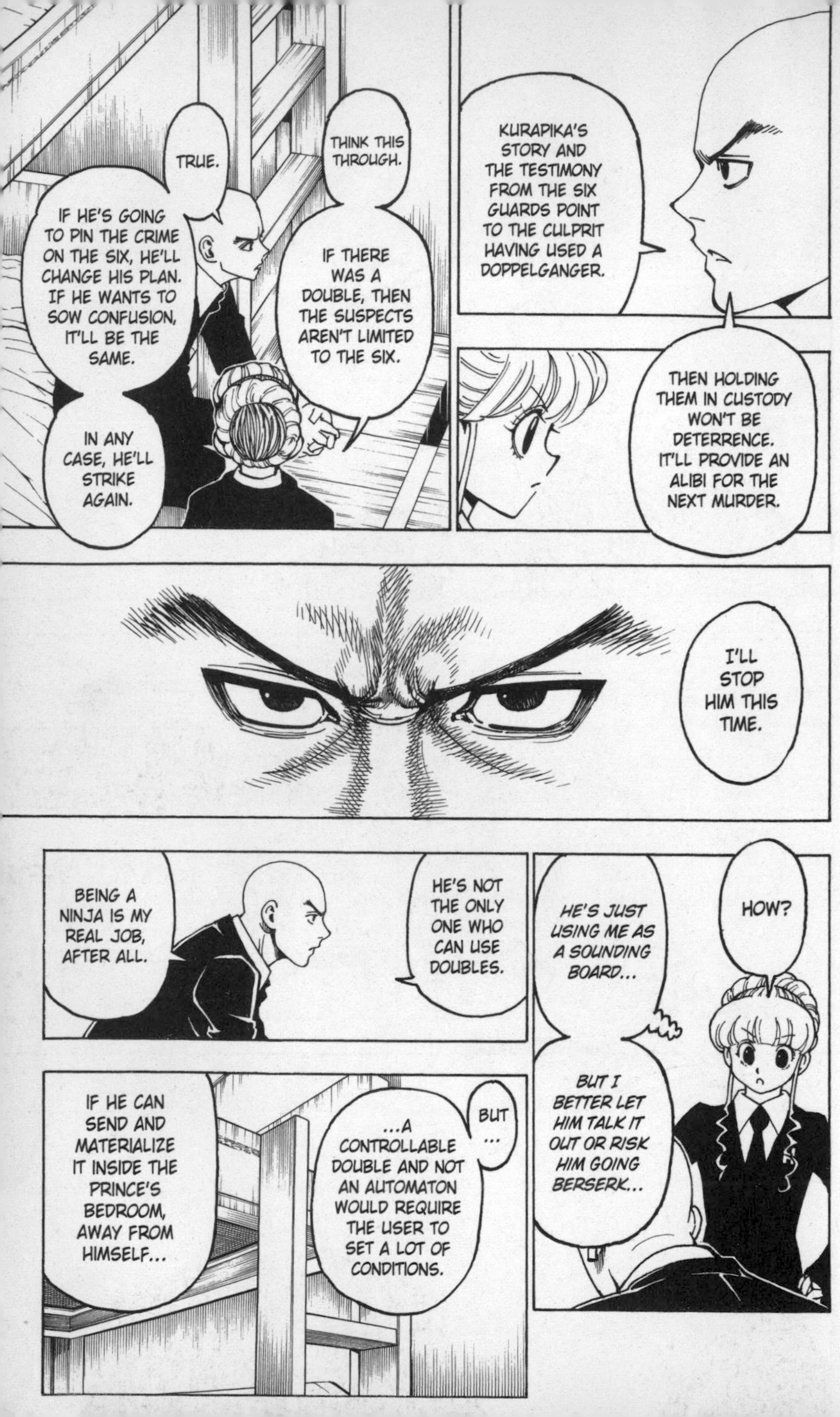
KURAPIKA'S STORY AND THE TESTIMONY FROM THE SIX GUARDS POINT TO THE CULPRIT HAVING USED A DOPPELGANGER.
THEN HOLDING THEM IN CUSTODY WON'T BE DETERRENCE. IT'LL PROVIDE AN ALIBI FOR THE NEXT MURDER.
THINK THIS THROUGH.
IF THERE WAS A DOUBLE, THEN THE SUSPECTS AREN'T LIMITED TO THE SIX.
TRUE.
IF HE'S GOING TO PIN THE CRIME ON THE SIX, HE'LL CHANGE HIS PLAN. IF HE WANTS TO SOW CONFUSION, IT'LL BE THE SAME.
IN ANY CASE, HE'LL STRIKE AGAIN.
I'LL STOP HIM THIS TIME.
HOW?
HE'S JUST USING ME AS A SOUNDING BOARD...
BUT I BETTER LET HIM TALK IT OUT OR RISK HIM GOING BERSERK...
HE'S NOT THE ONLY ONE WHO CAN USE DOUBLES.
BEING A NINJA IS MY REAL JOB, AFTER ALL.
BUT...
...A CONTROLLABLE DOUBLE AND NOT AN AUTOMATON WOULD REQUIRE THE USER TO SET A LOT OF CONDITIONS.
IF HE CAN SEND AND MATERIALIZE IT INSIDE THE PRINCE'S BEDROOM, AWAY FROM HIMSELF...

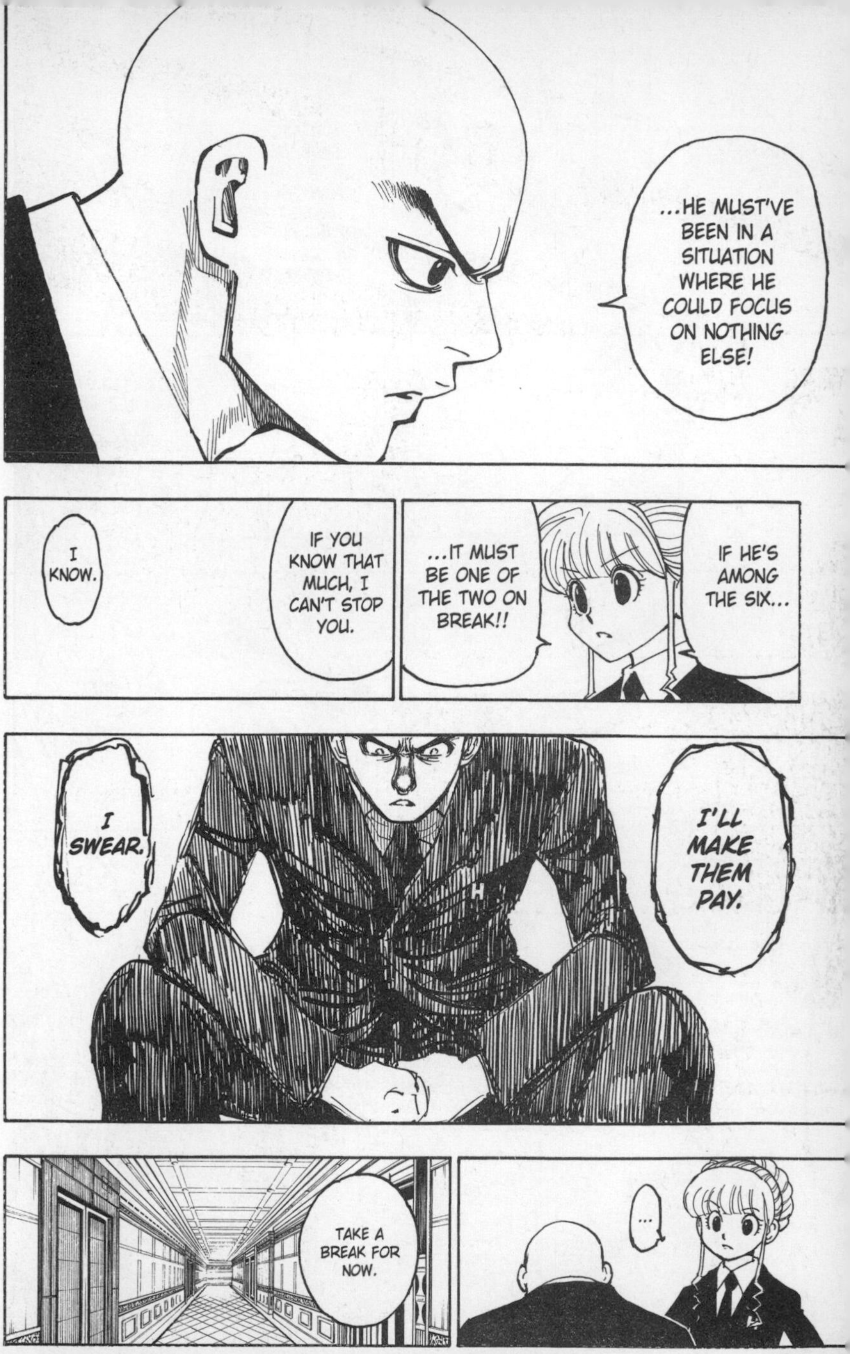
...HE MUST'VE BEEN IN A SITUATION WHERE HE COULD FOCUS ON NOTHING ELSE!
IF HE'S AMONG THE SIX...
...IT MUST BE ONE OF THE TWO ON BREAK!!
IF YOU KNOW THAT MUCH, I CAN'T STOP YOU.
I KNOW.
I'LL MAKE THEM PAY.
I SWEAR.
...
TAKE A BREAK FOR NOW.

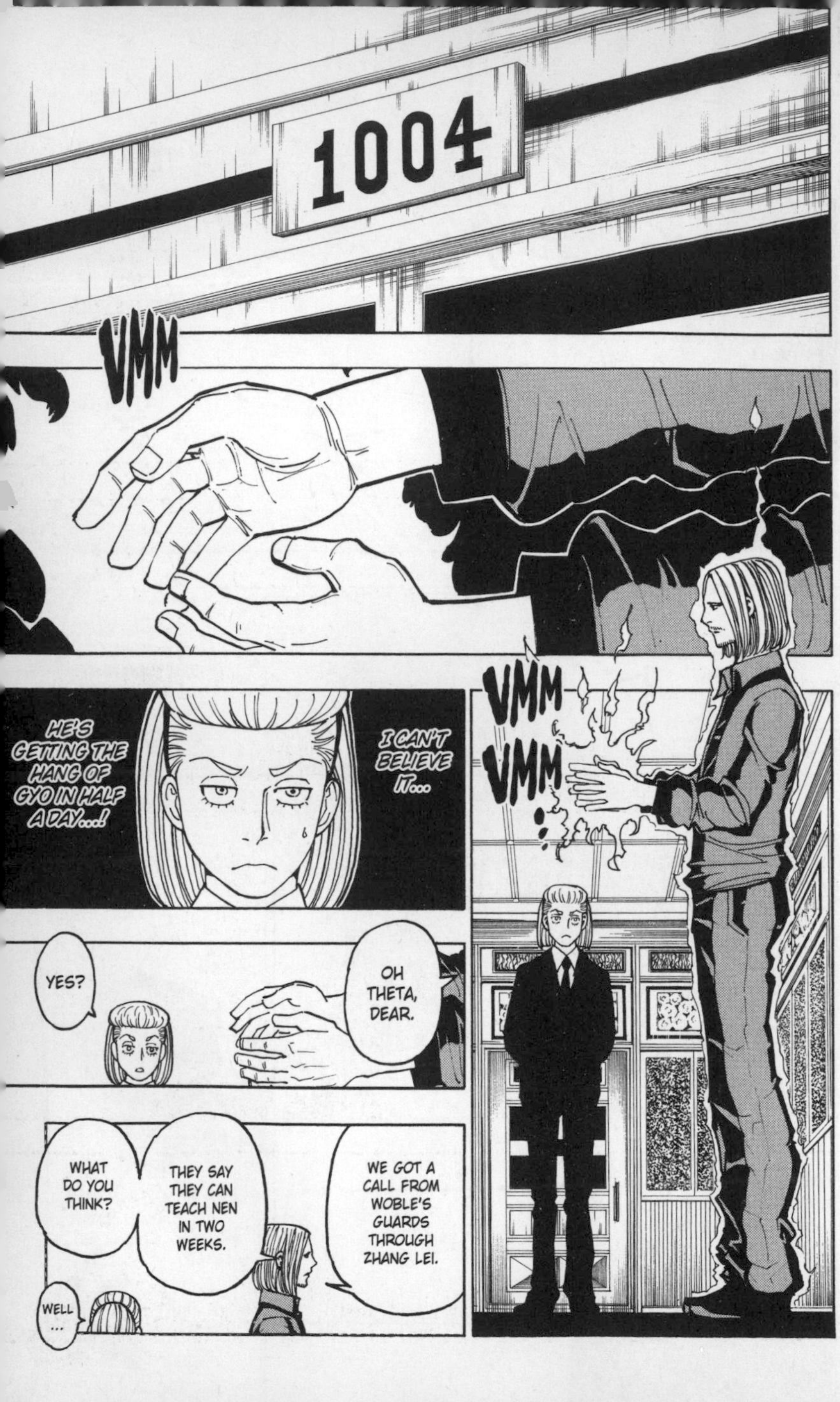
1004
VMM
VMM
VMM
I CAN'T BELIEVE IT...
HE'S GETTING THE HANG OF GYO IN HALF A DAY...!
OH THETA, DEAR.
YES?
WE GOT A CALL FROM WOBLE'S GUARDS THROUGH ZHANG LEI.
THEY SAY THEY CAN TEACH NEN IN TWO WEEKS.
WHAT DO YOU THINK?
WELL...

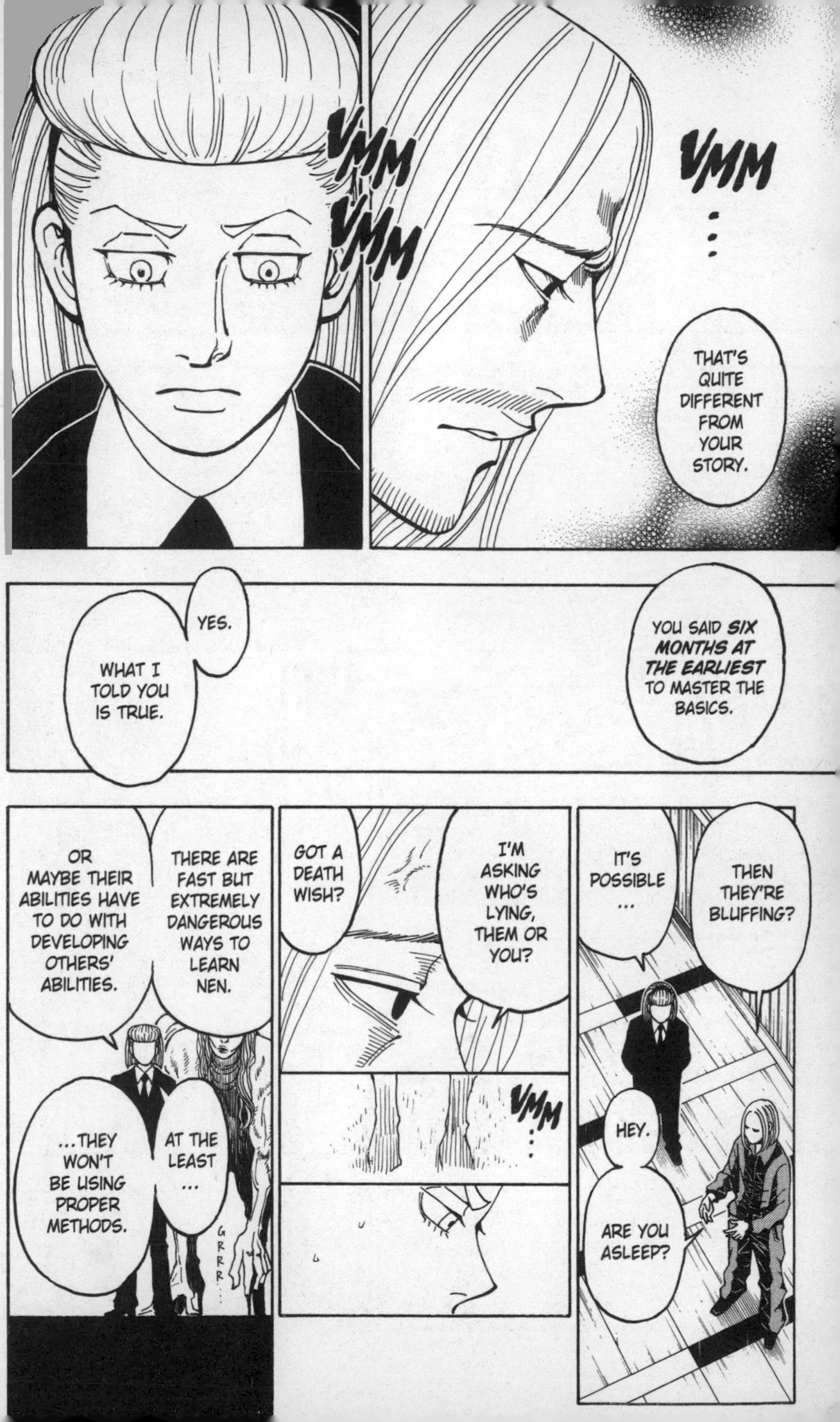
VMM
...
THAT'S QUITE DIFFERENT FROM YOUR STORY.
VMM VMM
YOU SAID *SIX MONTHS AT THE EARLIEST* TO MASTER THE BASICS.
YES.
WHAT I TOLD YOU IS TRUE.
THEN THEY'RE BLUFFING?
IT'S POSSIBLE ...
HEY.
ARE YOU ASLEEP?
I'M ASKING WHO'S LYING, THEM OR YOU?
GOT A DEATH WISH?
VMM
...
THERE ARE FAST BUT EXTREMELY DANGEROUS WAYS TO LEARN NEN.
OR MAYBE THEIR ABILITIES HAVE TO DO WITH DEVELOPING OTHERS' ABILITIES.
AT THE LEAST ...
...THEY WON'T BE USING PROPER METHODS.
GRRR...

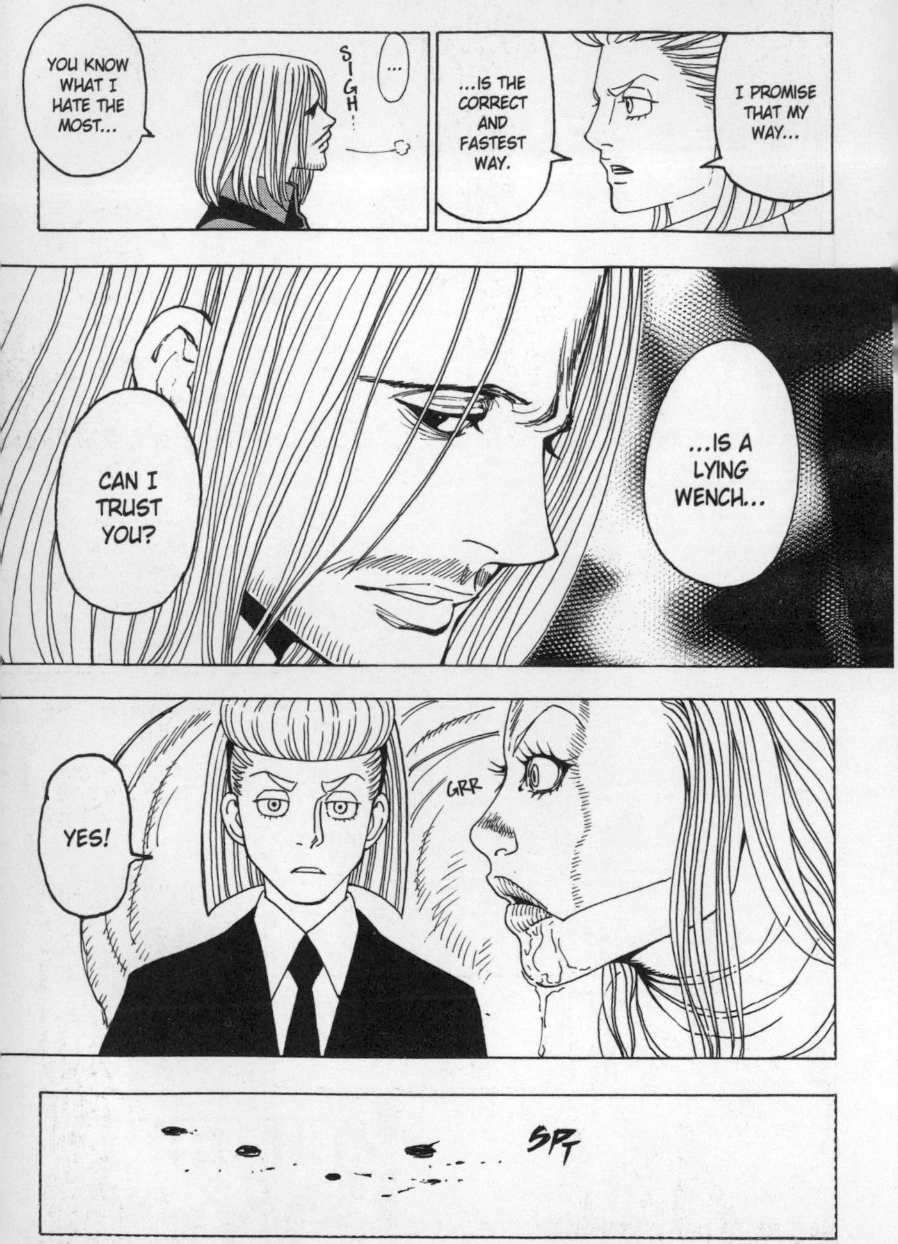
I PROMISE THAT MY WAY...
...IS THE CORRECT AND FASTEST WAY.
...
SIGH
YOU KNOW WHAT I HATE THE MOST...
...IS A LYING WENCH...
CAN I TRUST YOU?
GRR
YES!
SPT

HUNTER ハンター × ハンター HUNTER

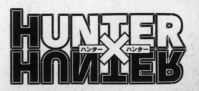

Chapter 369: Limits

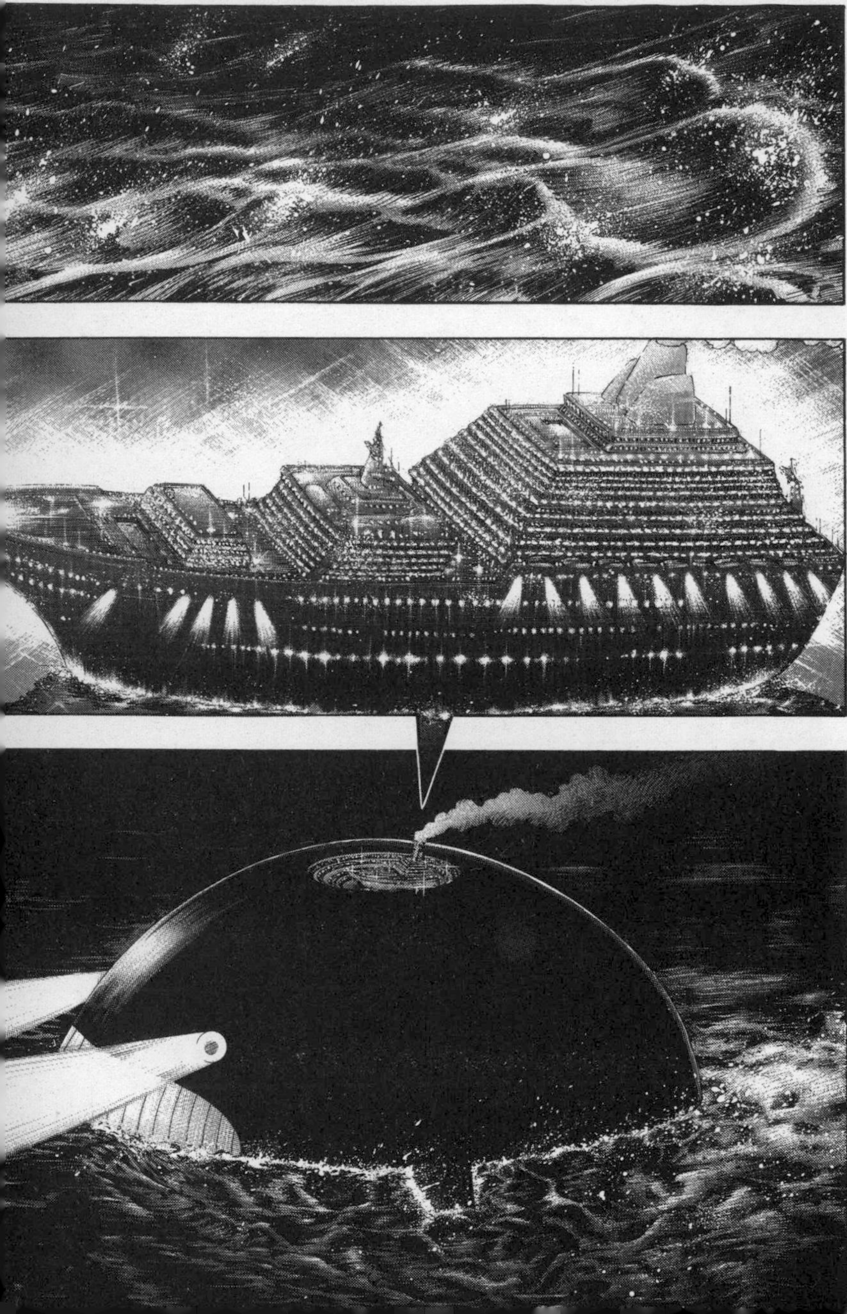

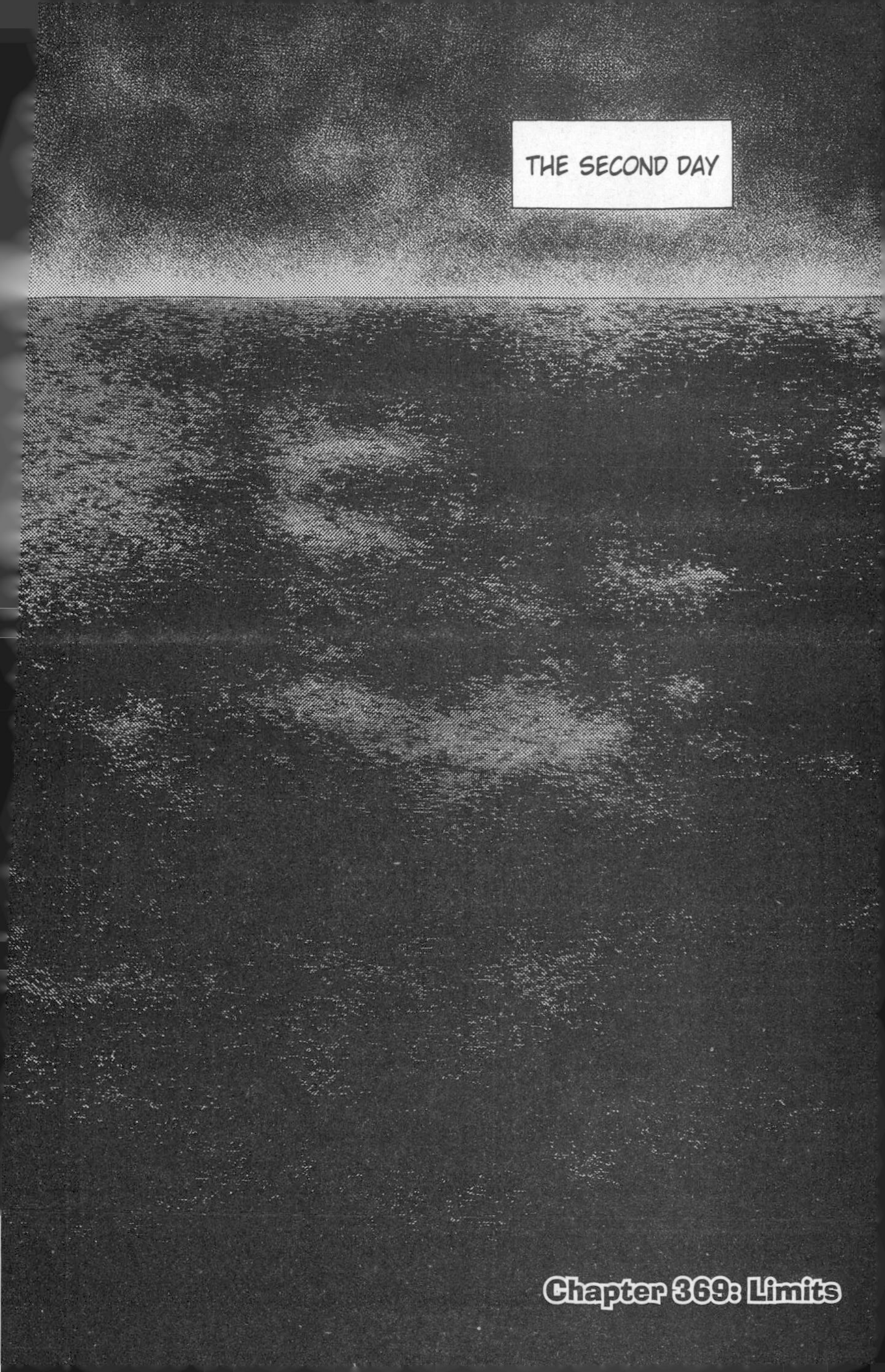
THE SECOND DAY
Chapter 369: Limits

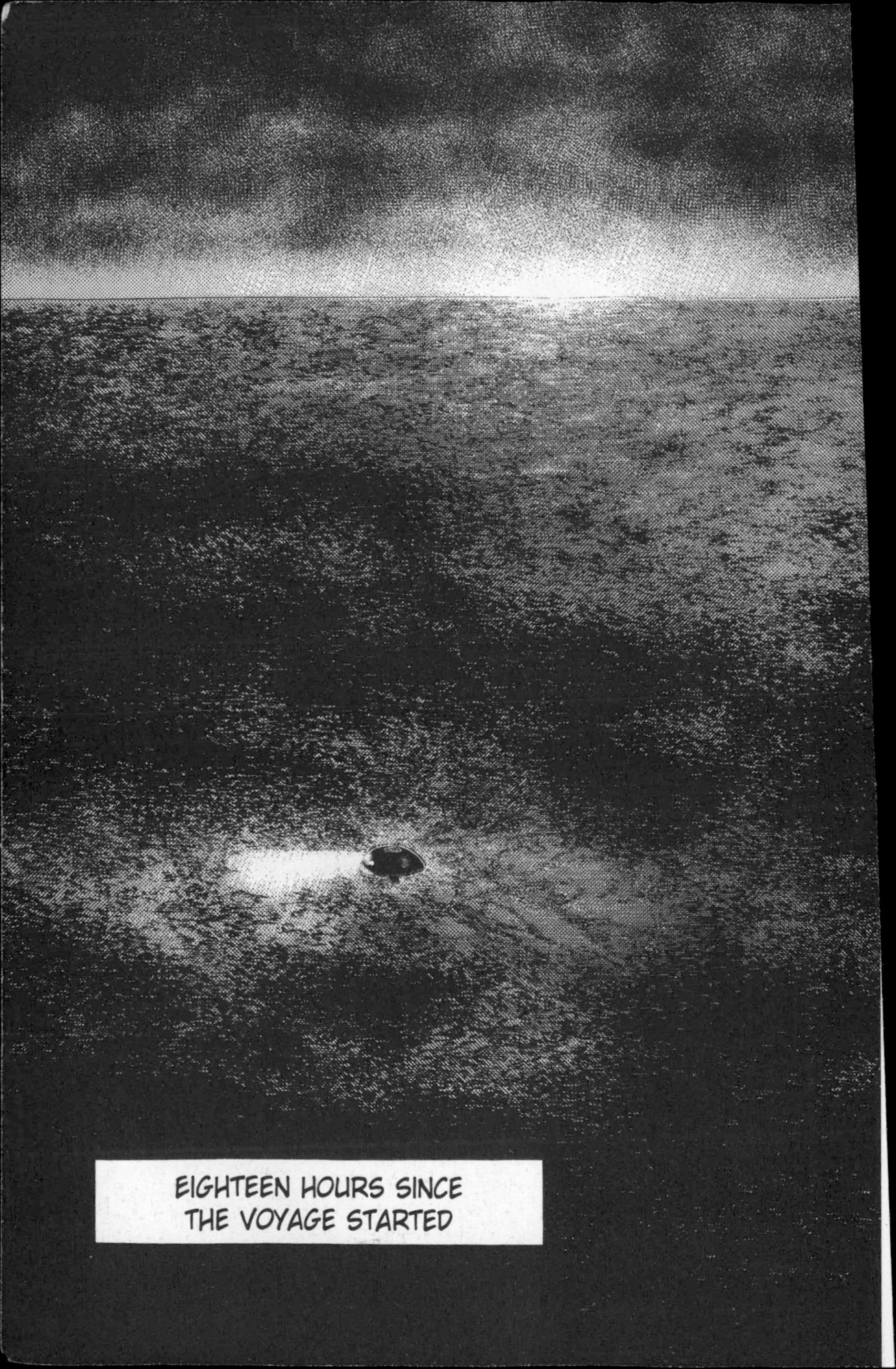
EIGHTEEN HOURS SINCE THE VOYAGE STARTED

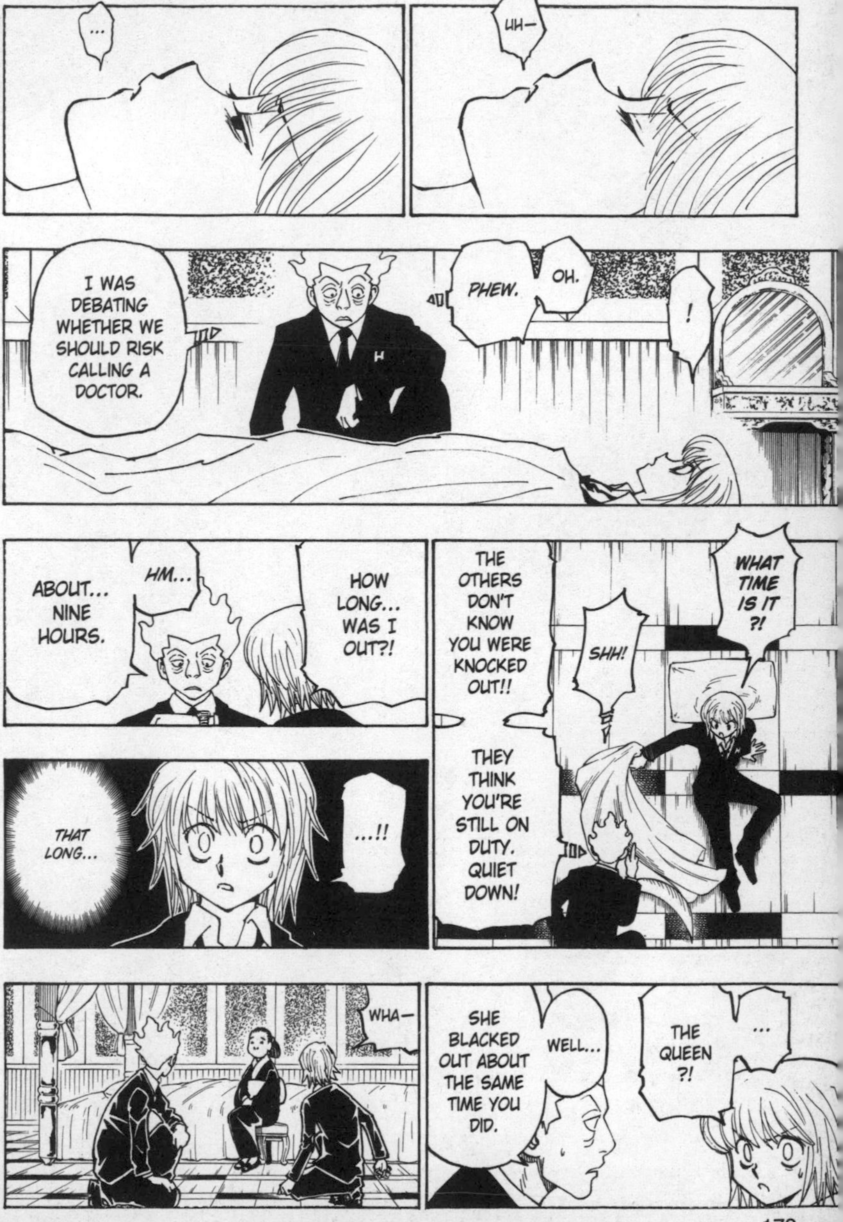
UH—
...
!
OH.
PHEW.
I WAS DEBATING WHETHER WE SHOULD RISK CALLING A DOCTOR.
WHAT TIME IS IT ?!
SHH!
THE OTHERS DON'T KNOW YOU WERE KNOCKED OUT!!
THEY THINK YOU'RE STILL ON DUTY. QUIET DOWN!
HOW LONG... WAS I OUT?!
HM...
ABOUT... NINE HOURS.
...!!
THAT LONG...
...
THE QUEEN ?!
WELL...
SHE BLACKED OUT ABOUT THE SAME TIME YOU DID.
WHA—

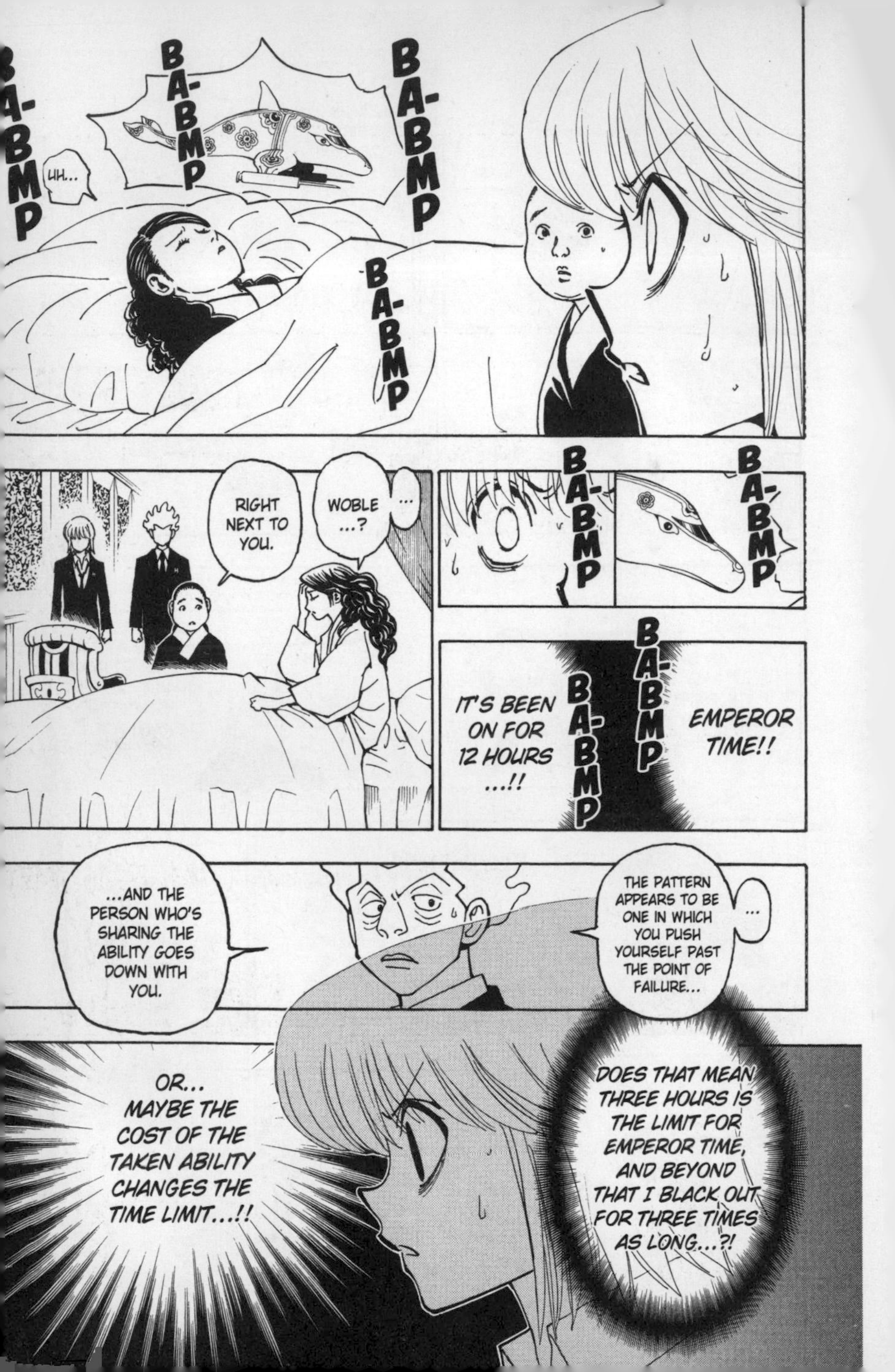
BA-BABMP
BA-BABMP
BA-BMP
UH...
BA-BABMP
BA-BABMP
BA-BABMP
EMPEROR TIME!!
BA-BABMP
BA-BABMP
IT'S BEEN ON FOR 12 HOURS ...!!
...
WOBLE ...?
RIGHT NEXT TO YOU.
...
THE PATTERN APPEARS TO BE ONE IN WHICH YOU PUSH YOURSELF PAST THE POINT OF FAILURE...
...AND THE PERSON WHO'S SHARING THE ABILITY GOES DOWN WITH YOU.
DOES THAT MEAN THREE HOURS IS THE LIMIT FOR EMPEROR TIME, AND BEYOND THAT I BLACK OUT FOR THREE TIMES AS LONG...?!
OR... MAYBE THE COST OF THE TAKEN ABILITY CHANGES THE TIME LIMIT...!!

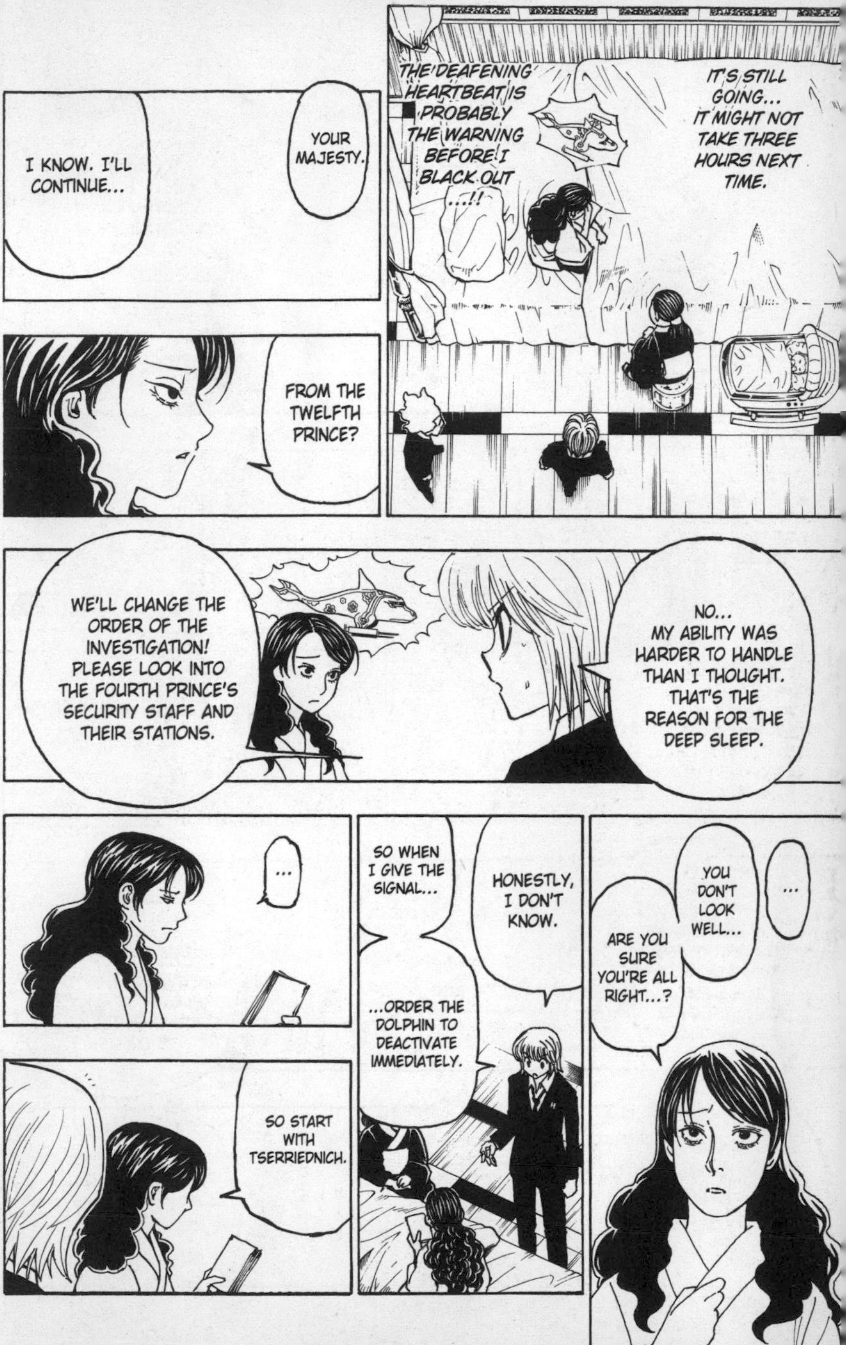
IT'S STILL GOING... IT MIGHT NOT TAKE THREE HOURS NEXT TIME.
THE DEAFENING HEARTBEAT IS PROBABLY THE WARNING BEFORE I BLACK OUT ...!!
YOUR MAJESTY.
I KNOW. I'LL CONTINUE...
FROM THE TWELFTH PRINCE?
NO... MY ABILITY WAS HARDER TO HANDLE THAN I THOUGHT. THAT'S THE REASON FOR THE DEEP SLEEP.
WE'LL CHANGE THE ORDER OF THE INVESTIGATION! PLEASE LOOK INTO THE FOURTH PRINCE'S SECURITY STAFF AND THEIR STATIONS.
...
YOU DON'T LOOK WELL...
ARE YOU SURE YOU'RE ALL RIGHT...?
HONESTLY, I DON'T KNOW.
SO WHEN I GIVE THE SIGNAL...
...ORDER THE DOLPHIN TO DEACTIVATE IMMEDIATELY.
...
SO START WITH TSERRIEDNICH.

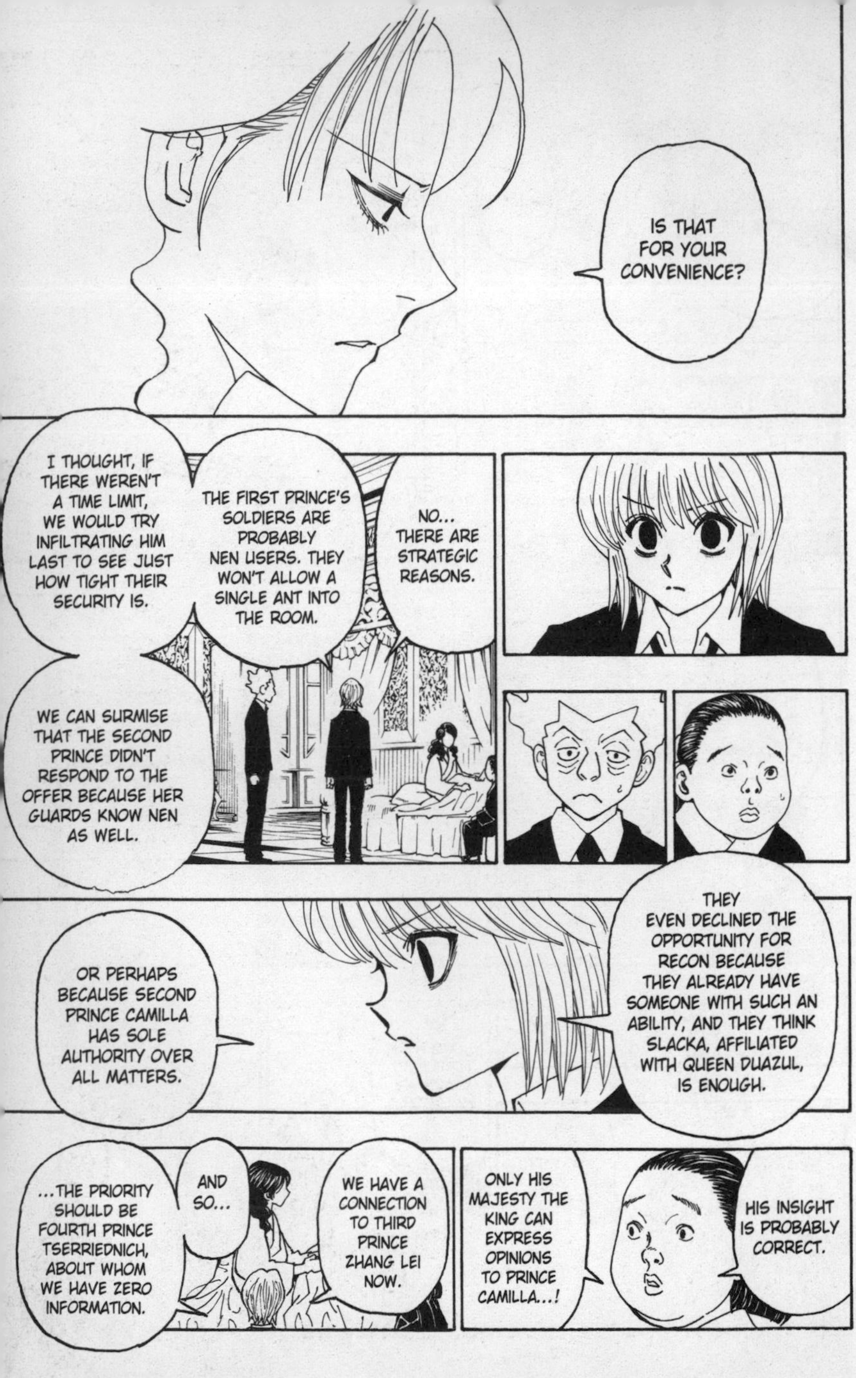
IS THAT FOR YOUR CONVENIENCE?
NO... THERE ARE STRATEGIC REASONS.
THE FIRST PRINCE'S SOLDIERS ARE PROBABLY NEN USERS. THEY WON'T ALLOW A SINGLE ANT INTO THE ROOM.
I THOUGHT, IF THERE WEREN'T A TIME LIMIT, WE WOULD TRY INFILTRATING HIM LAST TO SEE JUST HOW TIGHT THEIR SECURITY IS.
WE CAN SURMISE THAT THE SECOND PRINCE DIDN'T RESPOND TO THE OFFER BECAUSE HER GUARDS KNOW NEN AS WELL.
THEY EVEN DECLINED THE OPPORTUNITY FOR RECON BECAUSE THEY ALREADY HAVE SOMEONE WITH SUCH AN ABILITY, AND THEY THINK SLACKA, AFFILIATED WITH QUEEN DUAZUL, IS ENOUGH.
OR PERHAPS BECAUSE SECOND PRINCE CAMILLA HAS SOLE AUTHORITY OVER ALL MATTERS.
HIS INSIGHT IS PROBABLY CORRECT.
ONLY HIS MAJESTY THE KING CAN EXPRESS OPINIONS TO PRINCE CAMILLA...!
WE HAVE A CONNECTION TO THIRD PRINCE ZHANG LEI NOW.
AND SO...
...THE PRIORITY SHOULD BE FOURTH PRINCE TSERRIEDNICH, ABOUT WHOM WE HAVE ZERO INFORMATION.

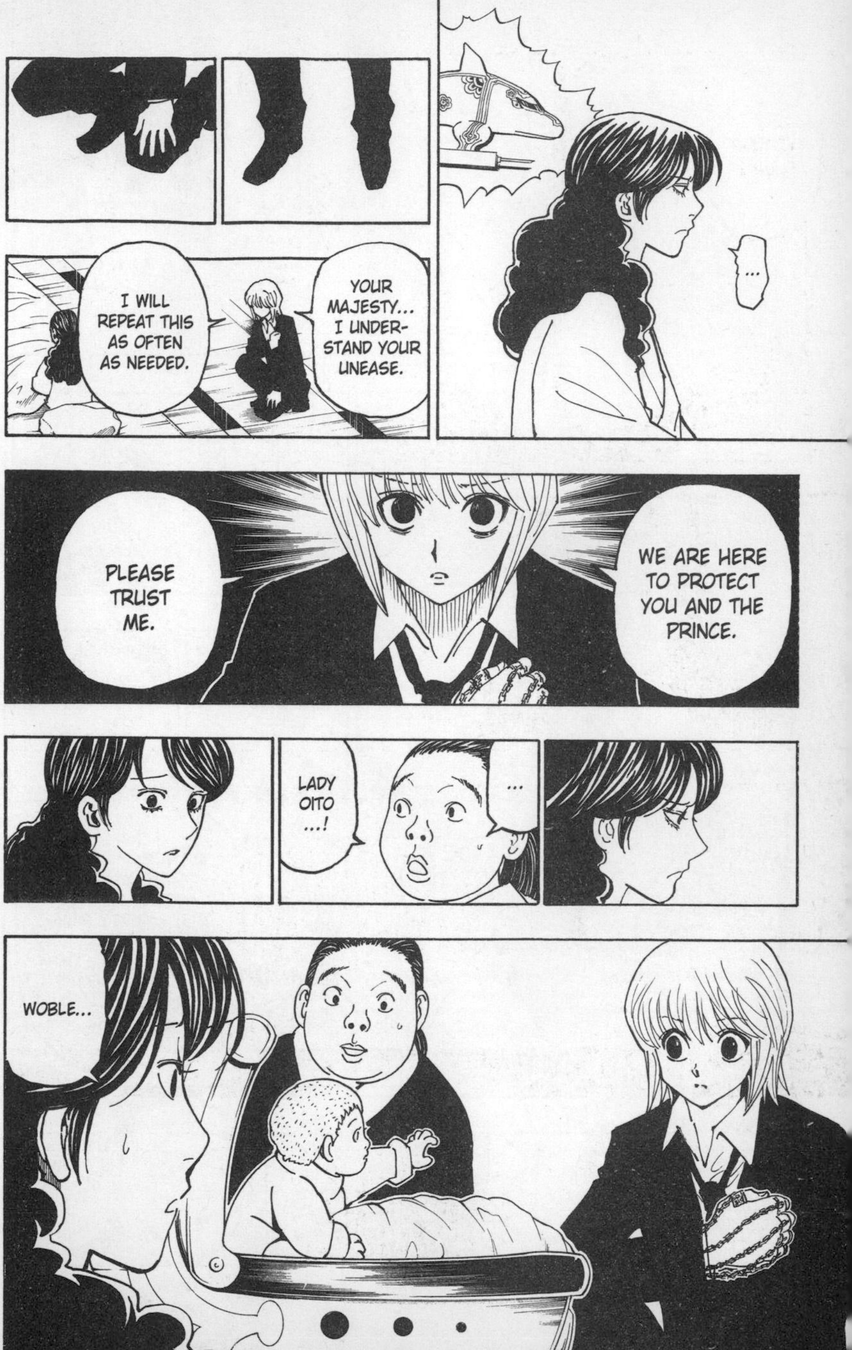
...
YOUR MAJESTY... I UNDERSTAND YOUR UNEASE.
I WILL REPEAT THIS AS OFTEN AS NEEDED.
WE ARE HERE TO PROTECT YOU AND THE PRINCE.
PLEASE TRUST ME.
...
LADY OITO ...!
WOBLE...

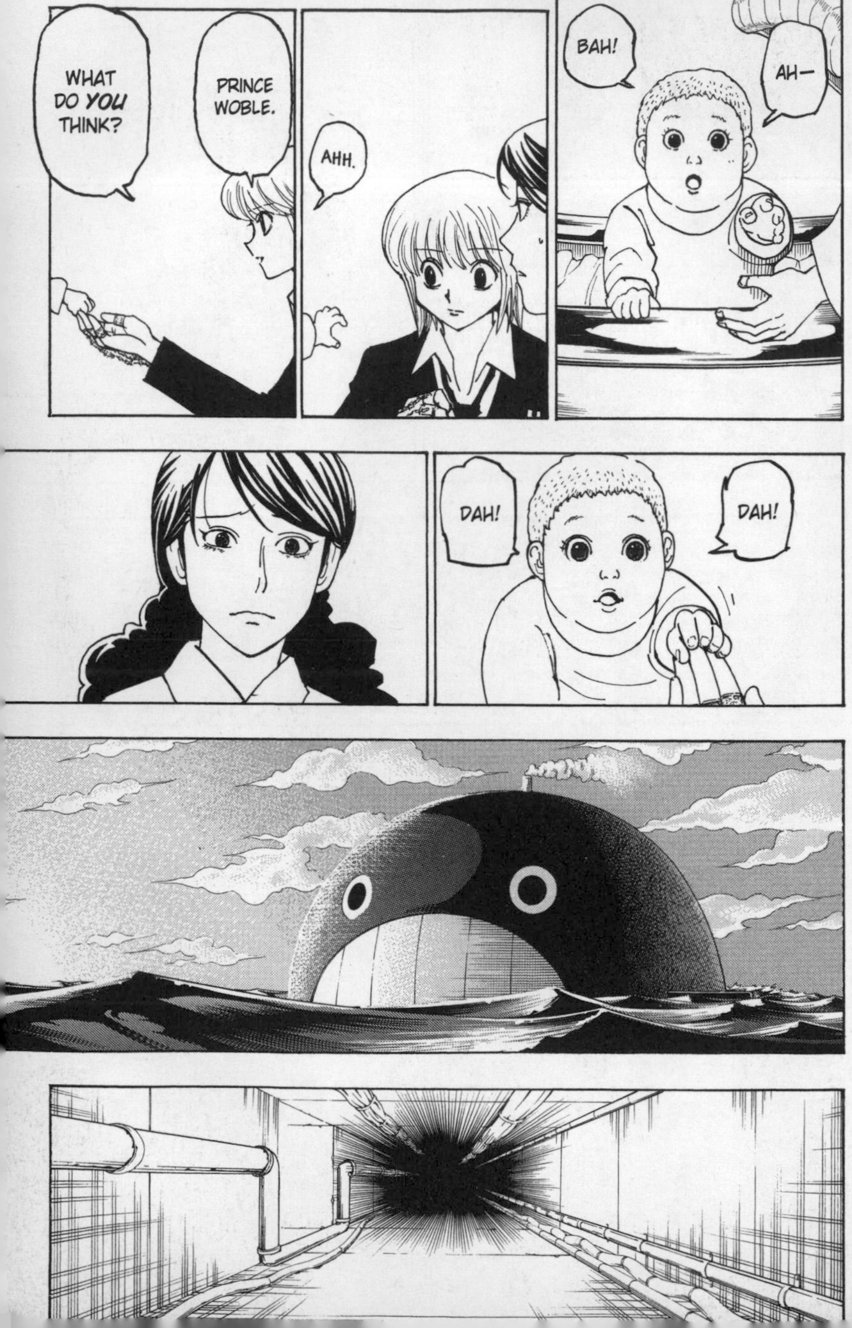
AH—
BAH!
AHH.
PRINCE WOBLE.
WHAT DO *YOU* THINK?
DAH!
DAH!

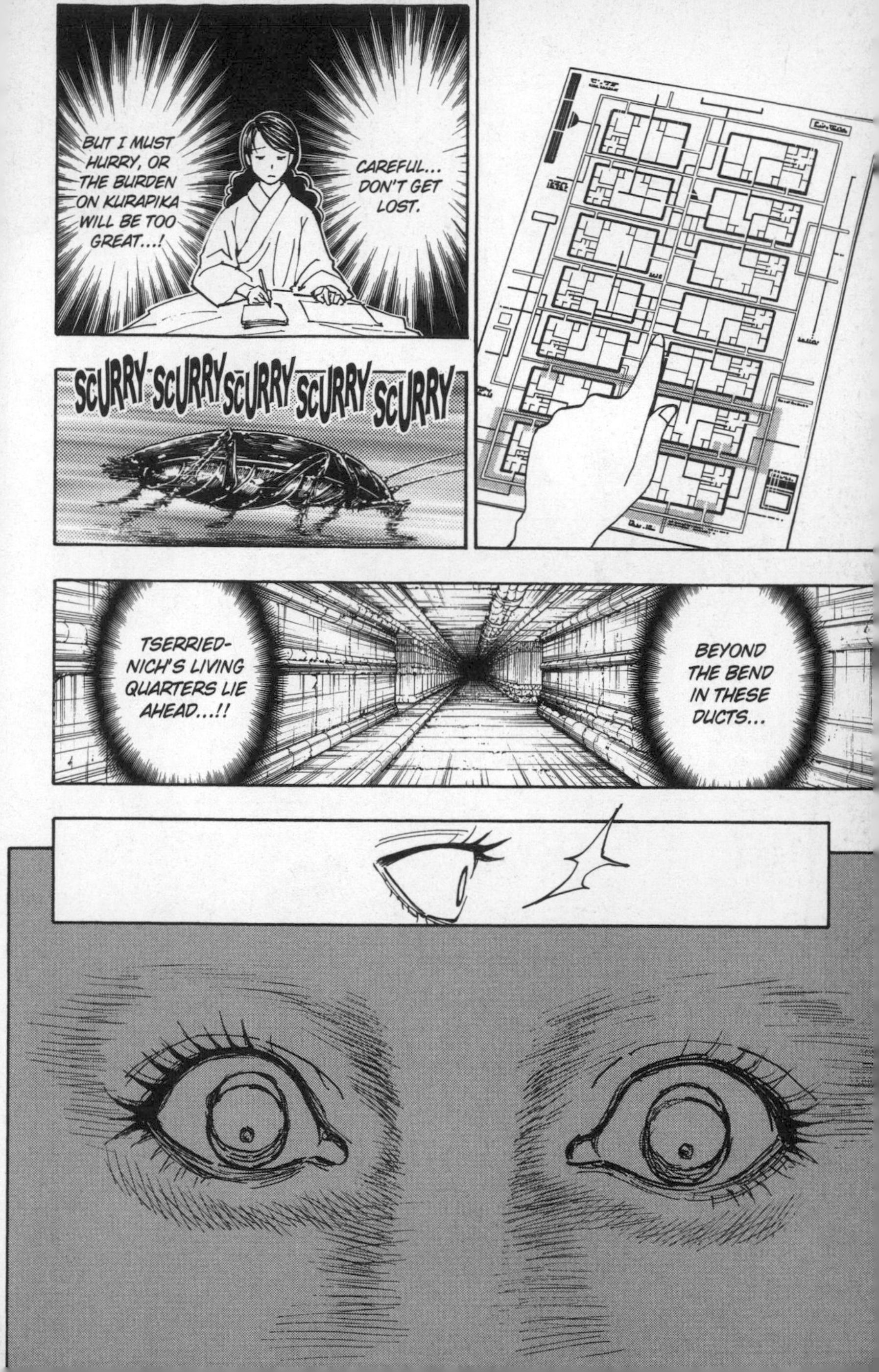
CAREFUL... DON'T GET LOST.
BUT I MUST HURRY, OR THE BURDEN ON KURAPIKA WILL BE TOO GREAT...!
SCURRY SCURRY SCURRY SCURRY SCURRY
BEYOND THE BEND IN THESE DUCTS...
TSERRIED-NICH'S LIVING QUARTERS LIE AHEAD...!!

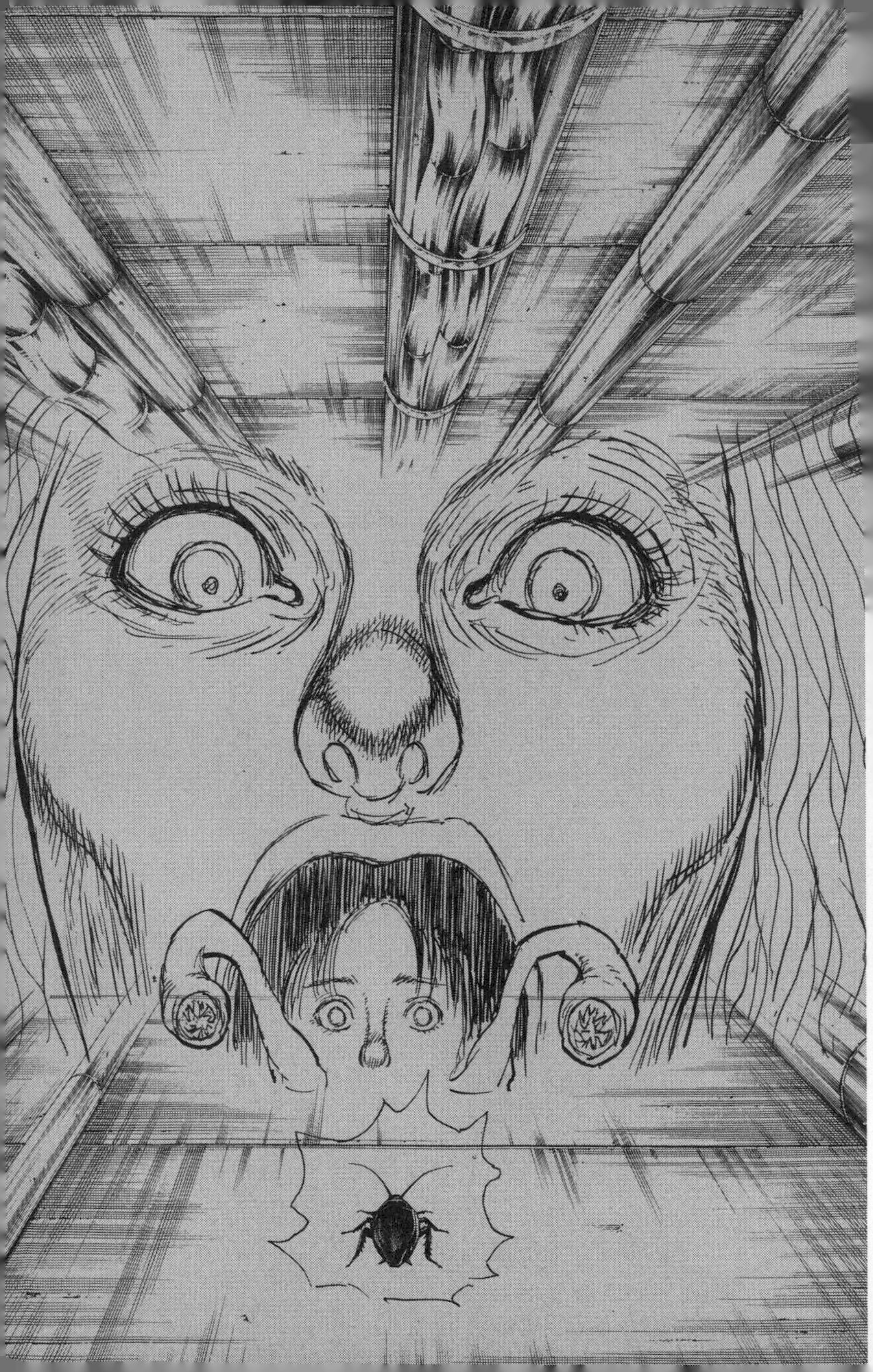

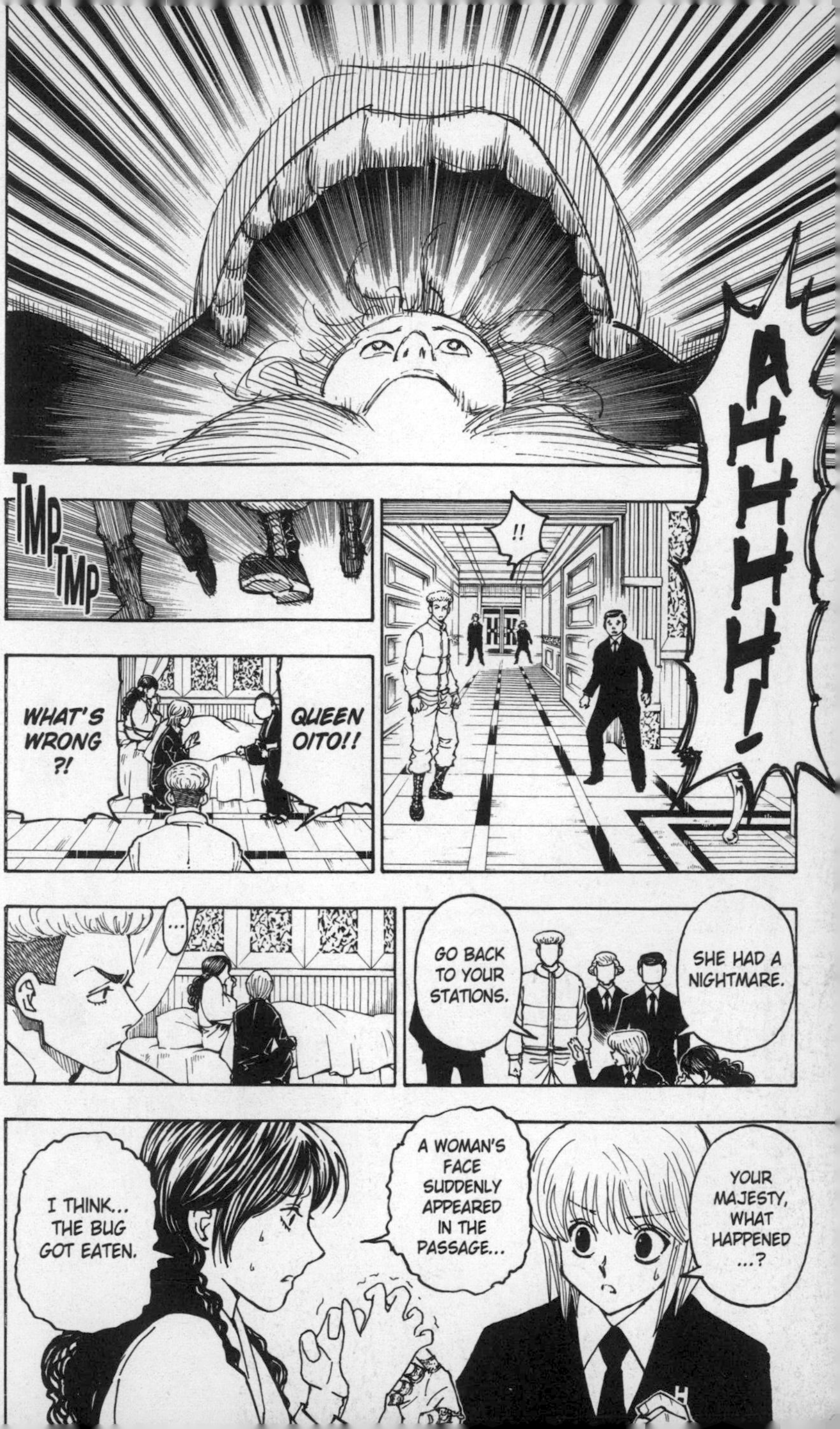
AHHHH!
!!
TMP TMP
QUEEN OITO!!
WHAT'S WRONG ?!
SHE HAD A NIGHTMARE.
GO BACK TO YOUR STATIONS.
...
YOUR MAJESTY, WHAT HAPPENED ...?
A WOMAN'S FACE SUDDENLY APPEARED IN THE PASSAGE...
I THINK... THE BUG GOT EATEN.

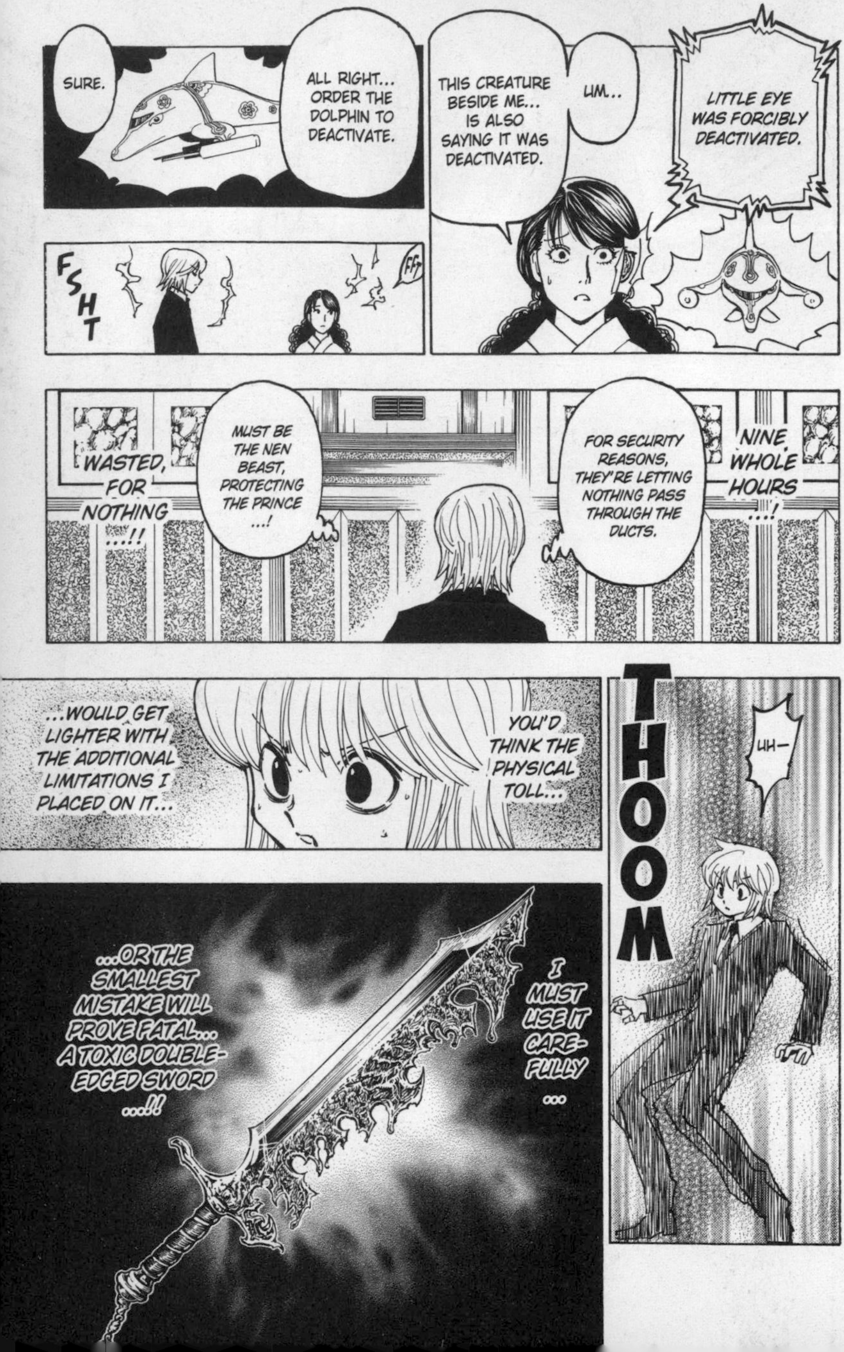
LITTLE EYE WAS FORCIBLY DEACTIVATED.
UM...
THIS CREATURE BESIDE ME... IS ALSO SAYING IT WAS DEACTIVATED.
ALL RIGHT... ORDER THE DOLPHIN TO DEACTIVATE.
SURE.
FF
FSHT
NINE WHOLE HOURS ...!
FOR SECURITY REASONS, THEY'RE LETTING NOTHING PASS THROUGH THE DUCTS.
MUST BE THE NEN BEAST, PROTECTING THE PRINCE ...!
WASTED, FOR NOTHING ...!!
THOOM
UH—
YOU'D THINK THE PHYSICAL TOLL...
...WOULD GET LIGHTER WITH THE ADDITIONAL LIMITATIONS I PLACED ON IT...
I MUST USE IT CARE-FULLY ...
...OR THE SMALLEST MISTAKE WILL PROVE FATAL... A TOXIC DOUBLE-EDGED SWORD ...!!

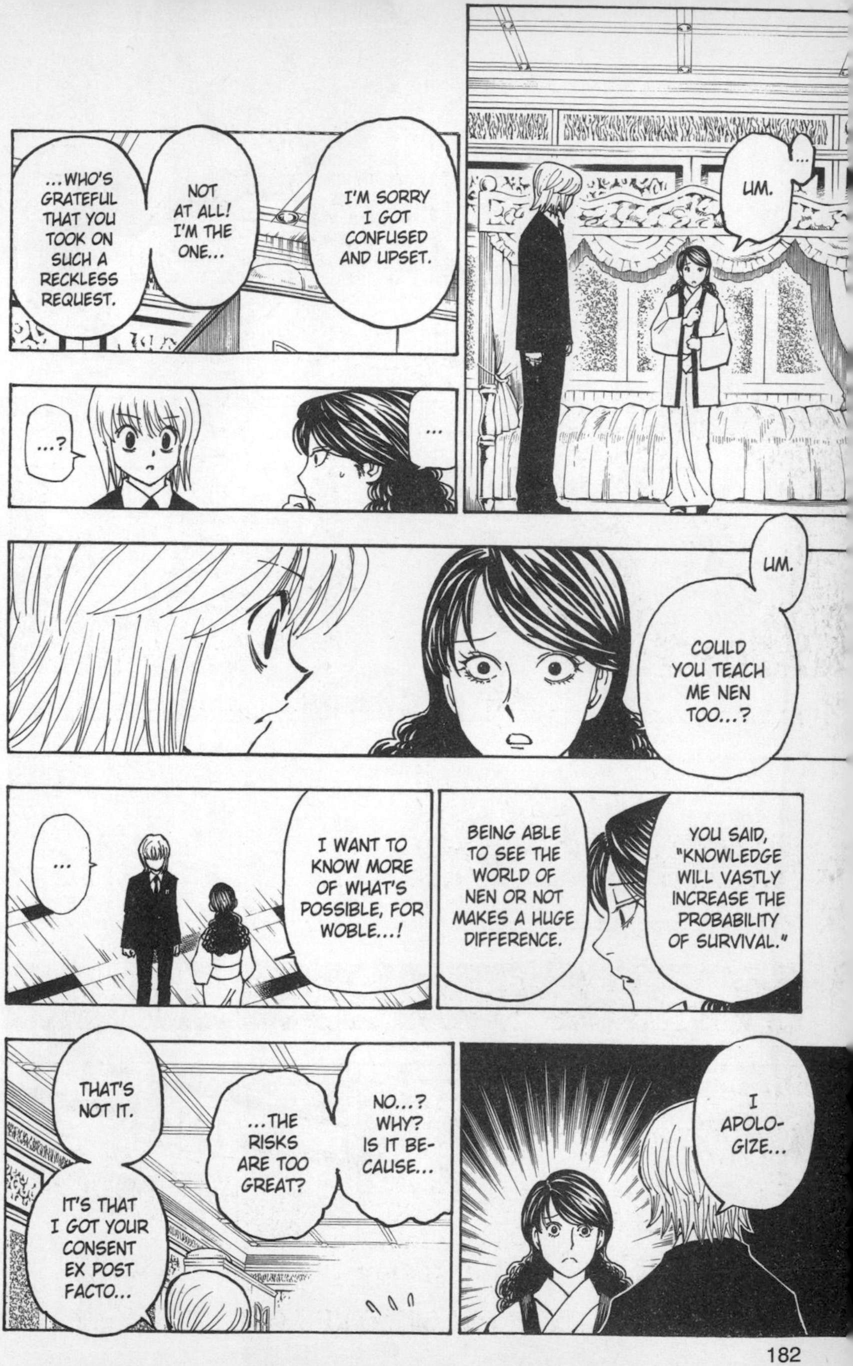
...
UM.
I'M SORRY I GOT CONFUSED AND UPSET.
NOT AT ALL! I'M THE ONE...
...WHO'S GRATEFUL THAT YOU TOOK ON SUCH A RECKLESS REQUEST.
...
...?
UM.
COULD YOU TEACH ME NEN TOO...?
YOU SAID, "KNOWLEDGE WILL VASTLY INCREASE THE PROBABILITY OF SURVIVAL."
BEING ABLE TO SEE THE WORLD OF NEN OR NOT MAKES A HUGE DIFFERENCE.
I WANT TO KNOW MORE OF WHAT'S POSSIBLE, FOR WOBLE...!
...
I APOLOGIZE...
NO...? WHY? IS IT BECAUSE...
...THE RISKS ARE TOO GREAT?
THAT'S NOT IT.
IT'S THAT I GOT YOUR CONSENT EX POST FACTO...

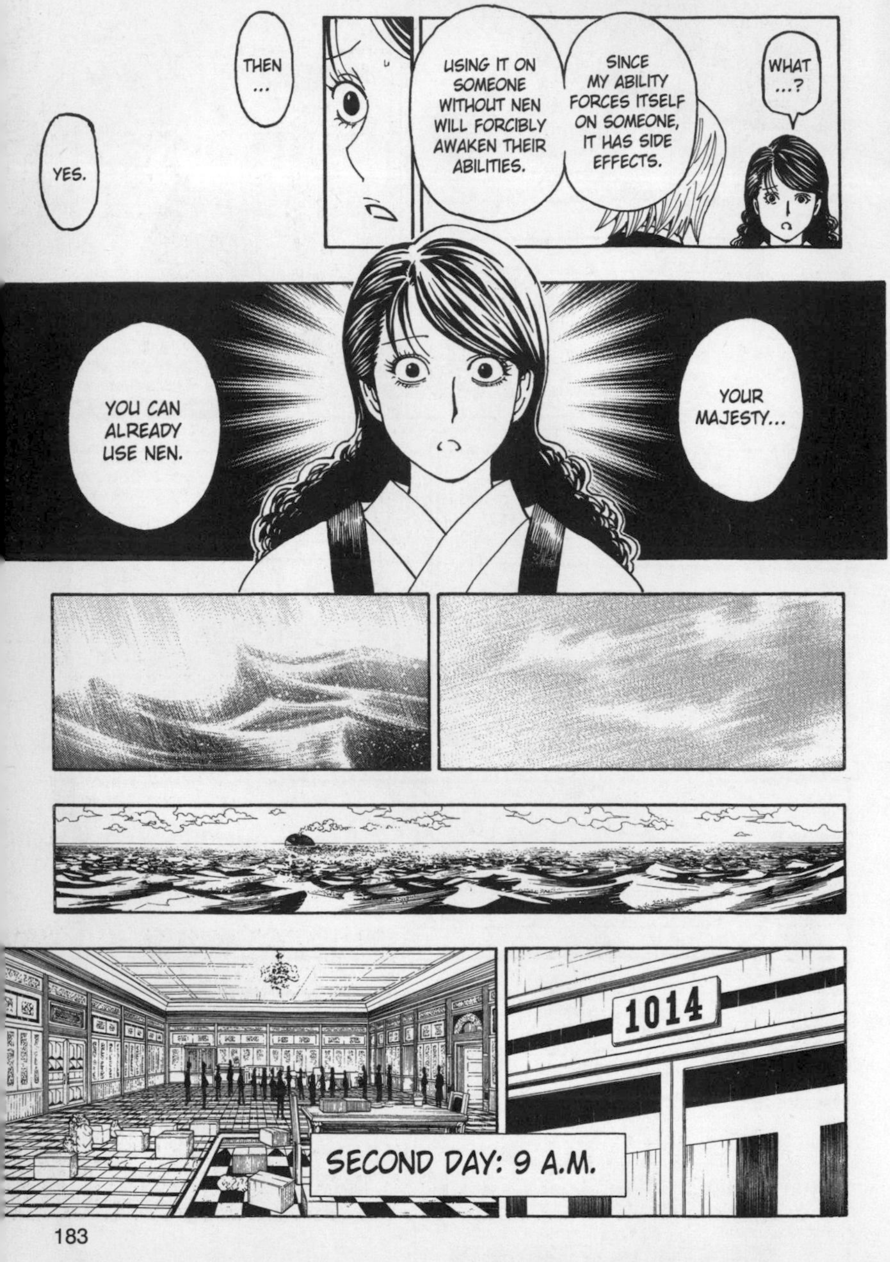
WHAT ...?
SINCE MY ABILITY FORCES ITSELF ON SOMEONE, IT HAS SIDE EFFECTS.
USING IT ON SOMEONE WITHOUT NEN WILL FORCIBLY AWAKEN THEIR ABILITIES.
THEN ...
YES.
YOUR MAJESTY...
YOU CAN ALREADY USE NEN.
1014
SECOND DAY: 9 A.M.

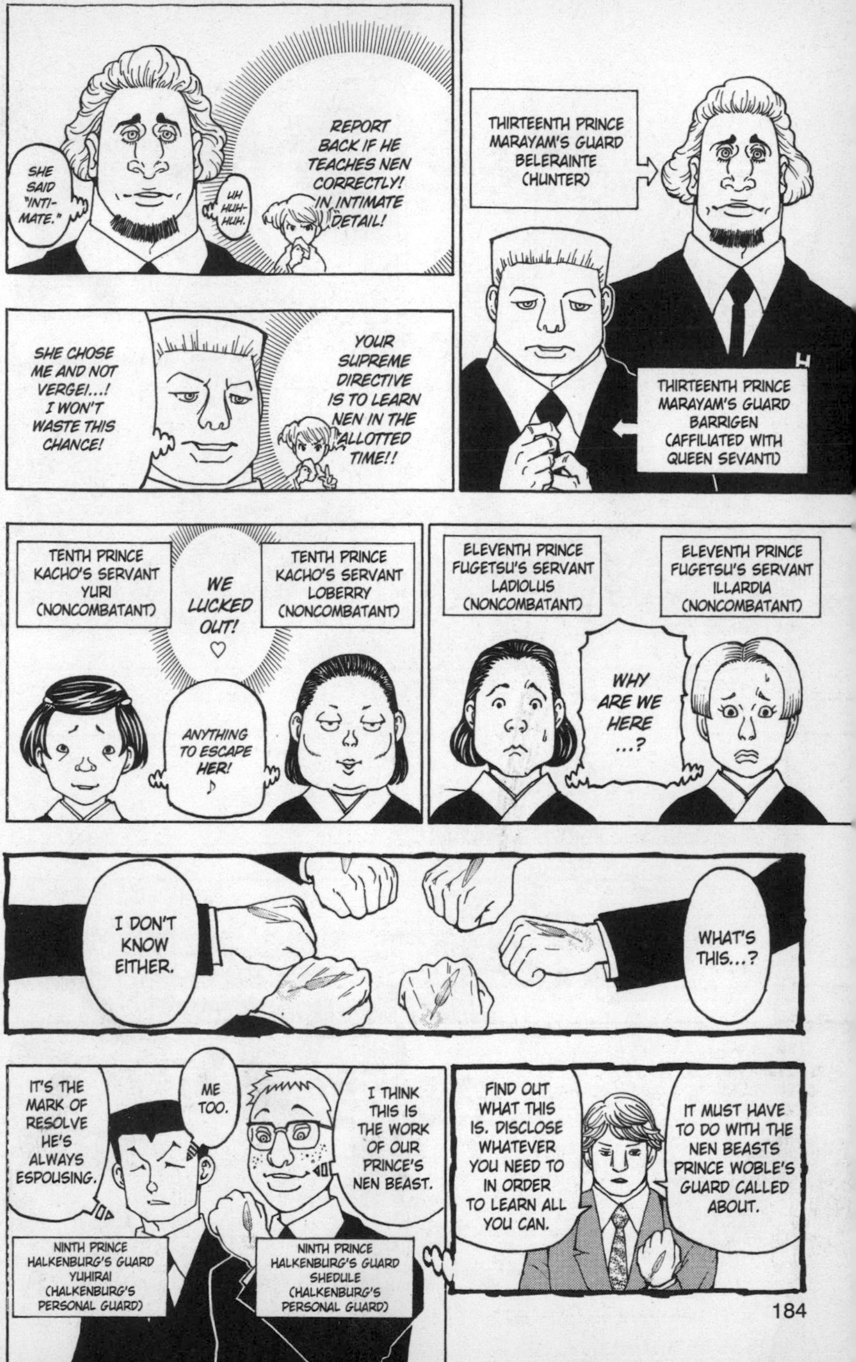

THIRTEENTH PRINCE MARAYAM'S GUARD BELERAINTE (HUNTER)
THIRTEENTH PRINCE MARAYAM'S GUARD BARRIGEN (AFFILIATED WITH QUEEN SEVANTI)
REPORT BACK IF HE TEACHES NEN CORRECTLY! IN INTIMATE DETAIL!
UH HUH-HUH.
SHE SAID "INTI-MATE."
YOUR SUPREME DIRECTIVE IS TO LEARN NEN IN THE ALLOTTED TIME!!
SHE CHOSE ME AND NOT VERGEI...! I WON'T WASTE THIS CHANCE!
ELEVENTH PRINCE FUGETSU'S SERVANT ILLARDIA (NONCOMBATANT)
ELEVENTH PRINCE FUGETSU'S SERVANT LADIOLUS (NONCOMBATANT)
WHY ARE WE HERE ...?
TENTH PRINCE KACHO'S SERVANT LOBERRY (NONCOMBATANT)
WE LUCKED OUT! ♡
TENTH PRINCE KACHO'S SERVANT YURI (NONCOMBATANT)
ANYTHING TO ESCAPE HER! ♪
WHAT'S THIS...?
I DON'T KNOW EITHER.
IT MUST HAVE TO DO WITH THE NEN BEASTS PRINCE WOBLE'S GUARD CALLED ABOUT.
FIND OUT WHAT THIS IS. DISCLOSE WHATEVER YOU NEED TO IN ORDER TO LEARN ALL YOU CAN.
I THINK THIS IS THE WORK OF OUR PRINCE'S NEN BEAST.
ME TOO.
IT'S THE MARK OF RESOLVE HE'S ALWAYS ESPOUSING.
NINTH PRINCE HALKENBURG'S GUARD SHEDULE (HALKENBURG'S PERSONAL GUARD)
NINTH PRINCE HALKENBURG'S GUARD YUHIRAI (HALKENBURG'S PERSONAL GUARD)

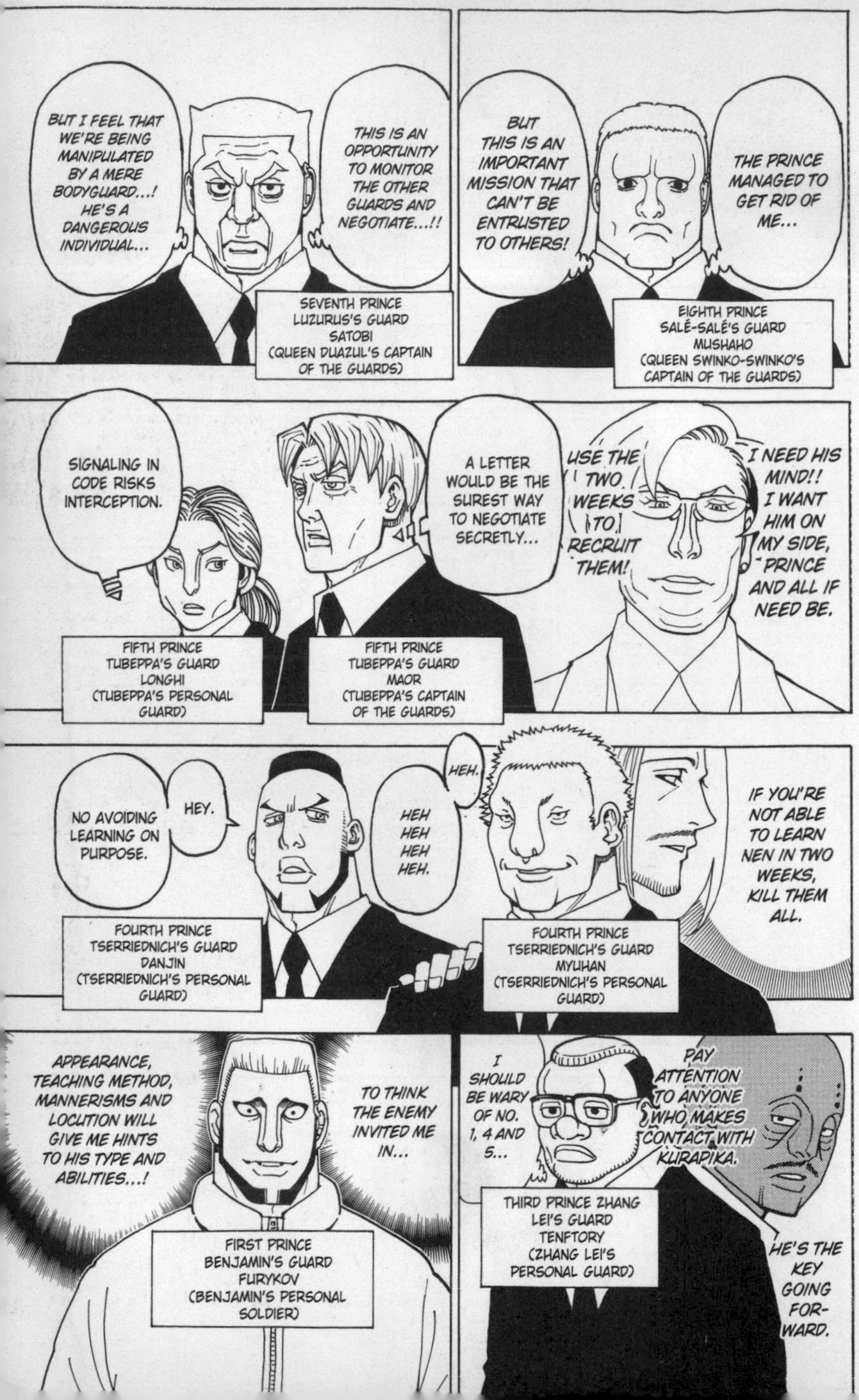
THE PRINCE MANAGED TO GET RID OF ME...
BUT THIS IS AN IMPORTANT MISSION THAT CAN'T BE ENTRUSTED TO OTHERS!
EIGHTH PRINCE SALÉ-SALÉ'S GUARD MUSHAHO (QUEEN SWINKO-SWINKO'S CAPTAIN OF THE GUARDS)
THIS IS AN OPPORTUNITY TO MONITOR THE OTHER GUARDS AND NEGOTIATE...!!
BUT I FEEL THAT WE'RE BEING MANIPULATED BY A MERE BODYGUARD...! HE'S A DANGEROUS INDIVIDUAL...
SEVENTH PRINCE LUZURUS'S GUARD SATOBI (QUEEN DUAZUL'S CAPTAIN OF THE GUARDS)
I NEED HIS MIND!! I WANT HIM ON MY SIDE, PRINCE AND ALL IF NEED BE.
USE THE TWO WEEKS TO RECRUIT THEM!
A LETTER WOULD BE THE SUREST WAY TO NEGOTIATE SECRETLY...
FIFTH PRINCE TUBEPPA'S GUARD MAOR (TUBEPPA'S CAPTAIN OF THE GUARDS)
SIGNALING IN CODE RISKS INTERCEPTION.
FIFTH PRINCE TUBEPPA'S GUARD LONGHI (TUBEPPA'S PERSONAL GUARD)
IF YOU'RE NOT ABLE TO LEARN NEN IN TWO WEEKS, KILL THEM ALL.
HEH.
FOURTH PRINCE TSERRIEDNICH'S GUARD MYUHAN (TSERRIEDNICH'S PERSONAL GUARD)
HEH HEH HEH HEH.
HEY.
NO AVOIDING LEARNING ON PURPOSE.
FOURTH PRINCE TSERRIEDNICH'S GUARD DANJIN (TSERRIEDNICH'S PERSONAL GUARD)
PAY ATTENTION TO ANYONE WHO MAKES CONTACT WITH KURAPIKA.
I SHOULD BE WARY OF NO. 1, 4 AND 5...
THIRD PRINCE ZHANG LEI'S GUARD TENFTORY (ZHANG LEI'S PERSONAL GUARD)
HE'S THE KEY GOING FOR-WARD.
TO THINK THE ENEMY INVITED ME IN...
APPEARANCE, TEACHING METHOD, MANNERISMS AND LOCUTION WILL GIVE ME HINTS TO HIS TYPE AND ABILITIES...!
FIRST PRINCE BENJAMIN'S GUARD FURYKOV (BENJAMIN'S PERSONAL SOLDIER)

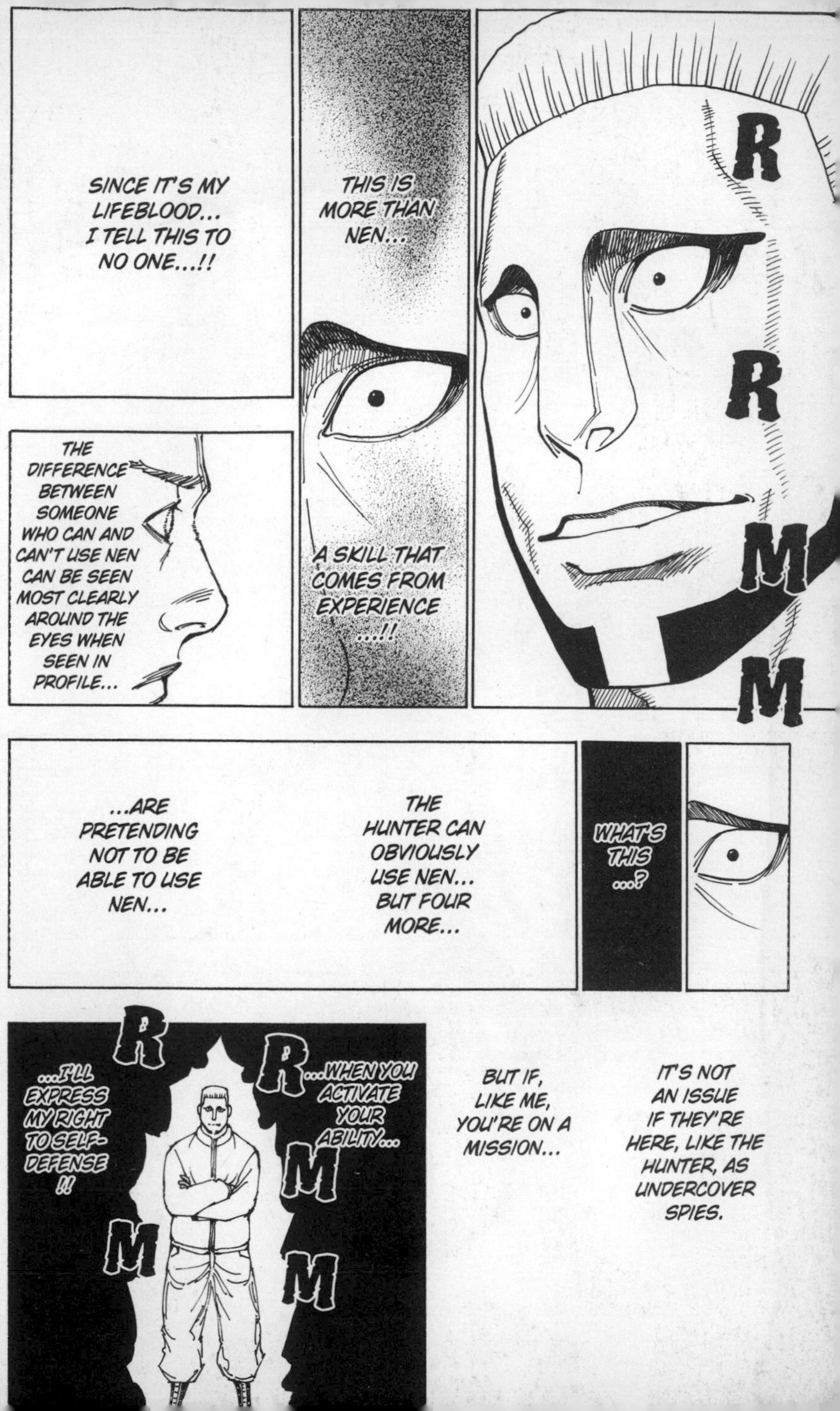
RRMM
THIS IS MORE THAN NEN...
A SKILL THAT COMES FROM EXPERIENCE...!!
SINCE IT'S MY LIFEBLOOD... I TELL THIS TO NO ONE...!!
THE DIFFERENCE BETWEEN SOMEONE WHO CAN AND CAN'T USE NEN CAN BE SEEN MOST CLEARLY AROUND THE EYES WHEN SEEN IN PROFILE...
WHAT'S THIS...?
THE HUNTER CAN OBVIOUSLY USE NEN... BUT FOUR MORE...
...ARE PRETENDING NOT TO BE ABLE TO USE NEN...
IT'S NOT AN ISSUE IF THEY'RE HERE, LIKE THE HUNTER, AS UNDERCOVER SPIES.
BUT IF, LIKE ME, YOU'RE ON A MISSION...
...WHEN YOU ACTIVATE YOUR ABILITY...
...I'LL EXPRESS MY RIGHT TO SELF-DEFENSE!!
RRMM

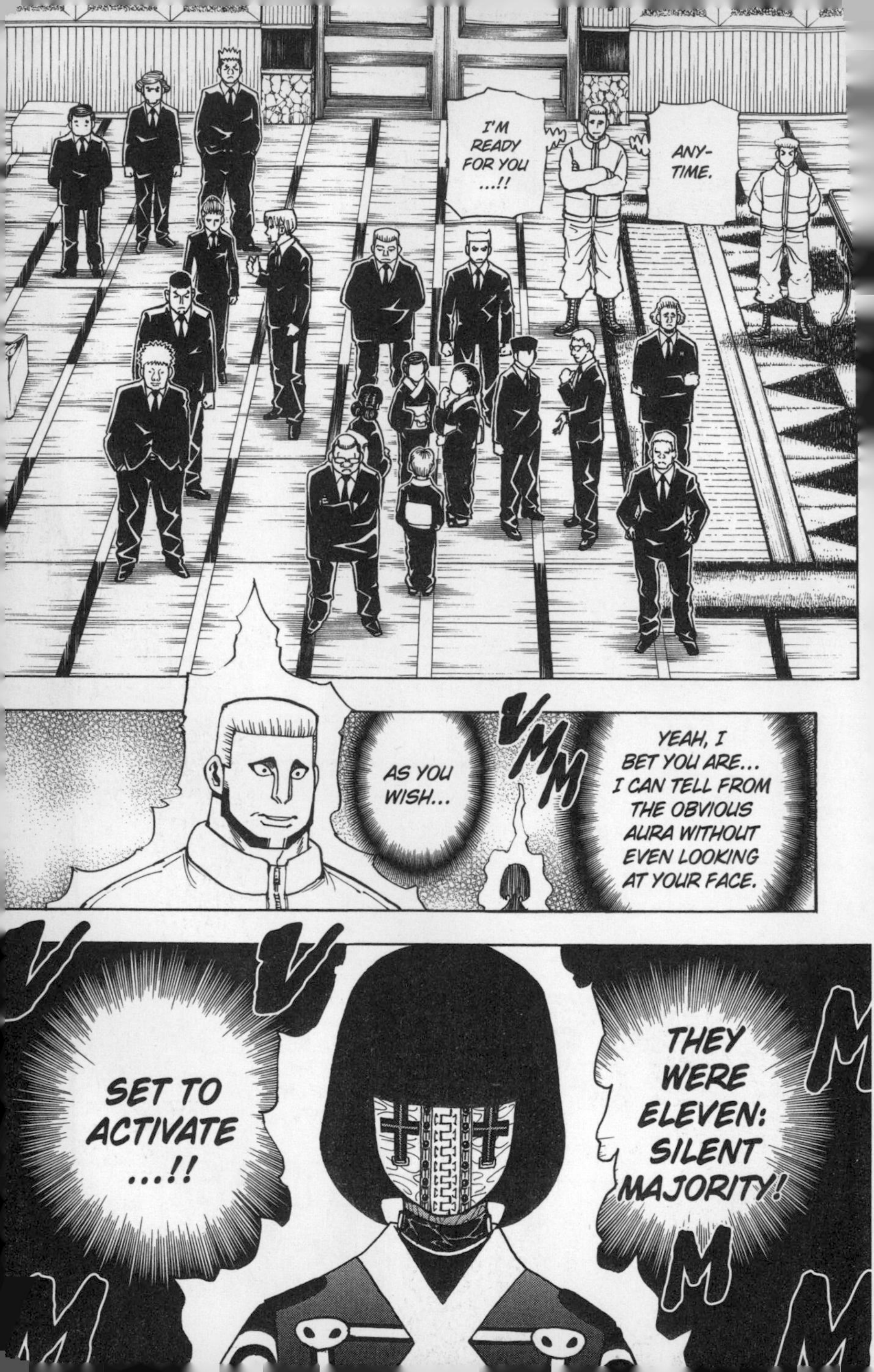
ANY-TIME.
I'M READY FOR YOU ...!!
YEAH, I BET YOU ARE... I CAN TELL FROM THE OBVIOUS AURA WITHOUT EVEN LOOKING AT YOUR FACE.
VMM
AS YOU WISH...
THEY WERE ELEVEN: SILENT MAJORITY!
SET TO ACTIVATE ...!!

HUNTER ハンター × ハンター HUNTER

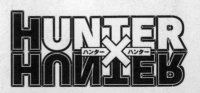

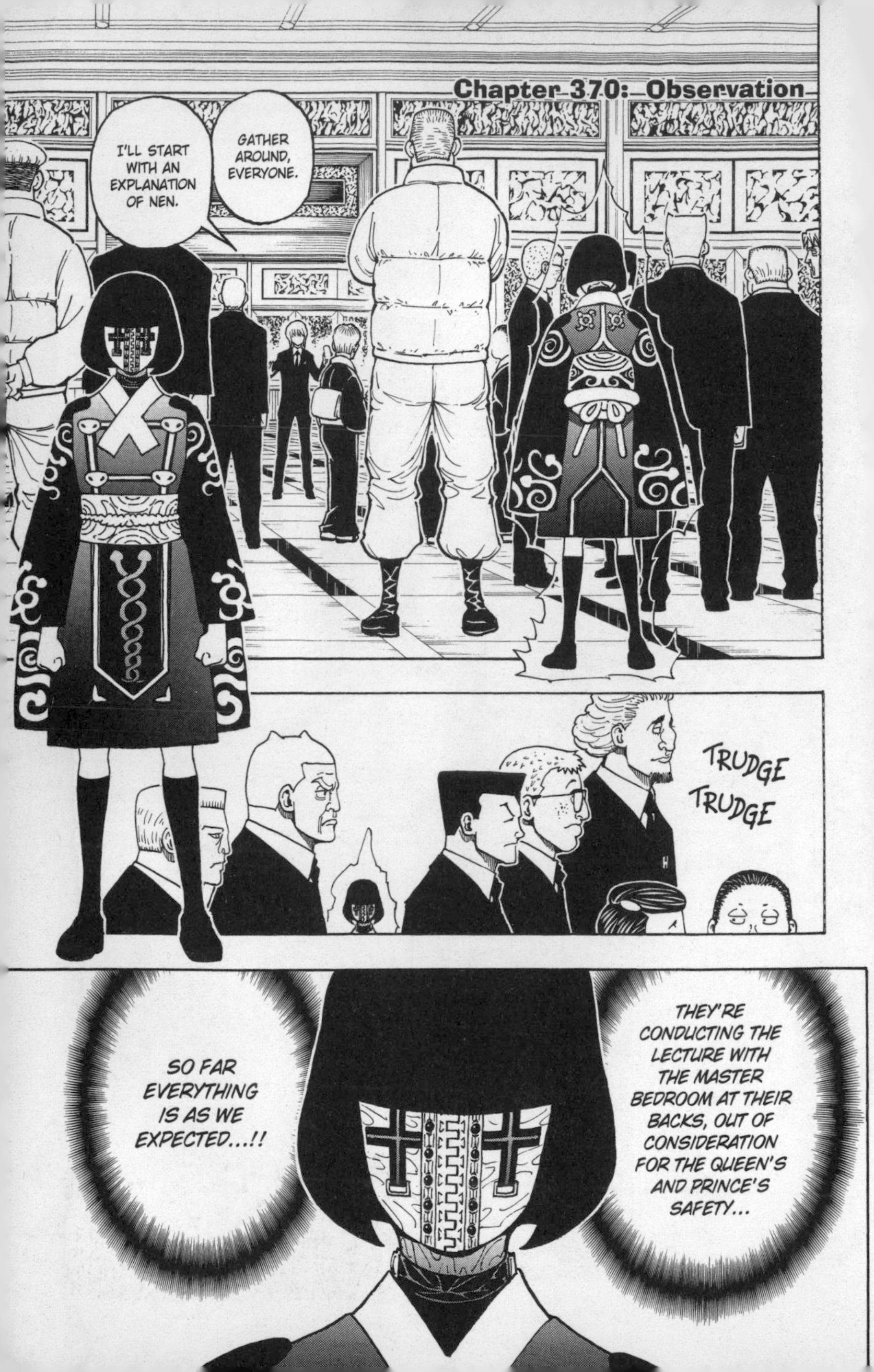
Chapter 370: Observation
GATHER AROUND, EVERYONE.
I'LL START WITH AN EXPLANATION OF NEN.
TRUDGE TRUDGE
THEY'RE CONDUCTING THE LECTURE WITH THE MASTER BEDROOM AT THEIR BACKS, OUT OF CONSIDERATION FOR THE QUEEN'S AND PRINCE'S SAFETY...
SO FAR EVERYTHING IS AS WE EXPECTED...!!

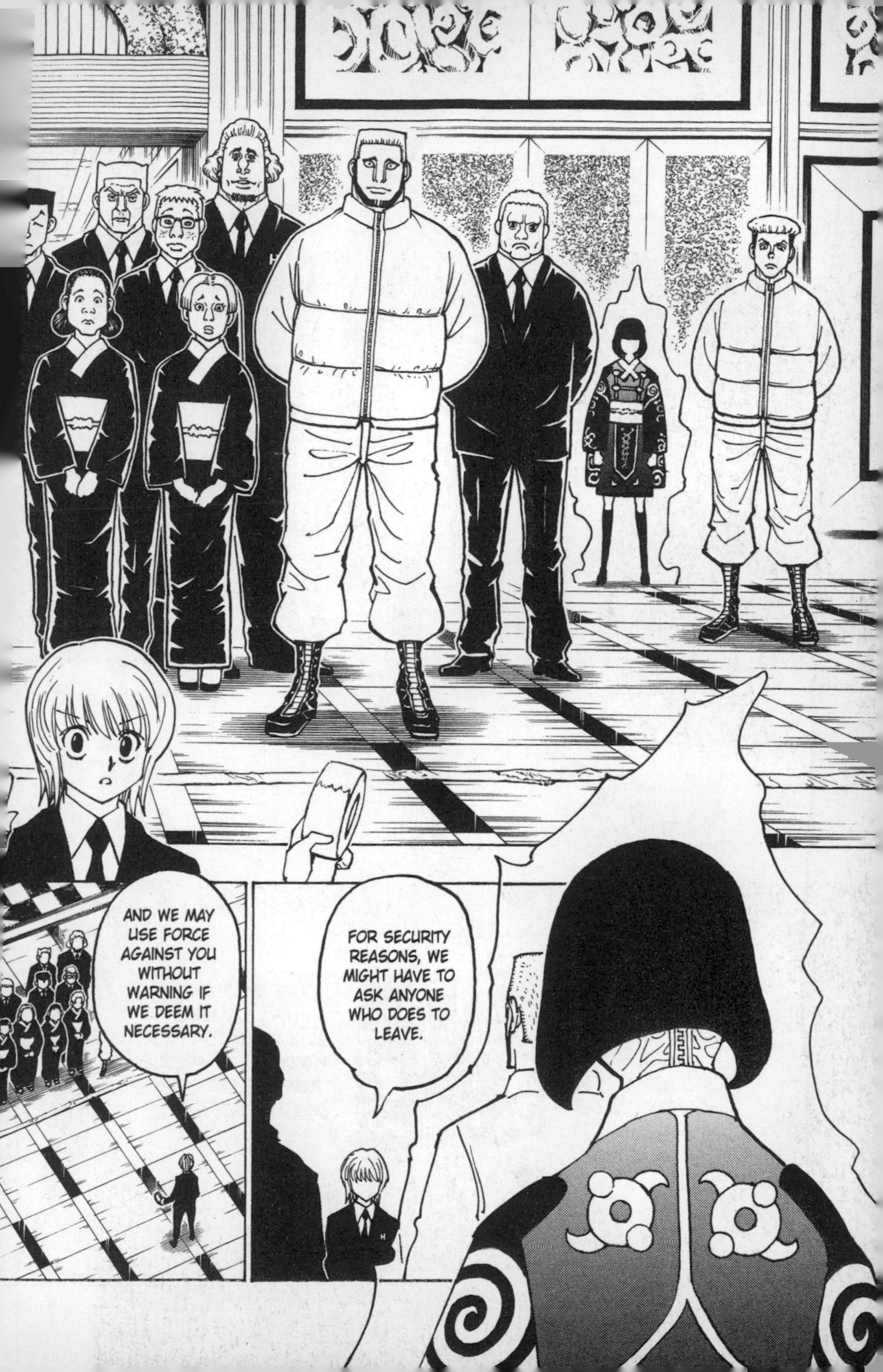
FOR SECURITY REASONS, WE MIGHT HAVE TO ASK ANYONE WHO DOES TO LEAVE.
AND WE MAY USE FORCE AGAINST YOU WITHOUT WARNING IF WE DEEM IT NECESSARY.

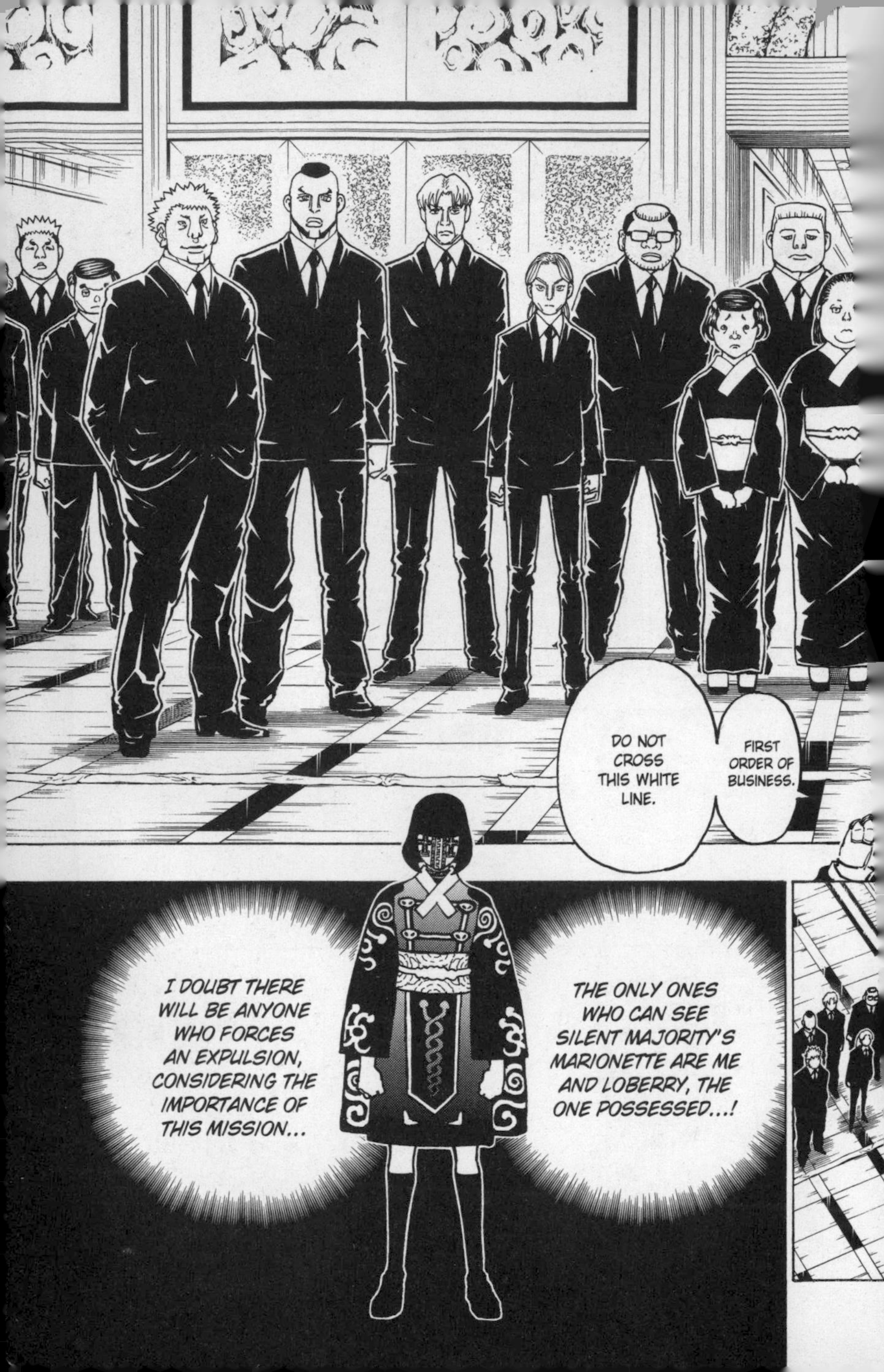
FIRST ORDER OF BUSINESS.
DO NOT CROSS THIS WHITE LINE.
THE ONLY ONES WHO CAN SEE SILENT MAJORITY'S MARIONETTE ARE ME AND LOBERRY, THE ONE POSSESSED...!
I DOUBT THERE WILL BE ANYONE WHO FORCES AN EXPULSION, CONSIDERING THE IMPORTANCE OF THIS MISSION...

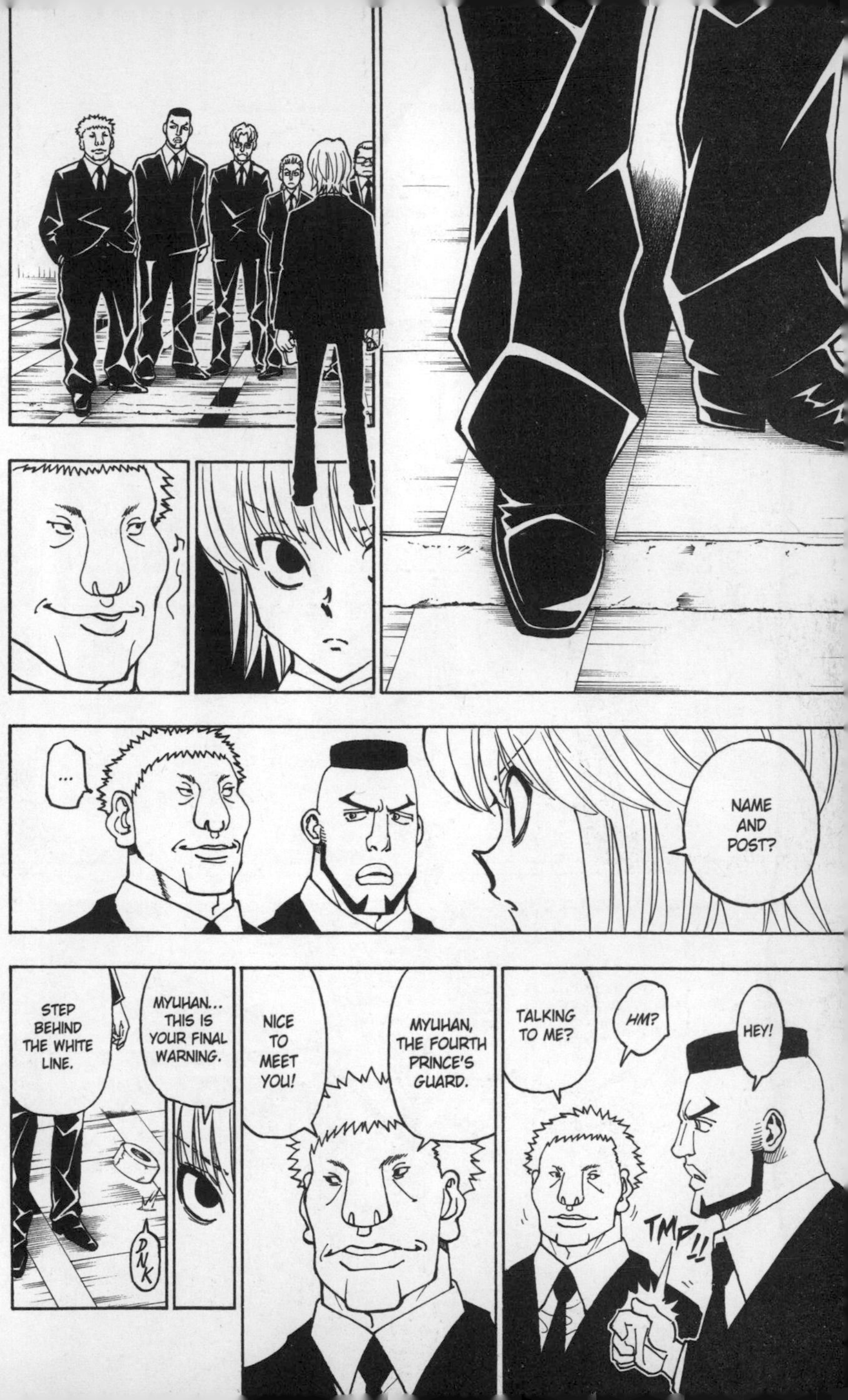
NAME AND POST?
...
HEY!
HM?
TALKING TO ME?
TMP!!
MYUHAN, THE FOURTH PRINCE'S GUARD.
NICE TO MEET YOU!
MYUHAN... THIS IS YOUR FINAL WARNING.
DNK
STEP BEHIND THE WHITE LINE.

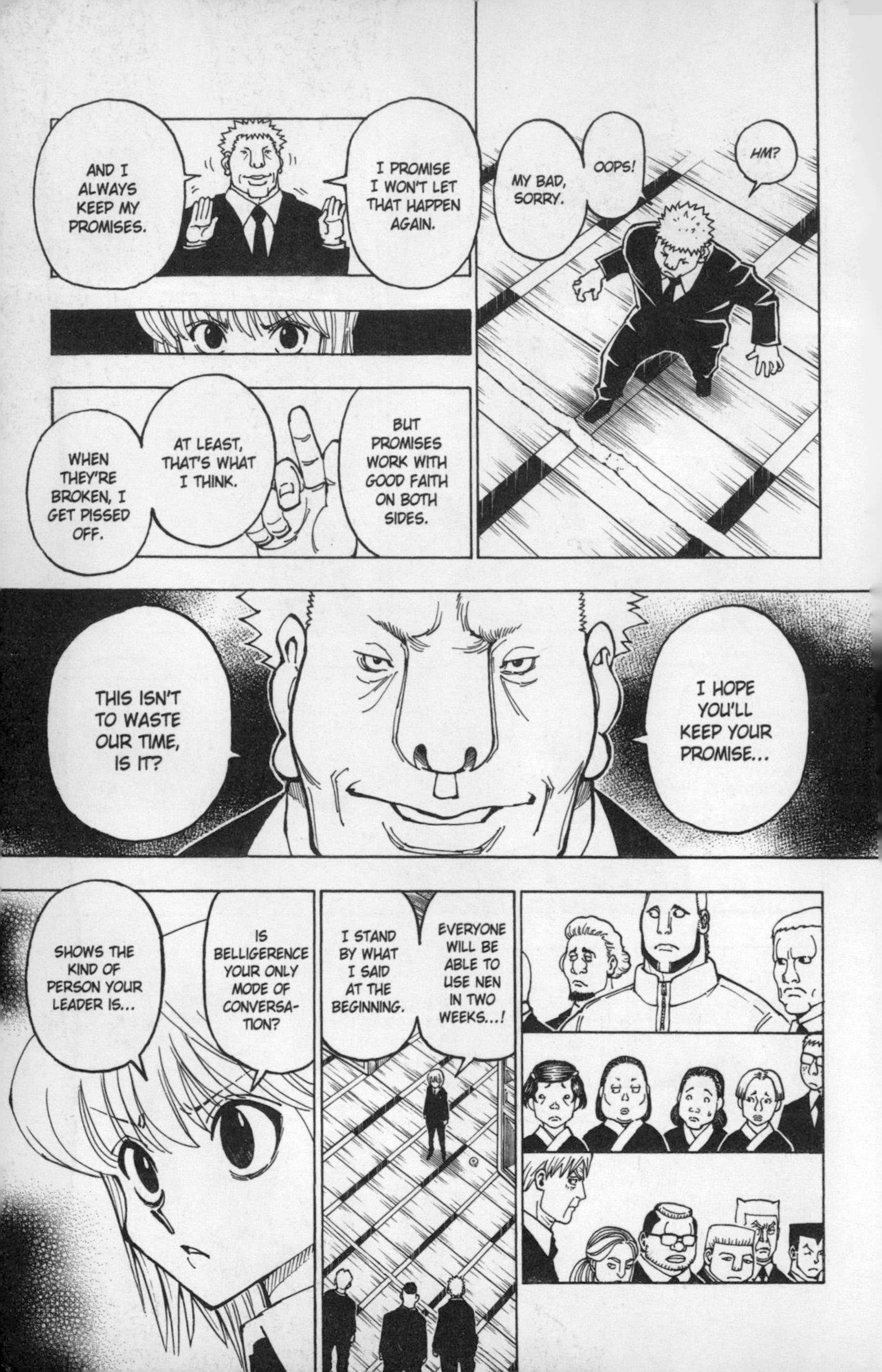
HM?
OOPS!
MY BAD, SORRY.
I PROMISE I WON'T LET THAT HAPPEN AGAIN.
AND I ALWAYS KEEP MY PROMISES.
BUT PROMISES WORK WITH GOOD FAITH ON BOTH SIDES.
AT LEAST, THAT'S WHAT I THINK.
WHEN THEY'RE BROKEN, I GET PISSED OFF.
I HOPE YOU'LL KEEP YOUR PROMISE...
THIS ISN'T TO WASTE OUR TIME, IS IT?
EVERYONE WILL BE ABLE TO USE NEN IN TWO WEEKS...!
I STAND BY WHAT I SAID AT THE BEGINNING.
IS BELLIGERENCE YOUR ONLY MODE OF CONVERSATION?
SHOWS THE KIND OF PERSON YOUR LEADER IS...

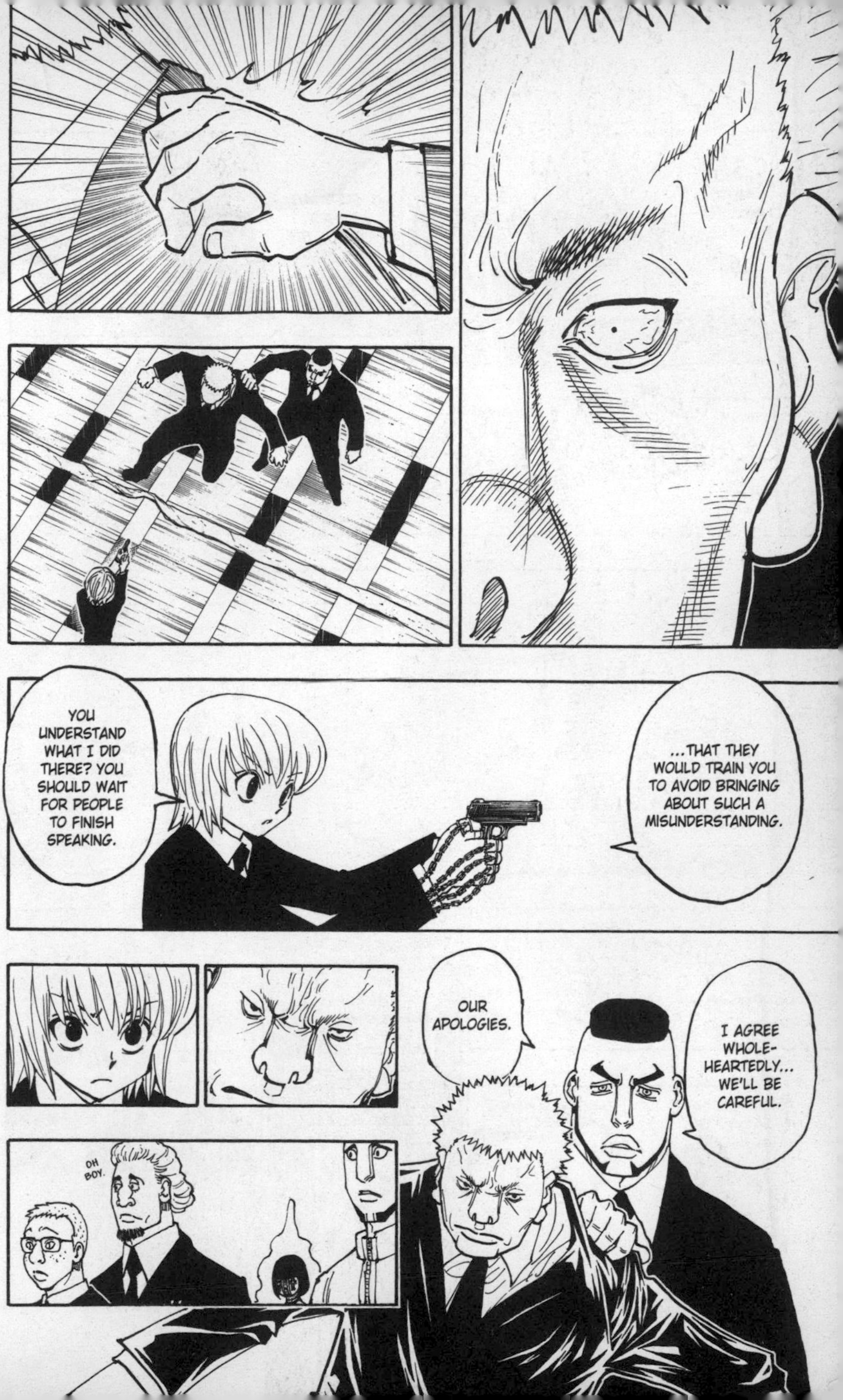
...THAT THEY WOULD TRAIN YOU TO AVOID BRINGING ABOUT SUCH A MISUNDERSTANDING.
YOU UNDERSTAND WHAT I DID THERE? YOU SHOULD WAIT FOR PEOPLE TO FINISH SPEAKING.
I AGREE WHOLE-HEARTEDLY... WE'LL BE CAREFUL.
OUR APOLOGIES.
OH BOY.

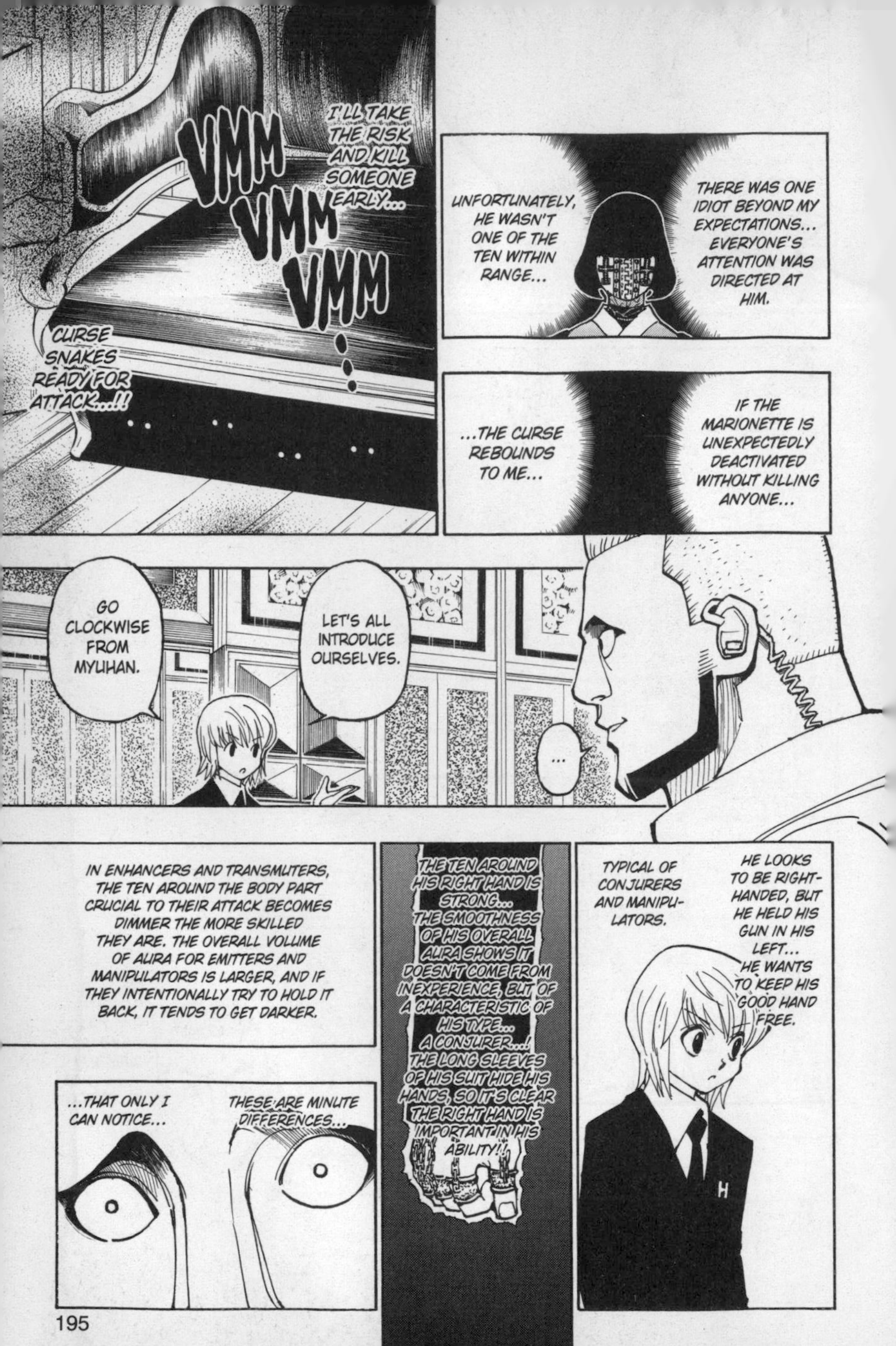
THERE WAS ONE IDIOT BEYOND MY EXPECTATIONS... EVERYONE'S ATTENTION WAS DIRECTED AT HIM.
UNFORTUNATELY, HE WASN'T ONE OF THE TEN WITHIN RANGE...
IF THE MARIONETTE IS UNEXPECTEDLY DEACTIVATED WITHOUT KILLING ANYONE...
...THE CURSE REBOUNDS TO ME...
I'LL TAKE THE RISK AND KILL SOMEONE EARLY...
VMM VMM VMM
CURSE SNAKES READY FOR ATTACK...!!
...
LET'S ALL INTRODUCE OURSELVES.
GO CLOCKWISE FROM MYUHAN.
HE LOOKS TO BE RIGHT-HANDED, BUT HE HELD HIS GUN IN HIS LEFT... HE WANTS TO KEEP HIS GOOD HAND FREE.
TYPICAL OF CONJURERS AND MANIPULATORS.
THE TEN AROUND HIS RIGHT HAND IS STRONG... THE SMOOTHNESS OF HIS OVERALL AURA SHOWS IT DOESN'T COME FROM INEXPERIENCE, BUT OF A CHARACTERISTIC OF HIS TYPE... A CONJURER...! THE LONG SLEEVES OF HIS SUIT HIDE HIS HANDS, SO IT'S CLEAR THE RIGHT HAND IS IMPORTANT IN HIS ABILITY!!
IN ENHANCERS AND TRANSMUTERS, THE TEN AROUND THE BODY PART CRUCIAL TO THEIR ATTACK BECOMES DIMMER THE MORE SKILLED THEY ARE. THE OVERALL VOLUME OF AURA FOR EMITTERS AND MANIPULATORS IS LARGER, AND IF THEY INTENTIONALLY TRY TO HOLD IT BACK, IT TENDS TO GET DARKER.
THESE ARE MINUTE DIFFERENCES...
...THAT ONLY I CAN NOTICE...

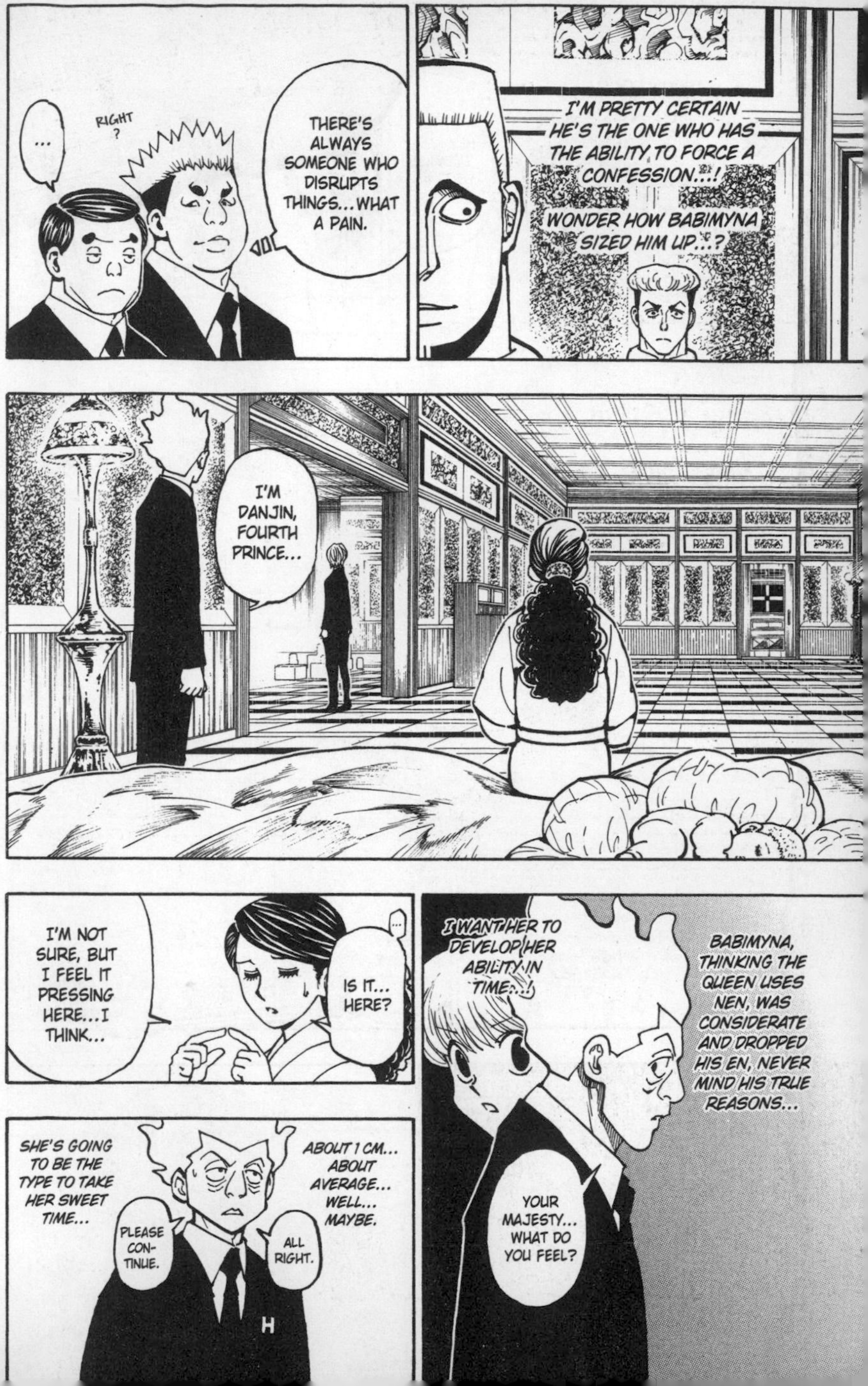
I'M PRETTY CERTAIN HE'S THE ONE WHO HAS THE ABILITY TO FORCE A CONFESSION...!
WONDER HOW BABIMYNA SIZED HIM UP...?
THERE'S ALWAYS SOMEONE WHO DISRUPTS THINGS...WHAT A PAIN.
RIGHT?
...
I'M DANJIN, FOURTH PRINCE...
BABIMYNA, THINKING THE QUEEN USES NEN, WAS CONSIDERATE AND DROPPED HIS EN, NEVER MIND HIS TRUE REASONS...
I WANT HER TO DEVELOP HER ABILITY IN TIME...!
YOUR MAJESTY... WHAT DO YOU FEEL?
IS IT... HERE?
...
I'M NOT SURE, BUT I FEEL IT PRESSING HERE...I THINK...
ABOUT 1 CM... ABOUT AVERAGE... WELL... MAYBE.
ALL RIGHT.
SHE'S GOING TO BE THE TYPE TO TAKE HER SWEET TIME...
PLEASE CONTINUE.

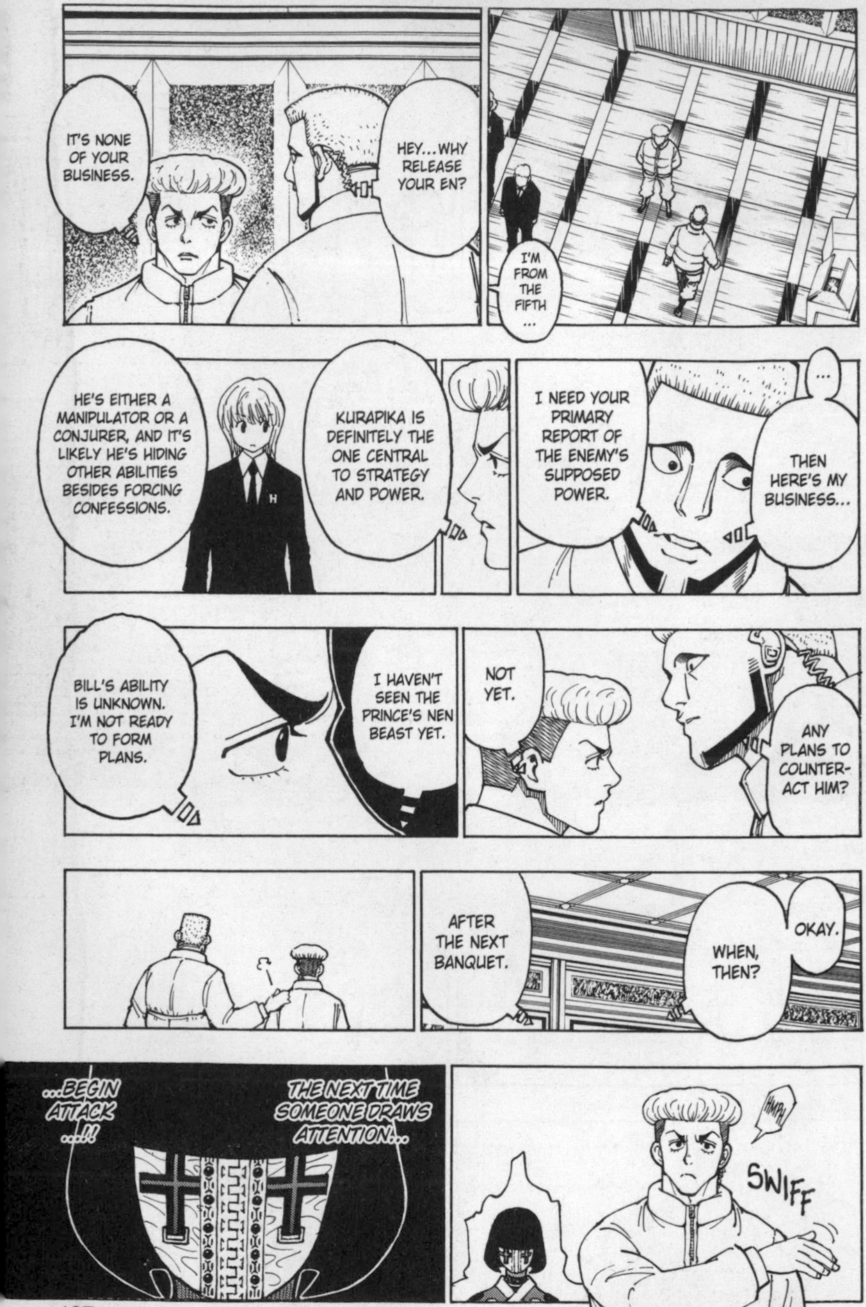
I'M FROM THE FIFTH ...
HEY...WHY RELEASE YOUR EN?
IT'S NONE OF YOUR BUSINESS.
...
THEN HERE'S MY BUSINESS...
I NEED YOUR PRIMARY REPORT OF THE ENEMY'S SUPPOSED POWER.
KURAPIKA IS DEFINITELY THE ONE CENTRAL TO STRATEGY AND POWER.
HE'S EITHER A MANIPULATOR OR A CONJURER, AND IT'S LIKELY HE'S HIDING OTHER ABILITIES BESIDES FORCING CONFESSIONS.
ANY PLANS TO COUNTER-ACT HIM?
NOT YET.
I HAVEN'T SEEN THE PRINCE'S NEN BEAST YET.
BILL'S ABILITY IS UNKNOWN. I'M NOT READY TO FORM PLANS.
OKAY.
WHEN, THEN?
AFTER THE NEXT BANQUET.
HMPH
SWIFF
THE NEXT TIME SOMEONE DRAWS ATTENTION...
...BEGIN ATTACK ...!!

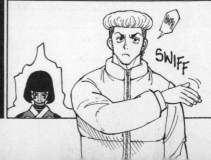

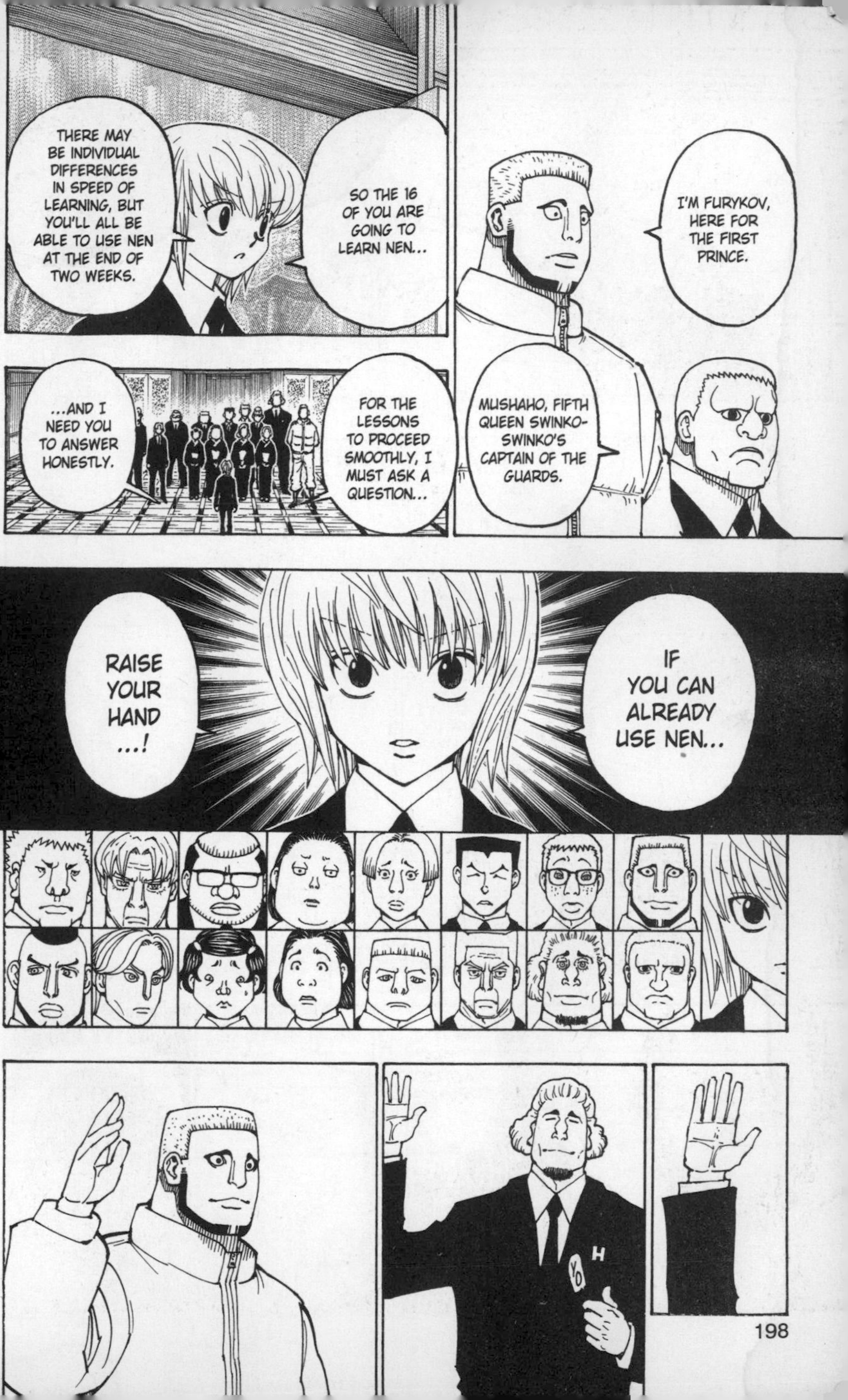
I'M FURYKOV, HERE FOR THE FIRST PRINCE.
SO THE 16 OF YOU ARE GOING TO LEARN NEN...
THERE MAY BE INDIVIDUAL DIFFERENCES IN SPEED OF LEARNING, BUT YOU'LL ALL BE ABLE TO USE NEN AT THE END OF TWO WEEKS.
MUSHAHO, FIFTH QUEEN SWINKO-SWINKO'S CAPTAIN OF THE GUARDS.
FOR THE LESSONS TO PROCEED SMOOTHLY, I MUST ASK A QUESTION...
...AND I NEED YOU TO ANSWER HONESTLY.
IF YOU CAN ALREADY USE NEN...
RAISE YOUR HAND ...!

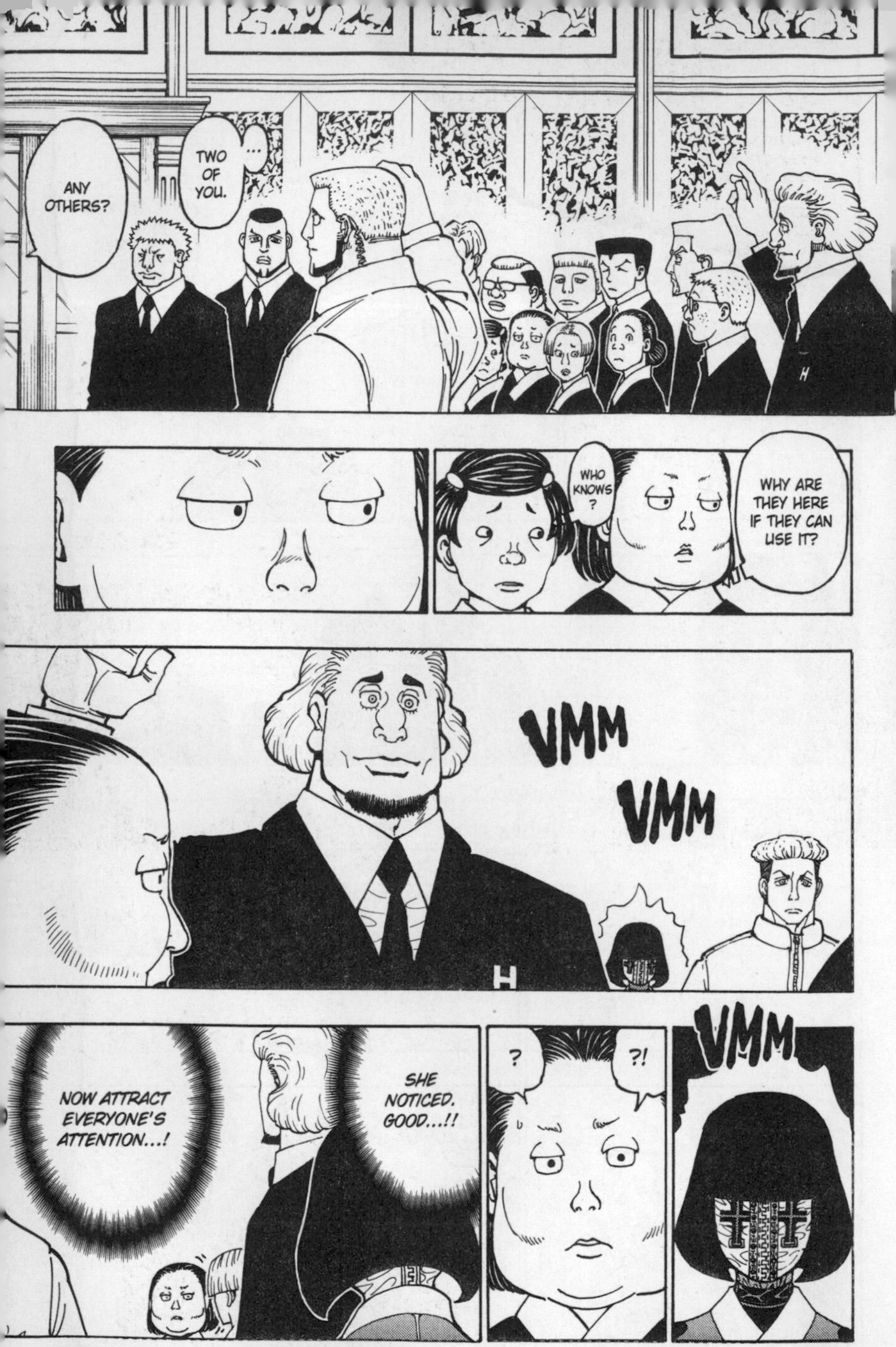
…
TWO OF YOU.
ANY OTHERS?
WHY ARE THEY HERE IF THEY CAN USE IT?
WHO KNOWS?
VMM
VMM
VMM
?!
?
SHE NOTICED. GOOD…!!
NOW ATTRACT EVERYONE'S ATTENTION…!

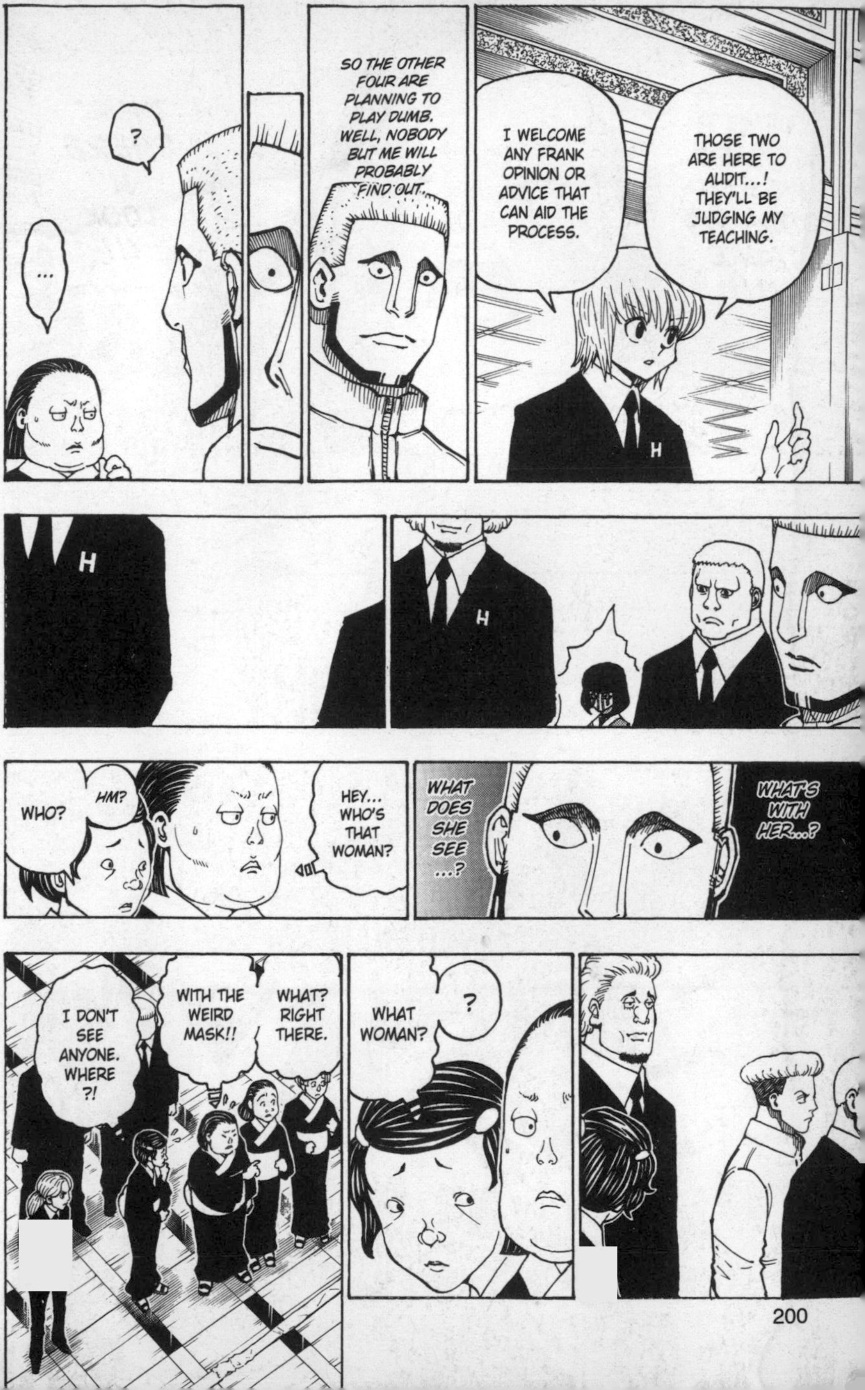
THOSE TWO ARE HERE TO AUDIT...! THEY'LL BE JUDGING MY TEACHING.
I WELCOME ANY FRANK OPINION OR ADVICE THAT CAN AID THE PROCESS.
SO THE OTHER FOUR ARE PLANNING TO PLAY DUMB. WELL, NOBODY BUT ME WILL PROBABLY FIND OUT.
?
...
WHAT'S WITH HER...?
WHAT DOES SHE SEE ...?
HEY... WHO'S THAT WOMAN?
HM?
WHO?
?
WHAT WOMAN?
WHAT? RIGHT THERE.
WITH THE WEIRD MASK!!
I DON'T SEE ANYONE. WHERE ?!

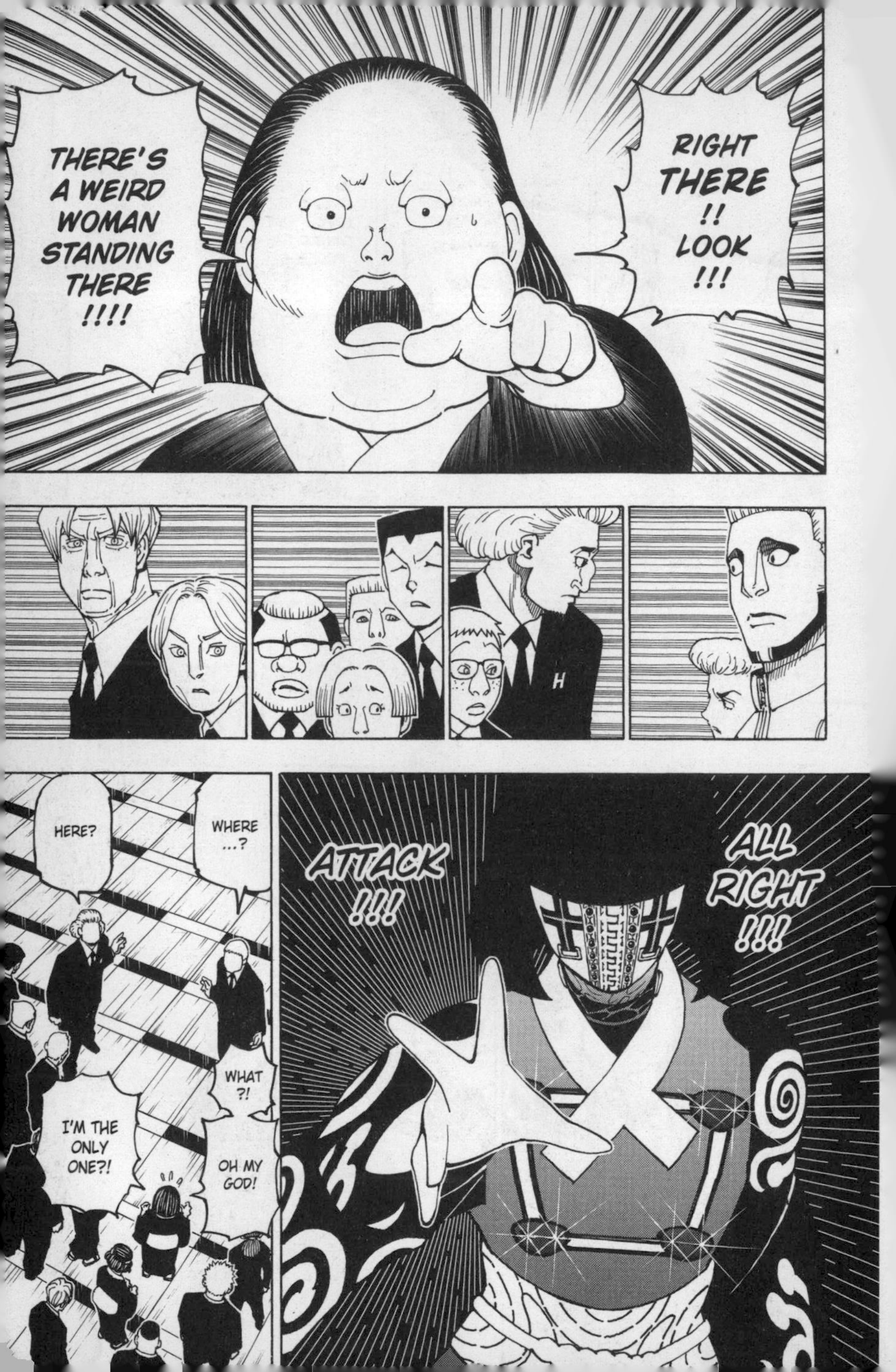
RIGHT THERE !! LOOK !!!
THERE'S A WEIRD WOMAN STANDING THERE !!!!
ALL RIGHT !!!
ATTACK !!!
WHERE ...?
HERE?
WHAT ?!
I'M THE ONLY ONE?!
OH MY GOD!

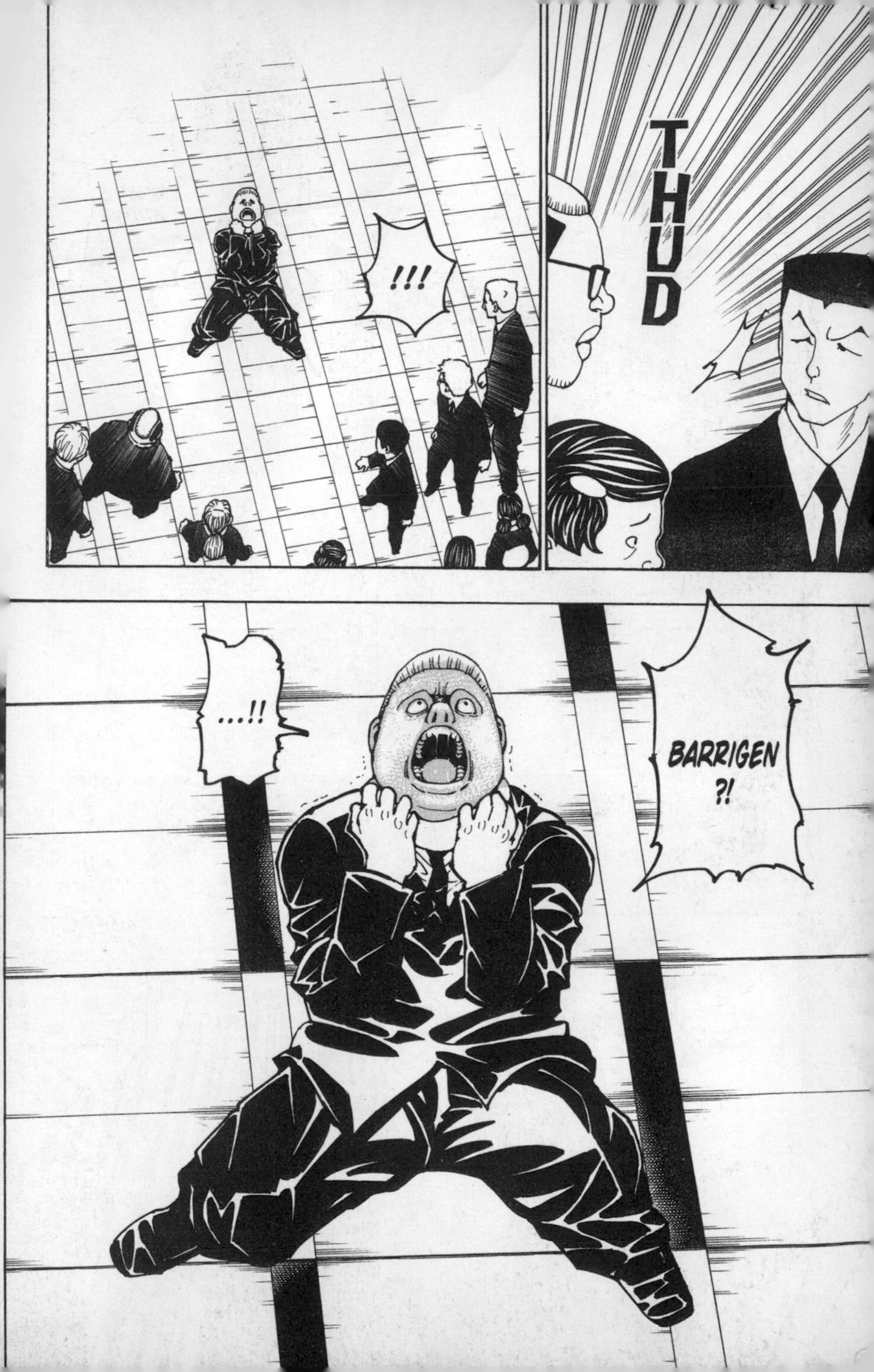
THUD
!!!
BARRIGEN ?!
...!!

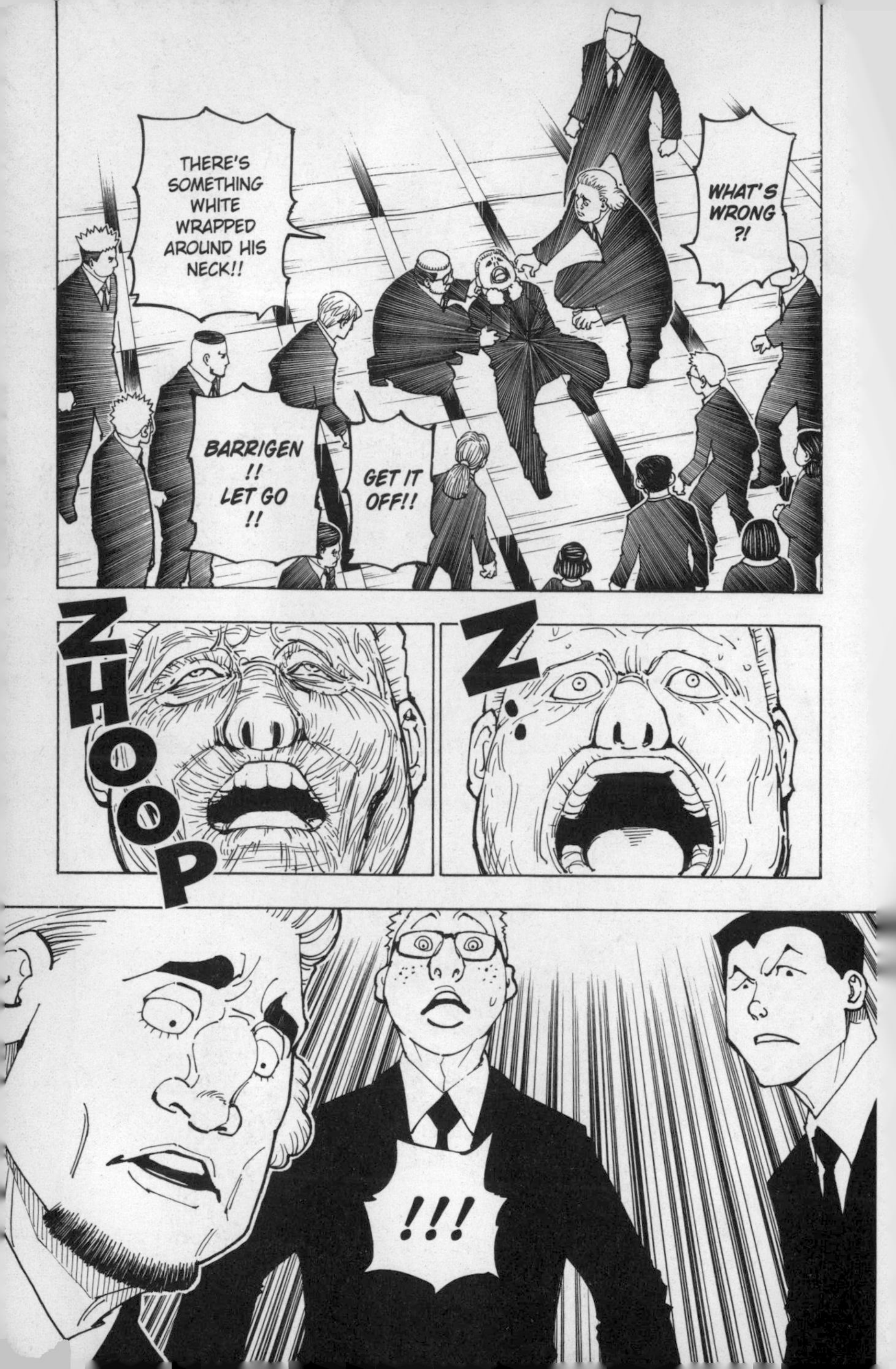
WHAT'S WRONG ?!
THERE'S SOMETHING WHITE WRAPPED AROUND HIS NECK!!
GET IT OFF!!
BARRIGEN !! LET GO !!
Z
ZHOOP
!!!

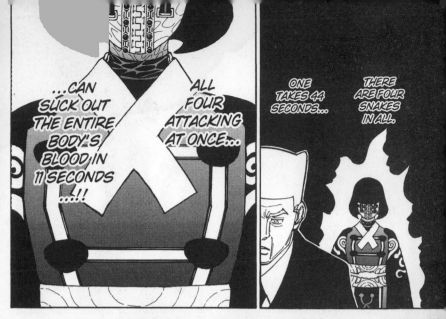

THERE ARE FOUR SNAKES IN ALL.
ONE TAKES 44 SECONDS...
ALL FOUR ATTACKING AT ONCE...
...CAN SUCK OUT THE ENTIRE BODY'S BLOOD IN 11 SECONDS ...!!
SLS
HSS...

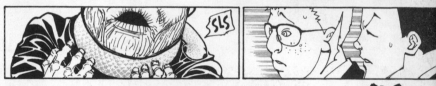

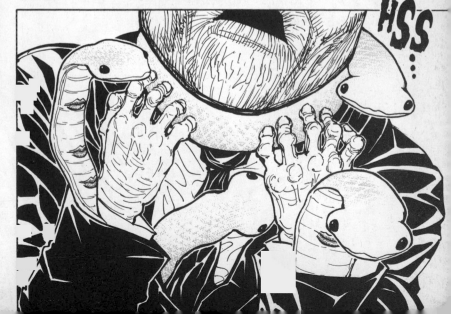

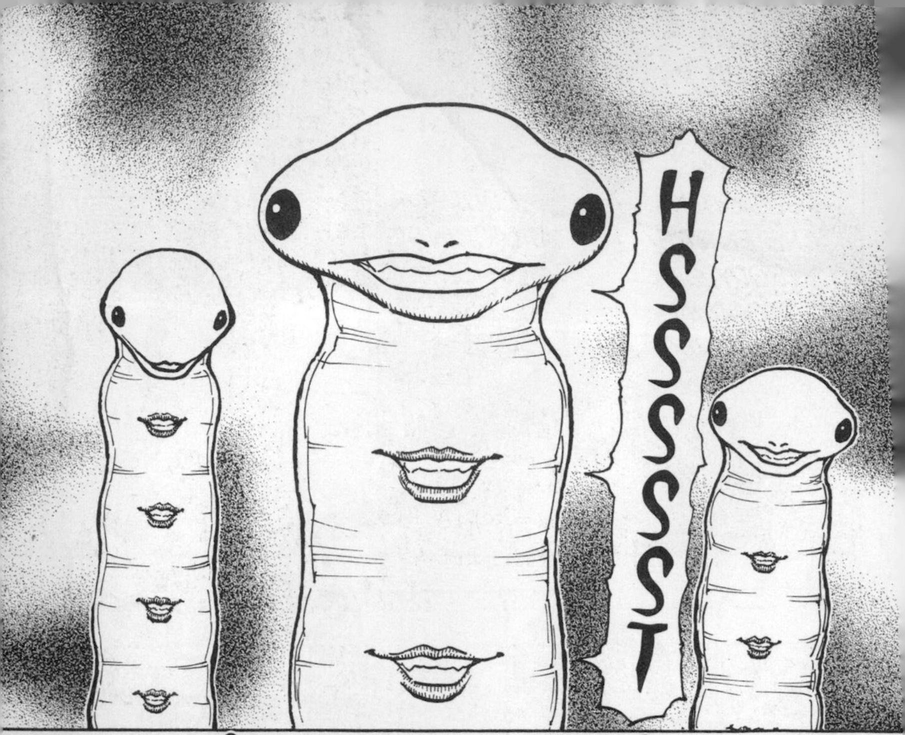
HSSSST

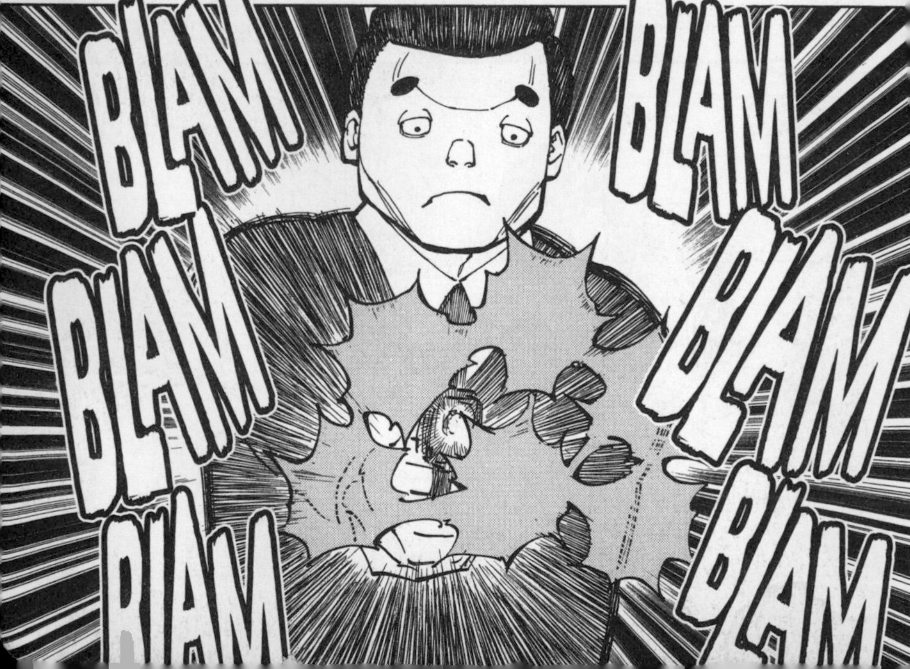
BLAM
BLAM
BLAM
BLAM
BLAM
BLAM

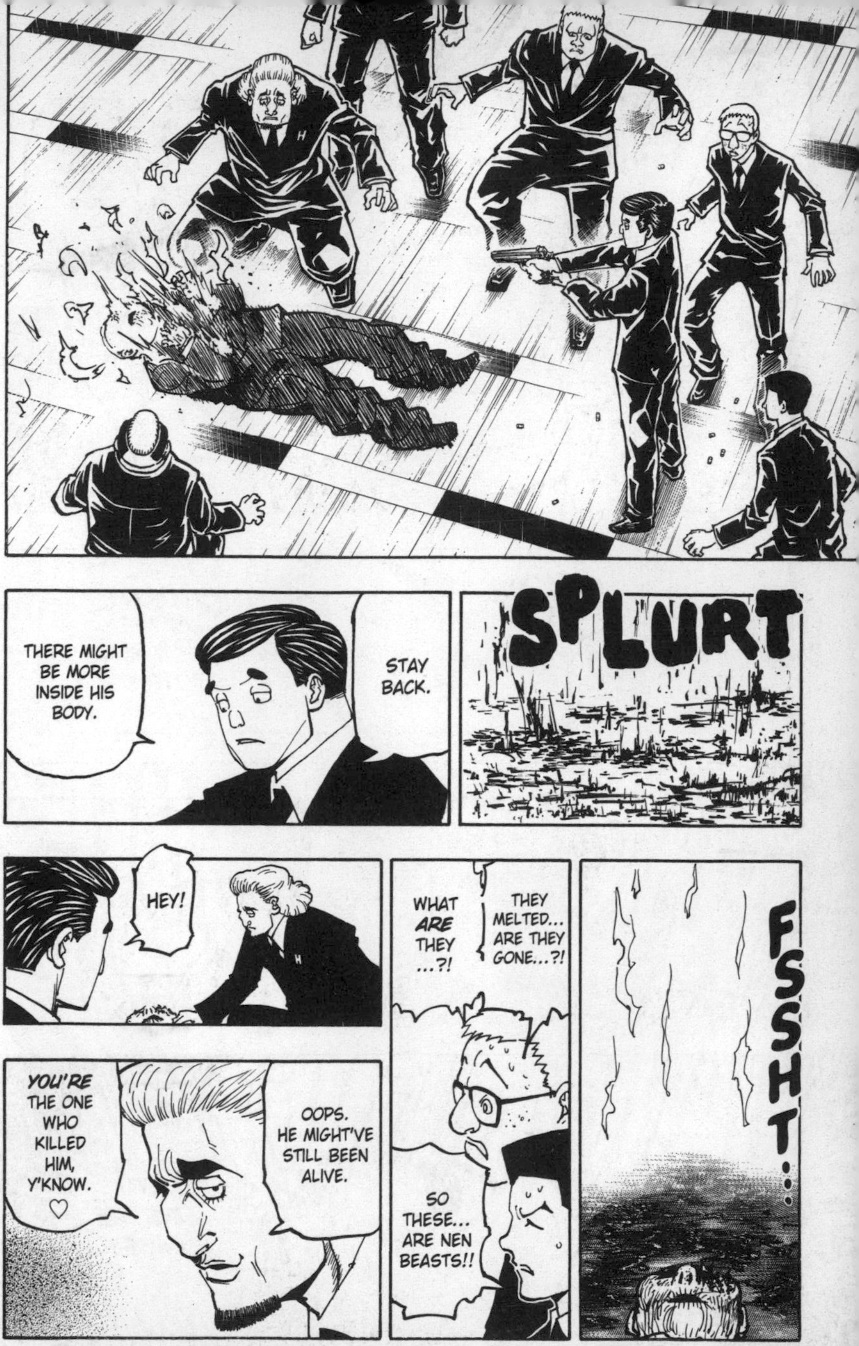
SPLURT
STAY BACK.
THERE MIGHT BE MORE INSIDE HIS BODY.
FSSHT...
THEY MELTED... ARE THEY GONE...?!
WHAT *ARE* THEY ...?!
SO THESE... ARE NEN BEASTS!!
HEY!
OOPS. HE MIGHT'VE STILL BEEN ALIVE.
YOU'RE THE ONE WHO KILLED HIM, Y'KNOW. ♡

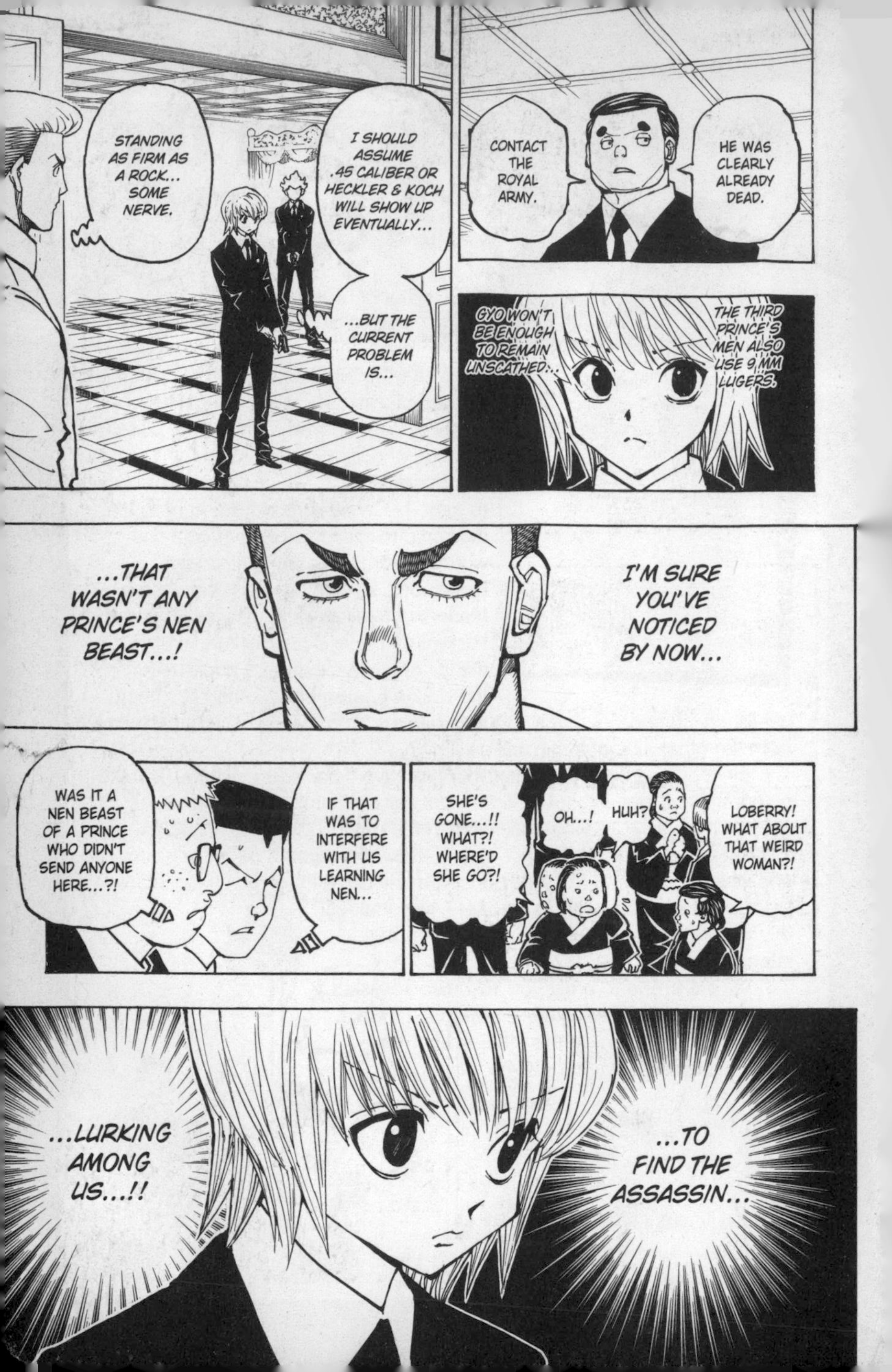
HE WAS CLEARLY ALREADY DEAD.
CONTACT THE ROYAL ARMY.
THE THIRD PRINCE'S MEN ALSO USE 9 MM LUGERS.
GYO WON'T BE ENOUGH TO REMAIN UNSCATHED...
I SHOULD ASSUME .45 CALIBER OR HECKLER & KOCH WILL SHOW UP EVENTUALLY...
...BUT THE CURRENT PROBLEM IS...
STANDING AS FIRM AS A ROCK... SOME NERVE.
I'M SURE YOU'VE NOTICED BY NOW...
...THAT WASN'T ANY PRINCE'S NEN BEAST...!
LOBERRY! WHAT ABOUT THAT WEIRD WOMAN?!
HUH?
OH...!
SHE'S GONE...!! WHAT?! WHERE'D SHE GO?!
IF THAT WAS TO INTERFERE WITH US LEARNING NEN...
WAS IT A NEN BEAST OF A PRINCE WHO DIDN'T SEND ANYONE HERE...?!
...TO FIND THE ASSASSIN...
...LURKING AMONG US...!!

You're Reading in the Wrong Direction!!

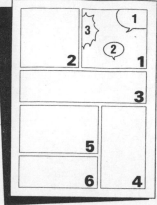

Whoops! Guess what? You're starting at the wrong end of the comic!

…It's true! In keeping with the original Japanese format, **Hunter x Hunter** is meant to be read from right to left, starting in the upper-right corner.

Unlike English, which is read from left to right, Japanese is read from right to left, meaning that action, sound effects and word-balloon order are completely reversed… something which can make readers unfamiliar with Japanese feel pretty backwards themselves. For this reason, manga or Japanese comics published in the U.S. in English have sometimes been published "flopped"— that is, printed in exact reverse order, as though seen from the other side of a mirror.

By flopping pages, U.S. publishers can avoid confusing readers, but the compromise is not without its downside. For one thing, a character in a flopped manga series who once wore in the original Japanese version a T-shirt emblazoned with "M A Y" (as in "the merry month of") now wears one which reads "Y A M"! Additionally, many manga creators in Japan are themselves unhappy with the process, as some feel the mirror-imaging of their art skews their original intentions.

We are proud to bring you Yoshihiro Togashi's **Hunter x Hunter** in the original unflopped format. For now, though, turn to the other side of the book and let the adventure begin…!

—Editor

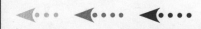

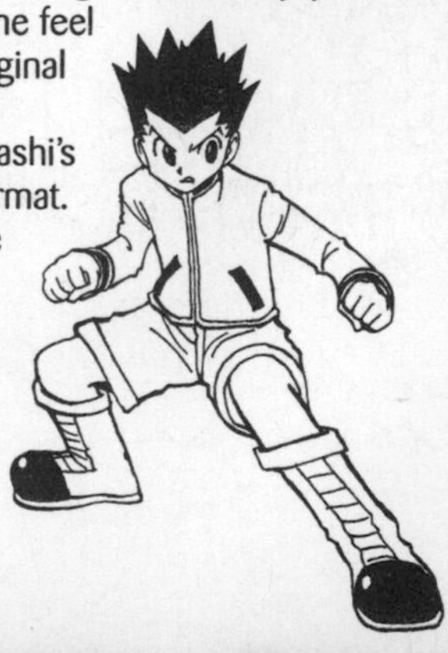